Social History of Western Civilization

Volume I

Readings from the Ancient World to the Seventeenth Century

SECOND EDITION

RICHARD M. GOLDEN

Clemson University

St. Martin's Press   New York

Acquisitions Editor: Louise H. Waller
Project management: Chad Colburn, Publication Services
Cover design: Leon Bolognese
Cover photo: "King Ashurbanipal on his chariot." © Archivi Alinari 1991.
 All rights reserved. Reproduction prohibited unless authorized
 by Art Resource, exclusive agent for Alinari.

For information, write:
St. Martin's Press, Inc.
175 Fifth Avenue
New York, NY 10010

ISBN: 0-312-03507-1

Acknowledgments

It is a violation of the law to reproduce these selections by any means whatsoever without
the written permission of the copyright holder.

"Formation of Western Attitudes toward Women" From *The Subordinate Sex: A History of
Attitudes Toward Women* by Vern L. Bullough, Brenda Shelton, and Sarah Slavin, pages
16–25, 27–35. Copyright © 1988 by The University of Georgia Press. Used by permission.

"Slavery in the Ancient Near East." Isaac Mendelsohn. From *Biblical Archaeologist*, volume 9,
December 1946, pages 74–88. Reprinted by permission.

"Afterlife: Ancient Israel's Changing Vision of the World Beyond." Bernhard Lang. From *Bible
Review*, February 1988, pages 12, 14–23. Courtesy of the Biblical Archaeology Society, 3000
Connecticut Avenue, NW, Suite 300, Washington, D.C. 20008.

"The Rites of Burial in Egypt." Pierre Montet. From *Everyday Life in Egypt in the Days of Ramses
the Great*, translated by A. R. Maxwell-Hyslop and M.S. Drowes, 1958, pages 300–303, 305–
319, 321–328. Reprinted by permission of Edward Arnold (Publishers) Ltd.

"Organized Greek Games." William J. Baker. From *Sports in the Western World*, 1982, pp.
14–23, 25–26. Reprinted by permission of Rowman & Littlefield Publishers.

"Marriage and the Family in Athens." Reprinted From W.K. Lacey, *The Family in Classical
Greece*. Copyright © 1968, Thames and Hudson. Used by permission of the publisher,
Cornell University Press.

"Classical Greek Attitudes to Sexual Behavior." K.J. Dover. In *Women in the Ancient World*,
The Arethusa Papers, volume 6, ed. by John Paradotto and J.P. Sullivan, 1984. Reprinted
by permission of the State University of New York Press.

"Roman Women" by Gillian Clark..(Abridged) From *Greece and Rome* volume 28 (1981) pp.
193–210. Reprinted by permission of Oxford University Press.

Acknowledgments and copyrights continue at the back of the book, on page 322, which
constitutes an extension of the copyright page.

 The text of this book has been printed on recycled paper.

Preface

Social History of Western Civilization, second edition, is a two-volume reader for Western Civilization courses. The twenty-five essays in each volume deal with social history because I believe that the most original and significant work of the past two decades has been in this area and because Western Civilization textbooks tend to slight social history in favor of the more traditional political, intellectual, and cultural history, though this bias is slowly changing. In the fifteen years that I have taught Western Civilization, I have used many books, texts, and readers designed specifically for introductory courses. I decided to compile this anthology because I perceived that other collections generally failed to retain student interest. My students found many of the essays in these other books boring, often because the selections assumed a degree of background knowledge that a typical student does not possess. To make this reader better suited to students, I have attempted to include essays that are both important and readable. This has not been an easy task, for many significant history articles, which have been written solely for specialists, are, unfortunately, simply too difficult for college undergraduates. I have gone through hundreds of articles searching for the few that are challenging, fascinating, important, and readable. To further enhance the readability of the selected articles, I have translated foreign words and identified individuals and terms that students might not recognize. All footnotes are therefore my own unless otherwise indicated. I, for one, do not understand why anthologies intended for college students do not routinely translate foreign expressions, phrases, and book titles and, moreover, seem to take for granted that students will be familiar with Tertullian, Gustavus Adolphus, or Pearl Buck, to mention some examples.

A Western Civilization reader cannot be all things to all instructors and students, but I have consciously tried to make these two volumes useful for as many Western Civilization courses as possible, despite the widely varying ways in which such courses are taught. The readings in these volumes cover many geographical areas and a broad range of topics in social history. Some historians argue that Western civilization began with the Greeks, but I have included in Volume One a section on the Ancient Near East for the courses that begin there. Both volumes contain material on the seventeenth century; indeed, Volume Two includes in its first selections some material that precedes the seventeenth century. This chronological overlap is intentional because Western Civilization courses break differently according to the policies of instructors and institutions.

To show how the articles in *Social History of Western Civilization* may be used in most Western Civilization courses, there is a correlation chart at the beginning of each volume that relates each essay to a relevant chapter in the major Western Civilization textbooks currently on the market. Though the textbooks do not always offer discrete discussions on all the subjects covered in the essays, they touch upon many of the subjects. As for the others, students will at least be able to place the articles in a historical context by reading the standard history of the period in the relevant textbook chapter, thereby gaining fresh insight into that historical period.

I have also provided introductions to the major periods in history for each volume as well as an introduction to each selection where I have asked pertinent questions in order to guide students through the essays and to encourage them to think about the problems and issues the authors of these essays raise. These introductions do not contain summaries and so may not be substituted for the reading of the selections.

The preparation of this reader was more time-consuming than I had originally thought possible. There always seemed to be somewhere a more attractive article on every topic. This was true for both the first and second editions. In the second edition, I have changed approximately one-quarter of the essays, substitutions based on my own searching, conversations over the past three years with historians around the country who adopted *Social History of Western Civilization* for their classes, and on the results from two dozen anonymous readers' reports solicited by the publisher. Many people also suggested essays to me, critiqued what I wrote, and helped in other ways as well. I thank Ove Andersen, Jay Crawford, Fara Driver, Phillip Garland, Laurie Glover, Tully Hunter, and Laurie McDowell. Especially generous with their time and comments were Philip Adler, William Beik, Robert Bireley, Richard Bulliet, Caroline Walker Bynum, Elizabeth D. Carney, Suzanne A. Desan, Lawrence Estaville, Hilda Golden, Leonard Greenspoon, Alan Grubb, Christopher Guthrie, George Huppert, Thomas Kuehn, Charles Lippy, Donald McKale, Steven Marks, Victor Matthews, John A. Mears, Edward Murnane, David Nicholas, Thomas F.X. Noble, D.G. Paz, James Sack, Carol Thomas, and Roy Vice. The editorial associates at St. Martin's Press—Vivian McLaughlin, Beverly Hinton, Kristen Heimstra, Miriam Foote, Abigail Scherer, Randi Israelow, and Huntley Funsten—have been gracious and efficient. I especially want to thank the four editors with whom I have worked on both the first and second editions of *Social History of Western Civilization:* Michael Weber, Andrea Guidoboni, Don Reisman, and Louise Waller. They have been tolerant of my lapses, supportive throughout, and wonderfully professional.

I would also like to thank the following individuals who reviewed this edition for St. Martin's Press: Anita Guerrini, University of California at Santa Barbara; Lawrence Manson, Ventura College; Marcelline Hutton, University of Texas—El Paso; John Rilling, University of Richmond; Carol Menning, University of Toledo; Bruce Kraig, Roosevelt University; and Bonnelyn Young Kunze, Clemson University.

Contents

Topical Table of Contents

URBAN LIFE

Correlation Chart for Western Civilization Texts and Volume I of Social History of Western Civilization

Text	Vern L. Bullough et al., *Formation of Western Attitudes toward Women*	Isaac Mendelsohn, *Slavery in the Ancient Near East*	Bernhard Lang, *Afterlife: Ancient Israel's Changing Vision of the World Beyond*	Pierre Montet, *The Rites of Burial in Egypt*	William J. Baker, *Organized Greek Games*	W.K. Lacey, *Marriage and the Family in Athens*
Winks et al., *A History of Civilization*, 7/e (1989)	1	1	1	1	2	2
Willis, *Western Civilization: A Brief Introduction* (1987)	1	1	1	1	2	2
Willis, *Western Civilization*, 4/e (1985)	1	1	1	1	2	2
Wallbank et al., *Civilization Past and Present*, 6/e (1987)	1	1	1	1	2	2
Strayer & Gatzke, *The Mainstream of Civilization*, 5/e (1989)	1	1	1	1	2	2
Spielvogel, *Western Civilization* (1991)	1	1	2	1	3	3
Perry et al., *Western Civilization: Ideas, Politics & Society*, 4/e (1992)	1	1	2	1	3	3
Perry, *Western Civilization: A Brief Survey* (1990)	1	1	2,3	1	3	3
Palmer & Colton, *A History of the Modern World*, 7/e (1992)				1		1
McNeill, *History of Western Civilization*, 6/e (1986)	I-A	I-A	L, A-5	L, A-3	II, A-3	II, A-4
McKay, Hill, Buckler, *A History of Western Society*, 4/e (1991)	1,2	1,2	2	2	3	3
Lerner et al., *Western Civilizations*, 11/e (1988)	2, 3	2	1	3	5	5
Kishlansky et al., *Civilization in the West*, (1991)	1	1	1	1	2	3
Kagan, Ozment, Turner, *The Western Heritage*, 4/e (1991)	1	1	1	1	2	3
Harrison, Sullivan, Sherman, *A Short History of Western Civilization*, 7/e (1990)	1,2,3	1,2,3	2	1,2	6	6
Greer, *A Brief History of the Western World*, 5/e (1987)	1	1	1	1	2	2
Goff et al., *A Survey of Western Civilization* (1987)	1	1	1	1	2	2
Darst, *Western Civilization to 1648* (1990)	2	2	2	2	3	4
Chambers et al., *The Western Experience*, 5/e (1991)	1	1	1	1	3	3
Bouchard, *Life and Society in the West* (1988)	1	1	1	1	2	2
Blackburn, *Western Civilization* (1991)	2, 3	1	1	1	3	3

	K.J. Dover, Classical Greek Attitudes to Sexual Behavior	Gillian Clark, Roman Women	Jérôme Carcopino, Gladiatorial Combat in Ancient Rome	G.E.M. de Ste. Croix, Why Were the Early Christians Persecuted?	Georges Duby, Rural Economy and Country Life in the Medieval West	Marc Bloch, The Life of the Nobility	Jean Gimpel, Environment and Pollution
Winks et al., *A History of Civilization*, 7/e (1989)	2	3	3	4	5	5	7
Willis, *Western Civilization: A Brief Introduction* (1987)	2	3	3	4	5	5	6
Willis, *Western Civilization*, 4/e (1985)	2	4	4	5	7	7	8
Wallbank et al., *Civilization Past and Present*, 6/e (1987)	2	3	3	5	8	8	9
Strayer & Gatzke, *The Mainstream of Civilization*, 5/e (1989)	2	4	4	4	9	9	11
Spielvogel, *Western Civilization* (1991)	3	5	6	6	9	9	11
Perry et al., *Western Civilization: Ideas, Politics & Society*, 4/e (1992)	3	7	7	8	9	9	10
Perry, *Western Civilization: A Brief Survey* (1990)	3	4	4	5	6	6	6
Palmer & Colton, *A History of the Modern World*, 7/e (1992)	1	1	1	1	3	3	3
McNeill, *History of Western Civilization*, 6/e (1986)	II, A-4	II-C	II-C II-D	II, D-2	II, B-1	II, B-1	III, B-2
McKay, Hill, Buckler, *A History of Western Society*, 4/e (1991)	3	5	6	6	10	10	11
Lerner et al., *Western Civilizations*, 11/e (1988)	5	7	7	8	10	10	10
Kishlansky et al., *Civilization in the West*, (1991)	3	5	6	6	8,9	9	9
Kagan, Ozment, Turner, *The Western Heritage*, 4/e (1991)	3	4,5	5	5	6,8	8	7
Harrison, Sullivan, Sherman, *A Short History of Western Civilization*, 7/e (1990)	6	10	10	12	17, 18	17, 18	18
Greer, *A Brief History of the Western World*, 5/e (1987)	2	3	3	4	5	5	5
Goff et al., *A Survey of Western Civilization* (1987)	3	6	7,8	9	12	12	12
Darst, *Western Civilization to 1648* (1990)	4	6	6	7	9	9	10
Chambers et al., *The Western Experience*, 5/e (1991)	3	4,5	5	6	8	9	
Bouchard, *Life and Society in the West* (1988)	2	3	3	4,6	6	7	
Blackburn, *Western Civilization* (1991)	3	5	5	5	7	7	8

Reading																			
David Herlihy, *Medieval Children*	8, 9	4,6,9	9,11	12	5,6	18	8	9	10,12	3	III, B-2	6,7	9,10	8, 12	11	9	8	6	7
Caroline Walker Bynum, *Fast, Feast, and Flesh: The Religious Significance of Food to Medieval Women*	8	11	13	10	6	22	7,8	10	10	4	III, B-2	7	9,10	10, 11	11	11	8	6	7
David Nicholas, *Vendetta and Civil Disorder in Late Medieval Ghent*	9	11	12	12	7	24	9	10	12	5	III, B-3	7	12	12	13	9	10	7	
Norbert Elias, *The Development of the Concept of Civilité*	10	12	18	13	8	27,29	10	11	13	6	III, B-3	8	13	13	16	13	11	7	10
David Herlihy, *The Family in Renaissance Italy*	10	12	18	13	8	26	10	11	13	6	III, B-3	8	13	13	16	13	11	7	11
Alfred W. Crosby Jr., *The Early History of Syphilis: A Reappraisal*	10	13	19	15	9	29	10	12	14	11	III, C-1	9	15	15	18	18	13	9	11
Mary Elizabeth Perry, "Lost Women" in Early Modern Seville	11	13	19	15	10	29	11,12	14	16	13	III, C-1	9	16	15	18	15	13	9	14
Merry Wiesner, *Nuns, Wives and Mothers*	11	14	20	14	9	30	11	14	14,15	9	III, C-1	8	14	14	17	14	12	8	13
Joseph Klaits, *Sexual Practice and Religious Reform in the Witch Craze*	11	16	21	15	9	30	12	14	15	28, 32	III, C-1	10	15	15	18	15	10	8	12
Natalie Z. Davis, *The Rites of Violence: Religious Riot in Sixteenth-Century France*	11	15	21	15	10	31	12	15	15	15	III, C-1	9	16	15	18	15	12, 15	8	15
Wendy Gibson, *Birth and Childhood in Seventeenth-Century France*	11	16	22	15		36	13	16	16	21	III, C-1	9	16	15	19	19	15	12	13
Michael MacDonald, *Insanity in Early Modern England*	11	17	24	15	10	37	13	16	16	34	III, C-2	9	17	15	21	15	15	11	15

Introduction

The social history of Western civilization seeks to include the complete fabric of human experience. Such comprehensiveness, like the quest for historical objectivity or the search for truth, is impossible to achieve. Nevertheless, the desire to learn about the totality of life differentiates social history from other subject areas such as military, intellectual, religious, cultural, diplomatic, biographical, economic, or art history. The social historian looks at groups or masses of people, at conditions that affected populations in everyday life. In part, this approach has been a reaction against biographies and the study of prominent people, usually military, political, or religious leaders, that dominated historical writing during the nineteenth century and the first half of the twentieth century. This history of elites ignores the vast majority of people and so implies that ordinary lives are unimportant. Hence, "history from the bottom up" seeks to rediscover previously neglected populations and lifestyles. But, ironically, social history, the history of aggregates, has sometimes become a history without names, that is, without the mention of individuals. Is it necessary to refer to anyone by name in discussing the agricultural system of the early Middle Ages or the effects of epidemics on human communities? On the other hand, discovering those "nameless" people and more intimate details constitutes the very humanness of history.

Though contemporary problems should not be the sole criterion for a historian's choice of a topic, the subjects that form the backbone of social history still exist today, though in different forms. In other words, the social history of ancient civilizations or the Middle Ages is intrinsically of interest to us as citizens of the twentieth century because it is often relevant, though it must be emphasized that relevance is not a goal of the social historian. Rather, awareness of concerns in present society has often led to investigations of similar problems in the past. Thus, primary topics in social history, all of which are discussed in this volume, include the family, marriage, children, death, disease, sports, violence, crime, women, persecution, food, sexuality, the environment, social behavior, religion, insanity, and the daily lives of various social groups. People in the past seem very different from us in Western civilization today; they thought and behaved in ways that appear alien to us, for the principles by which they ordered their universe are contrary to ours. The faceless masses, whom social historians are now beginning to see, fascinate precisely because they dealt with many of our problems—sex, for example—and our institutions—such as the family—in ways that from our vantage point seem superstitious, exotic, and neurotic. To appreciate social history, one must understand, not judge, and one must try to immerse oneself in the period studied and in the mentality of the people. The German poet Heinrich Heine said, "If one has no heart, one cannot write for the masses." To study the lives of the masses in history likewise requires heart; as the selections in this book reveal, the vast majority of people in past societies lived short, unhealthy lives, punctuated more often than not by violence, brutality, and exploitation. The study of social history needs empathy, the ability to place oneself in the hearts and minds of ordinary people in the past.

I

ANCIENT NEAR EAST

Where did Western civilization begin? Some argue that it began with the Greeks because they were so like us: they thought in terms of history, they reflected on the human predicament, and they questioned all areas of life. The Greeks invented history, drama, and philosophy and so were the first to tackle in a systematic way the perennial major questions basic to humanity: What are goodness, truth, beauty, justice, love? The Greeks were also the first to study nature as an autonomous and distinct entity, without reference to outside, supernatural forces. In history, science, and philosophy, the Greeks parted company with the earlier civilizations of the ancient Near East.

But a cogent argument could be made to include the ancient Near East in Western civilization. The cultures in what is today known as the Middle East, extending from Egypt to Iran, contributed writing, the alphabet, iron, astronomy, elements of common mathematics, agriculture, monumental architecture, cities, codes of law, and, with the Hebrews, a religion of ethical monotheism. All these influenced Graeco-Roman civilization, and thus our own.

Filling the universe with exotic gods, the minds of most Near Eastern people seem alien to us. In social life and personal relationships, nevertheless, they bear affinities with the Western cultures that followed them. Slavery, for example, was a feature of every ancient society, dying out in the modern West only in 1865 and in the Middle East in the 1970s. The belief in the inferiority of women and even in their relative equality could be found in the Near East. Echoes of these convictions are heard in rancorous debates in the twentieth century. Some attitudes toward children and education appear quite familiar to us, though others seem grotesque, if not inhuman.

Hebrew culture was not different from other cultures in its imperialism and in its unification of life around religion. The Hebrew religion was unusual—after all, it is the only ancient Near Eastern religion that has survived to our own day. Although there may be theological reasons for the continuation of Judaism, its penetration of every aspect of life certainly contributed to its longevity. Slavery, childrearing, and diet all bore the imprint of Hebraic religion.

The following selections on the ancient Near East address fundamental topics in the social history of Western civilization. They identify common as well as dissimilar features among Near Eastern civilizations. At the same time, they provide comparisons with conditions of life in later cultures.

1

Formation of Western Attitudes toward Women

VERN L. BULLOUGH,
BRENDA SHELTON, and SARAH SLAVIN

In order to understand later attitudes toward women in Western civilization, Vern L. Bullough, Brenda Shelton, and Sarah Slavin investigate and compare the role of women in Mesopotamia and ancient Egypt.

The inhabitants of the Tigris-Euphrates river valley, whether Sumerians, Babylonians, or Assyrians, treated women as property rather than as persons. What implications did this have for marriage, the treatment of adultery, and the lives of female slaves? That we know the names of only a few Mesopotamian women suggests the tight grip of male dominance; women were rarely able to distinguish themselves as individuals. Law codes indicated the very real subordination of women, and religion, always a cultural phenomenon, likewise preached female inferiority.

Women fared better in Egypt, though certainly there was no pretence of equality. But at least Egyptian women had greater standing in law than their Mesopotamian counterparts. What legal rights did Egyptian women have? Do you agree with Bullough's reasons for the comparatively higher status of women in Egypt? The most famous Egyptian woman, besides Cleopatra, was Hatshepsut, who reigned for approximately twenty years. How did her gender affect her rule? Her experience shows clearly an ingrained negative attitude toward women that would continue through Western civilization. Societies did not permit women to be warriors, for the military was a means to power. The only power attributed to women, other than that of mother, was the ability—or so men thought—to trap, delude, and steer men away from the right path.

The cradle of civilization, or at least of Western civilization, was the river valleys of the Near East (sometimes called the Middle East), particularly in the area extending from modern Egypt to modern Iraq. Attitudes formed in these areas were incorporated into Jewish, Greek, and later Western Roman and Christian attitudes. . . .

It has been said that man's vision of the gods reflects his own vision of himself and his activities. If there is any merit to this statement it seems clear that the inhabitants of the Tigris-Euphrates Valley quite early held man to be superior to woman, and in fact relegated her to being a kind of property. There are hints that in the beginning of Sumerian society women had a much higher status than in the heyday of Sumerian culture. Tiamat, a mother goddess, was a dominant figure, and it was her body that was used to form the earth and the heavens after she was killed by Enlil (called Marduk in the Babylonian versions and Asshur in the Assyrian ones). The blood of Tiamat's consort, Kingu, served to form individual humans. This death of a female goddess and her replacement by a dominant male figure is a common theme in the mythology of many peoples. The meanings of this matricide are unclear, and all we can say for certain is that by the time the Babylonian theology was organized into the form in which it has come down to us, the mother goddess was clearly subordinate to male gods.

The names and positions of the gods changed during different periods of Mesopotamian civilization as differing peoples achieved dominance. There were hundreds of deities but there were two major triads of gods: Anu, Enlil, and Ea; Sin, Shamash, and Ishtar. Over and above them was another god, Marduk or Asshur. The only female in the group was Ishtar, or in Sumerian, Inanna, goddess of war and of love. Like humans, the gods had wives and families, court servants, soldiers, and other retainers. Ishtar, however, remained unmarried. Her lovers were legion, but these unhappy men usually paid dearly for her sexual favors. She was identified with the planet Venus, the morning and evening star, and could arouse the amorous instinct in man, although she also had the power of causing brothers who were on good terms to quarrel among themselves and friends to forget friendship. If she perchance withdrew her influence, "The bull refuses to cover the cow, the ass no longer approaches the she-ass, in the street the man no longer approaches the maidservant." Part of her difficulty was that she did not really know her place. In the poem translated as *Enki and World Order* the god Enki (whose powers are similar to Ea's) assigned the gods various tasks. Ishtar, however, felt left out and complained to Enki. Her complaint applies to woman in general: "Me, the woman, why did you treat differently?/ Me, the holy Inanna, where are my powers?" She was given various tasks as a result, but because she was an unmarried and erotic figure it was no wonder that sacred prostitution formed part of her cult. When she descended to earth she was accompanied by courtesans and prostitutes. The implication might well be ... that woman was to be either wife and mother or an unmarried professional, a prostitute.

The mere presence of Ishtar, or Inanna, in the heavenly triad is probably striking evidence of the great strength of the forces of nature, which were so deeply rooted in primitive society. She represented the blending of several different characters into one, most obviously the lady of love and the lady of battles, although these different aspects of her powers were worshiped at different places. If Ishtar chose to favor a mere mortal, he could gain fame and riches, and she was much sought after. Sargon, the Akkadian conquerer who lived toward the end of the third millenium B.C., felt himself to be under the protection of Ishtar and believed it was through her influence that he became king. . . .

If the place of women in official mythology was somewhat circumscribed, it was even more so in actual life. Our chief source of information about actual conditions is the various law codes. These might be regarded as the official male view of women since they are essentially male social constructs. . . . Formal law codes are known from Ur-Nammu of the third dynasty of Ur [c. 2050 B.C.] and Lipit Ishtar of Isin [c. 1870]. Neither of these codes is preserved completely and their great importance to us lies in the influence they had on later laws. In the Semitic dialects the first law code was that of the town of Eshnunna, dating from about 1800 B.C. The best known, however, was that of Hammurabi (c. 1700 B.C.), which contained about 250 laws. Later from the Assyrian scribes there exists another legal corpus dating from 1100 B.C., which has a long section on women and marriage.

Women legally were property. They were neither to be seen nor heard. Monogamy was the normal way of life, but monogamy meant something different for the man than for the woman. A wife who slept with another man was an adulteress but a man could not only visit prostitutes but in practice also took secondary wives as concubines. Rich men and royalty often had more than one legal wife. Women were always under the control of a male. Until the time of her marriage a girl remained under the protection of her father, who was free to settle her in marriage exactly as he thought fit. Once married she was under the control of her husband. During the marriage ceremony a free woman assumed the veil that she wore from then on outside her home. In fact the veil was the mark of a free woman, and anyone who met a slave or courtesan wearing a veil had the duty of denouncing her. A concubine could only wear a veil on those occasions when she accompanied the legal wife out of doors. It was an offence for a woman to have any dealings in business or to speak to a man who was not a near relation.

Some scholars have argued that the earliest form of marriage required the bridegroom to purchase his bride, emphasizing even further the woman as property. . . .

The economic dependence of the woman upon the male was reinforced by the various provisions allowing her to remarry. In cases where a woman's husband was taken captive and he had not left enough for her to eat, she could live with another man as his wife. If her husband returned, though, she was to go back to him. Any children by the temporary husband remained with him. If, however, the absence of her husband was malicious, motivated by a "hatred of king and country," he had no further claim upon his wife if she took a second husband. Women could also hold property. An unmarried daughter, for example, could be given either a dowry, a share of her father's property, or the usufruct, the right to the profits from the land. She was free to dispose of her dowry as she wished, but in other cases her property rights upon her death reverted to her brothers, except under special conditions.

The purpose of marriage was by law procreation, not companionship. The wife's first duty was to raise her children and a sterile marriage was grounds for divorce. The wife who gave birth to children, particularly to sons, was accorded special protection. The man who divorced the mother of his sons or took another wife was committing a culpable act. Her childbearing responsibilities were emphasized by penalties to anyone injuring a woman sufficiently to cause a miscarriage and also by statutes against abortion.

Adultery was not a sin against morality but a trespass against the husband's property. A husband had freedom to fornicate, while a wife could be put to death for doing the same thing. Free women were inviolable and guarded; a man who gave employment to a married woman not closely related to him was in difficulty. A man caught fornicating with an adulterous woman could be castrated or put to death, while the woman could be executed or have her nose cut off. Offenses with unmarried free women were treated differently from those with married women because there was no husband. If the offender had a wife, she was taken from him and given to her father for prostitution and the offender was compelled to marry the woman who was his victim. If he had no wife, he had to pay a sum of money to the woman's father as well as marry her, although the father might accept money and refuse to give him his daughter. In any case, the payment was for damaging property, lessening the value of the woman. If a man could prove by oath that an unmarried woman gave herself to him, he was not compelled to surrender his own wife, although he still had to pay a sum of money for the damage he had caused. If a married woman was seized by a man in a street or public place and, in spite of her efforts to defend herself, was violated, she was regarded as innocent. If, however, she was acting as a prostitute either in a temple brothel or in the street, the man could be convicted of engaging in an adulterous relationship only if he was shown to have had guilty knowledge.

These laws applied to freewomen. There were other women, particularly slaves. A slave had no human personality but instead was real property. If she was injured, it was her master and not she herself who was entitled to compensation. A female slave was under obligation to give her purchaser not only her labor but also herself, without any counter obligation on his part. He could in fact turn her over to prostitution. Even when she became the purchaser's concubine and had children by him, she still remained a slave liable to be sold. At her owner's death, however, she and her children received liberty. If a female slave was bought by a married woman either as her servant or as a concubine for her husband (as in the case of a childless woman), she remained the property of the wife. A male slave could, with his master's consent, marry a freewoman, and even if she lacked a dowry, she and her children would still remain free. If she brought a dowry, she could keep it, but any increase from investment was split with her husband's master. There were also temple slaves who were not confined to the temple but worked in the towns and hired out to private employers. Their legal status was harsher than that of ordinary slaves since they had no hope of adoption, while their children automatically became the property of the gods. Children and wives of freemen were different from slaves, but the father still had almost total control. He could deposit his children with creditors, and apparently also his wife, although she could not be kept for more than four years. . . .

Specific laws dealt with women as tavernkeepers, priestesses, and prostitutes, occupations in which women could act outside conjugal or paternal authority. In general, however, the law failed to recognize women as persons. For example, a woman could be careless with animals just as a man could, but the law only refers to men. As far as priestesses and prostitutes were concerned, there were various kinds of both. At the head of the priestesses was the Entu, the wife of the gods, or the "lady [who is] a deity." They were of very high standing and the kings could make their daughters Entu of a god. They were expected to remain virgins, although they might eventually take husbands, perhaps after menopause. A second class of priestesses was the Naditu, who were lower in rank but who were also not expected to have children. The Hammurabic code had several provisions attempting to ensure the rights of a priestess to dowry and other shares of her father's goods. Apparently their conduct was rigidly circumscribed since any priestess who went to a tavern to drink could be put to death. Prostitutes seem to have been quite common and there was a considerable variety of harlots and hierodules.[1] . . .

With such a male-oriented society, few women emerged as real individuals in the history of the Mesopotamian civilizations. . . .

. . . It was only through their sons that women in the Mesopotamian civilizations seem to have had any influence at all. Even the wives of the king were not important enough to be regarded as queens since the use of the term was restricted to goddesses or to women who served in positions of power. The chief wife instead was usually called "she of the palace," and she lived along with the concubines and other wives in a harem guarded by eunuchs. Their way of life was carefully regulated by royal edicts, although in the last period of the Assyrian kingdom the influence of the king's wife and mother was somewhat greater than before.

Other than a few exceptional royal wives, only a handful of women managed to break through into the pages of history. There is an isolated reference to a woman physician at the palace in an Old Babylonian text, and we can assume that women attended other women in childbirth, but there is no further reference. The professional physician was usually a male. Women were also generally illiterate if only because in this period reading and writing were restricted to a professional class of scribes who underwent long training. Poetry, however, is a preliterate form of literature, and one of the most remarkable poets, in fact one of the few we know by name, was a woman, Enheduanna. She was the daughter of Sargon, whose administration marked the fusion of Semitic and Sumerian culture. As part of this fusion the Sumerian Inanna and the Akkadian Ishtar came

---

[1] Temple slaves.

together, and in this process Enheduanna played an important role, at least if her identification is correct. She was a high priestess of the moon god, the first of a long line of royal holders of this office, and in this capacity she wrote a poem usually entitled "The Exaltation of Inanna." Her poetry served as a model for much subsequent hymnography and her influence was so great that she later seems to have been regarded as a god herself.... Most of the cuneiform literature from the area is anonymous, or at best pseudonymous, so how many other women poets there were must remain unknown. The attitudes expressed about women in most of the poetry tend to indicate that they had male authors.

In one of the great classics of Mesopotamian literature, the Gilgamesh epic, it seems obvious that woman's duty was to keep man calm and peaceful. In the beginning of the account Gilgamesh was oppressing the city of Erech, taking the son from the father, the maiden from her lover. The people complained to the gods, who created a rival, Enkidu, from clay to deal with Gilgamesh. Enkidu was a wild man whose whole body was covered with hair, who knew neither people nor country. When the existence of Enkidu was reported to Gilgamesh he sent forth a temple harlot to ensnare the wild man: "Let her strip off her garment; let her lay open her comeliness;/ He will see her, he will draw nigh to her...." Then with his innocence lost he could be more effectively handled by Gilgamesh.

> *The prostitute untied her loin-cloth and opened her legs,*
>   *and he took possession of her comeliness:*
> *She used no restraint but accepted his ardour,*
> *She put aside her robe and he lay upon her.*
> *She used on him, the savage, a woman's wiles,*
> *His passion responded to her.*
> *For six days and seven nights Enkidu approached and*
>   *coupled with the prostitute.*
> *After he was sated with her charms,*
> *He set his face toward his game.*
> *[But] when the gazelles saw him, Enkidu, they ran away;*
> *The game of the steppe fled from his presence.*
> *Enkidu tried to hasten [after them, but] his body was*
>   *[as if it were] bound.*
> *His knees failed him who tried to run after his game.*
> *Enkidu had become weak, his speed was not as before.*
> *But he had intelligence, wide was his understanding.*

... The legend suggests that woman was designed to ensnare a man, to weaken him, to prevent him from realizing his full potentiality. In this forerunner of the stereotype of Eve, woman was both a source of pleasure and yet a delusion....

Woman, nonetheless, was designed to be at the side of man, and as a proverb stated, "a house without an owner is like a woman without a husband." The ideal wife was both passionate and able to bear sons: "May [the goddess] Inanna cause a hot-limbed wife to lie down for you; / May she bestow upon you broad-armed sons; / May she seek out for you a place of happiness." Even a good wife was a burden and responsibility: "The man who does not support either a wife or a child, / His nose has not borne a leash." Or in a more hostile vein: "As the saying goes: 'Were not my wife in the cemetery, and were not also my mother in the river, I should die of hunger.'" Women, as well as men, enjoyed sex. "Conceiving is nice," but "being pregnant is irksome." It was also recognized that the "penis of the unfaithful husband" was no better "than the vulva of the unfaithful wife," but in most things a woman was discriminated against. "A rebellious male may be permitted a reconciliation; / A rebellious female will be dragged in the mud." Obviously women were regarded as a mixed blessing, and it was thought best that they be kept in their place.

Life in Mesopotamia was harsh and unpredictable. There were floods, famine, scorching heat, and cloudbursts, and always the danger of invasions. It might well be that in such a society the strong man was admired while the weak woman was regarded as a liability but necessary because of her childbearing abilities. Inevitably the male was forced to assert himself, to man the armies, to do the fighting, to keep his womenfolk in subordination. Is this an adequate explanation for male dominance? The difficulty with such a thesis that these same attitudes are found in other cultures where environmental conditions are quite different. Nonetheless environment might have had some influence, since the place of women in Egyptian society seems to be quite different from that of Mesopotamian society.

. . . Most recent studies would not regard Egypt as a matriarchal society, but all would agree that the status of women was probably higher there than in Mesopotamia and that women had the right to own and transmit property. . . .

Part of the difficulty with reconstructing the real status of women in Egypt is that we lack the kind of comprehensive law codes present in ancient Mesopotamian society. We do, however, have numerous legal documents, particularly from the time of the Persians and the Greeks who occupied Egypt in the last half of the first millenium B.C. From these it would appear that women had the right to own property, to buy, sell, and testify in court. . . . [I]t is apparent that women not only enjoyed full equality to own property but also could go about their transactions in the same manner as men. Moreover, they were allowed to regain the property they brought with them as dowry if their marriage broke up. If, however, the woman had committed adultery, no such guarantee existed. Women were listed as taxpayers, and they could also sue. Apparently a woman did not need a guardian to be able to execute legal acts, nor did it matter whether she was married or not. A daughter, at least in the Ptolemaic period, was entitled to equal succession in the estate of her father. Women could acquire wealth or property through their parents or husbands or purchase it. A wife was entitled to a third of her husband's possessions after his death, whereas the other two-thirds had to be divided among the children and sisters and brothers of the testator. If a husband desired his wife to receive more, he had the right to donate it to her before he died.

The comparative economic independence of women may have given them greater freedom than in Mesopotamia. . . . Such independence must have been limited to the upper levels of society. The ordinary peasant, whether male or female, lacked many possessions, and the slave was even lower on the scale. Nevertheless, women of all classes were recognized as important, as is evidenced by the numerous goddesses. Particularly important were the triads of gods composed of a man, woman, and child, almost always a son. . . .

Since goddesses were so important it would seem to follow that royal women would also be important, if only because the pharaoh's first wife was the consort of a god. Inevitably, too, she became the "mother of the god" who would be the successor to her husband. At all periods in Egyptian society the queens were the first ladies of the land, and originally the tombs of some were as big and as elaborate as those of the kings. . . .

. . . [I]t was not until the eighteenth dynasty (c. 1570–1305) that the Egyptian queen achieved her highest prestige. The most influential of all was Hatshepsut (c. 1486–1468), who stole the throne from her young nephew and stepson, Thutmose III, and wielded the scepter for about twenty years. Hatshepsut, however, ruled as a king and not as a queen, an indication of the difficulties women had in ruling. The reigning monarch of Egypt had to be male: the titles, laudatory inscriptions, and ceremonies were all designed for men and were so deeply rooted in tradition and dogma that it was easier for a woman to adapt herself to fit the titles than to change the titles to fit her sex. Inevitably her reign is somewhat confusing since she is shown both in a man's kilt (and body) wearing the king's crown and artificial beard, and as a woman with feminine dress and queen's crown. She also has two tombs, one in her capacity as queen and one as king, the latter being larger. When she died or was driven from the throne by her nephew, Thutmose III, he destroyed almost anything Hatshepsut had ever touched, and even tried to obliterate all inscriptions which referred to her. Though Hatshepsut must have been a strong-willed woman, one of her great difficulties seems to have been her inability to lead an army. She recorded no military conquests or campaigns; her great pride was in the internal development of Egypt. Some would say she lacked military exploits because she may have been a leader of a peace party opposed to expansion. Actually there is nothing in a woman's biological makeup that would prevent a her from being a soldier or general, in fact; many women disguised themselves as males to serve in the American Civil War, but women almost without exception were not trained as soldiers. In the past, when kings had to lead their armies, this discrimination might have prevented more women from being rulers. Hatshepsut obviously was supported by the bureaucracy of the state, but civil powers can be diffused. In a military crisis, however, power must be centralized into the hands of one person, and though a woman might appoint a male to act as commander, there is little to stop him from turning against her, particularly if he has the loyalty of the troops. It might well be that Thutmose III used his military ability to regain the throne, since he either deliberately introduced military imperialism or was forced to expand in order to defend his country's borders.

Hatshepsut was not the only woman to sit on the throne. There were at least three others, although only as regents for their sons. . . . Women continued to exercise considerable influence down to the time of Cleopatra.[2] . . . Though Cleopatra was Greek rather than Egyptian, her importance emphasizes the continuing influence of women in Egyptian affairs, whether foreign or native.

The relative importance of the queen mother was no indication that the king was restricted to one wife. Concubines and harems were common, but such women seldom appeared in public. The size of the harem probably varied and at times reached remarkable numbers. Ramses II (1290–1224 B.C.), for example, had at least seventy-nine sons and fifty-nine daughters. The members of the royal harem lived apart from the rest of the court. Employees of the harem were not eunuchs, as in Mesopotamia, but included normal men, many of them married, as well as numerous women. In general the harem women were chosen by the pharoah either for political reasons or for their great beauty. It was through this last procedure that many nonroyal women gained admission and some became queens. There were also a number of women of foreign birth. Inevitably there were conspiracies in the harem as various wives tried to maneuver their sons into key positions. When women were not in the harem for political reasons, their chief purpose was to amuse their lord. They were instructed in dancing and singing and other arts designed to arouse and delight the male. Some of the richer Egyptians also had harems and concubines, but as a general rule Egyptians practiced monogamy if only because economic factors worked against polygamy. The husband could dismiss his wife if he wished to remarry or if his wife ceased to please him, but he had to return her dowry and give other forms of settlement. Women had no such freedom.

Like most societies, Egypt practiced a double standard. Concubinage existed but not polyandry. Maidservants belonged to their owner and adultery for the male was not considered a sin. Prostitution was wide-

[2]69–30 B.C.

spread. . . . If a married woman committed adultery, however, she could be deprived of her property and be subject to punishment. We have two folk-tales from the Middle and New Kingdom of women committing adultery: in the first the woman was burned to death; in the second her husband killed her and threw her corpse to the hounds. In other folktales women appeared as very sexual creatures, willing to betray their husbands, use various kinds of tricks, and do other things in order to get the men who attracted them physically into bed. . . .

. . . Instead of evidence of female promiscuity, such tales might only be male-oriented pornography, designed to arouse the male. By emphasis on female sexual desire, however, female insubordination might also be encouraged. Thus to reassert their control men emphasized clitoridectomies, allowing unlimited pleasure for the male but only limited temptation for females to be insubordinate. We also know that before this time the Egyptian woman was seldom pictured in any negative way in the literature. She was always portrayed as the faithful caring wife, the princess with many suitors, or the mistress praised by songs and poems. Motherhood was her revered function. Not to have children was a terrible and lamentable situation, and mother and children were depicted at all times in Egyptian tombs and pictures.

Women seldom appeared in public life although some women did hold public offices. There are records of a woman director of a dining hall, a manageress of a wig workshop, a headmistress of singers, a female supervisor of a house of weavers, and numerous mistresses of royal harems or superintendents of houses. In later Egyptian history wives of eminent persons or members of old noble families also were allowed to use honorary official titles. We know of at least one woman scribe who belonged to the household of a thirteenth-dynasty queen, and it is possible some queens and princesses knew how to write. Most women, even of the upper classes, could not. Women could also serve in the temples, and priestesses were recruited not only from the royal house, the civil services, or clergy, but also from the working class. Generally women served as musicians or dancers in the temple, although some might have become high priestesses.

Egyptians also believe that males rather than females were the key to procreation, and the male phallus was often portrayed. The female sex organs were not usually depicted in ancient Egypt. There was, however, a widespread belief that a women might succumb to hysteria if the womb remained barren long after puberty. . . .

The extant literature seems to be from the hands of males, and it reflects the various attitudes of men toward women. Ptah Hotep, the semi-legendary sage of the Old Kingdom who lived in the third millenium B.C., said: "If you are a man of note, found for yourself a household, and love your wife at home, as it beseems. Fill her belly, clothe her back; unguent is the remedy for her limbs. Gladden her heart, so long as she lives; she is a goodly field for her lord [that is, she will produce children if you cultivate her]. But hold her back from getting the mastery. [Remember that] her eye is her stormwind, and her vulva and mouth are her strength." Though wives were good if kept in their place, care should be exercised in their choice.... Women were also dangerous: "If you would prolong friendship in a house to which you have admittance, as master, or as brother, or as friend, into whatsoever place you enter, beware of approaching the women. It is not good in the place where this is done. Men are made fools by their gleaming limbs of carnelian. A trifle, a little, the likeness of a dream, and death comes as the end of knowing her."... Motherhood was especially revered. "Double the bread that thou givest to thy mother, and carry her as she carried [thee]. When thou wast born after thy months, she carried thee yet again about her neck, and for three years her breast was in thy mouth. She was not disgusted at thy dung, she was not disgusted and said not: 'What do I?' She put thee to school, when though hadst been taught to write, and daily she stood there [at the schoolhouse] ... with bread and beer from her house." When a man married he should keep the example of his mother in front of him. "When thou art a young man and takest to thee a wife and art settled in thine house, keep before thee how thy mother gave birth to thee, and how she brought thee up further in all manner of ways. May she not do thee harm nor lift up her hands to the Gods and may he not hear her cry."...

Women, in general, however, were a snare and a delusion. "Go not after a woman, in order that she may not steal thine heart away." In particular beware "of a strange woman, one that is not known in her city. Wink not at her... have no carnal knowledge of her. She is a deep water whose twisting men know not. A woman that is far from her husband, 'I am fair,' she saith to thee every day, when she hath no witnesses."

Yet a woman could also be a delight.

. . .

Lovely are her eyes when she glances,
Sweet are her lips when she speaks,
*   and her words are never too many!*
Her neck is long, and her nipple is radiant,
*   and her hair is deep sapphire.*
Her arms surpass the brilliance of gold,
*   and her fingers are like lotus blossoms.*
Her buttocks curve down languidly from her trim belly,
*   and her thighs are her beauties.*
Her bearing is regal as she walks upon the earth —
*   she causes every male neck to turn and look at her.*
Yes, she has captivated my heart in her embrace!
In joy indeed is he who embraces all of her —
*   he is the very prince of lusty youths!*

. . .

In sum, the Egyptian woman had a relatively pleasant life and we do not need to resort to questionable generalizations like that of primitive matriarchy in order to explain it. Her somewhat higher status than that of the Mesopotamian woman still did not mean that she was considered equal to men. Women were clearly subordinate, and compared to men's, their lives were circumscribed. It might well be that the very passivity of living in Egypt, owing to the great fertility of the soil and to the regularity of life, lent less emphasis to war and to the making of war. Women worked in the fields along with the men in ancient times, as they do now, although their assigned functions differed. Even the fact that women appeared as rulers does not mean that they had equality, since all apparently exercised their power in the name of a son or took a male name. It is also worthy of comment that most of the women rulers appeared at the end of a dynasty, apparently striving to keep the family in power either because their sons were young or their husbands were enfeebled. Hatshepsut, of course, was an exception. Some Egyptian women worked outside of their homes, but the professions were not open to them nor were any of the crafts, except the traditionally feminine ones. They were not priests, nor were they carpenters, sculptors, or scribes. Woman's place was in the home, and it was as mothers that they had their greatest influence. If Egypt is the example of the power that women had under what some have called a matriarchy, their status in times past must never have been very high. . . .

Slavery in the Ancient Near East

ISAAC MENDELSOHN

For people in antiquity, a society without slaves was virtually inconceivable. The trade in slaves linked cultures in the ancient Near East, as did the shared belief in the necessity and virtue of slavery. That belief was as widespread then as the feeling today that slavery is morally wrong.

Mendelsohn first discusses various ways—war, sale, and indebtedness—in which one could become a slave in the ancient Near East. War was endemic in that period; individuals and entire populations could suddenly lose their freedom. Omnipresent poverty was the cause of the sale of minors and the sale of oneself as well as the reason for people falling into debt and hence into slavery. Such a precarious existence for ancient Near Eastern peoples! Terrorized by vengeful and sometimes fickle gods, they received no relief from the sociopolitical world. Invading armies routinely crisscrossed the countryside from present day Iraq to Israel. Enormous disparities in wealth, poor weather, and erratic harvests help explain the plunge into slavery for those whose life-long poverty became destitution. How did slavery affect family relationships in these conditions?

Second, Mendelsohn analyzes the legal status of slaves, how they were treated by various law codes, particularly that of Hammurabi in Babylonia and the Bible. Were there significant differences between the Hebrew Bible and Hammurabi's Code concerning the regulation of slavery? Is there reason to believe that slaves were treated as the laws specified? How could a slave become free? Would slaves always desire liberty?

Third, in explaining the economic role of slavery, Mendelsohn shows that institution to be even more nuanced. Not only did slavery differ from culture to culture, but also according to the economic function of the slaves. Slaves worked for governments, temples, and private individuals, most often in agriculture or in industry. Historians of slavery are always drawn to the question of whether or not slavery was economically beneficial.

Finally, Mendelsohn looks at the attitude of religion toward slavery. Because religion is a product of culture, we should not be surprised to learn that Near Eastern religions accepted slavery as part of the natural order of things. But were there any seeds in religion that would later germinate to produce moral outrage against one person's owning another person?

The earliest Sumerian terms for male and female slaves are the composite signs *nita* + *kur* "male of a foreign country," and *nunus* + *kur* "female of a foreign country," indicating that the first humans to be enslaved in Ancient Babylonia were captive foreigners. That prisoners of war, spared on the battle field, were reduced to slavery is amply attested in the annals of the long history of the Ancient Near East. The Hammurabi Code[1] took this universal practice of the enslavement of war captives for granted and decreed that (1) a captive state official should be ransomed, in case he had no resources of his own, by his city temple or by the state, and (2) that a woman whose husband was taken prisoner may re-marry in case she had no means to support herself and her children. The Late Assyrian annals repeatedly mention large numbers of war captives "from the four corners of the world" who were dragged to Assyria and were compelled to perform forced labor. The small city-states of Syria in the middle of the second millennium B.C. employed the same procedure with regard to their war prisoners. In a war between the cities of Carchemish and Ugarit in which the former was victorious, many prisoners were taken. The king of Ugarit then requested the king of Carchemish to free one of the captives, offering him one hundred shekels as ransom. In answer to this request the king of Carchemish pointed out that he had already sold many prisoners for forty shekels a piece and that he could not be expected to free a high ranking captive for the small sum offered. The Tell el-Amarna letters (14th

---

[1]Main collection of law in Mesopotamia, named after the Babylonian king of the eighteenth century B.C.

century B.C.)[2] tell us of war captives being sent as "gifts" by Syrian and Palestinian princes to their Egyptian overlords. The Old Testament tells us that in their conquest of Palestine the Israelites enslaved many of their Canaanite enemies.

No sooner was this practice of enslaving foreigners established than it was carried over and applied to natives themselves. Man became a commodity and the total exploitation of his physical strength served as a new source of profit. Although captives of war and imported foreign slaves made up a substantial part of the slave population of the Ancient Near East, the bulk of the Babylonian, Assyrian, Canaanite, and Hebrew slaves originally came from the ranks of the free-born native population. The native-born slaves were recruited from the following three sources: sale of minors by their parents, voluntary self-sale by adults, and enslavement of defaulting debtors.

Poor parents who were either unable to support their children or were in need of money sold their offspring in the market. These sales were transacted in two ways: (1) unconditional sale; that is, the parent(s) handed the child over to the buyer and in return received the purchase price "in full," and (2) conditional sale or sale-adoption; that is, the parent(s) received the price and the sold minor was adopted by the purchaser. We have documentary evidence showing that the practice of the sale of minors was in use throughout the history of Babylonia and Assyria. Our evidence from Syria and Palestine, however, is very inadequate. Still, there are enough references to prove that this practice was also prevalent there. The Tell el-Amarna letters tell us that some people were forced to sell their children in order to procure food. From the Old Testament we learn that parents sold their daughters into conditional slavery (Ex. 21:7–11); that creditors seized the children of their deceased debtors (II Kings 4:1); and that debt-ridden farmers were forced to hand over their sons and daughters as slaves (Nehemiah 5:5).

The evidence of the existence of the second method of sale, namely, the sale of young girls into conditional slavery, comes from Nuzi[3] and Palestine. Nuzian and Hebrew parents often sold their daughters with the condition that the purchaser give them into marriage when the girls will have reached puberty. In Nuzi this type of sale was drawn up in the form of a fictitious adoption. The general scheme of a Nuzian sale-adoption contract runs as follows: (1) Preamble: Contract of daughtership and daughter-in-lawship. A has given his daughter B "into daughtership and daughter-in-lawship" to C. (2) Conditions: After [B has] reached puberty C shall give B into marriage either to a free-born man or to a slave. (The free-born man may be the purchaser himself, one of his sons, or a

[2]Correspondence uncovered at Tell Amarna in Egypt between Egyptian pharaohs and Syro-Palestinian rulers.

[3]Nuzi was a city in Assyria.

stranger "in the gate." In case the girl is given into marriage to one of her purchaser's slaves, she must remain in her owner's house as long as she lives.) (3) Price: The sum paid by the purchaser to the girl's father. The condition that the girl be married was fundamental. Fathers took the precaution to safeguard for their daughters a continuous marital status by inserting in the sale document a special clause (in case the condition was that the girl be married to a slave) to the effect that should her first slave-husband die, her master would give her into marriage to another one of his slaves. In some documents provisions are made for four husbands and in one for as many as eleven: "If ten of her husbands have died, in that case to an eleventh into wife-hood she shall be given."

This Nuzian practice had its parallel in Palestine. A section of the earliest Old Testament slave legislation, that of Exodus 21:7–11 reads:

> If a man sells his daughter to be an *amah* ("handmaid, female slave"), she shall not leave as the slaves do (i.e., in the seventh year). If her master dislikes her, although he had appointed her (as wife) for himself, then shall he let her be redeemed; to sell her (as a wife) to a stranger he shall have no power for he has dealt deceitfully with her. But if he has appointed her for his son, he shall treat her in the manner of daughters. If he takes to himself another (wife), he shall not diminish her food, her clothing, and her conjugal rights. If he does not do these three (things) to her, then she shall go out free without compensation. . . .

In view of the Nuzian practice, this Biblical law represents a fragment of a series of enactments which originally dealt with all cases of conditional sales of young girls. The section before us deals, to use the Nuzian terminology, with a "daughtership and daughter-in-lawship" sale. The conditions as set forth in this case are: (1) that the master himself marry the girl (hence the prohibition of treating her like a slave woman or selling her into marriage to a stranger); (2) in case he refuses, after she had reached puberty, to abide by the stipulation in the contract on the ground that the girl now does not find favor in his eyes, he may take recourse to one of the following alternatives: (a) he may let her be redeemed, (b) he may give her as wife to one of his sons, or (c) he may retain her as his concubine. Should he refuse, however, to comply with any of these alternatives open to him; then, as a penalty for breach of contract, "she shall go out free without compensation." . . .

Poverty or debt drove people to sell their children first and then themselves into slavery. In the absence of any state or community help for those driven from the soil by war, famine, or economic misfortune, a man or woman had only one recourse to save himself from starvation, and that was self-sale into slavery. Voluntary self-sale was a common phenomenon especially among strangers. From Nuzi we possess a number of documents relating to self-enslavement. These documents concern themselves mostly with the Habiru,[4] who not being able to find employment entered "of their own free will," singly or with their families, into the state of servitude. The term "servitude" is here used advisedly in preference to "slavery," because legally most of the Habiru self-sale cases in Nuzi differ fundamentally from the self-sale documents of Babylonia. In Babylonia the person who sold himself received his purchase price and as a result he became a slave, the property of another man. But in Nuzi no purchase price is paid to those who "sell themselves." The Habiru enter voluntarily into the state of servitude in exchange for food, clothing, and shelter.... These Habiru then, retain some kind of legal personality for in some documents it is expressly stated that only after desertion will they "be sold for a price," that is, be reduced to slavery.

Of all the ancient law codes, the Old Testament alone mentions the case of self-sale or voluntary slavery. Ex. 21:2–6 and Deut. 15:16–17 deal with the case of a Hebrew debtor-slave who refuses "to go out" after his six year term of service has been completed because he loves his master, his wife, and his children. The law provides that such a man (who prefers slavery with economic security to freedom with economic insecurity) shall have his ear bored through and shall remain a slave "forever." Leviticus 25:39–54 deals with a free Hebrew who, because of poverty, is forced to sell himself. In this case, the law provides that such a man, regardless of the fact that he had sold himself for ever, shall be freed in the year of the jubilee.

Although slaves were recruited from various indigenous and foreign sources, the basic source of supply for the ever mounting number of slaves in the Ancient Near East was the native defaulting debtor. Insolvency could be the result of many causes, such as drought, war, etc., against which the individual was powerless to act, but one of the chief factors leading to the foreclosure of property and man was unquestionably the exorbitant interest rate charged on loans. The average rate of interest in Ancient Babylonia was 20–25% on silver and 33 1/3% on grain. Assyria had no fixed or average rate. In Late Assyria the usurer had a free hand in determining the rate of interest. Interest on money varied from 20% to as high as 80% per annum. In addition to this general type there were two other kinds of loans current in Babylonia and Assyria. These were loans granted without interest by the temples and the landlords to their tenant-farmer and loans on which interest was charged only after the date of maturity. In the latter case the interest was enormous. In Babylonia the double of the principal, that is, 100% was charged; in Neo-Babylonia[5] we find 40% and also 100%; and in Late Assyria 100% and even 141% was charged. In Nuzi the average interest rate seems to have been 50% "till after the harvest." There is no information in the Old Testament as to the

[4]Possible ancestors of the Hebrews.

[5]Period of the eleventh dynasty (626–539 B.C.), when Babylonia achieved its greatest power.

rate of interest charged in Palestine. From the injunction against the taking of interest from a fellow Hebrew we may infer that a higher interest rate was charged and that Palestine was no exception to the rule.

The fate of the defaulting debtor was slavery. The creditor had the right to seize him and sell him into slavery. It was at this unlimited power of the creditor, which tended to reduce large numbers of free-born people into slavery, that . . . laws . . . of the Hammurabi Code were aimed. These laws demand that the defaulting debtor or his free-born pledge shall be released after three years of compulsory service. The right of seizure of the defaulting debtor by his creditor was in like manner exercised in Palestine. In II Kings 4:1–2 the creditor seized the children of a deceased debtor and the widow appealed to Elisha for help: "The creditor has come to take unto him my children as slaves." This practice of seizure and the subsequent sale into slavery of the unsolvent debtor is reflected in the prophetic literature: "Because they have sold the righteous for a pair of sandals" (Amos 2:6), and "Which of my creditors is it to whom I have sold you?" (Isaiah 50:1). Nehemiah 5:1 ff. shows that creditors foreclosed the land of their defaulting debtors and reduced pledged children to slavery. Like the Hammurabi Code, the Old Testament codes (Ex. 21:2–3 and Dt. 15:12–18) sought to arrest the power of the creditor by demanding that the Hebrew defaulting debtor should be released after six years of compulsory labor.

Legally the slave was considered a chattel. He was a commodity that could be sold, bought, leased, or exchanged. In sharp contrast to the free man, his father's name was almost never mentioned; he had no genealogy, being a man without a name. . . . Family ties were disregarded in the disposal of slaves. Husbands were separated from their wives, wives were sold without their husbands, and even young children were not spared. The only exception made was in the case of infants "at the breast" who were sold with their mothers.

Babylonia had a class legislation but it was not a caste state. The inequality and discrimination before the law, displayed in the Hammurabi Code in regard to the three main classes which constituted Babylonian society, were based not on race or birth but primarily on wealth. To be sold or to sell oneself into slavery, because of poverty or indebtedness, was a misfortune that could befall any man. This new status, however, was not irrevocable. The fact that the slave could, theoretically at least, be freed, made him a member of a low, dependent class, but not a member of a caste. However, as long as he remained a slave, he was subject to the wearing of a visible property mark . . . It may have been an incised mark upon the forehead, a tattooed sign upon some visible part of the body, or a small tablet of clay or metal hung on a chain around the neck, wrist, or ankle. In the Neo-Babylonian period the prevailing custom of marking slaves was to tattoo the name of the owner (and in case of a temple slave the symbol of the god) on the wrist of the slave. There is no evidence that the Assyrian slave was marked. . . .

The Biblical law prescribes that he who voluntarily submits to perpetual slavery shall have his ear pierced with an awl (Ex. 21:6; Dt. 15:17). . . . We may, therefore, conclude that just as in Babylonia, the Palestinian slaves were marked with a property sign either in the form of a suspended tag attached to the ear, or with a tattoo mark bearing the owner's name on the wrist.

While, legally, the slave was a mere chattel, classed with movable property, both law and society were forced to take into consideration the constantly self-asserting humanity of the slave. We thus have the highly contradictory situation in which on the one hand, the slave was considered as possessing the qualities of a human being while on the other hand, he was recognized as being void of the same and regarded as a mere "thing." The slave's status as a chattel, deprived of any human rights, was clearly and unmistakably emphasized in his relation to a third party. If injured, maimed, or killed by a third party, his owner was compensated for the loss, not the slave. The Biblical legislation mentions only the case of a slave who was killed by a goring ox and provides that the owner shall be compensated for his loss (Ex. 21:32).

. . . The slave's fate was in fact in his master's hand. Beatings and maltreatment of slaves seem to have been . . . common. . . . The Biblical legislation does not prohibit the maltreatment of a Hebrew slave by his master "for he is his money." It is only when the slave dies immediately (within three days) as a result of the beating that the master becomes liable to punishment (Ex. 21:20–21). In Ancient Babylonia a runaway slave was put in chains and had the words "A runaway, seize!" incised upon his face. The Hammurabi Code decrees the death penalty for those who entice a slave to flee from his master and also for those who harbor a fugitive slave. Furthermore, a reward of two shekels is promised to anyone who captures a fugitive slave and brings him back to his master.

The Old Testament slave legislations (Ex. 21, Dt. 15, Lev. 25) do not mention the case of the fugitive slave although the tendency to run away was prevalent in Palestine as it was in the adjacent countries. . . . Fugitive slaves were extradited when they fled into foreign countries (I Kings 2:39 f.). In view of these facts how should the Deuteronomic ordinance (chap. 23:16) "You shall not deliver a slave unto his master who escapes to you from his master" be interpreted? It is a most extraordinary law for its application in life would have spelled the end of slavery in Palestine. Perhaps this ordinance should be explained from a national-economic point of view. It was most probably drawn up in favor of Hebrew slaves who had fled from foreign countries. If this interpretation be correct, then the Deuteronomic law would have its parallel in . . . the Hammurabi Code according to which a native Babylonian slave who had been sold into a foreign country and fled from there was set free by the state . . . .

The slave enjoyed certain privileges which neither law nor society could deny him. According to the Hammurabi Code a slave could marry

a free-born woman and a female slave could become her master's concubine. In both cases the children born of such unions were free. The slave
could amass a peculium[6] and enjoy it during his life-time, though legally
it belonged to his master. And finally the slave could be manumitted. The
Hammurabi Code recognizes four legal ways by which a slave received his
freedom ipso facto: (1) wives and children sold, or handed over as pledges,
are to be freed after three years of service ...; (2) a slave concubine and
her children become free after the death of the master ...; (3) children
born of a marriage between a slave and a free woman are free ...; and
(4) a native Babylonian slave bought in a foreign country and brought
back to Babylonia is unconditionally freed.... In addition to these laws
which applied only to certain classes and to specific cases of slaves, there
were two other ways of manumission: release by adoption and by purchase. Release by adoption was, like that by purchase, a business transaction.... The manumitted slave entered into a sonship (or daughtership)
relation to his former master and took upon himself the obligation to support him as long as he lived. After the death of the manumitter, the fictitious relationship and the very real material support were terminated and
the "son" became completely free. If the adopted slave failed to live up to
his promise of support, that is, repudiated his "parents" by saying "you
are not my father" or/and "you are not my mother," the adoption was
annulled and the "son" reverted to his former slave status. The difference
between release by adoption with the condition to support the manumitter
(or release with the condition of support without adoption) and that of release by purchase is that in the former case the released slave still remains
in a state of dependency to his former master and becomes completely
free only after the death of his former master, while in the second case,
the slave severs all connections with his master and becomes immediately
and irrevocably free.

According to the Biblical law there were five ways by which a Hebrew
slave obtained his freedom. These were: (1) a debtor-slave is freed after six
years of service (Ex. 21:2, Dt. 15:12); (2) he who sold himself into slavery is
to be freed in the year of the jubilee (Lev. 25); (3) a free-born girl who was
sold by her father with the condition that her master or his son marry her,
is to be freed if the master refuses to abide by the conditions of the sale
(Ex. 21:7–11); (4) by injury (Ex. 21:26–27); and (5) by purchase (Lev. 25:47
ff.). The six-years service limit of the defaulting debtor has its parallel in
the Hammurabi Code ... which demands the release of a debtor-slave in
the fourth year. We have no evidence to prove that the Hammurabi law
was ever enforced in Ancient Babylonia. We have hundreds of documents
showing that this law was not enforced in Neo-Babylonia. Debtors were
foreclosed and sold into slavery if the loans were not paid on the date of
maturity. In view of the fact that we have no private documents from the

[6]Small savings.

Biblical period we cannot say whether the law of release of the debtor-slave was enforced in Palestine. . . . The law of the release of the Hebrew slave in the year of the jubilee is part of a great land reform utopia according to which all land, whether sold or given as security, must revert to its original owners in the year of the jubilee. . . . Was the law of the jubilee ever enforced in life? The sages of the Talmud[7] were very much in doubt about it. The law of release by injury presents considerable difficulties. The meaning of the law is, of course, quite clear. The loss of limb, as a result of beatings administered by the master, is considered sufficient ground for meriting release. . . . It seems . . . that the only plausible interpretation . . . would be to assume that the law . . . applies to the Hebrew defaulting debtor. From the point of view of the law, the Hebrew defaulting debtor is not a slave at all but merely a debtor temporarily in the service of his creditor. When such a debtor is permanently injured by his creditor, the loss of limb is considered to be the equivalent of the amount of the debt and hence he is to be released.

There were three main classes of slaves in the Ancient Near East, viz., state slaves, temple slaves, and privately owned slaves. Of these, the first group, recruited from war prisoners, was economically the most important. In Babylonia and Assyria the state slaves, with the assistance of corvee[8] gangs and hired laborers, constructed roads, dug canals, erected fortresses, built temples, tilled the crown lands, and worked in the royal factories connected with the palace. The small city-states of Syria and Palestine also had their state slaves. In the El-Amarna period (c. 1400 B.C.) Syrian and Palestinian "kings" sent large numbers of slaves and war captives . . . as gifts to their Egyptian overlords. . . . That this institution existed in Palestine from the days of David down to the period of Nehemiah and Ezra is attested by the numerous references to the state slaves in the Old Testament. Since this class of slaves (recruited from war captives and from the tribute paying Canaanites) was officially created by Solomon, they were appropriately called *abde Shelomo* ("Solomon's slaves"). Once formed, this class of state slaves remained in existence until the end of the Judaean kingdom.[9] . . . The end of independent statehood marked also the end of the institution of slavery.

Already at the dawn of history the Babylonian temple with its vast wealth constituted the richest agricultural, industrial, and commercial single unit within the community. It was a well organized and efficiently run corporation controlling extensive tracts of land, enormous quantities of raw material, large flocks of cattle and sheep, sizeable amounts of precious metal, and a large number of slaves. This was also true, though to a lesser degree, of the Assyrian, Syrian, and Palestinian temples. . . .

[7]The books of Jewish law.
[8]Forced labor.
[9]586 B.C.

Temple slaves were recruited from two sources: prisoners of war who were presented to the temples by victorious kings, and dedications of slaves by private individuals. The sanctuaries in Palestine recruited their slaves from the same sources. After the successful campaign against the Midianites,[10] Moses is reported to have taken one of every five hundred, or one of every fifty, prisoners, and presented them as a gift to Yahweh (Num. 31:25ff.). Joshua made the Gibeonites[11] "hewers of wood and drawers of water in the sanctuary" (chap. 9:21ff.). . . . We have no evidence to prove that privately owned slaves were dedicated to temples in Palestine. The case of young Samuel who was dedicated to the sanctuary of Shiloh, however, shows that this practice was known in Palestine. While the number of state and temple slaves was very large, their economic role must not be overestimated. The state . . . employed them in non-competitive enterprises and the temple used them primarily for menial work. In its two main branches of activity, agriculture and industry, the temple employed mostly free-born people and not slaves. The land was cultivated by free-born tenant-farmers, and free-born artisans worked in the shops.

Unlike Egypt, where the land belonged to the crown, private ownership of land was the rule in the Sumero-Semitic countries. The case of the Israelite farmer Naboth who chose death in preference to selling his ancestral plot to king Ahab was characteristic of the attitude of all peasantry in the Ancient Near East. With the exception of the large holdings of the crown and the temples, the land was owned by two classes of people: small farmers and large landowners. Since the land property of the average farmer was small and his family large there was no great need for outside help either in the form of hired laborers or of slaves. The labor situation was, of course, different in the second group. These large estates had to be worked with hired help. This help, however, was only to a very small degree drawn from the ranks of hired laborers and slaves. It was drawn primarily and overwhelmingly from the ranks of the dispossessed peasantry croppers. . . . Instead of buying, maintaining, and guarding considerable numbers of unwilling slaves, the large landowners (and to a degree even the kings and the temples) preferred to lease parcels of their land to free-born tenant-farmers. . . . Like the upper class in the cities, well-to-do farmers owned slaves and employed them on the land, but slave labor was not a decisive factor in the agricultural life of the Ancient Near East.

The counterpart of the free-born tenant-farmer in agriculture was the free-born "hired laborer" in industry. There was, of course, great competition between free laborers and slaves in the field of unskilled labor, but the skilled fields were dominated by the free artisans. The reasons for this phenomenon, that is, the small number of slave artisans in the Ancient

---

[10]Semitic people who invaded southern Palestine after 1200 B.C.

[11]Palestinian people who derived their name from the city, Gibeon.

Near East, were: (1) the apprenticeship period lasted from two to six years, a period during which the slave not only did not bring in any profit, but the owner had to spend money for his upkeep; (2) the number of slaves in well-to-do families averaged from one to three and therefore only a few of them could be spared to be used as an investment with a view to future returns; and finally (3) the general unwillingness of the employer to hire slaves because they could not be trusted to operate with expensive tools even when they possessed the skill to handle them. We thus come to the conclusion that the role played by slaves in the skilled industries was very insignificant indeed. Ancient Near Eastern craftsmanship was the product of free labor.

We have seen that economically the Ancient Near Eastern civilization was not based on slave labor. We have also seen that society was unable to maintain consistently the legal fiction that the slave was a mere chattel, and hence some freedom was accorded to him. There remains one more aspect to be considered and that is the attitude of religion toward slavery, the ownership of man by man. Nowhere in the vast religious literature of the Sumero-Accadian world is a protest raised against the institution of slavery, nor is there anywhere an expression of sympathy for the victims of this system. The Old Testament justifies perpetual slavery of the Canaanites, but demands the release of the Hebrew defaulting debtor in the seventh year and of those who sold themselves in the year of the jubilee. The first case—the release of the debtor-slave after a limited term of service—has a parallel in the earlier Hammurabi Code which also demands the release of the defaulting debtor. But in the second case where the release is demanded of even those who had sold themselves voluntarily into slavery, we have for the first time an open denial of the right of man to own man in perpetuity. This denial of the right of possession of man by man is as yet restricted to Hebrews only (cf. Nehemiah 5:8), but it is a step which no other religion had taken before. The first man in the Ancient Near East who raised his voice in a sweeping condemnation of slavery as a cruel and inhuman institution, irrespective of nationality and race, was the philosopher Job. His was a condemnation based on the moral concept of the inherent brotherhood of man, for

"Did not He that made me in the womb make him (the slave) also? And did not One fashion us in the womb?" (31:15)

Afterlife: Ancient Israel's Changing Vision of the World Beyond

BERNHARD LANG

Ancient Semites (Israelites and their Mesopotamian and Syro-Palestinian neighbors) viewed the world as containing the heavens, the earth, and the netherworld (Sheol). How did humans communicate with the gods of heaven and those of the underworld? What type of worship was familial and which rituals were community functions?

How did the ancient Semites bury their dead? Unlike the Egyptians, for example, the Semites did not express great interest in life after death, even though they evidently believed in some sort of afterlife. Why did they believe it necessary to venerate and placate dead ancestors? How did the living make contact with the dead? What was life in the netherworld like?

Religion is a cultural creation and changes over time. In what ways did Israel's vision of the world beyond develop? For instance, attitudes toward ancestor worship and toward the existence of other gods and goddesses underwent transformation. What was the "Yahweh-alone movement" and how did it bear on Israel's conceptions of the world beyond? How did it alter religious ritual? What effect did the destruction of the northern kingdom of Israel in 722 B.C. have on Hebraic religion? How did this religion now view the dead and their significance? In this regard, what was the import of the Book of Job? What did Sheol become in the minds of the Hebrews?

The ancient Hebrews, through their dietary laws, keeping of the Sabbath, and circumcision, cut themselves off from their neighbors. By eventually creating a this-worldly religion, Hebrew theology distanced itself from some of the other ancient Near Eastern religions. The Egyptians, for example, spent much religious energy on preparing for and worrying about a life after death. Hebraic religion concentrated on life above ground.

But Judaism continued to evolve. How did the Babylonian conquest of the southern kingdom of Judah in 586 B.C. lead the Hebrews to rethink their beliefs about the dead? How did the new Persian religion, Zoroastrianism, influence Judaism? By what means did Ezekiel link the new belief in individual bodily resurrection with national aspirations?

From an early date, the Hebrews were concerned with elaborating a theodicy, an attempt to explain the presence of evil in this world. Pain inflicted on sentient beings brought into question their god's attributes of omnipotence and perfect goodness, so Judaism rationally tried to explain how God would permit suffering to exist. How did the belief in resurrection provide a new answer to the problem of evil for some Jews?

Bernhard Lang argues that the Jews became seriously divided on their views of a life after death. What were the beliefs of those who accepted a philosophical and individualistic response to an afterlife? What new role did heaven play? How was heaven pictured? As a result of Greek influence, what ideas emerged about the immortality of the soul?

By the first century A.D., there were three distinct Jewish views of the afterlife. What were these interpretations?

Lang emphasizes the diversity and evolution of Jewish attitudes in the ancient world. The precise extent to which the populace, as opposed to simply a religious elite, held these views is impossible to determine, but, in light of the support that Jews gave to their religion, it is safe to assume that common Jews shared the various attitudes toward life after death and toward Sheol that Lang describes. The changing visions of the world beyond joined together Jewish religious thinkers and the population in an attempt to fathom the unfathomable.

The earliest Hebrew understanding of the cosmos grew out of prevailing Mesopotamian and Canaanite mythology. Even before the time of the Hebrews, ancient Semites pictured the world as a three-tiered structure: an upper realm of the gods (heaven), a middle world given by the gods to humans (earth) and a lower domain consisting of a great cave far below the surface of the earth (the netherworld or Sheol). While the gods inhabited heaven, and humans during life inhabited earth, Sheol housed both the dead and the infernal gods.

Although the ancients envisioned Sheol as a dark and silent place, we should not think of it as hell. A deity called Mot, "Death," reigned there and ruled over both the dead and the infernal gods.

Human beings living on earth, between heaven and Sheol, were affected and influenced by both the upper and lower worlds. Human communication with the deities of the upper world, as well as with the gods of the lower world, was of paramount importance. All the inhabitants of the earth—whether wealthy landlords, merchants, proud warriors, aristocrats, princes or fashionable ladies—had to regard themselves as essentially weak and dependent on the gods. Only by establishing temples, sponsoring priests and temple choirs, offering lavish sacrifices, chanting elaborate prayers, and heeding sorcerers and prophets could human beings be assured of divine benevolence. Fertile flocks, abundant harvests, victories in battle and success, prosperity and peace depended on the graciousness of the gods residing in either heaven or Sheol.

Ancient Near Eastern ritual was varied and complicated. Only priests, thoroughly trained in public and private ritual and lore, knew the intricacies of communication with the upper and lower worlds. Their ritual appealed either to the powers of heaven or to the gods of the netherworld and the dead who shared that habitation and who might influence the infernal gods with whom they lived. To appeal to the dead meant basically to call upon expired ancestors, residing in Sheol, to aid the living.

Ancestor worship—on behalf of genealogically related individuals— venerated forefathers and, perhaps, foremothers, from whom the living expected personal protection and, more important, numerous offspring. Gradually, formalized rituals developed to express the veneration of ancestors. In one such ritual, the living drank huge quantities of wine and also poured out wine for the dead, who were the objects of appeal; in this ritual everyone, including the dead, supposedly got drunk. Another, less elaborate, ritual consisted simply of placing offerings of water and food at the family tomb.

Ancestor worship did not involve the community at large; we may therefore refer to it as a private ritual. Small groups of family members would venerate their ancestors in private worship without the participation of any larger political or ethnic grouping.

However, when the gods of heaven, rather than the dead, were invoked, the entire community was involved. Priests in state temples offered regular sacrifices to the gods of heaven on behalf of the king, and, through him, on behalf of the whole society. These were public rituals that extended far beyond the confines of an individual family or family lineage. The more important public rituals celebrated the cycle of the agricultural year: the sowing and reaping of grain, or the eating of the first fruits of the season. These public rituals connected the people not with their dead relatives, but with the gods of the sky who were responsible for rain. Without this communion with the sky gods, they believed, no vegetation could grow in the arid zones of the ancient Near East.

Both kinds of ritual—the public one addressed to the celestial gods and the private one directed to the ancestors in the netherworld—coexisted. Indeed, they were practiced by the same people. The types of rituals depended not on what the supplicant hoped to gain, but for whom the gain was intended. If a family member would benefit, then a private ritual was performed. If the community as a whole benefited, a public ritual was conducted.

In this cosmic conception, to die meant to change one's place in the ritual universe. But transfer to the netherworld required some earthly actions. The family was required to bury the body, thereby removing it from the sight of the celestial gods and bringing it into contact with the dead person's new realm of being. Burial usually occurred in an underground vault or was carried out simply by covering the body with earth. Although the flesh decayed and the bones dried out, a shadowy replica of the deceased became manifest and descended into the vast underground mausoleum where it would continue its existence.

What was life like there? The ancient Semites, unfortunately for 20th-century students of the past, have left us no speculations about life in Sheol. The ancients were apparently uninterested in this question. Their concern was with establishing ritual contact with the world of the dead. Hence, we do not know what they believed existence was like in Sheol. We know only of their belief that in the netherworld the dead would meet their own ancestors, a belief that may have prompted the biblical expression that a person who dies "goes to his fathers [ancestors]" (see Genesis 15:15) or is "gathered to his people [kin]" (Genesis 25:8).

The shadowy life of the dead was permanent and did not fade away. There were, however, different degrees of life in the netherworld, depending on one's past earthly existence and on the regularity with which one's descendants engaged in certain rituals. Someone who died in ripe old age and who received regular offerings of food and water (placed near the tomb) achieved the best fate. Residing in the upper, and perhaps somewhat lighter part of Sheol, such an ancestor could assist his or her descendants by bestowing powerful blessings. But ancestors could also become angry and withhold blessings and cause harm. The ancestors thus became like "gods" who could affect the lives of the living in dramatic ways (see 1 Samuel 28:13).

If earthly relatives neglected their ancestor offerings, the fate of the dead worsened. Rather than residing in the lighter parts of Sheol, they would descend to the lower and more unpleasant parts of the netherworld. People who died the death of criminals or on the battlefield without having their bodies properly buried populated the lowest regions.

Isaiah provides us with a vivid picture of the lower parts of Sheol in a prophecy against Babylon. The king of Babylon will be brought down by Yahweh, the prophet tells us, and Israel will sing a song of scorn to taunt her former oppressor (Isaiah 14:3). The song, a mock dirge, describes how the king of Babylon will die:

> How you are fallen from heaven,
>   O Day Star, son of Dawn!
> How you are cut down to the ground,
>   you who laid the nations low!
> You said in your heart,
>   'I will ascend to heaven;
> above the stars of God
>   I will set my throne on high;
> I will sit on the mount of assembly
>   in the far north;
> I will ascend above the heights of the clouds,
>   I will make myself like the Most High.'
> But you are brought down to Sheol,
>   to the depths of the pit.
>
> Isaiah 14:12–15

On his arrival in Sheol, the king of Babylon is met by the kings who preceded him. They are mere shades, leading shadowy lives of their own, with dreamy pomp and ceremony. The king of Babylon is to lie in mud and filth, covered with worms.

> Sheol beneath is stirred up
>   to meet you when you come,
> it rouses the shades to greet you,
>   all who were leaders of the earth;
> it raises from their thrones

all who were kings of the nations.
All of them will speak
  and say to you:
'You too have become as weak as we!
  You have become like us!'
Your pomp is brought down to Sheol,
  the sound of your harps;
maggots are the bed beneath you,
  and worms your covering.

Isaiah 14:9–11

The king of Babylon will live in Sheol like one who has been unburied:

Those who see you will stare at you,
  and ponder over you:
'Is this the man who made the earth tremble,
  who shook kingdoms,
who made the world like a desert
  and overthrew its cities,
  who did not let his prisoners go home?'
All the kings of the nations lie in glory,
  each in his own tomb;
but you are cast out, away from your sepulchre,
  like a loathed untimely birth,
clothed with the slain, those pierced by the sword,
  who go down to the stones of the Pit,
  like a dead body trod under foot
You will not be joined with them in burial,
  because you have destroyed your land,
  you have slain your people.

Isaiah 14:16–20

The living contacted the dead in Sheol not only through ancestor worship, but also through mediums, sorcerers, witches and necromancers who had special access to the netherworld. In one episode described in the Bible, King Saul, nearly deranged, seeks to learn the outcome of an imminent battle with the Philistines by consulting the witch of En-dor. After his normal channels of communication with the divine realm—dreams, priestly manipulation of lots, the advice of prophets—fail, Saul, desperate and disguised, pays a nocturnal visit to a necromancer. The witch of En-dor digs a hole in the crust of the earth so that the world of the living may be joined to the realm of the dead. At Saul's request, the witch raises the Prophet Samuel, once Saul's supporter—who anointed him king and who is now his sworn detractor. The scene is one of high drama and emotion:

Then Samuel said to Saul, 'Why have you disturbed me by bringing me up?' Saul answered, 'I am in great distress; for the Philistines are warring against me, and God has turned away from me and answers me no more, either by prophets or by dreams; therefore I have summoned you to tell me what I shall do.'

And Samuel said, 'Why then do you ask me, since the Lord has turned from you and become your enemy?'

'The Lord has done to you as he spoke by me; for the Lord has torn the kingdom out of your hand, and given it to your neighbor, David. Because you did not obey the voice of the Lord, and did not carry out his fierce wrath against the Amalek,[1] therefore the Lord has done this thing to you this day. Moreover the Lord will give Israel also with you into the hand of the Philistines; and tomorrow you and your sons shall be with me; the Lord will give the army of Israel into the hand of the Philistines.'

Then Saul fell at once full length upon the ground, filled with fear because of the words of Samuel (1 Samuel 28:15–20).

Although this communication occurred between Saul and Samuel, only the medium could see the dead Samuel. Saul had to ask the medium, "What do you see? . . . What is his appearance?" (1 Samuel 28:13,14). She describes "an old man wrapped in a robe."

After the conversation with Saul, the fading spirit returns to the darkness and silence of Sheol. Saul, of course, dies as foretold during the consultation.

The episode gives us a glimpse of an afterlife in which the dead, although apparently deprived of material substance, retain such personality characteristics as form, memory, consciousness and even knowledge of what happens on the other side. While life in the netherworld is less than appealing, the dead have the power to aid or to harm the living. Such powers permit the dead to function as gods. Private rituals, conducted by kin, emphasize the bonds between the residents of earth and the residents of the netherworld. These private rituals contrast with public rituals that focus on the concerns of the larger community.

Although our knowledge of this early stratum of Semitic thought is sketchy, we can discern a belief in a shadowy afterlife in which the status of the dead depends on the veneration of the living; conversely, the state of the living may be influenced by the gods of the netherworld.

Later biblical writers condemned ancestor worship and necromancy as an inherently pagan practice that cannot be a legitimate part of the religion of Israel. Note that the author of 1 Samuel 28 has Saul outlawing resort to such necromancers, although Saul is recklessly violating his own prohibition.

Ancestor worship was outlawed in the eighth century B.C. as a part of a new prophetic movement. At that time, the powerful Assyrian empire was exerting increasingly intolerable pressure on the small vassal kingdoms of Israel and Judah. In this situation of almost permanent crisis, a prophetic movement formed that advocated the exclusive worship of one

---

[1]In Exodus 17:8–16, the Amalekites attacked the Israelites shortly after they crossed the Red Sea. For that reason, God cursed the Amalekites and commanded their annihilation.

God, Yahweh. The worship of all other gods and goddesses was to be abandoned.

According to this prophetic movement, Israel's God Yahweh, the only one with real power, would eventually intervene and alter the political scene in favor of his people. This new religious movement has been called by scholars the "Yahweh-alone movement." It not only banned the worship of the sky gods but also outlawed the cult of the dead.

The Yahweh-alone-ists outlawed ancestor worship because they perceived it as a magical deviation from true worship. . . . [M]agic "is not part of an organized [communal] worship, but private, secret, mysterious" and is therefore often prohibited by the controlling group. The Yahweh-alone-ists believed that ancestor worship, which gave preference to kin, slighted national concerns. For them, national and public matters assumed clear priority over private and family affairs.

Ironically enough, after the Assyrians conquered and destroyed the northern kingdom of Israel in 722 B.C., the Yahweh-alone-ists became even more convinced of their cause. They attributed the military disaster at the hands of the Assyrians to the neglect of the one God whose exclusive worship they advocated. In the now truncated Israel—the small southern kingdom of Judah alone survived—the Judahite king Hezekiah (716–687 B.C.) attempted a cultic and legal reform, emphasizing the exclusivity of Yahweh worship.

King Hezekiah's reform either failed or remained partially unimplemented. In any event, almost a century passed before the Yahweh-alone-ist movement became the decisive factor in official Judahite policy. In 623 B.C., the Judahite king Josiah proclaimed that Yahweh was the only god to be worshipped, apparently accomplishing the aim of the earlier reform. The biblical report of Josiah's reform tells us that "Josiah got rid of all the mediums and necromancers [literally, those who called up the ghosts and spirits of the dead], of all household gods and idols, and all the abominations" (2 Kings 23:24).

By taking this decisive step toward monotheism, Josiah drastically reduced private worship, and especially ritual activities relating to the dead. The placing of food near or in the tomb as a funerary offering—a ritual that formerly was a real sacrifice to the gods of the underworld—was reduced to a simple gesture of convention or tradition. The ritual was stripped of its cosmological significance. The dead could be fed and thereby kept vital, but any other contact was forbidden by the reformers. Denied their exercise of influence over the living, the ancestors faded into the distance, into the eternal darkness of Sheol.

While King Josiah's reform outlawed certain traditional practices concerning the dead, it did not create new beliefs to replace earlier traditions regarding life after death. A more philosophical examination of the meaning of death and the afterlife appears, however, in the Book of Job, which dates from the fifth century B.C. Continuing the trend begun in the eighth century with King Hezekiah, the Book of Job devalues the role of the dead. It recognizes that, when one's earthly life ceases, one is cut off permanently from life on earth, without communication either way, and, perhaps worse, one is cut off from God himself. Job, in his suffering, longs to go to Sheol until the time when God will remember him, but he knows that will not be; there is no hope of this. The Book of Job proclaims that the dead have no knowledge of the living; they cannot influence those on earth. Although a dead man's descendants may honor him, he knows nothing of it (Job 14:21). The communication between ancestor and offspring, so vital in polytheistic thought and ritual, disappears. The living and the dead are eternally separated:

> For there is hope for a tree,
>> if it be cut down, that it will sprout again,
>> and that its shoots will not cease.
> Though its root grow old in the earth,
>> and its stump die in the ground,
> yet at the scent of water it will bud
>> and put forth branches like a young plant.
> But man dies, and is laid low;
>> man breathes his last, and where is he?
> As waters fail from a lake,
>> and a river wastes away and dries up,
> So man lies down and rises not again;
>> till the heavens are no more he will not awake,
>> or be roused out of his sleep.
> Oh that thou wouldest hide me in Sheol,
>> that thou wouldest conceal me until thy wrath be past,
>> that thou wouldest appoint me a set time, and remember me!
> If a man die, shall he live again?
>> All the days of my service I would wait,
>> till my release should come.
> Thou wouldest call, and I would answer thee;
>> thou wouldest long for the work of thy hands.
> For then thou wouldest number my steps,
>> thou wouldest not keep watch over my sin;
> my transgression would be sealed up in a bag,
>> and thou wouldest cover over my iniquity.
> But the mountain falls and crumbles away,
>> and the rock is removed from its place;
> the waters wear away the stones;
>> the torrents wash away the soil of the earth;
>> so thou destroyest the hope of man.
> Thou prevailest for ever against him, and he passes;
>> thou changest his countenance, and sendest him away.
> His sons come to honor, and he does not know it;
>> they are brought low, and he perceives it not.

Job 14:7–21

Job and his contemporaries agreed with older, pessimistic traditions of the Semitic world that the fate of the dead was a deplorable one. Who wants to exist in "a land of gloom and chaos, where light is as darkness" (Job 10:22; 3:17–19)? We are reminded of the Old-Babylonian epic of Gilgamesh, which portrays the netherworld as "the house wherein the dwellers are bereft of light, where dust is their fare and clay their food." Despite this gloomy view of the land of the dead, at least death ends our earthly misery, as Job points out in a skillful eulogy (Job 3:17–19). Death also resolves the problem of social inequality by releasing us from servitude. Since the dead cannot help the living, the dead are released from the burden of being involved in human troubles. Sheol, if not a place of happiness, is at least free from the trials of earth.

But for the devout worshipper of Yahweh, Sheol held another deprivation. Even Yahweh is not worshipped there.

"Who will praise the Most High in Sheol?" asks Ecclesiasticus,[2] written in the second century B.C. "When a man is dead and ceases to be, his gratitude dies with him" (Ecclesiasticus 17:27,28). There can thus be no relationship between Yahweh and the dead.

The two taboos—prohibiting relating to any deity but Yahweh and prohibiting a relationship between the dead and Yahweh—condemned the dead to a meaningless existence. They could not even ask for consolation from the living. Since the realms of the living and the dead were completely separated, no communication could take place between them. The residual veneration in the form of funerary offerings notwithstanding, the dead expected nothing from their descendants. And those on earth no longer waited for their ancestors' help. Priests especially avoided any ritual connection with the dead; they were not even allowed to attend the funerals of their own parents (Leviticus 21:11).

In contrast to the earlier Semitic ritual universe, the ritual universe created by King Josiah's seventh-century B.C. reform ultimately sealed off the netherworld. Israelite rituals simply excluded the dead from ritual consideration. Instead of being powerful and influential ancestors, the deceased became weak shadows of negligible vitality. Not being able to praise the only God, they were doomed to a meaningless existence in the eternal silence of Sheol. Israelite theology focused on the practices of a this-worldly religion rather than on the futile speculations of the life of the dead. The pious who meet with unfortunate circumstances on earth had to be promised rewards in this life. Job, faced with a miserable earthly existence, is not promised rewards after death. Whatever other messages his story presents, the implications of its last page are clear: God rewards Job for his patience and devotion with health, family and wealth. Job

---

[2]Ecclesiasticus, or the Book of Sirach, is part of the Catholic canon and is contained in the Septuagint, the first translation of the Bible from Hebrew to Greek—made for the Jews of Alexandria in about the third century B.C. Ecclesiasticus is in the apocrypha of Jews and Protestants. (Author's note.)

receives his blessing—"twice as much as he had before"—*on earth and not in the afterlife* (Job 42:10). The Judaism of King Josiah's reform held no promise for the dead.

The Babylonian destruction of Jerusalem in 586 B.C. brought the kingdom of Judah to an abrupt end. Israel no longer existed on the political map of the Near East. In the centuries that followed, many Jews of course continued to dream of an independent Israel restored by divine intervention. Especially in times of political upheavals and turmoil, the fire of independence flared; whenever one superpower vanished, giving way to new rulers—the Babylonians to the Persians, the Persians to the Greeks, and, eventually, the Greeks to the Romans—the hope of a national restoration swelled.

The most extreme version of this hope assumed that Yahweh not only intended to restore Israel as a state but would also permit the dead to live in the new Jewish commonwealth. The belief in a "bodily resurrection" held that the dead must not be deprived of the blessings of the new age that was to come. Restored fully to bodily life, they would live for many years in the new world, enjoying a renewed life.

The concept of a bodily resurrection and life in a restored world had nothing in common with the views of the afterlife reflected in King Josiah's reform. Indeed, the concept of bodily resurrection was borrowed from the ancient Iranians. It first appears in the teachings of the Iranian prophet Zoroaster (about 1500 B.C.). According to Zoroaster, the soul's fate after death depended on the character of its life on earth; after death, the soul would be judged, and either rewarded in heaven or punished in a less pleasant place, hell. Complete happiness, however, required more than this: Some day the souls of the just would be reunited with their bodies, not in a heavenly paradise, but on earth. Zoroaster anticipated a general resurrection of the dead, following a universal divine judgment and an eventual cleansing of the earth. Restored to its original perfection and beauty, the world would then serve as the eternal kingdom of Ahura Mazda, the creator. In this new world, men and women would live forever.

Jews living in Babylonia, later Persia, and other areas within the orbit of Iranian influence in the sixth century B.C., absorbed Zoroastrian beliefs and adapted them to their own aspirations. Iranian religion helped Jewish theologians shape their own tradition.

The idea of a bodily resurrection in Israel first appears in the prophecies of Ezekiel (c. 585–568 B.C.). Ezekiel delivered a series of oracles of hope that included visions of a gloriously rebuilt Jerusalem with a magnificent temple. In one of his visions, Ezekiel saw a vast plain covered with dry human bones, bleached by the sun (Ezekiel 37:1–15). A plain with dried bones is reminiscent of a Zoroastrian funeral ground where the bodies of the dead remained unburied. Worshippers of Ahura Mazda allowed the bodies to lie in the sun for a year until the rains turned the flesh into carrion and the birds devoured it, leaving only the bones. According to Zoroastrian doctrine, at a later resurrection the creator would reassemble the scattered parts of the body. Similarly in Ezekiel, after the prophet is shown the plain covered with human bones, he is commanded to prophesy to the bones and announce their resurrection; immediately the skeletons reassemble themselves and form bodies. God then tells Ezekiel to order the winds to breathe into the bodies—and the bodies come back to life. The resurrected people return to their homeland in Israel from their exile in Babylonia.

Zoroastrian resurrection was of course adapted to the religious and political outlook of Jews at the time. Ezekiel linked the idea of resurrection to national concerns, rather than to universal, cosmological expectations. The original Iranian doctrine implied the end of human history, as well as the end of death; Ezekiel, however, related resurrection to a miracle that would inaugurate a new era in Israel's national life. Ezekiel expected not a new universe, but a renewed Jewish commonwealth free from foreign oppression.

In later centuries, in times of persecution or when the spirit of national pride was rekindled, religious leaders and political rebels alike would envision a national revival accompanied by a bodily resurrection.

The Book of Daniel, written in the second century B.C. during a time of Greek persecution, anticipated a national revival when "many of those who sleep in the dust of the earth will awake" (Daniel 12:2).

While the kingdom God would create would be never-ending and eternal, the life span of the resurrected would be limited. According to the Book of Enoch,[3] for instance, the resurrected would live "five hundred years" or as "long life on earth as [their] fathers lived." Their "fathers" were not their immediate ancestors, but rather the biblical patriarchs who, according to Genesis, lived to ripe old ages like 895, 987, etc. After a long and peaceful second life on earth, which would more than make up for the difficulties encountered in their first life, the resurrected would eventually die.

The expectation of resurrection, with its accompanying establishment of the divine kingdom, provided an answer to the question of why God did not intervene on behalf of his suffering people. Far from being indifferent to Israel's political fate, God was simply waiting for that special day that he, in his wisdom, had chosen. Then would the faithful be resurrected, fully restored to bodily life, and God's universal kingdom on earth established.

Not all Jews, of course, shared this hope. Many simply made their peace with their various overlords and accepted foreign rule. As long as their overlords allowed them freely to exercise their religion, they saw no reason to be dissatisfied. Many such Jews, especially those with a more philosophical outlook, explored the fate of the dead in a way vastly dif-

---

[3] A non-biblical book that originated in third-century B.C. Judaism. (Author's note.)

ferent from that of the nationalists. For them, the idea of a glorious communal future with a restored Israelite nation faded into the background. They focused instead on the post-mortem future of individuals.

The earliest effort to formulate a more philosophical, individualistic response to life after death may be found in Psalms 73 and 49. The authors of these psalms are troubled by the seeming prosperity of the wicked and the ease of the rich. The poet-author of Psalm 73 laments that the wicked "are always at ease, they increase in riches. All in vain have I kept my heart clean" (Psalm 73:12–13). But then he realizes that eventually the wicked will be "destroyed in a moment, swept away utterly" (Psalm 73:19). The psalmist, on the other hand, having led a righteous life, will be with God (Psalm 73:23): "Afterward [that is, after life on earth] thou will receive me with glory. Whom have I *in heaven*, but thee?" (Psalm 73:24–25).

Psalm 49 is even more explicit. The rich, boastful and arrogant will be unable to bargain with God. They will perish and be sent to Sheol, without their riches and denied any glimpse of light. As for the righteous psalmist, however, God "will take me from the power of Sheol . . . he will receive me" (Psalm 49:15).

Both psalms reveal a strong personal element; they reflect personal concerns; they speak in the first person, "I."

By proclaiming that God will eventually "receive" them after their deaths, these individualistic poets are boldly reusing vocabulary traditionally associated with figures like Enoch (the sixth descendant after Adam) and the prophet Elijah. Enoch and Elijah did not die; God bodily assumed them into heaven (Genesis 5:24 and 2 Kings 2:11). From the viewpoint of the authors of Psalms 73 and 49, what was possible for Enoch and Elijah was possible for others as well. Thus, the concept of heavenly assumption was redefined in less extraordinary terms. God "received" his faithful "after" death, without having to resort to the miraculous procedure of taking them away while still alive. Searching the Scriptures, the psalmists found the ancient myth of heavenly assumption and creatively expanded it. They translated the myth of heaven, once only possible for the special few like Enoch and Elijah, into a hope and expectation for the many.

The psalmists, however, give no description of this heavenly realm, where the righteous would go. The psalmists speak only of a continuing fellowship with God and refer only vaguely to future glory. Their reflections were "but jets of religious feeling, spasmodic upleapings of the flame of love of existence." . . . Convinced of the love of God for the righteous, the psalmists made the bold assertion that God recognizes the goodness of his creatures and has the power to place them in a celestial realm.

The psalmists combined an ethical argument—that righteousness must be rewarded—with a mythical argument—that God confers upon the righteous the privilege of residence in heaven instead of in Sheol. Eventually these two notions were supplemented by a third—the immortality of the soul. Wherever Diaspora Jews met Greek intellectuals, the idea of an immortal soul surfaced. In cities like Alexandria, Jewish philosophers confronted the notion that an immortal and immaterial soul existed quite independently from the body. This soul was not subject to decay and eventual death. Moreover, it was the soul that contained the essence of the individual. Unlike Jewish tradition, in which the person continued after death as a shade—a weak, emaciated replica of the individual, Greek tradition held that the soul, which was immortal, contained the most vital aspects of the person. Once released from the restrictions of the body, the soul became not weaker but stronger and more powerful. It tended to ascend upwards, rather than to sink into the netherworld. Under favorable circumstances, the individual soul not only survived death, it found its ultimate home in the transcendent, celestial realm of Platonic ideas.

The Greek belief in an immortal soul made a lasting impression on Jewish thought, and eventually on Christian beliefs. Both the Book of Wisdom (also called the Wisdom of Solomon) (first century B.C.)[4] and the work of the Jewish philosopher Philo of Alexandria (20 B.C.–45 A.D.) reflect a deep concern with the nature of the soul. The Wisdom of Solomon accepts the soul's immortality as a simple fact. Philo, on the other hand, developed a unique synthesis of Platonic philosophy and biblical traditions. For Philo, death restored the soul to its original, prebirth state. Since the soul belongs to the spiritual world, life in the body was nothing but a brief, often unfortunate, episode. While many human souls lose their way in the labyrinth of the material world, the true philosopher's soul survives bodily death and assumes "a higher existence, immortal and uncreated."

In heaven, Philo tells us, the soul joins the incorporeal inhabitants of the divine world, the angels. In certain cases the soul advances even higher and lives in the world of ideas. If it moves still higher, it can live with the deity itself. Enoch, according to Philo, lived among pure ideas; only the soul of Moses, however, entered the very highest realm, to live with God.

But the soul might also descend again into the material world. By adopting the Platonic view that "some, longing for the familiar and accustomed ways of mortal life, again retrace their steps," Philo recognized the possibility of reincarnation.

Hellenistic Jews, like Philo of Alexandria, showed no interest in recreating a Jewish national state. They considered Judaism a philosophy, a system of belief, rather than the ideology of a state. Ideally, the Jew would be a philosopher, who like Philo led the retired life of a thinker, preparing his soul for its celestial ascent. Preparation for death, rather than hope for a resurrected society, served as a basis for mediation with life here on earth.

Philo and his fellow Hellenistic Jews deepened the musings of the poets who composed Psalms 73 and 49, discussed above. These Psalmists

[4]The Book of Wisdom, or Wisdom of Solomon, is part of the Catholic Bible. It reflects the concerns of Jewish intellectuals living in first-century B.C. Alexandria, Egypt. (Author's note.)

sang of the mercy and justice of a God whose powers saved them from a meaningless existence in Sheol. They did not explain, however, how this would be done. Platonic thought provided the system for transforming the weakened shade trapped in Sheol into an immortal soul destined for the highest realms of existence. For some Hellenistic Jews who retreated from the idea of overthrowing the seemingly endless stream of colonial rulers, an individualistic heaven appeared more appealing—and more realistic— than the promise of a renewed kingdom of Israel where people lived to be 900 years old. They rejected both the early Israelite idea of the futility of any afterlife and the nationalistic hope for a restored communal existence. Instead, they answered their questions about life after death by a belief in the immortal individual soul freed from its bodily confines.

By the first century A.D., in the period before the Roman destruction of the Temple in 70 A.D., three Jewish responses to the question of afterlife competed with one another in the major Jewish sects or religious divisions. The ancient sources are sketchy in their details, but the broad outlines are clear.

The first group originated with the Josianic reform movement of the seventh century B.C., whose heirs were the Sadducees.[5] According to the Jewish historian Josephus (37–100 A.D.), the Sadducees held "that the soul perishes with the body." Because all ancient sources concerning the Sadducees are unsympathetic to them and do not attempt to understand their perspective on death, we can offer only a tentative and somewhat speculative evaluation of why they held this belief. Tradition attributes to the Sadducees a this-worldly attitude, reporting that they "use vessels of silver and gold all their lives" and do not "afflict themselves in this world" as did ascetic-minded Jews. Paul viewed the necessary conclusion of a disbelief in the soul as "Let us eat and drink, for tomorrow we die" (1 Corinthians 15:32).

While the Sadducees expressed their skepticism on the soul's fate after death, the Jewish sect of Pharisees probably shared the view of some of the prophets who predicted a glorious reestablishment of a renewed state of Israel and the destruction of her enemies. This popular movement sought to reconstruct Judaism as a culture whose identity was shaped by meticulous observance of religious law, especially regulations concerning purity.

We can only speculate about how the Pharisees viewed the possibility of life after death. The sources give only fleeting indications of their beliefs concerning the afterlife. From Acts, we learn that the Pharisees accepted the resurrection of the dead. Paul, who admitted to being a Pharisee "born and bred," must already have developed a perspective on the resurrection before becoming a Christian (Acts 23:6ff.). According to Josephus, the

---

[5]A Jewish sect that represented the priesthood and the wealthy and that stood for a strict interpretation of Mosaic law.

Pharisees maintained that every soul was imperishable, "but the soul of the good alone passes into another body." Did the doctrine of the resurrection supplement the Pharisees' expectation of a restored Jewish nation? Our sources do not provide a clear answer.

A third Jewish movement adopted a more individualistic perspective on the afterlife. The philosophic view that at death the immortal soul ascended to heaven, appealed not only to cosmopolitan Hellenistic Jews. Some evidence indicates that the Essenes too hoped for freedom from bodily constraints and eventual rest in a heavenly kingdom. Unlike Philo, the Essenes seem to have speculated about a new Jewish state under the leadership of a messianic king. Yet, they withdrew from active anticolonial politics and led their lives in such secluded communities as Qumran, an isolated site in the Judean Wilderness near the Dead Sea. The Essenes rejected the skepticism of the Sadducees as well as the crude, materialistic notions implied in the belief in a future resurrection. According to Josephus, the Essenes held that "the body is corruptible," while the soul is "immortal and imperishable." As in Philo's thought, the Essenes believed that, at death, souls are released "from the prison house of the body . . . and are borne aloft." For the virtuous, "there is reserved an abode beyond the ocean, a place which is not oppressed by rain or snow or heat but is refreshed by the ever gentle breath of the west wind coming from the ocean." Like the philosophers, the Essenes looked forward to a calm and comfortable hereafter.

The ancient Jewish attitude toward the afterlife reflects the complicated and developing relationship among individual, family and national concerns and theological concepts. Far from being static, belief in the nature of Sheol, and eventually heaven, changed considerably over the centuries. Religious reform movements found new meanings in the nature of God as they coped with the demise of Israel as a state, and tried to survive under non-Jewish governments. They also formed new ideas on life after death.

The Rites of Burial in Egypt

PIERRE MONTET

Blessed with the regular flooding of the Nile and surrounded by waters and deserts that for the most part impeded invaders, ancient Egypt was a relatively isolated, prosperous, and optimistic society. Egyptians loved life and prepared for a death that was to mirror life. While Egyptian literature sometimes spoke of injustice, oppression of the poor and the weak, and corruption by public officials, one theme that seems to prevail is that even if there is no hope of receiving justice in this life, it will surely

*be given by the gods of the world of the dead. Yet, although convinced of the pos-
sibility of immortality, Egyptians were in no hurry to breathe their last. Compared
to other civilizations of the Near East, life was not particularly harsh and old age
was revered. When an Egyptian felt death approaching, how did he or she attempt to
gain release from past sins and to ensure salvation? What steps did Egyptians take
to prepare their tombs?*

*Egypt was not an egalitarian society in life or in death. In what ways did a
pharaoh's pyramid differ from the tomb of a private individual? There are problems
in talking about the rites of burial in ancient Egypt because archaeologists have uncovered complete tombs only in the south where the desert has preserved them. In
the north, where the Nile delta spills into the Mediterranean, evidence of burial sites
has disappeared. Does Montet concern himself with this difficulty or with the burial
habits of Egyptian peasants or slaves?*

*Wealthy and powerful Egyptians lined their tombs with ornate furnishings and
considerable food. How did the Egyptians' views of an afterlife explain the manner
in which they filled their burial chambers? Why did they place statuettes and wall
decorations inside tombs? What precautions did Egyptians take to ensure that their
"house of eternity" would provide the desired peace and security?*

*Why and how did the Egyptians resort to mummification? As with the prepa-
ration of the tomb and mummification, the funeral itself was an elaborate and carefully planned spectacle. Did Egyptian religion demand that so much time and effort
be placed on the death of a person? Did eternal life require an elaborate tomb and
funeral? What obligations did the living owe to the dead? Was there any boundary
between the natural and the supernatural, between the living and the dead? What,
according to Egyptians, should be the proper relationship between the living and the
dead? Were Egyptians motivated by fear or pity when they honored their dead relations? Overall, do you find that the rites of burial in ancient Egypt made its inhabitants anxious and fearful or calm and assured?*

The maxims of the sage Ptahhotep[1] and the tale of the adventures of
Sinuhe[2] make no attempt to sentimentalize over old age. It is a time of
ugliness and of physical and moral weakness; of failing sight and hearing and memory, and of growing weariness, when food does the eater no
good. Nevertheless the Egyptians shared the universal desire of mankind
not to quit this vale of tears before they must. The old man who by dint
of infinite pains had managed to preserve the appearance of youth and
to keep his faculties unimpaired was the object of universal admiration.
The high priest Romeroy admits that he had been exceptionally blessed
in reaching old age in the service of Amūn.[3] 'My limbs are healthy, my

[1]Vizier of King Izezi of the fifth dynasty (c.2450 B.C.), who produced a piece of wisdom
literature that served as a guide for correct behavior.

[2]Middle Kingdom official of the royal household of Pharaoh Amenemes I (d.1961 B.C.),
whose memoirs of his exile in Palestine provide a picture of the tribal peoples living in that
area.

[3]God of generation and fertility, associated with the city of Thebes. During the Middle
Kingdom (2160–1785 B.C.) Amūn was combined with the sun god Rê to produce the new state
god Amūn-Rê.

sight is good and the food of his temple remains in my mouth.' The court had once buzzed with talk of an old man aged 110 who thought nothing of eating 500 loaves and a shoulder of beef and of drinking 100 jars of beer 'up to this day': though we are not told whether this feat had taken him a day, a month, a season, or a year. . . .

A happy old age required something more than a mere absence of physical infirmity; it needed wealth, or at least a comfortable income. Anyone who had attained to the state of *amakhou*[4] was not merely certain not to starve in old age but could rely on a first-class burial. When Sinuhe returned from exile he was given an estate and a house fit for a courtier. Many workmen were engaged on its construction and the wood used in it was new and not taken from a demolished building. 'I was brought food from the palace, three and four times each day, besides what the children of the royal household gave me in perpetuity.' Thereupon Sinuhe, who had been the recipient of the royal funerary offering, supervised the building of his house of eternity. He furnished it and made the most detailed arrangements for every aspect of the upkeep of his tomb and his funerary cult. This was the kind of pleasure in which any elderly man might indulge, at least if he were a friend of the king, who could at his pleasure grant or withhold the coveted title of *amakhou*. But a monarch who, according to his panegyrists, was as good and as just as he was omnipotent and omniscient, could be relied on not to deny it to anyone who had done him good service. Furthermore, every great man modelled his behaviour upon that of the king. Governors of towns and provinces, First Prophets and leading soldiers all had considerable staffs: and as his servants and dependants grew old a kindly master would see to it that they had a job within their failing powers and would guarantee them food and shelter while they awaited death. It was in order not to deprive Sinuhe of these essentials that Pharaoh, who had refused to pardon him for his flight while he was still in the prime of life, allowed him to return when he learned that he was getting old. Egypt took equal care of her old people and her children. I could not swear that on no occasion in this kindly land did an impatient heir ever curtail the span of an elderly relative who proclaimed too loudly his determination to live to the age of 110; some kings were, after all, deposed. But it is worth remembering that Amenemmes I,[5] on handing over the effective control of affairs to his son after a reign of twenty years, lived peacefully for a further decade, during which he had leisure to compose some fairly cynical maxims: while Apries,[6] though defeated and dethroned, could have saved his life had he not enraged

---

[4]Venerable, revered; an honorable title that grants the holder the right to be buried at the pharaoh's expense.

[5]Middle Kingdom pharaoh, 1991–1961 B.C.

[6]Pharaoh, 588–568 B.C.

public opinion by acts of senseless cruelty. Taking it by and large, Egypt was a good country for the elderly.

It would be a great mistake to imagine that the Egyptians regarded the prospect of dying with any pleasure. They knew that death would give ear to no complaint and could not be moved by prayer. It was vain to proclaim one's youth, for 'death seizes the child at his mother's breast as readily as the man that is grown old.' . . .

On entry to *Amentit*, the next world, all the dead had to undergo a formidable experience: the weighing of their actions. The aged king who compiled his instructions for Merikarê[7] warned his son against judges that oppress the poor, and this led him to speak of other judges. 'Do not believe that all will be forgotten in the day of judgement, and put not your trust in the length of years. They (the gods) regard life as but an hour. After death man continues to exist and all his deeds are piled up beside him. He that shall come without sin before the judges of the dead, he shall be there as a god, and will walk in freedom with the lords of eternity.' Setna, the son of Ramesses Ousirmarê,[8] had the extraordinary good fortune to make his way into *Amentit* while yet alive, where he saw 'Osiris[9] the great god seated on his throne of pure gold and crowned with the twin-plumed diadem: the great god Anubis[10] on his left hand and the great god Thoth[11] on his right: the gods of the council of the people of *Amentit* on his left hand and on his right the scales set up in full view among them all, where they weighed evil deeds against meritorious deeds, while the great god Thoth acted as the recorder and Anubis addressed them.' The accused were divided into three groups. Those whose evil deeds outweighed their good were thrown to the bitch-monster Amait. Those whose good deeds outweighed their evil were received among the council of the gods. The man whose good and evil deeds were of equal weight had to serve Sokar Osiris,[12] covered with amulets.

The Egyptians believed that only a very few sinless mortals would come before the supreme judge and it was accordingly necessary to win from the gods the boon that misdeeds should be cancelled and the sinner purified. This hope was very widely held and often finds expression in

[7]Son of pharaoh during the First Intermediate Period (c.2100 B.C.). This twelfth dynasty king wrote a set of instructions to his son on how to rule wisely.

[8]Throne name of Ramses II, New Kingdom pharaoh (c.1301–1234 B.C.).

[9]Legendary ruler of Egypt; judge and ruling god of the underworld.

[10]Dog-headed god of cemeteries who ensured proper burial and who was the master of embalmment.

[11]Ibis-headed god; scribe of the other gods; lord of wisdom and magic.

[12]Sokar and Osiris are gods of the underworld. Sokar was associated with Memphis during the Old Kingdom, but he was combined with Osiris during the Middle Kingdom.

funerary literature: 'My sins are cleansed, my faults are swept away, my iniquities are destroyed. Thou layest down thy sins at Nen-Nisou.'[13]

'The great enchantress purifies thee. Thou confessest thy sin which shall be destroyed for thee to make things according to all that thou has said. Homage to thee, O Osiris of Dedou,[14] thou hearest men's words. Thou washest away his sins. Thou justifiest his voice against his foes and he is strong in his court of justice on earth.' . . .

Did the Egyptians really believe that nothing was needed to erase their sins from the memory of gods and man, save to deny them in writing? . . . It could be maintained that the very fact that an Egyptian insisted so strongly on his purity and innocence showed that he had rid himself of the burden of his sin during his lifetime, and that it was this conviction which released him from fear of the next world.

The essential aim was to be declared *maa kherou,* or 'just of voice', a title which could only be gained as a result of having pleaded one's case before the judges. . . .

I think . . . that the Egyptians could become *maa kherou* during their active lifetimes; but the question remains how they had succeeded in doing so. The first *maa kherou* had been Osiris who, after being restored to wholeness and life by the devotion of his wife, hounded his murderer Seth until he had brought him to the divine seat of judgement presided over by the god Rê[15] and there had him condemned. Isis[16] had never wanted her struggles and the evidence of her devotion to be lost in oblivion and she had therefore instituted mysteries of the utmost sanctity to serve at once as a memorial of her labours and as a consolation to mankind. . . . The next scene represented the mystery of judgement, and chapter eighteen of the Book of the Dead[17] lists the towns which enjoyed the privilege of seeing this ceremony enacted, namely On, Didou, Imit, Khem, Pé and Dep, Rekhti in the Delta, Ro Setaou (a district of Memphis), Narèf at the mouth of the Fayyum, and Abydos in Upper Egypt. All the evidence suggests that a pious Egyptian could ensure his salvation by imitating Osiris. The end of chapter 125 contains a rubric which must have been addressed to the living. 'To utter this chapter purely and correctly, wearing ceremonial garb, shod in white sandals, with eyes dusted with black powder, and anointed with the finest incense after making a full and complete offering of oxen and birds, terebinth, bread, beer and vegetables.' And the sacred

---

[13]City just south of Memphis in Lower Egypt; present day Ahnas. Site of the appeal of the "eloquent peasant" in Middle Kingdom literature.

[14]City associated with the worship of Osiris, also known as Busiris, located in the central Nile Delta region.

[15]Falcon-headed sun god, combined with Amūn during the Middle Kingdom.

[16]Goddess of fertility and wife and sister of Osiris.

[17]A collection of magical spells, dating from the eighteenth to twenty-first dynasties (1550–950 B.C.), intended to help the dead in their passage through the netherworld.

text continues 'He who has done as much for himself, he shall be green (i.e. shall flourish) and his children shall be green. He will be looked on with favour by the king and the great ones. He shall want for nothing and shall at the last join the company of Osiris.'

We can now form a picture of this mystery of the judgement in which the Egyptians succeeded in gaining release from their sins. All those who felt that their days on earth were numbered, either from old age or sickness or because they had been visited by one of the secret warnings sometimes sent by Osiris to those who were destined soon to join his kingdom, would hasten to throng one of the towns named in the previous paragraph and there take the stipulated precautions, being particularly careful to provide a full and complete offering. . . .

His mind thus at peace, every Egyptian could devote his whole attention to his 'house of eternity'.

The Pharaohs always gave this their attention in good time. The building of even quite a modest pyramid was a considerable undertaking and what were virtual expeditionary forces had to be dispatched to bring the blocks of granite or alabaster to the plains of Gizeh or Saqqara. By the beginning of the New Kingdom[18] the royal necropolis had been moved to the Valley of the Kings, which lay to the west of Thebes. Though the descendants of Ramesses I[19] had originally come from the Delta, they followed the practice of the dynasty whom they had supplanted and continued to cut their tombs into the mountain of Thebes. These subterranean vaults, or hypogea, might be as much as a hundred yards in length. Although the walls of their passages and chambers were covered with strange scenes, depicting the mighty voyage of Rê in the twelve regions of the underworld and his struggle against the enemies of light, there was nothing to recall what the king had done during his lifetime, nor anything designed for the eye of the visitor. In truth the royal tomb was not intended to be visited. It was an enclosed domain whose very entrance had to be kept secret.

In this it differed completely from the tombs of private individuals, which usually consisted of two quite separate parts. A chamber hollowed from the rock at the bottom of a shaft was designed as the resting place of the dead. When he was laid there in his sarcophagus and the last rites had been performed, the entrance to the chamber was walled up, the shaft filled in and no one, in theory, should ever disturb his repose. But above the chamber there stood a substantial building, open to those who survived him. The façade stood at the far end of a courtyard in which stelae[20] proclaimed to later generations the dead man's merits and services. Sometimes palm-trees and sycamores had been induced to grow near a

[18] 1580–1085 B.C.

[19] New Kingdom pharaoh, 1314–1312 B.C.

[20] Stones used as monuments or tablets inscribed with a commemorative or funerary text.

pool of water in the courtyard, which in turn gave access to an enchantingly decorated room, generally greater in width than in length. Even the ceiling was decorated with plant motifs or with brightly coloured geometrical patterns, and the pillars and walls were covered with paintings of the most characteristic moments in the dead man's life. A big landowner would be shown watching men at work in the fields, or hunting antelope in the desert or water birds with the boomerang or the hippopotamus with the harpoon, or fishing. . . . He might be portrayed being received in audience by the king, or introducing into the palace long lines of envoys from countries which knew not Egypt, who had come bowed with the weight of the gifts they bore to beg the breath of life. After making a circuit of this ante-room, the visitor would enter a wide passage. One wall carried a picture of the dead man voyaging by boat to Abydos, the other, scenes from the full burial ritual. This passage led into an inner chamber entirely devoted to displaying the dead man's piety and showing him worshipping the gods, pouring a libation of water in their honour, offering a lighted brazier and reciting hymns. The reward for his piety and forethought was to ensure an eternally renewed supply of food.

Naturally the sarcophagus occupied the place of honour among the articles of funerary furniture. Neferhotep[21] paid more than one visit during his lifetime to the workshop in which his own was being fashioned; there he saw his future resting place supported on two stools and the workmen, standing or sitting, busily engraving, polishing and painting it. He saw too the priest who was sprinkling it with holy water. The king and the wealthy were not content with a single coffin. The mummy of King Psousennes[22] not only wore a mask of gold but was enclosed in a silver sarcophagus shaped like a mummy, which in turn fitted tightly into another sarcophagus of black granite of similar shape. This was completely enclosed in a huge rectangular box decorated inside and out with figures of divinities keeping watch over the mummy. Along the upper surface of the curved lid lay the figure of the dead man with the attributes of Osiris, while on the under side hung Nout, the goddess of the sky, surrounded by the barques of the constellations. Her slender and graceful body lies a few inches above the black granite sarcophagus. With his eyes of stone the king could gaze with endless delight on the lovely goddess bestowing an eternal kiss on him. This fulfilled one of the wishes of every Egyptian for eternity, namely to dwell in heaven and wander among the stars that knew not rest and the planets that knew no destination. The sides of the sarcophagus were also carved both with eyes, with whose aid he could see as keenly as Rê and Osiris, and with doors through which he could leave or re-enter his palace at his pleasure.

[21]Priest and scribe of the god Amūn during the reign of Pharaoh Hor-em-heb (c.1349–1319 B.C.).

[22]Pharaoh of the Tanite dynasty (c.1085 B.C.) who enclosed the central district of Tanis with a wall.

The richness and diversity of the tomb furnishings naturally varied with the means of its occupant. Tutankhamūn's[23] tomb, for example, baffles description with its ceremonial couches and beds, chariots and boats, coffers and chests, arm-chairs, plain chairs, stools, every kind of weapon, every variety of walking-stick then known, ornaments, games, metal and stone vessels and ritual objects. As a member of the kingdom of Osiris, the king would have to repeat the acts of piety which he had performed during his lifetime, while as head of a family and sovereign respectively he would have to continue to receive and entertain his children, relatives, friends and subjects. This accounts for the large quantity of dishes. Certain articles from the royal sideboard were put on one side to be laid in the tomb, and birds, meat, fruit, cereals, liquids and indeed every conceivable kind of food and drink were all prepared for consumption.

The complement to the sarcophagus was formed by a chest of wood or stone and four jars of the type wrongly known as Canopic, intended to contain the organs removed from the body during the process of mummification and laid under the protection of four gods and four goddesses. The four gods were Amset,[24] Hâpi,[25] Douamoutef[26] and Qebehsenouf,[27] with the heads of man, dog, jackal and falcon respectively. Some people indulged in the further refinement of making miniature coffins of gold or silver, with separate bodies and lids, to hold little mummified packets of viscera. The coffins would then be enclosed in the alabaster jars.

The fields of Yalou, the realm of Osiris ... —the most beautiful place on earth, but one which had to be ploughed, sown, weeded and harvested like an estate on earth. Not only must the irrigation canals be kept in repair but a number of operations whose utility escapes us had to be performed, such as moving the sand from one bank to the other. These operations, which a landowner would accept as pure routine, were on the contrary regarded as quite insupportable by those who had lived out their lives in idleness or had not followed an agricultural career. The Egyptians had a unique capacity for believing that the image of a thing or a person possessed to some degree the abilities and properties of the original, and the obvious way to deal with the problem was to make statuettes which could do the necessary work in the dead man's stead. These statuettes, of glazed faience[28] or occasionally of bronze, were shaped like a mummy.

[23]New Kingdom pharaoh (c.1350 B.C.), whose unrobbed tomb has provided more information on Egyptian burial customs than any other.

[24]One of four gods who guard the jars containing the internal organs of the mummy; has a bearded man's head—primary responsibility was the liver.

[25]Dog-headed god of the Nile, one of four gods who guard the jars containing the internal organs of the mummy—primary responsibility was the lungs.

[26]Jackal-headed god, one of four gods who guard the jars containing the internal organs of the mummy—primary responsibility was the stomach.

[27]Falcon-headed god, one of four gods who guard the jars containing the internal organs of the mummy—primary responsibility was the intestines.

[28]A fine kind of glazed and painted earthenware, sometimes used as a substitute for lapis lazuli or turquoise in jewelry or as tile.

The faces sometimes have sufficient character to make it probable that the artist intended a portrait. But even if no likeness was intended it did not matter, since an inscription gave at least the name and title of the person whose place it was to take.... Quite frequently a ... text defines the job which the statuette would be expected to perform. 'The Osiris N.,[29] he says: "O statuette (*oushebti*), if the Osiris N. is counted, called by name and summoned to do all the tasks which must be done there in the necropolis, as a man does them on his own behalf, to make the fields fertile, to make water flow through the channels, to carry the sand from east to west or from west to east, to pull up the weeds, like a man on his own behalf, you must say 'I will do it, here am I.' "

Once this idea had caught on, there was no end to the manufacture of these statuettes which were designed to ensure permanent freedom from the dreadful threat of this forced labour. Tools were carved in their hands, and bags on their backs. Statuettes not only of manual workers but also of scribes and overseers were manufactured, since close in the background of every gang of labourers lurked the inevitable official. Ultimately there developed a regular industry in the manufacture of a large range of miniature objects and tools in faience or bronze for the statuettes to use; yokes for the carriers of sand or water, large and small baskets, picks and mallets, each article inscribed with the name of the appropriate statuette to ensure that it was not stolen or used in defiance of its original's wishes.

By an extension of the same idea, a number of statuettes of naked women were also made for the dead. Kings and princes had concubines and had no intention of doing without them in the next world. Examples were found in the antechamber of the tomb of Psousennes, some inscribed with the king's name, others with that of a woman. But he would deserve our sympathy if the concubines he enjoyed in his lifetime were anything like the puppets he chose for his tomb.

Mummies loved adornment just as much as the living. Quite frequently indeed, a mummy was decked with the jewels which the dead man had worn in his lifetime, but it was more usual to make new ones. The following list shows what was essential for a king or a high dignitary.

A mask, of gold for kings and princes of the blood, of papier mâché and painted plaster for private persons.

A collar formed of two stiff plaques of enamelled gold in the shape of a vulture with outspread wings.

One or more necklaces of gold, precious stones or faience beads, consisting of several rows of beads or pendants fastened with one or two clasps, occasionally fitted also with a pendant, usually of gold and precious stones graded in size, sometimes of faience....

Bracelets, flexible and rigid, hollow or solid, to be worn on wrists, arms, thighs and ankles.

---

[29] A name (abbreviated N.) and title of the person whose place is taken in the tomb by a statuette.

Finger stalls for each finger and toe.

Sandals.

Amulets and statuettes of gods which would have been hung round the neck or attached to the pectoral.

Among the gods, Anubis and Thoth were specially responsible for watching over the dead man, on account of the part they played in the weighing of his deeds, but the choice was by no means confined to them. Their place might sometimes be taken by falcons or vultures with out-spread wings or serpent heads (the serpent was the keeper of the bolt which barred the doors of the different sections of the next world), or by the fetishes of Osiris and Isis, or the magical eye-amulet, *oudja*.

Besides all these ornaments there were also a number of tiny repro-ductions of walking-sticks, sceptres, weapons, and attributes of royalty or divinity which it was always useful to have around.

To choose such an elaborate and expensive outfit, and to make sure that it was really well made, must have meant a great deal of work. For, whatever a few cynics might say, the future of the dead man largely de-pended upon the trouble he had taken over the preparation, furnishing and decoration of his 'house of eternity'. The next world was by no means a place of peace and quiet; it was full of traps into which it was all too easy to fall unless every conceivable precaution had been taken.

Our elderly Egyptian had now watched the construction of his future 'house of eternity', decorated it in accordance with his taste and means and commissioned a variety of tomb furnishings from the cabinet-maker and the joiner. From the goldsmith he had ordered a large quantity of ornaments, talismans and amulets—everything, he judged, that he could need in the next world. But he still had to ensure that his descendants should not fail in displaying due piety towards him, not merely by paying him their last respects and seeing that he was fittingly bestowed in his new dwelling, but throughout all generations to come. 'I made over my duties to my son while I was still alive,' says one Egyptian nobleman. 'I have bequeathed him more than my father left me. My house is firmly founded and my estates are in good order; all is stable and all my possessions are where they should be. It is my son that will make my heart to live on this stele; he has been an heir to me as a good son should.' The funerary texts often express the belief that a son would keep alive the name of his father, and even of his forefathers. Hâpidjefai, the governor of Siout, appointed his son as his *ka*-priest[30] or 'priest of the Double'—practically equivalent to his executor. Goods inherited by the son in this capacity were privileged and were not shared with other children; and the son in turn would not divide them among his own children, but would bequeath them intact to the son appointed to be responsible for his grandfather's tomb and for supervising and participating in the ceremonies performed in his memory.

[30]*Ka*: a person's vital force, his soul, his double.

These ceremonies were generally held on New Year's Day and in connexion with the festival known as *Wâg*, which was held eighteen days later at the tomb, in the temples of Wepwawit, lord of Siout, and of Anubis, lord of the necropolis.

Five days before New Year's Day the priests of Wepwawit would go to the temple of Anubis and each deposit a loaf for the statue which stood there. On the last day of the old year an official of the temple would give the priest of the Double a candle which had already been used in the temple. The high priest of Anubis did likewise and gave a candle which had been used to help light the temple to an individual known as the chief of the staff of the necropolis. His duty was to make his way to the tomb with the keepers of the mountain, where they would meet the priest of the Double and gave him this candle.

On New Year's Day each priest of Wepwawit had to present a loaf in honour of the statue of Hâpidjefai after the illumination of the temple had ceased. They would then form up in a procession behind the priest of the Double and celebrate his memory: while for their part the chief of the necropolis and the keepers would offer bread and beer and conduct a similar celebration. In the evening of the same day the officials of the temple who had presented a candle on the previous evening would present another. So would the high priest of Anubis and, as on the previous evening, the statues of the dead man would be illuminated with candles already sanctified by their earlier use.

The same cycle of ceremonies with minor variations was due to be repeated for the *Wâg* festival. In the temple of Wepwawit each priest presented a white loaf in honour of the statue and formed a procession behind the priest of the Double in honour of Hâpidjefai, and a third candle would burn all night long before the statue. The priests of Anubis would go in procession, singing the god's praises as they went, as far as the monumental staircase leading to the tomb, and each would lay a loaf before the freshly illuminated statue that stood there.

After the officiating priest had performed the requisite ceremonies in the temple, he would offer loaves and beer in honour of this same statue. A second personage, namely the overseer of the desert hills, would also lay loaves and jugs of beer for the statue between the hands of the priest of the Double.

Hâpidjefai took good care not to be forgotten at the festivals held at the beginning of each season which, though less solemn than that on New Year's Day, were none the less of some significance. On these occasions the chief of the necropolis and the desert patrols would assemble near the garden of his tomb and carry to the temple of Anubis the statue that stood there. Now came his last and final behest. Since he was the head of the priesthood of Wepwawit, Hâpidjefai used to receive on every feast day . . . meat and beer. He gave orders that after his death these should be carried to his statue, under the supervision of the priest of the Double.

   Attentions on this scale were bound to cost money, and to pay for them Hâpidjefai renounced some of the natural advantages which he enjoyed either as governor or as head of the priesthood of Wepwawit, mortgaging his offices for the purpose with a sublime egotism, and thus reducing the income they would yield, since his successor would be obliged to expend each year twenty-seven 'days of the temple'—i.e. twenty-seven three hundred and sixty-fifths, or nearly one fourteenth, of the temple's total annual revenue. No doubt the temple of Wepwawit was simply a provincial shrine, but its revenue was nevertheless considerable, and his heirs, obliged as they would be to forfeit something like $7\frac{1}{2}$ per cent of the temple staff's normal income, were likely to find their standard of living depressed, the more so because the capital sum itself had been further diminished by the devising of various estates. On this basis the upkeep of the tomb looked unpleasantly like being more expensive than its original cost and the whole of Egypt would gradually become crippled by a self-imposed burden. The indifference to this aspect of his wishes displayed by Hâpidjefai is emphasized by the fact that no princes in later generations would have the right to vary any arrangements made by a prince like himself with the priests of his own day. But in point of fact even the most elaborate funerary foundations usually failed after two or three generations—or rather their income was diverted to the benefit of those who had died more recently. . . .

   Once an Egyptian, after due warning from Osiris, had had enough time to build and fit out his 'house of eternity', and had done everything that piety and respect for tradition required, there was nothing to keep him on earth. The day when he 'crossed to the other bank' (Egyptians disliked the word 'die' and this was the common euphemism) his relations went into mourning for at least seventy days, during which they did no active work and lived at home in silent grief. If they had to go out of doors, they smeared their faces with mud . . . and incessantly beat the top of their head with both hands. But they still had to perform the urgent duty of handing over the body to the embalmers and of selecting the method to be employed, of which . . . there were three. What might be called first-class embalming required much time and care, involving as it did the removal of the brains and all the internal organs except the heart; these were then treated separately and tied up in four separate packages to be put in the four Canopic jars. The body cavity was then cleaned out twice and filled up with aromatic spices. It was next pickled in natron, which . . . was used for a wide variety of purposes, particularly for domestic cleaning. After seventy days the body was again washed and then wrapped in bandages which were cut from a roll of linen soaked in glue. As many as fifteen separate products were required for the complete operation: bees-wax to cover ears, eyes, nose, mouth and the incision made by the embalmer, cassia, cinnamon, cedar oil (actually derived from the juniper-tree), gum, henna, juniper berries, onions, palm wine, various types of resin, sawdust, pitch, tar and, of course, the indispensable natron. Several of these items came from abroad, especially pitch and resin, which was extracted from the conifers of Lebanon, so that when the sea traffic to Byblos was interrupted, the embalmers and their wealthy clientele were in despair at the thought of being driven to find substitute materials.

After the whole process was finished the body was virtually a skeleton enclosed in a shrivelled skin, but the face was still recognizable despite its sunken cheeks and wizened lips. . . .

It was now time to dress and adorn the mummy. It was hung with necklaces, pectorals and amulets and decked with bracelets, finger stalls, rings and sandals. The incision through which the internal organs had been removed was covered with a thick gold sheet engraved or inlaid with the *oudja,* the sacred eye which had the power of healing wounds, and the four deities that protected the Canopic jars. Between the legs was laid a copy of the Book of the Dead, that indispensable guide to the underworld. Then body and limbs were completely wrapped in linen bands, and the mask was laid over the face. In the case of private people it was made of cloth and stucco: but for kings and a few high dignitaries it was of gold and in some cases attached by threads to a beaded garment. The whole was then wrapped in an outer shroud which was secured by parallel strips. . . . Provided that during the interval the cabinet-makers, joiners, armourers and all the various specialist craftsmen who had their part to play in making the funerary furniture had worked at full speed, it was possible to proceed two and a half months after the death to the actual closing of the coffin and the interment.

An Egyptian funeral was a spectacle at once mournful and picturesque. The members of the family would weep and gesticulate unashamedly throughout its progress. Both male and female mourners would have been hired for the occasion, no doubt from fear that too little grief might be manifested, and the women in particular were indefatigable. With faces smeared with mud, breasts bare and garments rent, they groaned and struck their heads incessantly. The more sober members of the procession were less abandoned in their gestures, but as they walked they would recall the virtues of the deceased. . . . Thereafter a funeral procession must have looked very like moving house. The leading group of servants carried cakes and flowers, pottery and stone vases, and boxes slung on either end of a yoke, containing the figurines and their tools. A second and larger group bore such normal articles of furniture as seats, beds, chests and cup-boards, not to mention the chariot. A third group was responsible for the personal effects—chests for the Canopic jars, sticks, sceptres, statues and sunshades. Jewels, necklaces, falcons or vultures with outspread wings, human-headed birds and other valuables were displayed on dishes or carried ostentatiously in open defiance of the crowds of idlers who watched the cortège pass. The sarcophagus itself was hidden beneath a catafalque drawn by a pair of cows and several men, and consisting of movable wooden panels or a framework hung with curtains of embroidered material or leather. It was mounted on a boat and flanked by statues of Isis and Nephthys,[31] the boat itself being mounted on a sledge.

The procession made its way slowly to the banks of the Nile, where it was met by a number of boats. The main vessel, whose prow and stern curved gracefully backwards and ended in papyrus umbels, was constructed with a very large cabin, the inside of which was hung with embroidered material and strips of leather. In this cabin the catafalque was laid, together with the statues of Nephthys and Isis. A priest with a panther's skin draped round his shoulders burned incense while the female mourners bowed their heads. The crew consisted of a single sailor who took soundings with a long pole, since the boat bearing the catafalque was to be towed by another vessel with a large crew under the command of a captain who stood in the bows with a steersman in charge of the rudder posted at the stern. This latter vessel also had a large cabin, on the roof of which the female mourners, with bare breasts, continued to cry and gesticulate in the direction of the catafalque. One of their dirges ran as follows: 'Let him go swiftly to the west, to the land of truth. The women of the Byblite boat weep sorely, sorely. In peace, in peace, O praised one, fare westwards in peace. If it please the god, when the day changes to eternity, we shall see thee that goest now to the land where all men are one.' We may well wonder what the Byblite boat..., designed for the open sea, is doing here, when the boat with the catafalque was designed simply to make the crossing of the Nile. They had something in common, for when Isis in Byblos had succeeded in regaining the sacred tree which contained the body of her husband Osiris, she carried it on to a boat that was on the point of leaving for Egypt in which she held it in her arms and bedewed it with her tears. In the same way the women of the family wept bitterly while their boat crossed the Nile.

Those who wanted to accompany the dead man to his journey's end, together with the funerary furniture, were embarked on four other boats. Others, who wished to go no farther, remained on the bank and uttered a last wish to their friend. 'Mayest thou fare to the west of Thebes in peace' or 'To the West, to the West, the land of the just. The place thou didst love groans and laments.' This was the moment when the widow's sorrowful voice was heard: 'Oh my brother, oh my husband, oh my friend! Stay, rest in thy place, leave not the place where thou dost abide. Alas, thou goest hence to cross the Nile. Oh, ye sailors, hasten not, let him be: ye shall return to your houses, but he is going to the land of Eternity.'...

At last the procession completed its laborious journey and stood before the tomb. Here too there were little stalls at which men were preparing braziers with handles and putting water in large jars to keep cool. Near the stele the invisible presence of the goddess of the West was symbolized by

---

[31]Goddess who was the companion of her sister Isis; wife of the god Seth.

a falcon on its perch. The sarcophagus was removed from the catafalque and set upright against the tomb stele, and a woman knelt beside it and clasped it in her arms. On its head a man placed a scented cone similar to those placed on the heads of guests at a party. The weeping and head-beating of the relations, children and female mourners were intensified. But the priests had an important task to perform. They had already laid on the table not merely the ingredients of a meal—bread and jugs of beer—but a number of strange implements: an adze, a curved knife shaped like an ostrich feather, an imitation leg of beef, a palette ending in two scrolls. Their object was to empower the priest to counteract the effects of the embalming and to restore to the dead man the use of his limbs and his missing organs, so that he might once more be able to see, to open his mouth and speak, to eat and to move his arms and legs.

The moment of parting had nearly been reached. The cries of grief rose to a climax. The wife cried: 'Oh my lord, it is thy wife, Meryt-Rê, that speaks. Leave me not! Dost thou wish that I should be parted from thee? If I depart thou wilt be alone, and none will be left to follow thee. Though thou wast wont to be merry with me, now thou art silent and speakest not.' Her women echoed her cries: 'Woe, woe, thrice I say, mourn without respite! The good shepherd is departed to the land of eternity. The crowd of people departs from thee, and now thou art in the land which loves solitude. Thou who didst love to walk freely, now thou art held fast, a prisoner swathed in thy bands. Thou who hadst a great store of fine stuffs now sleepest in the linen of yesterday.'

It only remained to descend into the tomb and there bestow the sar-cophagus and all the funerary furniture. The catafalque was left empty, and the priests, who had hired it out for the ceremony, took it back to the town, where it had already been booked by a fresh set of clients. The mummiform coffin was laid in its square stone receptacle which had long before been cut, carved and lowered into its place. Various objects— sticks, weapons and possibly some amulets—were placed around it, and then the heavy stone lid was manoeuvred into position. Near the sarcoph-agus were laid the chest with the Canopic jars, the boxes of *oushebtiou*[32] and all the rest of the furniture. It was especially important not to forget what would be most useful of all after death—food for the dead man and what we call the sprouting Osiris figures, i.e. wooden frames in the shape of a mummified Osiris, with a base of coarse material and filled with a mixture of barley and sand. They were watered regularly for several days, whereupon the barley germinated and grew thickly. When it had reached a height of about two or three feet it was allowed to dry off and was finally wrapped in a linen cloth. The hope was thereby to encourage the dead man's resurrection, since Osiris himself had sprouted in the same way at the moment when he had been resurrected. . . .

[32]Statuettes placed in tombs to substitute for living servants.

When the vault had been duly arranged, the priest and his assistants were free to withdraw and the mason walled up the doorway. The relations and friends, however, who had accompanied the dead man to his 'house of eternity' had no intention of separating and returning home forthwith. Their emotional orgy had sharpened their appetites, and the porters, besides the considerable load they had carried for the dead man's benefit, had had the foresight to include some food for the sustenance of the living. The company would gather either in the tomb or in the courtyard immediately in front of it or occasionally a little way off among the temporary stalls.

A harpist then entered from the direction in which the mummy lay. He opened his performance by recalling that, thanks to everything that had been done for him, the dead man was faring excellently well. . . .

This is a description of the funeral of a wealthy Egyptian. Needless to say, those of the poor were far less elaborate affairs. The embalmer did not bother to open up the body and remove the internal organs but simply injected a fatty liquid, derived from the juniper, through the rectum and pickled the body in natron. In the case of the very poor, the juniper oil was replaced by an even simpler disinfectant. After these preparations the mummy was put in a coffin and carried to a disused tomb, stacked with coffins to the roof, which had been turned into a communal burying place. But even in these cases the mummy was not entirely deprived of all that it would need in the next world: and the coffin would contain tools, sandals of woven papyrus, several bronze or faience rings, bracelets, amulets, scarabs, *oudjas*,[33] and miniature figures of gods, also of faience. There were some folk who were even poorer still: they were destined for the common burial pit. A paupers' burial place lay in the middle of the rich cemetery district of Assassif in Thebes. Into this the mummies, wrapped in a coarse cloth, were thrown, covered with a thin layer of sand and another body quickly thrown on top. Fortunate indeed were those among the poor that were named or depicted on the walls of a tomb of a vizier or a Viceroy of Kush,[34] for they would continue to serve their master in the next world as they had done on earth, and since all work earned payment, they could live on the proceeds. To some extent they could enjoy in perpetuity the advantages promised to the favourites of fortune who were also men of justice.

Anyone who thought of *Amentit*[35] as a place of peace and quietness was in danger of disillusionment. The dead were suspicious and vindictive, fearful alike of robbers attracted by the gold and silver deposited in the tomb, and of the malice or even the indifference of the countless sight-

[33]An *oudjat* was the Eye of Horus, a potent amulet. Horus was the sky god, god of goodness and light. He was the son of Osiris and Isis and he avenged his father's death by defeating the god of evil, Seth.

[34]The desert-like country south of Egypt; modern Sudan, biblical Ethiopia.

[35]The realm of the gods of the dead.

seers that ventured to wander among the vast necropolis city of the west, and mistrustful of the officials responsible for its upkeep. They threatened the direst punishment on those who might neglect their duties in this respect. 'He will give them over to the fire of the king in the day of wrath . . . they will capsize in the sea which will engulf their bodies. They shall not receive the honours which are owed to men of virtue. They shall be unable to consume the offerings of the dead. No man shall pour for them libations of water from the flowing river. They shall have no son to succeed them. Their wives shall be raped before their eyes . . . they shall not hear the words of the king when he is joyful. . . . ' But if, on the contrary, they keep good guard over the funerary foundation . . . 'may they enjoy all possible good. Amon-Rê, king of the gods, shall favour you with length of days. . . . The king that shall reign in those days shall reward you as he alone can do. Office shall be added to office for you, which you shall receive from son to son and heir to heir . . . they shall be interred in the necropolis after reaching the age of one hundred and ten, and offerings shall be multiplied for them.'

Others among the dead were ill-disposed, some perhaps because they had been abandoned by their descendants, and others for no better reason than a love of malice. The gods ought to have prevented them from doing any harm, but they had managed to evade their watchful eyes and left their tombs to make the lives of the living a misery. They might belong to either sex and most illnesses were ascribed to them. The mother feared that they might harm her child: 'If thou art come to take this child in thy arms, I will not let thee take him. If thou art come to put him to rest, I will not let thee put him to rest. If thou art come to take him away I will not let thee take him.'

Whether inspired by fear or piety, the Egyptians paid frequent visits to the houses of eternity. Parents, children and the widowed alike would scale the hill, bringing with them a few provisions and a little water to be laid on an offering table which stood in front of the stele or between the palm trees which overshadowed the entrance court, while to satisfy the wishes of the dead they would repeat the following rubric: 'Thousands of loaves of bread and jugs of beer, oxen and birds, oil and incense, linen and ropes, all things pure and good which the Nile brings, which the earth creates and on which the god lives, for the *ka* of (so and so), justified.' . . .

. . . During the Middle Kingdom[36] the letter to the dead man was generally written on the package containing the food offered to him, to ensure that it was not overlooked. For example, we find a grandfather being informed of the existence of a plot to cheat his grandson of his inheritance. The dead man was assumed to be anxious to thwart such manoeuvres and was therefore expected to summon the members of his family and his friends to the victim's aid, since in setting up house a son established the

[36]2160–1785 B.C.

household of his forefathers and so endowed their name with life, and his ruin involved his ancestors no less than his descendants.

But however great the piety of the Egyptians towards their dead might be, it could not suffice for the upkeep of all those who lay in the necropolis. Whatever an individual might resolve to do in honour of his parents or his grandparents, no threats or curses could make him decide to do the same for his more distant forebears. One day what the harpist foresaw and the seer of old had foretold, would come to pass. 'Those that have builded there in granite, those who have fashioned a chamber within a pyramid ... their offering tables are as bare as the tables of them that die in misery on the open field with none to survive them.' Accordingly the necropolis tended to become the meeting place of the curious who walked past the tombs and idly read their inscriptions. Some of them inevitably felt the itch of the modern tourist to leave some evidence of their visit, though they would record that their motives were pious: for example, 'Scribes A and B have come to visit this the tomb of Antefoker; and many, many are the prayers that they have uttered.' Others were content to report that the tomb was well kept: 'They found it like the sky in its inner chambers.' . . .

II

CLASSICAL GREECE
AND ROME

In the eighteenth century, Voltaire, the French intellectual, wrote that true glory belonged only to "four happy ages" in the history of the world. The first was ancient Greece, specifically the fifth and fourth centuries B.C., and the second the Rome of Julius Caesar and Augustus, the first emperor. (The other two were Renaissance Italy and Louis XIV's France.) Voltaire praised classical Greece and Rome because he believed them civilized, holding the arts, literature, and refined living in high regard. The social historian, aware of the underside of classical civilization, cannot share Voltaire's optimism.

There is much to admire in Greek civilization. The political competition of its many independent city-states promoted some freedom of experimentation, evidenced in art, in literature, and in the diversities of philosophical schools. Greek social life too was more heterogeneous than that of other cultures, such as Egypt. Yet Greek civilization was rooted in slavery and oppression; life was difficult for most Greeks, and warfare among the city-states was constant. The Olympics and other games show that the Greeks admired brawn as well as brains. In Athens, the cradle of democracy and the center of classical Greek civilization, well-to-do males virtually locked up for life their wives and daughters. The family in Athens is as distinguishable historically as its philosophy and art are distinguished. Greek sexuality is also rather notorious and the subject of much speculation, if not myths.

Law, engineering, architecture, and literature bear witness to the glories of Rome; gladiatorial combats, mass murders in the Colosseum, and the persecution of Christians remind us of the streak of cruelty that was as Roman as an aqueduct. The Roman historian Tacitus remarked about imperial conquest: "Where they make a desert, they call it peace." Slavery, infanticide, and other brutalities were basic features of life in Roman civilization, as they had been in Greece and in the Near East. Women in Rome, however, seem to have fared better than their counterparts in Athens.

Certainly much has been written about the legacy of Greece and Rome to Western civilization. One of the great developments in classical Rome was the rise of Christianity, which has had a tremendous impact on Europe until the present day. Historians have documented the classical heritage in the Middle Ages, in seventeenth-century France, eighteenth-century Germany, Victorian Britain, and in American universities. When the term renaissance *is applied to a culture such as twelfth-century France or fifteenth-century Italy, it refers to a rebirth of classical art, literature, style. But social structures, people's attitudes, and lifestyles are as significant and as rich as the cultural developments more commonly studied.*

Organized Greek Games

WILLIAM J. BAKER

The history of sports, like women's history and the history of children, is a relatively new area of interest for scholars. A culture's games and its perception of sports and athletes tell us much about that society's priorities, values, and beliefs. No longer do historians view sports and leisure activities as unimportant.

Virtually everyone knows that the modern Olympics are patterned on the Olympic Games of ancient Greece, yet few people have more than a hazy understanding of the original Olympics. This selection describes the Greek games and points out their differences from the modern games (which date only from 1896).

One should bear in mind that, while the ancient Olympics were the most famous athletic contests in Greece, there were other games, including some limited to women. Baker is careful to use Greek athletics as a means to raise larger questions about Greek culture. Why were women excluded from the Olympic Games? What was the relationship between religion and athletics in Greece? How did Greek philosophers perceive the role of athletics? Answers to such questions lead one to conclude that sports were not a mere sideshow but a basic component of Greek civilization.

If that is so, then the Greeks were violent, for wrestling, boxing, and the pancration were more brutal than any modern Olympic contest (of course, such current professional sports as boxing, ice hockey, and rugby are violent). On the other hand, some events, such as footraces, appear almost identical to those staged today. The professionalism of the athletes and the honor they derived from their victories resemble the culture of sports in our society. On balance, were the ancient games vastly different from our Olympics? What does the role of games in ancient civilization suggest about the significance of sports in any society?

The story of organized athletics in the ancient world is primarily the story of Greece. A land of sunshine, mild climate, and rugged mountains rimmed by sparkling seas, Greece spawned philosophers and civic leaders who placed equal value on physical activity and mental cultivation. A vast array of gymnasiums and palaestras (wrestling schools) served as training centers for athletes to prepare themselves to compete in stadiums situated in every major city-state.

For more than a thousand years athletic festivals were an important part of Greek life. Originally mixtures of religious ceremony and athletic competition, hundreds of local festivals were held each year throughout the country and in Greek colonies in Egypt, Sicily, and on the banks of the Bosporus. By the fifth century B.C. four major festivals dominated the scene, forming a kind of circuit for ambitious athletes. The Pythian Games, held every fourth year at the sacred site of Apollo in Delphi, crowned victory with a laurel wreath. The Isthmian Games at Corinth in honor of Poseidon, the god of the sea, were conducted every other year, providing a victor's wreath of pine from a nearby sacred grove. The Nemean Games at Nemea, honoring Zeus every second year, awarded a sacred wreath of celery. The oldest and most prestigious of all the festivals, the Olympic Games, bestowed the olive wreath every four years in honor of Zeus.

The Olympics were the Super Bowl, the World Cup, the Heavyweight Championship of Greek athletics. By Olympic standards were the other festivals judged; at Olympia the sweet "nectar of victory" filled athletes with self-esteem and accorded them public acclaim. . . .

The Olympic Games originated in a most unlikely place. Far removed from Athens, Corinth, and Sparta, the teeming centers of Greek culture and power, Olympia was a little wooded valley in the remote district of Elis on the northwestern tip of Peloponnesus (the peninsula that makes up the southern half of Greece). . . . Mount Olympus, a site readily associated with the gods, lay far to the northeast. Yet according to ancient lore, little Olympia was the place where gods and heroes mingled to accomplish feats worthy of immortal praise.

The origins of the Olympic Games are shrouded in mystery and legend. According to one yarn, Hercules founded the games in celebration of his matchless feats. Some Greeks insisted that their two mightiest gods, Zeus and Cronus, contested for dominance on the hills above Olympia, and that the games and religious ceremonies held later in the valley were begun in commemoration of Zeus's victory. Others clung to the legend of Pelops, who won his bride in a daring chariot escape. The girl's father was an expert with the spear, and according to tradition, thirteen suitors had met death while attempting to steal the daughter away. But Pelops was shrewd. He loosened the axle of his adversary's chariot, took off with his prize, and breathed a sigh of relief when his lover's father broke his neck in the ensuing crash. . . . [S]upposedly on that hallowed ground Pelops instituted the games and religious sacrifices in celebration of his god-given victory.

Significantly, all these tales involve competition, physical aggressiveness, and triumph. . . . [L]ike most sporting activities in the ancient world, the competitive games associated with Olympia grew out of religious ceremonies and cultic practices. With all their emphasis on man and his achievements, the Greeks were extremely religious. Polytheists, they looked to particular gods for assistance and blessing in every sphere of life. . . . Most of all they feared the wrath and sought the favor of Zeus, the mightiest of the gods.

In prayers, processions, and sacrifices, the ancient Greeks sought diligently to appease their gods. Religious festivals, accompanied by feasts, music, dancing, and athletic contests, were scattered throughout the Greek world. About 1000 B.C. Olympia became a shrine to Zeus. In addition to their religious ceremonies, young Greeks competed athletically in honor of Zeus, himself reckoned to be a vigorous warrior god who cast his javelin-like thunderbolts from on high. Competitors at Olympia swore by Zeus that they would play fair and obey all the rules. When they broke their oaths, they were required to pay fines, which in turn were spent to erect statues to Zeus.

The actual date of the first competitive games at Olympia is unknown. But the year 776 B.C. stands as a milestone, for in that year the Greeks first recorded the name of the victor in a simple footrace. For a time the footrace—a sprint of about 200 meters—was the only event associated with the religious festival at Olympia. In 724 B.C., however, a "double race" (400 meters) was added, and in 720 B.C. a long-distance race of 4,800 meters became a fixture. Within the next hundred years other events were established: wrestling and the pentathlon in 708 B.C., boxing in 688 B.C., chariot races in 680 B.C., and boys' footraces, wrestling, and boxing between 632 and 616 B.C. Finally in 520 B.C. the Olympic program was completed with the introduction of a footrace in armor. For almost a thousand years the list of events remained essentially intact. Every four years, strong, young Greeks gathered to compete, to strive for the victory wreath of olive branches.

In the beginning, however, Olympia was a simple site unadorned with buildings. A few scattered stone altars to Zeus stood in the *altis,* the sacred grove. . . . Competitive events were held in randomly selected open spaces, as near to the *altis* as possible. Not until about 550 B.C. were buildings constructed. . . . Finally a hippodrome and stadium were constructed, the latter . . . providing space for about 40,000 spectators. A gymnasium and palaestra completed the athletic complex.

In the spring of every fourth year three heralds departed from Olympia to traverse the Greek world, announcing the forthcoming games and declaring a "sacred truce." By the authority of Zeus, competitors and spectators making their way to Olympia were allowed to pass safely through the countryside, even in times of war. The athletes and their trainers arrived in Olympia a month before the games. First they had to prove their eligibility—that they were Greek, freeborn (not slaves), and without criminal records. Then they had to swear by Zeus that they had been in training for the previous ten months. Participation in the Olympic Games was no lighthearted matter. Strict judges supervised a grueling month-long training program in order to ensure the fitness of prospective competitors, and they arranged elimination heats for those events that had attracted an unusually large number of athletes. . . .

While the athletes sweated and grunted through their preparatory exercises, little Olympia and the surrounding countryside took on a carnival atmosphere. Spectators came from all directions, and official delegations from Greek city-states arrived with gifts for Zeus. Food and drink vendors did a brisk business, as did hawkers of souvenirs and pimps with their prostitutes. Jugglers, musicians, dancers, and magicians displayed their talents, and soothsayers dispensed their wisdom. Deafening noise and stifling dust added to the midsummer heat, making attendance at the Olympic Games something of an ordeal.

Until late in the history of the games, tiny Olympia was ill-prepared to cope with the crowds. A few springs and the nearby rivers provided water for drinking and bathing, but sanitation and planned water facilities were not available until the second century A.D. Flies were everywhere. As one first-century visitor complained, life at the Olympics would have been unbearably crude and unpleasant were it not for the excitement of the games themselves: "Do you not swelter? Are you not cramped and crowded? Do you not bathe badly? Are you not drenched whenever it rains? Do you not have your fill of tumult and shouting and other annoyances? But I fancy that you bear and endure it all by balancing it off against the memorable character of the spectacle."

The athletes fared little better. Although they ate well during their month's training, they, too, received scant provision for physical comfort. Housing, or the lack of it, was a main problem. Servants of wealthy spectators and official delegations pitched richly embroidered tents on the hillsides, but most athletes simply wrapped themselves in blankets, slept under the stars, and hoped it would not rain. Not until about 350 B.C. was housing provided for the athletes, and even then it was too spartan for comfort. Certainly nothing approximating a modern Olympic village was ever constructed. . . .

For three centuries after the first recorded Olympic victor in 776 B.C., the sequence and duration of the games fluctuated from Olympiad to Olympiad according to the whims of the judges. In 472 B.C., however, the games were reorganized and fixed into a pattern that remained virtually unchanged for the next eight hundred years. The duration of the entire festival was set at five days, with only two and a half days devoted to the games themselves. The first day was given to religious ceremony: oaths, prayers, sacrifices, and the singing of hymns. Some athletes presented gifts and offered prayers to the statues of past victors who had been deified, at the shrines of various patron gods, and especially to the several statues of Zeus.

On the second day the sports competition began. Spectators gathered at the hippodrome, a level, narrow field about 500 meters long, to witness the chariot race. Amid great fanfare, splendid two-wheeled chariots pulled by four horses lined up in staggered starting places. Here was the most costly and colorful of all the Olympic events, a signal to the world that the owners were men of great wealth. Their drivers, decked out in finely embroidered tunics, tensely awaited the start. They could scarcely afford to relax. Their course was not a rounded oval but rather around posts set at each end of the hippodrome about 400 meters apart, requiring 180-degree turns for twelve laps. Rules forbade swerving in front of an opponent, but bumps and crashes and even head-on collisions around the posts were inevitable. In one race only one of forty chariots finished intact.

As soon as the dust settled and battered chariots were removed from the hippodrome, single horses and their jockeys moved into starting positions. Riding without saddles or stirrups, the jockeys were nude. Even more than the charioteers, jockeys got little credit if they won. They were the hirelings of wealthy owners, whose names were recorded as the winners of the race. Even the olive crown was placed on the owner's head, not the jockey's.

The morning having been given to these equestrian events, the afternoon was devoted to an altogether different contest, the pentathlon. Spectators crowded onto the grassy slopes of the stadium. Except for a few marble slabs provided for the Olympic officials, no seats were ever built. Through a narrow passageway at one end of the stadium the competitors entered. Naked and bronzed by the sun, they more than any of the other contestants at Olympia represented the Greek ideal of physical beauty. Pentathletes had to be fast as well as strong, with muscles well-proportioned and supple but not overdeveloped. . . .

Like the modern decathlon, the pentathlon rewarded the versatile athlete. First he had to throw the discus, a round, flat object originally made of stone and later of bronze. Five throws were allowed, and only the longest counted. Next came the javelin throw. About six feet long, the javelin had a small leather loop attached near the center of gravity. The athlete inserted one or two fingers in the loop, wound the thong around the javelin, and thus obtained leverage to make the javelin spin in flight. In the third event, the standing broad jump, the athlete carried weights in his hands, swung them forward to shoulder height, and then down as he leaped. Made of stone or metal in the shape of small dumbbells, the weights both increased the distance and helped the jumper to keep his balance when landing. A 200-meter sprint and a wrestling contest were the last two events in the pentathlon, but they were often not held: The athlete who first won three of the five events was declared the victor without further contest.

As the sun set on that second day of the Olympic festival, attention turned from athletic competition to religious ceremony. In honor of the hero-god Pelops, a black ram was slain and offered as a burnt sacrifice — always as the midsummer full moon appeared above the *altis*. On the following morning were religious rites, followed by a magnificent procession of priests, Olympic judges, representatives from the Greek city-states, the athletes and their kinsmen, and trainers. All finally arrived at the altar of Zeus, where one hundred oxen were slain and their legs burned in homage to Zeus. The carcasses were cooked and eaten at the concluding banquet on the final day of the festival.

On the afternoon of the third day, the footraces were held: 200-meter sprints the length of the stadium, 400-meter dashes around a post and back, and long-distance runs of 4800 meters (twelve laps). Marble slabs provided leverage for quick starts, and a trumpet blast served as the starting signal. . . .

The fourth day of the festival brought on the "heavy" events: wrestling, boxing, the pancration, and armored footraces. The first three were especially violent, brutal contests of strength and will. There were few rules, no time limit, and no ring. More important, there were no weight limits, thus restricting top-level competitors to the largest, best-muscled, and toughest men to be found throughout Greece. In the wrestling contests biting and gouging were prohibited, but not much else. A wrestler won when he scored three falls, making his opponent touch the ground with his knees. Wrestlers therefore concentrated on holds on the upper part of the body and tripped their opponents when possible. . . .

Yet wrestling was mild exercise compared to boxing. Boxers wound heavy strips of leather around their hands and wrists, leaving the fingers free. They aimed primarily for the opponent's head or neck, rather than the body. Slapping with the open hand was permissible, and it was often done to divert the attention, cut the face, or close the eyes of the opposition. The fight went on without a break until one of the competitors was either exhausted or knocked out, or until one raised his right hand as a sign of defeat. Blood flowed freely. Scarcely an Olympic boxer finished his career without broken teeth, cauliflower ears, a scarred face, and a smashed nose. He was lucky if he did not have more serious eye, ear, and skull injuries.

As if boxing and wrestling were not brutal enough, the Greeks threw them together, added some judo, and came up with the contest most favored by spectators at Olympia—the pancration. Pancratiasts wore no leather thongs on the fists, but they could use their heads, elbows, and knees in addition to hands and feet. They could trip, hack, break fingers, pull noses and ears, and even apply a stranglehold until tapped on the back, the sign that the opponent had given up. In 564 B.C. a pancratiast who had won in two previous Olympics found himself in both a leg scissors grip and a strangle-hold. Literally in the process of being choked to death, he frantically reached for one of his opponent's toes and broke it. As he gasped his final breath, his opponent, suffering excruciating pain, gave the signal of capitulation. So the strangled pancratiast was posthumously awarded the crown of victory, and in the central square of his native village a statue was erected in his honor.

After the deadly serious business of wrestling, boxing, and the pancration, the final Olympic contest added a farcical touch to the festival. The 400-meter footrace in armor pitted naked men clad only in helmets, shin guards, and shields, a fitting though ludicrous reminder of the military origins of most of the games. Although the armored footrace remained on the Olympic program from its introduction in 520 B.C. until the end, it was never a prestigious event. Apparently it provided comic relief at the end of a gory day.

The fifth and final day of the festival was devoted to a prize-giving ceremony, a service of thanksgiving to Zeus, and a sumptuous banquet at which the sacrificial animals were consumed. . . .

. . . [S]ome of the limited features of the Olympic Games should be noted. In the first place, the athletic program was narrowly confined to two equestrian contests, six track-and-field events, three physical-contact sports, and the armored footrace. From a modern point of view, conspicuously absent were relay races, hurdles, pole vaults, high jumps, running broad jumps, weight lifting, and shot puts. Nothing approximating a modern marathon ever appeared on the ancient Olympic program. . . .

Given the fact that Greece is a peninsula and half of it virtually an island, it is surprising to find no water sports such as swimming, diving, sailing, or rowing in the ancient Olympic program. . . . Less apparent was the reason for the lack of competitive ball games. In fact, the Greeks played a number of individual and team games of ball. At Sparta "ball player" and "youth" were synonymous. . . . Without doubt the Greeks played a kind of field hockey game. . . . Most common of all competitive ball play in Greece, however, was the game of *episkyros,* a team sport in which opposing sides threw a ball back and forth "until one side drives the other back over their goal line."

Why, then, were no ball games ever played in the ancient Olympics? When the Olympics began in the eighth century B.C., most ball play was still mere exercise, keep-away games at most. . . . [T]hey were played by women, children, and old men, but not by serious athletes. Not yet rough mock forms of combat, ball games were considered child's play compared to the warrior sports of chariot racing, javelin throwing, wrestling, and the like. By the time competitive ball play became respectable for adult males, the Olympic program was already set on its traditional course. . . .

Another limitation of the Olympics that more tellingly reflected the mentality of ancient Greek society was the exclusion of women from the games. In that patriarchal world, matters of business, government, and warfare were reserved for men. A woman might attend the theater if accompanied by a man, but even in the home she lived in separate quarters. Except for the honorary presence of the priestess of Demeter, women were altogether excluded from the Olympic Games, as spectators as well as competitors. Apparently only one woman ever broke the taboo, and her ploy provoked a rule change. In 404 B.C. a mother who wanted to see her son box slipped into the stadium disguised as a trainer. But when the boy won his match, she leaped over the barrier to congratulate him and in so doing gave herself away. Horrified Olympic officials immediately laid down a new rule: trainers henceforward must appear in the stadium stark naked, like the athletes.

Barred from the Olympic Games, women held their own competitive contests at Olympia in honor of Hera, the sister-wife of Zeus. Their competition was largely in the form of footraces, wrestling, and chariot races.

Apparently these Heraean Games even predated the Olympic Games as fertility rites representing an early matriarchal society. During the history of the Olympic Games, however, Olympic officials proved to be a highly conservative group of men committed primarily to maintaining a successful formula, thus inadvertently protecting traditional male interests. Their conservatism is best seen by comparison with the other major Panhellenic games. As Greek women increasingly became emancipated (primarily in the cities) toward the end of the pre-Christian era, short-distance races for girls were introduced as an integral part of the program in the Pythian, Isthmian, and Nemean Games.

Olympia's relation to the other festivals on the athletic "circuit" calls to mind another myth long entertained about athletes in the ancient world: Olympic victors received no cash prizes or other material rewards with their olive crowns; thus it would appear that they were purely amateur, competing for the honor of victory. The appearance was a mere shadow of reality. Throughout the history of the Olympics, only aristocrats could afford the horses and chariots for the equestrian events. For the first 300 years or so, the games were dominated by athletes from wealthy families who could afford trainers and coaches, a proper diet (plenty of meat), full-time training, and travel. Around 450 B.C., however, lower-class athletes began participating in the track-and-field and physical-contact sports. Financed by local patrons and public funds drawn from taxes on wealthy citizens, they ran and fought to bring honor to their city-states as well as to themselves. Their city-states, in turn, rewarded them with cash prizes, free food, and lodging. Therefore, although the Olympic Games paid no direct material rewards, they existed in a maze of commercial enterprise. A victory at Olympia dramatically raised an athlete's value as he went off to sell his talents and brawn for further competition at the Pythian, Isthmian, and Nemean Games. Whether or not he received money for his Olympic exploits is beside the point. Well paid for his full-time efforts, he was a professional athlete.

A sure sign of this professionalism was the emergence of athletic guilds in the second century B.C. Like today's unions or players' associations, the guilds originated on the principle of collective bargaining. And bargain they did: for the athletes' rights to have a say in the scheduling of games, travel arrangements, personal amenities, pensions, and old-age security in the form of serving as trainers and managers.

When Greek poets, philosophers, and playwrights turned a critical eye on the athletes of their day, they seldom attacked professionalism.... Yet athletics were scarcely beyond criticism. For well-born, highly cultured Greeks, athletics appeared to be a lamentably easy way for lower-class citizens to rise quickly to affluence, then to fall back into poverty once the strength of youth waned....

Worse still, the successful athlete had to specialize to such an extent that he made a poor soldier....

Yet of all the barbs directed against Greek athletics, the most common had to do with the glorification of physical strength to the detriment of mental and spiritual values. To the philosopher and satirist Xenophanes, it was "not right to honor strength above excellent wisdom." . . . Milo of Croton was the butt of numerous jokes and slurs on the mindlessness of the muscle-bound athlete. "What surpassing witlessness," declared a moralist when he heard that Milo carried the entire carcass of a bull around the stadium at Olympia before cutting it up and devouring it. Before it was slaughtered, the bull carried its own body with much less exertion than did Milo. "Yet the bull's mind was not worth anything—just about like Milo's." The image of the "dumb jock" is as old as athletics.

. . . "How very unlike an athlete you are in frame," Socrates once chided a young Athenian weakling. "But I am not an athlete," retorted the literal-minded youth. "You are not less of an athlete," shot back the wise Socrates, "than those who are going to contend at the Olympic Games. Does the struggle for life with the enemy, which the Athenians will demand of you when circumstances require, seem to you to be a trifling contest?" For Socrates, the key words were *contend, struggle,* and *contest.* Moreover, for Socrates the athlete provided the model for the principle that "the body must bear its part in whatever men do; and in all the services required from the body, it is of the utmost importance to have it in the best possible condition."

Socrates' prize pupil, Plato, agreed fully with his master. Plato, in fact, trained under the best wrestling teacher in Athens and reportedly competed in the Isthmian games. Originally his name was Aristocles, but his wrestling teacher changed it to Plato, meaning "broad shouldered." In *The Republic,* Plato set up a dialogue with Socrates to argue logically that gymnastic exercise was the "twin sister" of the arts for the "improvement of the soul." His ideal was the body and mind "duly harmonized."

This sense of balance between the physical and the mental prompted the third of the great Greek philosophers, Aristotle, to devote several sections of his *Politics* to the training of children to be good Greek citizens. "What is wanted," he insisted, "is not the bodily condition of an athlete nor on the other hand a weak and invalid condition, but one that lies between the two." Coming to manhood a hundred years or so after Socrates, Aristotle was more critical of "the brutal element" involved in organized athletics. Yet he, too, held the Olympic victors in awe. . . .

Critical as they were of overspecialized athletes, the great philosophers still did not reject athletics. For them, the association of body and mind was literally intimate: gymnasiums were places where men not only exercised, but gathered to hear the lectures of philosophers and itinerant orators. Plato's Academy and Aristotle's Lyceum in Athens were, in fact, gymnasiums, centers of training "for the body and the soul." Ironically, the terms "academy" and "lyceum" have come to refer solely to intellectual pursuits, wholly divorced from physical training. . . .

Marriage and the Family in Athens

W. K. LACEY

In the last two decades, historians of the family have demolished any lingering no-tion that families have not changed appreciably over time. Recent studies demon-strate that husbands, wives, and children, and their relationships with one another and with society at large, possess a complex past. In the long history of the family, that of classical Athens stands out because of its rigidity and connection to the poli-tics of the city.

For example, one would be hard-pressed to think of another society that kept women of wealthy families hidden. Athenian men felt their betrothed had to be vir-gins and their wives chaste. Why were Athenian males so uncompromising in these matters? How did the laws of the state serve to maintain the virtue of citizens' wives? Citizenship was the key, and the concept of citizenship affected marriage and children. Attitudes toward adultery also related to worries about citizenship.

Athens may have been the "cradle of democracy," but it was a very limited democracy. In what ways did Athenian legislation concerning the family discrimi-nate against those groups, such as foreigners or slaves, excluded from the democratic system? What kind of "democratic" values could be nurtured in such families?

Finally, how did Athenian males treat their wives, children, and parents? What explains their behavior and attitudes toward those groups? Is there evidence of love in these relations?

... In 451 Pericles[1] persuaded the assembly[2] to modify the rules for enti-tlement to citizenship by a law which decreed that a man's parents must both be citizens for him to be a citizen.... The motives for Pericles' law have been much discussed; selfishness—*i.e.* not wanting to share the prof-its of empire; race-consciousness—*i.e.* fear of diluting the Athenian au-tochthonous stock; ... but, from the point of view of the family, much the most convincing reason was the desire of Athenian fathers to secure husbands for their daughters....

Prior to the law Athenians had always been able to contract legal mar-riages with non-Athenian women....

That is not to say that there were no such people as illegitimate chil-dren before Pericles' day; bastards are known in the Homeric poems, mostly the children of slave girls or concubines begotten by the great heroes...; but their status and rights depended upon the decision of their father about them while he lived, or of their kinsmen when he had died. When a man had no son by his recognized wife he might adopt a bastard as his heir....

---

[1]Dominant Athenian statesman, 495–429 B.C.

[2]Popular assembly made up of all male citizens eighteen and older; only legislative body in Athens.

Slave girls' children, and the children of common prostitutes, must always have been classed as bastards, and so, presumably, were the offspring of parents who did not live together, such as the children of the victims of rape or seduction. . . .

Pericles' law, however, added a new class of persons to the illegitimate, by declaring the offspring of unions with non-citizen mothers non-citizens . . . however formal the marriage agreement had been, and thus the procreation of legitimate children became impossible except from the legitimate daughter of an Athenian. . . .

The law required that an Athenian's marriage should be preceded by either a betrothal agreement . . . or a court judgment. . . . This latter was the legal process whereby a man's claim to be the legitimate husband of an *epikleros*[3] was established. Otherwise the normal process . . . was for a girl's *kyrios*[4] to pledge her to a prospective bridegroom. The pledge was a formal one, and witnesses were present on both sides; it also stated what her dowry was to be as one of its conditions. It is uncertain at what age this agreement was normally made for girls. . . . But it is quite certain that betrothal, though obligatory, did not itself make a marriage. . . . This was because, if a child's mother was not properly married, the child was a bastard, and suffered severe disabilities in respect of the capacity to succeed to property, and exclusion from civic privileges as a citizen.

Marriages within the *anchisteia* or wider family were extremely common; they were prescribed by the law for *epikleroi*,[5] we hear of half-brothers marrying their half-sisters, and uncles often married their nieces; . . .

The normal age for men to marry seems to have been about thirty, an age approved by the philosophers as suitable, but there were sound family reasons as well as those of imaginary eugenics. These lay in the Athenian custom of old men retiring from the headship of (or at least from economic responsibility for) their families in favour of their sons, and the son's marriage was an appropriate moment for this to occur. . . . A man who married at about thirty would be about sixty when his son reached thirty; fifty-nine was the age at which a man's military service ended and he was therefore considered an old man.

Girls were married much younger; philosophers and other writers recommended about eighteen or nineteen as suitable. . . . In Athens, girls were presented to the *phratry*[6] on . . . the third day of the Apatouria,[7] when a sacrifice was made by their (new) husband; this is associated with the boys'

[3] A woman to whom property was attached. She was thus an attractive bride.

[4] The male guardian of a woman. An Athenian woman was an eternal minor; she always had a guardian.

[5] Plural of *epikleros*.

[6] Tribe or clan.

[7] An annual festival.

sacrifice on the same day, made on the occasion of their cutting their hair as indicating the end of their childhood. Therefore it will have been not later than about sixteen, and the Greeks' fanatical emphasis on premarital virginity will have made it tend to be earlier than this rather than later.

A few instances are known in which a woman is said to have chosen her own husband, but in every case it is clear that it was most unusual. . . . It is important to stress that all these women belonged to the highest social class, in which the women have always had markedly more independence than among the bulk of the population.

Society demanded that a man procure marriages for his daughters, and, if necessary, sisters; it was regarded as a slight on his excellence if he did not do so. Nature, however, ordained . . . that more girl-babies than boys should survive infancy, and battle casualties were at least as numerous as deaths in childbirth; the excess of brides seeking husbands therefore created a competitive situation for the fathers of girls, which ensured that a dowry was an invariable accompaniment (though by no means a legal requirement) of a marriage. Girls who had no dowry could not get married, and therefore to marry a girl without a dowry, or with only a very small one, was to do her a very great honour, and was a matter for self-congratulation by orators, especially when the girl was an *epikleros*. Unmarried girls had either to remain at home, or enter the world of the demimondaines[8] if they were destitute orphans. After marriage, however, a girl seems to have had more ability to determine her lot. . . . [For] most married couples divorce was easy, and widows were often remarried.

In the choice of their second husband widows were certainly sometimes able to exercise some element of choice. . . . There can be little doubt, however, that young widows, even if they had children, were expected to remarry.

Moreover, Athenian women had as much right to divorce their husbands as their husbands had to divorce them, and we even hear of a father taking his daughter away when he quarrelled with his son-in-law; divorce by consent was also possible, especially in connection with a suit for an *epikleros*. In all cases, however, the woman's dowry had to be repaid to her *kyrios,* and a large dowry is said to be something which protects a woman and prevents her being divorced. It is therefore alleged that a woman whose citizenship was doubtful would necessarily have a large dowry so that her husband would not easily get rid of her.

The dowry was a field in which it is accepted that a man would express his self-esteem. . . . Nobody failed to give a dowry if he could help it; an uncle, it is said, guardian to four nieces and one nephew, would be sure to see that the girls were given dowries; friends gave dowries to the daughters of the poor; the daughters of *thetes,* the lowest financial class, who lacked brothers had by law to be given dowries by their relatives in

---

[8]Women who lost social standing owing to their sexual promiscuity.

accordance with their means; even the state stepped in very occasionally (in return for outstanding public services) to dower a man's daughters. . . . Dowries consisted of cash, or real-estate valued in cash. . . . Widows on their remarriage received dowries in exactly the same way as unmarried girls, and this is only natural since a woman's dowry was deemed to be her share of her paternal estate, a share set apart for her maintenance, and it is an unfailing principle of Athenian law that the head of the family who had a woman's dowry in his possession had to maintain her. . . .

. . . [A] dowry was intended primarily for a woman's maintenance. It remained in her husband's control while he lived; if he predeceased her and there were no children, it returned with her to her own family; if there were children, it was part of the children's inheritance provided that they supported their mother if adult, or their guardian did if they were infants. . . .

After the betrothal . . . came the wedding . . . , at which the bride was brought to the bridegroom's house and the marriage really began . . . , so that the various songs of the wedding were then appropriate. It was living together which made a marriage a marriage; its existence was therefore essentially a question of fact. Living together . . . is the Greek for being married, and the procreation of children was its explicit object. Xenophon's[9] Socrates says: 'Surely you do not suppose that it is for sexual satisfaction that men and women breed children, since the streets are full of people who will satisfy that appetite, as are the brothels? No, it is clear that we enquire into which women we may beget the best children from, and we come together with them and breed children' . . .

The Athenians were even a bit sentimental about children, if about anything; weeping children were a stock-in-trade of the defendant at a trial. . . .

Formal marriage and the birth of children from it also had a public side; this was due to the importance of asserting the child's legitimacy. With this in view a marriage was registered with the *phrateres*,[10] the husband's *phrateres* in most cases, but also, when the girl was an *epikleros*, with her family's. Similarly, when a child was born, it was exhibited at least to relatives on the tenth day festival, at what seems to have been a big celebration; and on this occasion the father named him . . . . [T]he father swore 'that he knew that the child had citizen-status, being born to him from a citizen mother, properly (*i.e.* formally) married'.

Children who could not substantiate their claim to legitimacy were bastards; they not only lacked rights of succession after 403 . . . they were also excluded from the family religious observances, and they did not enjoy citizen-rights. This did not mean that they had no rights. . . . Bastards

[9]A student of Socrates who, like Plato, wrote an *Apology* (a work purporting to be what Socrates said on his own behalf at his trial).

[10]Tribe or clan (phratry).

resembled outsiders . . . in that they lacked the right to claim citizens' estates, but they must have had rights at law. . . .

. . . Apollodorus[11] cites a law forbidding a foreigner to live with a citizen woman as his wife . . . and a foreign woman to live with a citizen, on pain of enslavement or a heavy fine; clearly this did not mean a prohibition of sexual intercourse across these boundaries, nor a prohibition on keeping a concubine, or, in the case of a woman, a lover, but it prohibited such people from pretending that they were formally married, and from claiming to breed citizen children. . . .

During the Peloponnesian War, after the Sicilian disaster in 413, we are told that the Athenians temporarily abandoned their rules about requiring a child's father and mother to be formally married because of the shortage of men, and citizens were allowed to marry one wife, and breed children (that is, legitimate children) from another. This has shocked commentators, . . . but it accords fully with the Athenian view of marriage—as an arrangement for maintaining the *oikoi*,[12] and (in the case of the city) for replenishing the supply of citizen-soldiers. . . .

The importance of being able to prove legitimacy had two principal results; it made adultery a public as well as a private offense, and it made the Athenians excessively preoccupied with the chastity of their womenfolk, with the result that they were guarded in a manner nowadays thought to be intolerable.

Adultery in Athens (it is sometimes said) meant 'the sins of a wife'. The evidence is not quite so unequivocal; in the first place, the punishment of death is prescribed for the adulterer and not the adulteress—she was punished, naturally, but it is odd that, if the offense was only hers, her lover should be put to death, not she.

Secondly, . . . it is stated that a man may with impunity kill an adulterer caught in the act with any of the women in his *kyrieia*[13]—his mother, sister and daughter are mentioned as well as his wife. . . .

. . . Plato's laws on sexual matters are revealing. They were intended to be as severe for men as for women, but, as he admitted, he had to compromise; though he wished to brand all sexual intercourse with anyone other than a wife as adultery, and claimed that the law of nature was to preserve virginity until the age of procreation, then to remain faithful to one's mate, he admitted that most men, both Greeks and non-Greeks, did not do this; he therefore fell back on 'the possible', which was to prohibit all sexual intercourse with freeborn or citizen women other than a man's wedded wife, to forbid sodomy, and impose secrecy on intercourse with any other (*i.e.* non-free) woman on pain of disfranchisement. Obviously Plato was reacting against contemporary attitudes, which did allow men

[11]Important only because of his involvement with a famous legal case.

[12]Households or families.

[13]Headship of a family.

extra-marital sexual relations provided that they were not with women in the *kyrieia* of other citizens. This is to say that adultery was not *solely* an offense by a female; a man was punishable as an adulterer if he seduced a woman he was forbidden to seduce, and his punishment was apt to be more severe, as his liberty of action was greater.

Athenian women had no sexual liberty, but the explanation of the Athenians' attitude was primarily civic, not moral. Euphiletus[14] says that 'the lawgiver prescribed death for adultery' (though not for rape) '. . . because he who achieves his ends by persuasion thereby corrupts the mind as well as the body of the woman . . . gains access to all a man's possessions, and casts doubt on his children's parentage'. This was the point; if an Athenian had an affair with a citizen-woman not his wife, a baby would not have any claim on his property or family or religious associations, nor impose on them a bogus claim for citizenship; but the woman would be compelled to claim that her husband was the father, and his kinship-group and its cult was therefore deeply implicated, since it would be having a non-member foisted upon it, and if she were detected, all her husband's children would have difficulty in proving their rights to citizenship if they were challenged. An unmarried Athenian girl who had been seduced could be sold into slavery according to Solon's laws; Hypereides[15] implies that it was more usual 250 years later merely to keep her at home unmarried — when he hints that neither she nor a widow who had been seduced would be able to get a husband.

Death for an adulterer, even if caught in the act, was quite certainly not always demanded; comedy speaks of payment, depilation and other humiliating, vulgar but comical indignities being inflicted on an adulterer, which would prevent him appearing in public, certainly from appearing in the wrestling-school, for some time. Divorce for a woman taken in adultery was compulsory, but we may be pretty certain that the demand was not always complied with; a woman with a large dowry would have to have it repaid, and this might be impossible for her husband, or be something he was unwilling to do. . . .

Non-citizens could contract legally valid marriages and dower their daughters to non-citizens, and the Athenian law upheld their contracts; what the Athenian law was concerned to prevent was non-citizens claiming to be citizens, and making claims on the property of citizens. . . .

The attitude of the Athenians to old age was somewhat unusual. On the one hand they hated old age with its loss of the youthful beauty which they so much admired, and they dreaded the time when they would no longer have the strength to earn their daily bread. Senility moreover was one of the causes which made an Athenian's acts invalid at law in that it was deemed that he was out if his mind if senile. . . . On the other

[14] An aggrieved husband in a famous Athenian law case dealing with adultery.

[15] Mid-fourth–century speech writer and orator.

hand the city laid it on children as a legal obligation, not merely a moral duty, to ensure that their parents were looked after when they were old. Maltreatment of parents ranks with maltreatment of orphans and *epikleroi* as a prosecution in which a prosecutor ran no risk of punishment. . . . [E]xpectations did not stop at refraining from maltreatment; positive services were required, especially the provision of food-supplies. . . . Hence getting children in order to have someone to tend their old age is a frequently mentioned motive for parenthood, and equally for adoption.

The state also made provision for looking after old women; here the law was explicit; the person who had charge of her dowry had the obligation to maintain her. . . . The class of people most obviously concerned are widows, whose situation at the death of their husbands was possibly that they could remain in their husband's *oikos* and be maintained by its new *kyrios*, who was sometimes a son, sometimes the guardian of an infant, or (if she were childless) a relative; alternatively the widow could return to her own family, if she had no children, and get her dowry back, or interest on it at a prescribed rate, or, if she were young enough, she could be remarried with an appropriate dowry . . . , or she could be adjudicated as *epikleros* if her situation warranted it. But whatever happened, the person who was *kyrios* of her dowry had to support her.

On the other hand, one effect of the law about senility was that fathers of adult sons often handed over the management of their *oikos* to their sons, and virtually stepped down from the management of the house. . . .

Throughout his life an Athenian was essentially a part of his *oikos;* as a baby his birth had to be accepted by the *kyrios* of his *oikos* (his father) and registered by the *phrateres* of the phratry to which his *oikos* belonged—the city was not interested in him directly until he was ready to be trained to serve it in war; as a man he married usually at an age at which his father was ready to retire from economic responsibility for the *oikos,* and his *phrateres* took note of his marriage, so that his son in turn would readily be accepted as a member of the *oikos;* when he retired in his turn, his *oikos* continued to support him under its new *kyrios,* his son. An Athenian woman was equally a part of her *oikos* until she married, at which time she removed into her husband's *oikos* taking with her a portion out of the possessions of her own *oikos;* this was designated for her support until her dying day whether she was wife or mother or widow or even divorcée. All the Athenian law was framed with this membership of the *oikos* in view; a man's *oikos* provided both his place in the citizen body and what measure of social security there was, and this helps to account for that passionate determination to defend the *oikoi* alike against foreigners and against grasping individual Athenians which is characteristic of the democratic period.

Classical Greek Attitudes to Sexual Behavior

K. J. DOVER

In this article, K.J. Dover analyzes Greek standards of sexual morality. Male citizens had numerous opportunities for sexual activity, yet there were restrictions. Why? How were Greek adolescents supposed to behave sexually? How did the city and family influence the adolescents' sexual activity? At an early age, males learned responsibility and moral values. What were those values? How did the Greeks view love and love-making?

Homosexuality (more properly, bisexuality) is a frequently noted feature of ancient Greece. Dover offers a nuanced interpretation of the sexual relationship between men, or between men and boys. How do you account for the Greeks' tolerance of homosexuality? Why were men so attracted to other men? What qualities did the Greeks praise in men?

What did Greek males think of women as sexual beings? Did they believe that women had different sexual appetites? Dover discusses the sexual roles that daughters, wives, slaves, and prostitutes played in ancient Greece. Why was there a double standard?

Dover's sources for this essay include public speeches, the theatre, art, and the works of philosophers. Do these sources present different views of Greek attitudes toward sex? Dover notes that the reality of sexual activity may have been different from attitudes expressed in speech and in writing.

The Greeks regarded sexual enjoyment as the area of life in which the goddess Aphrodite[1] was interested, as Ares was interested in war and other deities in other activities. Sexual intercourse was *aphrodisia*, 'the things of Aphrodite.' Sexual desire could be denoted by general words for 'desire,' but the obsessive desire for a particular person was *eros*, 'love' in the sense which it has in our expressions 'be in love with...'...and 'fall in love with....'... Eros, like all powerful emotional forces, but more consistently than most, was personified and deified....

Eros generates *philia*, 'love'; the same word can denote milder degrees of affection, just as 'my *philoi*' can mean my friends or my innermost family circle, according to context. For the important question 'Do you love me?' the verb used is *philein*, whether the question is put by a youth to a girl as their kissing becomes more passionate or by a father to his son as an anxious preliminary to a test of filial obedience.

Our own culture has its myths about the remote past, and one myth that dies hard is that the 'invention' of sexual guilt, shame and fear by the Christians destroyed a golden age of free, fearless, pagan sexuality. That

[1]Goddess of love and beauty.

most pagans were in many ways less inhibited than most Christians is undeniable. Not only had they a goddess specially concerned with sexual pleasure; their other deities were portrayed in legend as enjoying fornication, adultery and sodomy. A pillar surmounted by the head of Hermes[2] and adorned with an erect penis stood at every Athenian front-door; great models of the erect penis were borne in procession at festivals of Dionysus,[3] and it too was personified as the tirelessly lascivious Phales.[4] The vase-painters often depicted sexual intercourse, sometimes masturbation (male or female) and fellatio, and in respect of any kind of sexual behaviour Aristophanic[5] comedy appears to have had total license of word and act. . . .

There is, however, another side of the coin. Sexual intercourse was not permitted in the temples or sanctuaries of deities (not even of deities whose sexual enthusiasm was conspicuous in mythology), and regulations prescribing chastity or formal purification after intercourse played a part in many Greek cults. Homeric epic, for all its unquestioning acceptance of fornication as one of the good things of life, is circumspect in vocabulary, and more than once denotes the male genitals by *aidos*, 'shame,' 'disgrace.' . . . Poets (notably Homer) sometimes describe interesting and agreeable activities—cooking, mixing wine, stabbing an enemy through a chink in his armour—in meticulous detail, but nowhere is there a comparable description of the mechanisms of sexual activity. Prose literature, even on medical subjects, is euphemistic ('be with . . .' is a common way of saying 'have sexual intercourse with . . .') . . .

Linguistic inhibition, then, was observably strengthened in the course of the classical period; and at least in some art-forms, inhibition extended also to content. These are data which do not fit the popular concept of a guilt-free or shame-free sexual morality, and require explanation. Why so many human cultures use derogatory words as synonyms of 'sexual' and reproach sexual prowess while praising prowess in (e.g.) swimming and riding, is a question which would take us to a remote level of speculation. Why the Greeks did so is a question which can at least be related intelligibly to the structure of Greek society and to Greek moral schemata which have no special bearing on sex.

As far as was practicable . . . , Greek girls were segregated from boys and brought up at home in ignorance of the world outside the home; one speaker in court seeks to impress the jury with the respectability of his family by saying that his sister and nieces are 'so well brought up that they are embarrassed in the presence even of a man who is a member of the family.' Married young, perhaps at fourteen (and perhaps to a man

[2]Messenger of the gods.

[3]God of wine and fertility.

[4]Personification of the phallus, often said to accompany Dionysus.

[5]Aristophanes (c.448–c.380 B.C.) was an Athenian writer of comedy.

twenty-years or more her senior), a girl exchanged confinement in her father's house for confinement in her husband's. When he was invited out, his children might be invited with him, but not his wife; and when he had friends in, she did not join the company. Shopping seems to have been a man's job, to judge from references in comedy, and slaves could be sent on other errands outside the house. Upholders of the proprieties pronounced the front door to be the boundaries of a good woman's territory.

Consider now the situation of an adolescent boy growing up in such a society. Every obstacle is put in the way of his speaking to the girl next door; it may not be easy for him even to get a glimpse of her. Festivals, sacrifices and funerals, for which women and girls did come out in public, provided the occasion for seeing and being seen. They could hardly afford more than that, for there were too many people about, but from such an occasion (both in real life and in fiction) an intrigue could be set on foot, with a female slave of respectable age as the indispensable go-between.

In a society which practices segregation of the sexes, it is likely that boys and girls should devote a good deal of time and ingenuity to defeating society, and many slaves may have co-operated with enthusiasm. But Greek laws were not lenient towards adultery, and *moikheia*, for which we have no suitable translation except 'adultery,' denoted not only the seduction of another man's wife, but also the seduction of his widowed mother, unmarried daughter, sister, niece, or any other woman whose legal guardian he was. The adulterer could be prosecuted by the offended father, husband or guardian; alternatively, if caught in the act, he could be killed, maltreated, or imprisoned by force until he purchased his freedom by paying heavy compensation. A certain tendency to regard women as irresponsible and ever ready to yield to sexual temptation . . . relieved a cuckolded husband of a sense of shame or inadequacy and made him willing to seek the co-operation of his friends in apprehending an adulterer, just as he would seek their co-operation to defend himself against fraud, encroachment, breach of contract, or any other threat to his property. The adulterer was open to reproach in the same way, and to the same extent, as any other violator of the laws protecting the individual citizen against arbitrary treatment by other citizens. To seduce a woman of citizen status was more culpable than to rape her, not only because rape was presumed to be unpremeditated but because seduction involved the capture of her affection and loyalty; it was the degree of offense against the man to whom she belonged, not her own feelings, which mattered.

It naturally follows from the state of the law and from the attitudes and values implied by segregation that an adolescent boy who showed an exceptional enthusiasm for the opposite sex could be regarded as a potential adulterer and his propensity discouraged just as one would discourage theft, lies and trickery, while an adolescent boy who blushed at the mere idea of proximity to a woman was praised as *sophron*, 'right-minded,' i.e.

unlikely to do anything without reflecting first whether it might incur punishment, disapproval, dishonour or other undesirable consequences.

Greek society was a slave-owning society, and a female slave was not in a position to refuse the sexual demands of her owner or of anyone else to whom he granted the temporary use of her. Large cities, notably Athens, also had a big population of resident aliens, and these included women who made a living as prostitutes, on short-term relations with a succession of clients, or as *hetairai*, who endeavoured to establish long-term relations with wealthy and agreeable men. Both aliens and citizens could own brothels and stock them with slave-prostitutes. Slave-girls and alien girls who took part in men's parties as dancers or musicians could also be mauled and importuned in a manner which might cost a man his life if he attempted it with a woman of citizen status. . . .

It was therefore easy enough to purchase sexual satisfaction, and the richer a man was the better provision he could make for himself. But money spent on sex was money not spent on other things, and there seems to have been substantial agreement on what were proper or improper items of expenditure. Throughout the work of the Attic orators,[6] who offer us by far the best evidence on the moral standards which it was prudent to uphold in addressing large juries composed of ordinary citizens, it is regarded as virtuous to impoverish oneself by gifts and loans to friends in misfortune (for their daughters' dowries, their fathers' funerals, and the like), by ransoming Athenian citizens taken prisoner in war, and by paying out more than the required minimum in the perfomance of public duties (the upkeep of a warship, for example, or the dressing and training of a chorus at a festival). This kind of expenditure was boasted about and treated as a claim on the gratitude of the community. On the other hand, to 'devour an inheritance' by expenditure on one's own consumption was treated as disgraceful. Hence gluttony, drunkenness and purchased sexual relations were classified together as 'shameful pleasures.' . . . When a young man fell in love, he might well fall in love with a hetaira or a slave, since his chances of falling in love with a girl of citizen status were so restricted, and to secure the object of his love he would need to purchase or ransom her. A close association between eros and extravagance therefore tends to be assumed, especially in comedy; a character in Menander[7] says, 'No one is so parsimonious as not to make some sacrifice of his property to Eros.' More than three centuries earlier, Archilochus[8] put the matter in characteristically violent form when he spoke of wealth accumulated by long labour 'pouring down into a whore's guts.' A fourth-century litigant venomously asserts that his adversary, whose tastes were predominantly homosexual, has 'buggered away all his estate.'

[6] Athenians who wrote or gave speeches in law courts or in the assembly.

[7] Greek writer of comedy, 342?–291? B.C.

[8] Greek poet of the mid-seventh century B.C.

We have here another reason for the discouragement and disapproval of sexual enthusiasm in the adolescent; it was seen as presenting a threat that the family's wealth would be dissipated in ways other than those which earned honour and respect from the community. The idea that one has a right to spend one's own money as one wishes (or a right to do anything which detracts from one's health and physical fitness) is not Greek, and would have seemed absurd to a Greek. He had only the rights which the law of his city explicitly gave him; no right was inalienable, and no claim superior to the city's.

Living in a fragmented and predatory world, the inhabitants of a Greek city-state, who could never afford to take the survival of their community completely for granted, attached a great importance to the qualities required of a soldier: not only to strength and speed, in which men are normally superior to women, but also to the endurance of hunger, thirst, pain, fatigue, discomfort and disagreeably hot or cold weather. The ability to resist and master the body's demands for nourishment and rest was normally regarded as belonging to the same moral category as the ability to resist sexual desire. Xenophon[9] describes the chastity of King Agesilaus[10] together with his physical toughness, and elsewhere summarises 'lack of self-control' as the inability to hold out against 'hunger, thirst, sexual desire and long hours without sleep.'

The reasons for this association are manifold: the treatment of sex—a treatment virtually inevitable in a slave-owning society—as a commodity, and therefore as something which the toughest and most frugal men will be able to cut down to a minimum; the need for a soldier to resist the blandishments of comfort (for if he does not resist, the enemy who does will win), to sacrifice himself as an individual entirely, to accept pain and death as the price to be paid for the attainment of a goal which is not easily quantified, the honour of victory; and the inveterate Greek tendency to conceive of strong desires and emotional states as forces which assail the soul from the outside. To resist is manly and 'free'; to be distracted by immediate pleasure from the pursuit of honour through toil and suffering is to be a 'slave' to the forces which 'defeat' and 'worst' one's own personality.

Here is a third reason for praise of chastity in the young, the encouragement of the capacity to resist, to go without, to become the sort of man on whom the community depends for its defence. If the segregation and legal and administrative subordination of women received their original impetus from the fragmentation of the early Greek world into small, continuously warring states, they also gave an impetus to the formation of certain beliefs about women which served as a rationalization of segregation and no doubt affected behavior to the extent that people tend to

[9]Greek general and historian, 430?–355? B.C.
[10]Spartan King (444–360 B.C.) who begin his reign in 399.

behave in the ways expected of them. Just as it was thought masculine to resist and endure, it was thought feminine to yield to fear, desire and impulse. 'Now you must be a *man;*' says Demeas[11] to himself as he tries to make up his mind to get rid of his concubine, 'Forget your desire, fall out of love.' Women in comedy are notoriously unable to keep off the bottle, and in tragedy women are regarded as naturally more prone than men to panic, uncontrollable grief, jealousy and spite. It seems to have been believed not only that women enjoyed sexual intercourse more intensely than men, but also that experience of intercourse put the woman more under the man's power than it put him under hers, and that if not segregated and guarded women would be insatiably promiscuous.

It was taken for granted in the Classical period that a man was sexually attracted by a good-looking younger male, and no Greek who said that he was 'in love' would have taken it amiss if his hearers assumed without further enquiry that he was in love with a boy and that he desired more than anything to ejaculate in or on the boy's body. I put the matter in these coarse and clinical terms to preclude any misapprehension arising from modern application of the expression 'Platonic love' or from Greek euphemism (see below). . . . Aphrodite, despite her femininity, is not hostile to homosexual desire, and homosexual intercourse is denoted by the same term, *aphrodisia*, as heterosexual intercourse. Vase-painting was noticeably affected by the homosexual ethos; painters sometimes depicted a naked woman with a male waist and hips, as if a woman's body was nothing but a young man's body plus breasts and minus external genitals, and in many of their pictures of heterosexual intercourse from the rear position the penis appears (whatever the painter's intention) to be penetrating the anus, not the vagina.

Why homosexuality—or, to speak more precisely, 'pseudo-homosexuality,' since the Greeks saw nothing surprising in the coexistence of desire for boys and desire for girls in the same person—obtained so firm and widespread a hold on Greek society, is a difficult and speculative question. Segregation alone cannot be the answer, for comparable segregation has failed to engender a comparable degree of homosexuality in other cultures. Why the Greeks of the Classical period accepted homosexual desire as natural and normal is a much easier question: they did so because previous generations had accepted it, and segregation of the sexes in adolescence fortified and sustained the acceptance and the practice.

Money may have enabled the adolescent boy to have plenty of sexual intercourse with girls of alien or servile status, but it could not give him the satisfaction which can be pursued by his counterpart in a society which does not own slaves: the satisfaction of being welcomed *for his own sake* by a sexual partner of equal status. This is what the Greek boy was offered by homosexual relations. He was probably accustomed (as often happens with boys who do not have the company of girls) to a good deal

[11]Character in a play by Menander.

of homosexual play at the time of puberty, and he never heard from his elders the suggestion that one was destined to become *either* 'a homosexual' *or* 'a heterosexual.' As he grew older, he could seek among his juniors a partner of citizen status, who could certainly not be forced and who might be totally resistant to even the most disguised kind of purchase. If he was to succeed in seducing this boy (or if later, as a mature man, he was to seduce a youth), he could do so only by *earning* hero-worship.

This is why, when Greek writers 'idealize' eros and treat the physical act as the 'lowest' ingredient in a rich and complex relationship which comprises mutual devotion, reciprocal sacrifice, emulation, and the awakening of sensibility, imagination and intellect, they look not to what most of us understand by sexual love but to the desire of an older for a younger male and the admiration felt by the younger for the older. It is noticeable also that in art and literature inhibitions operate in much the same way as in the romantic treatment of heterosexual love in our own tradition. When physical gratification is directly referred to, the younger partner is said to 'grant favours' or 'render services'; but a great deal is written about homosexual eros from which the innocent reader would not easily gather that any physical contact at all was involved. Aeschines,[12] who follows Aeschylus[13] and Classical sentiment generally in treating the relation between Achilles and Patroclus in the *Iliad*[14] as homoerotic, commends Homer for leaving it to 'the educated among his hearers' to perceive the nature of the relation from the extravagant grief expressed by Achilles at the death of Patroclus. The vase-painters very frequently depict the giving of presents by men to boys and the 'courting' of boys (a mild term for an approach which includes putting a hand on the boy's genitals), but their pursuit of the subject to the stage of erection, let alone penetration, is very rare, whereas depiction of heterosexual intercourse, in a variety of positions, is commonplace.

We also observe in the field of homosexual relations the operation of the 'dual standard of morality' which so often characterizes societies in which segregation of the sexes is minimal. If a Greek admitted that he was in love with a boy, he could expect sympathy and encouragement from his friends, and if it was known that he had attained his goal, envy and admiration. The boy, on the other hand, was praised if he retained his chastity, and he could expect strong disapproval if he was thought in any way to have taken the initiative in attracting a lover. The probable implication is that neither partner would actually say anything about the physical aspect of their relationship to anyone else, nor would they expect any question about it to be put to them or any allusion to it made in their presence.

---

[12] Athenian orator 397?–322? B.C.

[13] Athenian tragic poet, 525–456 B.C.

[14] Achilles was the great hero and Patroclus his friend in the *Illiad*, Homer's epic poem.

Once we have accepted the universality of homosexual relations in Greek society as a fact, it surprises us to learn that if a man had at any time in his life prostituted himself to another man for money he was debarred from exercising his political rights. If he was an alien, he had no political rights to exercise, and was in no way penalized for living as a male prostitute, so long as he paid the prostitution tax levied upon males and females alike. It was therefore not the physical act *per se* which incurred penalty, but the incorporation of the act in a certain deliberately chosen role which could only be fully defined with reference to the nationality and status of the participants.

This datum illustrates an attitude which was fundamental to Greek society. They tended to believe that one's moral character is formed in the main by the circumstances in which one lives: the wealthy man is tempted to arrogance and oppression, the poor man to robbery and fraud, the slave to cowardice and petty greed. A citizen compelled by great and sudden economic misfortune to do work of a kind normally done by slaves was shamed because his assumption of a role which so closely resembled a slave's role altered his relationship to his fellow-citizens. Since prostitutes were usually slaves or aliens, to play the role of a prostitute was, as it were, to remove oneself from the citizen-body, and the formal exclusion of a male prostitute from the rights of a citizen was a penalty for disloyalty to the community in his choice of role.

Prostitution is not easily defined—submission in gratitude for gifts, services or help is not so different in kind from submission in return for an agreed fee—nor was it easily proved in a Greek city, unless people were willing (as they were not) to come forward and testify that they had helped to cause a citizen's son to incur the penalty of disenfranchisement. A boy involved in a homosexual relationship absolutely untainted by mercenary considerations could still be called a prostitute by his family's enemies, just as the term can be recklessly applied today by unfriendly neighbours or indignant parents to a girl who sleeps with a lover. He could also be called effeminate; not always rightly, since athletic success seems to have been a powerful stimulus to his potential lovers, but it is possible (and the visual arts do not help us much here) that positively feminine characteristics in the appearance, movements and manner of boys and youths played a larger part in the ordinary run of homosexual activity than the idealization and romanticisation of the subject in literature indicate. There were certainly circumstances in which homosexuality could be treated as a substitute for heterosexuality; a comic poet says of the Greeks who besieged Troy for ten years, 'they never saw a hetaira . . . and ended up with arseholes wider than the gates of Troy.' . . . A sixth-century vase in which all of a group of men except one are penetrating women shows the odd man out grasping his erect penis and approaching, with a gesture of entreaty, a youth—who starts to run away. In so far as the 'passive partner' in a homosexual act takes on himself the role of a woman, he was open to the suspicion, like the male prostitute, that he abjured his prescribed role as a future soldier and defender of the community.

The comic poets, like the orators, ridicule individuals for effeminacy, for participation in homosexual activity, or for both together; at the same time, the sturdy, wilful, roguish characters whom we meet in Aristophanes are not averse to handling and penetrating good-looking boys when the opportunity presents itself, as a supplement to their busy and enjoyable heterosexual programmes... [T]here is one obvious factor which we should expect to determine different sexual attitudes in different classes. The thorough-going segregation of women of citizen status was possible only in households which owned enough slaves and could afford to confine its womenfolk to a leisure enlivened only by the exercise of domestic crafts such as weaving and spinning. This degree of segregation was simply not possible in poorer families; the women who sold bread and vegetables in the market—Athenian women, not resident aliens—were not segregated, and there must have been plenty of women... who took a hand in work on the land and drove animals to market. No doubt convention required that they should protect each other's virtue by staying in pairs or groups as much as they could, but clearly... the obstacles to love-affairs between citizens' sons and citizens' daughters lose their validity as one goes down the social scale. Where there are love-affairs, both boys and girls can have decided views... on whom they wish to marry. The girl in Aristophanes' *Ecclesiazusae*[15] who waits impatiently for her young man's arrival while her mother is out may be much nearer the norm of Athenian life than those cloistered ladies who were 'embarrassed by the presence even of a male relative.' It would not be discordant with modern experience to believe that speakers in an Athenian law-court professed, and were careful to attribute to the jury, standards of propriety higher than the average member of the jury actually set himself.

Much Classical Greek philosophy is characterized by contempt for sexual intercourse.... Xenophon's Socrates, although disposed to think it a gift of beneficent providence that humans, unlike other mammals, can enjoy sex all the year round, is wary of troubling the soul over what he regards as the minimum needs of the body.... One logical outcome of this attitude to sex is exemplified by Diogenes the Cynic, who was alleged to have masturbated in public when his penis erected itself, as if he were scratching a mosquito-bite. Another outcome was the doctrine (influential in Christianity, but not of Christian origin) that a wise and virtuous man will not have intercourse except for the purpose of procreating legitimate offspring, a doctrine which necessarily proscribes much heterosexual and all homosexual activity.

Although philosophical preoccupation with the contrast between 'body' and 'soul' had much to do with these developments, we can dis-

---

[15]The play, *The Assembly of Women*.

cern, as the ground from which these philosophical plants sprouted, Greek admiration for invulnerability, hostility towards the diversion of resources to the pursuit of pleasure, and disbelief in the possibility that dissimilar ways of feeling and behaving can be synthesised in the same person without detracting from his attainment of the virtues expected of a selfless defender of his city. It is also clear that the refusal of Greek law and society to treat a woman as a responsible person, while on the one hand it encouraged a complacent acceptance of prostitution and concubinage, on the other hand led to the classification of sexual activity as a male indulgence which could be reduced to a minimum by those who were not self-indulgent. . . .

Roman Women

GILLIAN CLARK

Although historians lack good evidence about Roman women, there is enough to illuminate many aspects of their lives. In this article, Gillian Clark explores their standing in law, customs relating to child-bearing and child-raising, female education, and the nature of marriage.

Clark seeks to know if women were oppressed in this society. Information about female mortality provides one part of the answer. Why were women more likely to be killed at birth and to die young? Today, women outnumber men, but Roman society had more males than females. How did this fact affect arrangements for marriage? What was married life like? Did well-born Roman husbands treat their wives differently than did Athenian husbands? What options were available to women who were not free or who did not marry in a society that reserved education and political activity, save in rare instances, exclusively for men? What can the family life of Romans tell us about their success in conquering and maintaining an extensive empire?

Clark often cites the opinions of Roman literary figures and physicians. How did they regard women and women's lives? Some of the beliefs are timeless, hardly peculiar to ancient Rome. The medical ideas often appear fanciful, but they do help explain the condition of women in Roman society.

From the very beginning of their lives, women had great disadvantages, though Clark argues that many of them probably were reasonably content with their situations in life. Perhaps only in upper-class marriages did women find some measure of happiness. That happiness, as Clark concludes, can be measured in relation to how the women fulfilled men's expectations of them as ideal mothers and wives. The women who were not slaves, prostitutes, poor, or the victims of infanticide, may have achieved success—insofar as that could be achieved—in an uneventful marriage, occupied with a loving husband and several children (but probably only one daughter!). In the ancient world, a solvent security attached to an enduring boredom may have been the most for which women could strive.

. . . What did Roman women do all day, besides getting dressed? How did they feel about it? What else could they have done? Were they oppressed, and did they notice? Why do we know so little about half the human race?

. . . We are still working with evidence strongly biased towards the upper classes and the city of Rome. The lives of women not in, or in contact with, the senatorial class, can only be guessed at from inscriptions, if someone troubled to put one up. And even within the senatorial class, it was not the women who wrote. . . . [T]he only extended work of literature to survive from the period I shall concentrate on, that of the late Republic and early Empire, is the elegies of Sulpicia.[1] . . . Moreover, there is little Roman literature which is concerned with the daily life and experience of particular people: the lives of women tend to be incidental to oratory or history or philosophy or agriculture, or to the emotions of an elegiac poet.

What then can be said? . . . To begin at the beginning: a girl's chances of being reared were less than her brother's. *Patria Potestas*[2] . . . was uniquely strong in Rome, and if a father decided that his new-born child was not to be reared there was no law (before the time of the Severi)[3] to prevent him. . . . Cicero[4] . . . and Seneca[5] . . . reveal that deformed babies were exposed . . . , and it was part of a midwife's training to decide which babies were worth rearing. Healthy but inconvenient babies might also be left to die. Musonius Rufus . . . in the mid-first century A.D. devoted one of his lectures on ethics to the question whether one should rear all one's children. The rich do not, he says, so that there shall be fewer children to share the family property. . . . Since the law required property to be shared among *sui heredes*,[6] it must have been a temptation. Among the poor, there was no question of splitting up an estate. Pliny[7] . . . praises Trajan's[8] extension of the grain-dole to children:

'There are great rewards to encourage the rich to rear their children, and great penalties if they do not. The only way the poor *can* rear their children is through the goodness of the *princeps*.'[9]

If a family did, from greed or necessity, expose a child, it would probably be a girl. Dionysius of Halicarnassus,[10] writing his *Antiquities of Rome* . . . under Augustus,[11] included a 'constitution of Romulus' which

[1] Roman poet, late first century B.C.

[2] The father's power.

[3] Line of emperors, 193–235 A.D.

[4] Roman orator and politician 106–43 B.C.

[5] Roman statesman and philosopher. 3 B.C.–65 A.D.

[6] His heirs.

[7] Pliny (the Younger)—statesman and civil servant, 61/2–113 A.D.

[8] Emperor, 98–117 A.D.

[9] Official title, meaning "first citizen," what we refer to as emperor.

[10] Greek historian, first century B.C.

[11] First Roman emperor, 27 B.C.–14 A.D.

has strong links with first-century thought. It provides that citizens must rear all male children (except those who are acknowledged by five neighbours to be deformed)—and the first girl. Apuleius[12] . . . has a prospective father instruct his wife: 'si sexus sequioris edidisset fetum, protinus quod esset editum necaretur.'[13] (This father, like those who speak now of 'the product of conception', is not prepared to acknowledge the child's humanity.) Some odd facts about sex-ratios make it likely that Dionysius and Apuleius reflect a general tendency. We simply do not hear of spinsters, except the Vestals[14]—and Augustus found it difficult enough to recruit them. (Even they could marry at the end of their term of office, aged 36–40, though they tended not to.) There is not even a normal word for a spinster. . . . Unmarried women were young *virgines*—and there were no nunneries for the women who did not marry.

Some families did, of course, raise more than one daughter. The daughter of L. Aemilius Paullus Macedonicus had three daughters and three sons; Appius Claudius Pulcher, cos.[15] 79 B.C., also had three daughters. . . . But tombstones in general record many more men than women, and this again suggests that either more males were reared or they mattered more to their families. Sometimes there is information about a specific group. A list of aqueduct maintenance men and their families . . . includes two families with two daughters each, but shows a very low proportion of daughters to sons overall. Trajan's alimentary scheme at Veleia supported only 36 girls out of 300 places: this cannot be used straightforwardly as evidence for sex-ratios, since girls got a smaller food-allowance and a family would obviously claim for a boy if it could, but does suggest that there were few families satisfied with daughters alone. Most impressive . . . is Augustus' concession that 'well-born men, other than senators and senators' sons, might marry *libertinae*.[16] Dio[17] . . . says there were just not enough women of good family to go round—and if this is true, after several decades of bloody civil war, then people must have been choosing not to rear daughters. But is Dio guessing? The senate, according to him, said that young men were not marrying because of . . . their failure to settle down, not because they could not find wives.

There are, of course, other causes than selective infanticide for a relative shortage of women. Many must have died in childbirth, from infection or difficult births, or because they were just too young. Soranus . . . , the

---

[12]Rhetorician and writer, mid-second century A.D.

[13]"If she bears a foetus of the inferior sex, that which she bore is to be killed immediately."

[14]Priestesses dedicated to the goddess of the hearth, Vesta, and sworn to remain virgins for thirty years.

[15]Consul, one of the two chief executives of the Roman state.

[16]Freed women.

[17]Dio Cassius, statesman and historian, late second to early third century A.D.

second-century A.D. physician whose work was the basis of gynaecology until well on in the nineteenth century, thought fifteen was the earliest suitable age for conception: most gynaecologists now would add three years to that. Child mortality too was alarmingly high, as it has been at all times and places except for some privileged Western countries in the twentieth century.... Girls are usually tougher than boys, but some societies undernourish them, either because they value girls less or because they think (wrongly) that girls need less. Roman governmental schemes like that at Veleia, and several private schemes, gave girls a smaller food-allowance. But these factors have affected other societies which do not show the same apparent shortage of women: so perhaps we do have to come back to parents not rearing girls.

How could they bear it? Even abortion, in this society, is tolerable only so far as we can avoid seeing the foetus as a baby: once the child is born, even for some time before birth, her rights are protected. But the father's right to decide the fate of his own infant probably seemed as obvious as, now, a woman's right to decide about her own body: so infanticide was not made criminal, even though low birth-rate was a persistent anxiety. Besides, Roman parents could not plan their families with much success. Contraceptives varied from quite effective spermicides and pessaries... to decoctions of herbs (and worse), faith in douches and wriggling, and entirely magical beliefs. The ovum was undiscovered and the relation between menstruation and fertile periods was misunderstood; this is less surprising in that conception can occur before the first menstruation if a girl marries before she reaches puberty. Observers may also have been confused by amenorrhea (failure to menstruate), which is a common reaction to stress and poor diet and which gets a lot of space in ancient medical textbooks. Soranus... held that the best time for conception was at the end of a menstrual period, when (he says) a women's desire is strongest, and suggested a rhythm method based on this belief. No wonder Augustus' daughter played safe, and never took a lover unless she was legitimately pregnant.... And no wonder abortion was also practiced. Doctors used herbal baths, suppositories, and potions first; then purges, diuretics, massage, violent exercise, and hot baths after drinking wine. If these ancient equivalents of gin, hot baths, and jumping off the kitchen table failed, there seem to have been back-street abortionists using the knitting-needle technique.

Abortion, like infanticide, was not a crime before the time of the Severi, and then the crime was not against the foetus, who was not a person in law, but against the defrauded husband. Why was it not made illegal before? There was strong feeling against abortion, which was taken to be proof of vanity ... or, worse, of adultery ... on the part of the mother. Perhaps it was simply too difficult to prove deliberate as against spontaneous abortion: Soranus' ... list of causes for the latter make one wonder how anyone ever managed to have a baby.

An unwanted pregnancy may yet produce a wanted child, but there were some practices which may have prevented, at least among the upper classes, the emotional bonding of mother and baby. Many mothers did not breast-feed, because it is tiring, but expected to use a wet-nurse. The wet-nurse's own baby had perhaps died, or been exposed, or was expected to manage on some substitute for breast-milk—which last was a major cause of child mortality in the nineteenth century. If Soranus' instructions . . . reflect general practice, the new-born was washed, swaddled, and then put somewhere to be quiet, and to be fed, if at all, the equivalent of glucose (boiled honey and water): Soranus advocated breast-feeding but thought colostrum was bad for babies. So the mother might scarcely have seen the child before the decision to expose it. Poorer people could not afford luxuries of feeling. It may have seemed better to expose the child and hope for the fairy-story to come true and the child to be rescued by some wealthy childless couple. Just occasionally it did. Slavery or a brothel . . . were more likely fates, but even that may have seemed more like putting a child to be raised 'in service', where the chances were better and at least there was food.

If, then, a Roman girl survived her parents' possible indifference, or resignation, to her death, and if she did not despite their best efforts die anyway, what would her life be like?

If she were a slave, she might have little time with her parents: she, or they, could be sold at any time, and there are epitaphs of very young children who had been freed by someone other than the master who freed either parent. But it may have been a relative who bought out the child, since at least the family was united enough for the epitaph to be made. Some slave families did manage gradually to buy the freedom of spouses and children. What a slave girl did depended on the size and type of household to which she belonged. She was most likely to be an *ancilla*, which may mean anything from a maid-of-all-work to a lady's maid— obviously the second was a better chance, since she could collect tips and win her mistress' (or master's) favour. She might have special skills: some slave-girls were dressers, hairdressers, dressmakers, woolworkers, and some perhaps worked in small factories rather than for the household stores. Some were childminders . . . , which was a job not regarded as needing skill, or, if they were lactating, wet-nurses.

Some households were brothels, and so in effect were some eating- and drinking-places. . . . A few slave-girls, who had other abilities for entertaining, were trained to dance, sing, and act . . .

If a slave-girl were freed, it did not much enlarge the possibilities: she might be a prostitute, a *mima*, or, if she were lucky, a housewife, doing much the same work as an *ancilla* did but in her own home. If she had caught the fancy of someone of high social status, she would be his *concubina* not his wife: it was not respectable to marry a *libertina*, though it had been known to happen even before Augustus allowed it for non-senators. Housework was hard: there was spinning and weaving and sewing and mending, cooking and cleaning, and water-carrying and baby-minding. Doubtless one reason for child mortality was the impossibility of keeping a swaddled baby clean on the fourth floor of a tenement with the water-supply at the end of the street. Soranus . . . said babies should be bathed and massaged once a day; the undersheets should often be aired and changed and one should watch for insect bites and ulceration. It sounds optimistic. If the housewife had learnt a trade before she married—baking, brickmaking, selling vegetables—she would probably go on with it, often working with her husband. The nearest approach to a professional woman would be a woman doctor, or the midwife who was called in for female complaints, though their social status was not high.

Rich girls had to learn to run a household rather than doing its work, but they too had spinning and weaving. By the first century B.C. there were ready-made fabrics for those who could afford them . . . , but *lanificium*[18] was part of traditional devotion to the home and was still, for most women, an essential part of household economy. A bride carried a spindle and distaff . . . : this is one marriage custom with an obvious relevance. Whether *lanificium* was an enjoyable craft skill or an exhausting chore depended on how much one had to do. Livy's[19] picture . . . of the virtuous Lucretia, sitting up with her maids doing wool-work by lamplight, needs to be supplemented by Tibullus'[20] . . . of the weary slave falling asleep over her work, and the neglected old woman who has no other resource. Too much woolwork, despite the lanolin in the wool, hardened the hands—a point to bear in mind when choosing a midwife. . . . But the custom was kept up by ladies of old-fashioned virtue. There were looms in the *atrium* of M. Aemilius Lepidus[21] when thugs broke in on his admirable wife; Augustus' women-folk kept him in homespun, though Livia[22] had a large staff of skilled workers. *Lanificium*, for ladies, perhaps took the place of the 'accomplishments'—music, drawing, fine sewing—which young ladies of the nineteenth century learnt before marriage and used to fill idle hours after. . . .

Little is heard of more intellectual pursuits. There was a chance of picking up some education from parents, brothers, even a sympathetic husband. The younger Pliny and his friend Pompeius Saturninus, who were civilized people, both continued the literary education of their wives. . . . Pompeius' wife wrote letters which sounded like prose Plautus[23]

---

[18]The making of wool.

[19]Titus Livy, Roman historian, 59 B.C.–17 A.D.

[20]Roman poet, 48–19 B.C.

[21]Late Republican Roman politician. His wife was the sister of Marcus Brutus, the assassin of Julius Caesar.

[22](58 B.C.–29 A.D.), wife to the first Roman emperor, Augustus.

[23]Roman playwright, c.254–184 B.C.

or Terence,[24] so pure was their Latin (Pliny was inclined to give Pompeius the credit). Pliny's wife set his verses to music with no tutor but Love, which sounds less promising. . . .

Some girls may have gone to school, at least for primary schooling, and some had private tutors. Pompeius' wife Cornelia had been taught literature, music, and geometry, and had 'listened with profit' to lectures on philosophy—which may mean ethics or physics. . . . Pompeius' daughter had a tutor for Greek. . . . Pliny's friend Fundanius had *praeceptores*[25] for his daughter, but he was a progressive: a philosopher, a friend of Plutarch[26] who wrote on the education of women, a pupil of Musonius[27] who argued for equal education for girls. These people may be exceptions. . . .

Some girls learnt music and singing, and the dramatic recitations which rose to a form of ballet and could be very strenuous, but it was not proper for them to aim at a professional standard. Scipio Aemilianus[28] had been shocked, as early as 129 B.C., to find well-born boys and girls at a dancing class; . . . Horace[29] thought it was part of the rot that grown girls should learn *Ionicos motus*.[30]

Some women, then, were reasonably well-educated: Quintilian[31] . . . cites as shining examples Cornelia (mother of the Gracchi),[32] and Hortensia and Laelia who were daughters of orators. . . . But at the age when a boy was going on to the secondary education which trained him in the use of language and prepared him for public life, a girl was entering her first marriage. . . .

Fourteen was evidently a proper age for marriage. It was assumed to be the age of menarche, though if a girl had not reached puberty the marriage might well be arranged anyway, and menstruation encouraged by massage, gentle exercise, good food, and diversion. The legal minimum age of marriage, as fixed by Augustan legislation which followed Republican precedent, was 12: earlier marriage was not penalized, but was not valid until the girl reached 12. (It followed that she could not be prosecuted for adultery.) Some marriages were certainly pre-pubertal. Augustus' own first wife was *vixdum nubilis*,[33] and Suetonius[34] . . . found it worth

[24]Roman comic poet, c.190–159 B.C.

[25]Tutors.

[26]Greek moralist and biographer, c.46–120 A.D.

[27]Roman philosopher, c.30–c.101 A.D.

[28](185–129 B.C.), often known as Scipio the Younger, Roman statesman and general responsible for the final destruction of Carthage.

[29]Roman poet, 65–8 B.C.

[30]Ionic dance (a type of Greek dancing).

[31]Roman teacher and rhetorician, 35–95 A.D.

[32]Tiberius Gracchus (163–133 B.C.) and Gaius Gracchus (153–121 B.C.), brothers who were Roman statesmen and reformers.

[33]Scarcely nubile.

[34]Roman biographer and civil servant, c.69–c.140 A.D.

recording that he sent her back *intacta*.[35] One girl . . . was 'taken to her husband's bosom' at 7: perhaps the marriage was not consummated, though Petronius[36] . . . relates (in order to shock?) the defloration of a seven-year-old. . . .

Plutarch, not surprisingly, thought that Roman girls married too young, and that Lycurgus[37] was right in ensuring that brides should be ready for childbearing. Romans, he says, were more concerned to ensure an undefiled body and mind. . . . Evidently they thought they had to catch the girls young to be sure. Doctors supposed that sexual desires began at puberty, especially in girls who ate a lot and did not have to work; society made provision for such desires instead of trying to sublimate them. Epictetus[38] remarks sadly that when girls are fourteen they begin to be called *kuria*,[39] the address of a grown woman: then they see that there is nothing for it but to go to bed with men, and begin to make themselves pretty in hopes. (His solution is for them to learn that men really admire them for modesty and chastity—and then, one supposes, they may go to bed with philosophers.) So marriage at fourteen was, in one sense, practical. But were girls in any sense ready for it? Physically, no: teenage pregnancies were known to be dangerous, and Soranus . . . stoutly disagrees with the school of thought which held that conception is good for you. . . . [O]ne striking contrast between Roman and Greek *mores:* the *materfamilias*[40] was at the centre of the household's social life. Visitors found her in the *atrium* (maybe even doing her wool work) and conversed with her; she went out shopping, to visit friends, to temples, theatres, and games. Decorum might require her to be suitably dressed and chaperoned, and restrained to the point of discourtesy in returning a greeting, but decorum is not always observed. Probably she had her daughters with her on some of these occasions; she may even have taken them to dinner-parties, though some people thought that girls learnt rather too much when out to dinner. A society which did not segregate women, and which praised wives for being pleasant company, gave married life a far better chance than did the conventions of classical Athens. A fourteen-year-old who had grown up in it, expecting to be grown up at fourteen, might well be reasonably mature. And where the expectation of life was nearer 30+ than 70+, there was no use in delaying recognized adulthood to 16 or 18.

The pressure of mortality was the underlying reason for early marriage. Tullia, Cicero's cherished daughter, was engaged at 12, and married at 16, to an excellent young man. She was widowed at 22, remarried at

[35]Intact, that is, still a virgin.

[36]Roman satirist, mid-first century A.D.

[37]Legendary founder of the Spartan constitution.

[38]Stoic philosopher, c.55–135 A.D.

[39]Term for a mature woman.

[40]Mother of the family.

23, divorced at 28; married again at 29, divorced at 33—and dead, soon after childbirth, at 34. The evidence of inscriptions shows that she was not untypical. So the fathers who arranged the marriages had good reason to start making alliances, and getting grandchildren, fast.

Fathers arranged marriages: but that was not all there was to it. A father's consent was necessary to the marriage of a daughter in his *potestas*,[41] though he was presumed to have given it unless he explicitly refused. The mother's consent was not relevant. The daughter's consent was necessary, but could be refused only if her father's choice were morally unfit—and, in practice, if she could get relatives and neighbours to back her up.... But, in practice, mothers and daughters might well have a say in the matter. Cicero, admittedly an indulgent father, wondered whether Tullia would accept the suitor suggested by Atticus...; Tullia and Terentia presented him with a *fait accompli* and her engagement to Dolabella,[42] though indeed Cicero was out of Italy at the time, and Tullia was a woman entering her third marriage, not a girl of twelve.... Anyone who reads Victorian novels will have a picture in mind of the complexities of family feeling and economic necessity which affect the choice of a husband—and of how much can be achieved by helpless young ladies and wives without civil rights. But it seems fair to ask whether the character of a *jeune fille*[43] got much consideration. Pliny... was delighted to find the ideal husband for the niece of Junius Mauricus.... Minicius, he says, is of a most respectable family, worthy of that into which he will marry. He has already held office, so they will not have the bother of canvassing for him. He is good-looking: Pliny thinks this deserves a mention (other people evidently would not) as a sort of reward for the bride's virginity. He is also rather well off. A very proper display of feeling, which makes no mention of the girl: she had not met her future husband. Another letter... congratulates a friend on his choice of son-in-law and his future grandchildren, but says nothing about the expected happiness of the friend's daughter. It may be relevant that nowhere in the *Aeneid*[44] are Lavinia's[45] views on her future husband considered: she does, once, blush.... A suitable connection for the family is what mattered: in the absence of social mobility and Social Security, a family is too much affected by the marriages of its members to leave them to romance.

An arranged marriage, with goodwill and similar expectations on both sides, may have as good a chance of happiness as a romantic marriage.... Roman marriages were expected to be happy. Musonius... rates

---

[41] Legal power.

[42] An unscrupulous late Republican politician known as a womanizer, who was a member of an opposing faction to that of Cicero, c.80–43 B.C.

[43] Young girl.

[44] Roman epic poem, late first century B.C., composed by Virgil.

[45] Character in the *Aeneid* who marries Aeneas, the mythical founder of the Roman people.

the mutual affection of husband and wife above all other ties. . . . In the proscription,[46] . . . wives showed greater loyalty than sons or slaves. The husband of the lady known as Turia recorded . . . his acute distress when she offered him a divorce (they were childless), though he said that marriages as happy and long-lasting as theirs, uninterrupted by death or divorce, were a rarity. Augustus and Livia had one. . . . The ideal was long-lived, harmonious, fertile marriage. But the death rate was not the only impediment. . . .

A woman who married *cum manu*[47] did indeed pass out of her father's *potestas* and into her husband's, on a par with his daughter—with two major exceptions. A daughter could not compel her father to anything, but a wife could compel her husband to divorce; and although a husband with *manus*[48] over his wife controlled all that she possessed and inherited, and need surrender only her dowry if they divorced, wives do seem to have kept control over some property (perhaps by sheer force of character or connections). A woman married *sine manu*,[49] as seems to have been the norm by the mid-first century B.C., remained in her father's *potestas*, needed his consent to any major financial transaction, and might have her marriage ended by him even against her wish. . . .

Divorce could in fact end the commitment of wife to husband very easily. There was no need to prove breakdown of marriage; guilty parties needed to be established only in so far as there might be a financial penalty in the divorce settlement (apparently for an adulterous wife or for the spouse who took the initiative in divorcing). There would, of course, be financial tangles over the repayment of dowry and in sorting out the assets which the couple had managed in common, and these might well be enough to ensure that, among poorer people, marriage contracts would be respected: it is difficult to find clear evidence of divorce at that economic level. But legal tangles and massive debts seldom discouraged upper-class Romans, and the financial patterns of marriage *sine manu* suggest that . . . they were prepared for a break-up.

It is often suggested that the move from marriage *cum manu* to marriage *sine manu* was prompted by the demands of late Republican women for greater freedom. . . . The marriage law of the late Republic is said to have given women exceptional freedom and dignity: 'for the first time in human civilization . . . a law founded on a purely humanistic idea of marriage, as being a free and freely dissoluble union of two equal partners for life.' Now marriage either *cum manu* or *sine manu* gave women more hope of release, if the marriage was unhappy, than indissoluble marriage,

[46]During the period of the civil wars in the first century B.C., the proscription was a list proclaiming certain people public enemies.

[47]Literally, "with legal control." A woman who marries *cum manu* passed from the legal control of her father to her husband.

[48]Legal control.

[49]Without legal control.

which was believed to have been the rule in the early Republic. (As always, there were those who thought it was still the best solution to marital problems—especially the problem of how to stop women causing trouble.) And if one's object was to be *sui iuris*,[50] independent but for the nominal control of a guardian, one's father was likely to release one from his *potestas* by dying sooner than one's husband was, so marriage *sine manu* was a better bet. But it does not appear that women were in a position to make a free choice. A *filiafamilias*[51] could not choose her husband unless she could get round her father; could not divorce him without her father's economic support; and could not prevent herself from being divorced at the instigation of her husband, her father, or his father. She was, indeed, almost her husband's equal in this: he too was subject, at least in theory, to his father's financial control, required his consent to marry (but could refuse his own) and perhaps to divorce, and could be made to divorce: but sons had, in practice, more scope. A woman *sui iuris*, like a man, could make independent decisions, allowing for family and financial constraints. But she had one major disadvantage. If she decided for divorce, she would lose her children, for they belonged to the father's family. Women cannot adopt, say the jurist Gaius . . . , for not even the children of their own bodies are in their *potestas*.

The father presumably decided who actually looked after the children of broken marriages. . . .

Women did not vote, did not serve as *iudices*,[52] were not senators or magistrates or holders of major priesthoods. They did not, as a rule, speak in the courts. . . . As a rule, women took no part in public life, except on the rare occasions when they were angry enough to demonstrate, which was startling and shocking. . . .

Women might, then, have considerable influence and interests outside their homes and families, but they were acting from within their families to affect a social system managed by men: their influence was not to be publicly acknowledged. Why were women excluded from public life? The division between arms-bearers and child-bearers was doubtless one historical cause, but the reasons publicly given were different. Women were alleged to be fragile and fickle, and therefore in need of protection; if they were not kept in their proper place they would (fragility and fickleness notwithstanding) take over. As the elder Cato[53] . . . said in defense of the *lex Oppia*:[54]

'Our ancestors decided that women should not handle anything, even a private matter, without the advice of a guardian; that they should always

---

[50]Literally, "under your own law."

[51]Daughter of the family.

[52]Judges.

[53]Cato the Elder (234–149 B.C.), a statesman of the Roman Republic.

[54]A wartime law, lasting from 215–195 B.C., limiting the freedom and luxuries of Roman women.

be in the power of fathers, brothers, husbands. . . . Call to mind all those laws on women by which your ancestors restrained their license and made them subject to men: you can only just keep them under by using the whole range of laws. If you let them niggle away at one law after another until they have worked it out of your grasp, until at last you let them make themselves equal to men, do you suppose that you'll be able to stand them? If once they get equality, they'll be on top.' . . .

A social system which restricted women to domestic life, and prevailing attitudes which assumed their inferiority, must seem to us oppressive. I know of no evidence that it seemed so at the time. The legal and social constraints detailed above may have frustrated the abilities of many women and caused much ordinary human unhappiness. But there evidently were, also, many ordinarily happy families where knowledge of real live women took precedence over the theories, and women themselves enjoyed home, children, and friends. There were some women who enjoyed the political game, and who found an emotional life outside their necessary marriages. And there were certainly women who found satisfaction in living up to the standards of the time. They were, as they should be, chaste, dutiful, submissive, and domestic; they took pride in the family of their birth and the family they had produced; and probably their resolution to maintain these standards gave them the support which women in all ages have found in religious faith. But the religious feelings of Roman women, as opposed to the acts of worship in which they might take part, are something of which we know very little. . . .

The son of Murdia,[55] in the age of Augustus, made her a public eulogy. Some of what he said has happened to survive . . . , and, since we should not otherwise know of her existence, may make the best epitaph for the women who did not make the history books.

'What is said in praise of all good women is the same, and straightforward. There is no need of elaborate phrases to tell of natural good qualities and of trust maintained. It is enough that all alike have the same reward: a good reputation. It is hard to find new things to praise in a woman, for their lives lack incident. We must look for what they have in common, lest something be left out to spoil the example they offer us. My beloved mother, then, deserves all the more praise, for in modesty, integrity, chastity, submission, woolwork, industry, and trustworthiness she was just like other women.'

[55]Roman woman distinguished only by the fact that her son made a eulogy of her.

Gladiatorial Combat in Ancient Rome

JÉRÔME CARCOPINO

In the first century A.D., *the population of the city of Rome may have approached
one million. The city faced many problems, but the major one for the emperors was
the potential for revolt in the hundreds of thousands of Romans who were poor and
unemployed. In order to keep the masses contented, the government distributed free
food, mainly grain, but other products as well. In addition, the population could
look forward to lavish spectacles, which might keep their minds off the wretched and
filthy living conditions in the Roman metropolis. Thus did the government follow the
policy of "bread and circuses."*

    *Jérôme Carcopino is awestruck at the sheer horror of the spectacles that pan-
dered to the bloodlust of the populace. Why were the Romans not horrified? Why did
the Romans prefer above all else the sport of men killing one another? But perhaps
sport is not always the proper term, for Carcopino outlines practices that simply
slaughtered people, often in grotesque and gruesome ways.*

    *The appeal of the combats was evident, as the Roman Colosseum filled up with
50,000 frenzied spectators. What sorts of combat did they witness? Who appeared in
the arena? If it is difficult to appreciate the cruelty of the crowd, it is likewise perplexing why many men chose to become gladiators. Who became gladiators? What
were their lives like? What rewards went to the victors?*

    *Most Romans, of course, accepted gladiatorial contests and public killings as
justifiable. What arguments did Romans offer in support of the fights? Was the Roman fondness for such cruelty unique historically?*

Revisiting the arenas of Rome after nearly two thousand years of Christianity, we feel as if we were descending into the Hades of antiquity. The
amphitheatre demands more than reproach. It is beyond our understanding that the Roman people should have made the human sacrifice, the
munus, a festival joyously celebrated by the whole city, or come to prefer
above all other entertainment the slaughter of men armed to kill and be
killed for their amusement. . . . By the first century B.C. the populace had
grown so greedy for these sights that candidates sought to win votes by
inviting the people to witness spectacular scenes of carnage. In order to
put an end to corrupt practices the Senate in 63 B.C. passed a law disquali-
fying for election any magistrate who had financed such shows for the two
years preceding the voting. It was natural that aspirants for the imperial
throne should play on the people's passion to promote their own ambitious aims. Pompey[1] even sated his fellow-citizens with combats; Caesar
freshened their attraction by the luxury with which he surrounded them.
Finally the emperors, deliberately pandering to the murderous lust of the

---

[1]Roman general, rival of Julius Caesar.

crowds, found in gladiatorial games the most sure, if also the most sinister, of their instruments of power.

Augustus was the first. Outside the city itself, he adhered to the posthumous laws of Julius Caesar and continued to limit the municipal magistrates to offering one annual *munus*. Within the city, he ordered the praetors[2] to give annually two *munera* limited to 120 gladiators. In 27 A.D., Tiberius[3] forbade any private person with a fortune less than an "equestrian capital" of 400,000 sesterces[4] to give a *munus*. Claudius[5] transferred the duty of providing the public gladiatorial shows from the praetors to the more numerous quaestors,[6] at the same time again limiting them to 120 gladiators per spectacle.

This restriction aimed less at curbing the passion of his subjects than at enhancing the prestige of their sovereign. For while thus regulating the giving of the public *munera*, Augustus recognized no limit save his own caprice to the number of "extraordinary" *munera*, which he offered the people three times in his own name and five times in the names of his sons and grandsons. By the incomparable splendour of these private gladiatorial spectacles, he practically monopolized the right to provide "extraordinary" *munera*, which was accomplished later by the formal prohibitions of the Flavians.[7] Thus the decrees of Augustus made the *munera* the imperial show par excellence, as official and obligatory as . . . the theatre and the circus. At the same time the empire provided grandiose buildings specially suited to their purpose. The design of these buildings, improvised more or less by chance, and repeated in hundreds of examples, seems to us today a new and mighty creation of Roman architecture—the amphitheatre. . . .

The first permanent amphitheatre was that built in 29 B.C. at Rome . . . and was destroyed in the great fire of 64 A.D. The Flavians decided almost at once to replace it by a larger one of the same design. It was started by Vespasian,[8] completed by Titus,[9] and decorated by Diocletian.[10] Since 80 A.D. neither earthquakes nor the Renaissance plunderers who carried off its blocks of stone . . . have seriously damaged it. . . . This is the Flavian amphitheatre, better known since the Middle Ages as the Colosseum. By the year 2 B.C. Augustus, after much costly labour on the right bank of the Tiber, had supplemented the amphitheatre of Taurus, which had

---

[2]Judges.

[3]Emperor, 14–37 A.D.

[4]The fortune needed to qualify for membership in the equestrian social order.

[5]Emperor, 41–54 A.D.

[6]Financial agents of the government.

[7]Emperors from 69–96 A.D.

[8]Emperor, 69–79 A.D.

[9]Emperor, 79–81 A.D.

[10]Emperor, 284–305 A.D.

been built only for land combats, by a *naumachia*[11] intended for the representation of naval battles. Its exterior ellipse . . . enclosed not an arena of beaten earth covered with sand, but a sheet of water cut by an artificial island and curving through thickets and gardens. Though the *naumachia* of Augustus covered an area almost treble that of the Colosseum, . . . the public soon became dissatisfied, and Trajan[12] was forced to build first the supplementary Amphitheatrum Castrense, . . . and then the supplementary Naumachia Vaticana. . . . Of the two *naumachiae* and of the Amphitheatrum Castrense almost nothing but the memory remains. But the ruins of the Colosseum suffice to show the typical arrangement of the Roman amphitheatre in its most perfect form.

The Colosseum was built of blocks of hard travertine[13] stone extracted from the quarries of Albulae near Tibur (the modern Tivoli) and brought to Rome by a wide road specially constructed for the purpose. The building forms an oval, 527 metres in circumference, with diameters of 188 and 156 metres, and rears its four-storied walls to a height of 57 metres. . . . The seats began four metres above the arena with a terrace or *podium* protected by a bronze balustrade. On the *podium* were ranged the marble seats of the privileged, whose names have been handed down to us. Above these were the tiers for the ordinary public. . . .

. . . [I]t is calculated that the number of sitting places was 45,000 and of standing places 5,000. . . .

The arena, 86 by 54 metres in diameter, enclosed an area of 3,500 square metres. It was surrounded by a metal grating, 4 metres in front of the base of the *podium,* which protected the public from the wild beasts which were loosed into the arena. Before the gladiators entered through one of the arcades of the longer axis, the animals were already imprisoned in the underground chambers of the arena. This basement was originally fitted with a water system which in 80 A.D. could flood the arena in a twinkling and transform it into a *naumachia.* Later—no doubt at the time when Trajan built his *Naumachia Vaticana*—it was provided with cages of masonry, in which the animals could be confined, and also with a system of ramps and hoists, so that they could either be quickly driven up or instantaneously launched into the arena. . . . Every detail of its internal arrangement is a triumph of technical ingenuity. Its solidity has defied the centuries and it still inspires the beholder with the sense of utter satisfaction that one feels in gazing on the Church of Saint Peter—the sense of a power so great as to be overwhelming, an art so sure that the infallible proportions blend into perfect harmony. But if its charm is to hold us, we must forget the inhuman ends for which this monument was raised, the spectacles of unpardonable cruelty for which the imperial architects of old created it.

[11]Building designed to hold simulated sea battles.
[12]Emperor, 98–117 A.D.
[13]A light-colored limestone.

At the period which we are studying, the organisation of these bloody games left no room for improvement. In the Italian *municipia*[14] and in the provincial towns, the local magistrates whose duty it was annually to provide the *munera* called in the expert advice of specialist contractors, the *lanistae*. These contractors, whose trade shares in Roman law and literature the same infamy that attaches to that of the pander or procurer . . . , were in sober fact Death's middlemen. The *lanista* would hire out his troupe of gladiators . . . , at the best figure he could command, . . . for combats in which about half were bound to lose their lives. He maintained his "family" at his own expense, under a system of convict discipline which made no distinction between the slaves he had purchased, starving wretches whom he had recruited, and ruined sons of good family. These young ne'er-do-wells were lured by the rewards and fortune they would win from the victories he would ensure them, and by the certainty of being well and amply fed in his "training school." . . . They discounted the premium which he was to pay them if they survived the term of their contract, and hired themselves out to him body and soul, abandoning all their human rights . . . and steeling themselves to march at his command to the butchery.

At Rome on the other hand there were no longer any *lanistae*. Their functions were performed exclusively by the *procuratores*[15] of the princeps. These agents had special official buildings . . . at their disposal. . . . They were also in charge of the wild and exotic animals which subject provinces and client kings, even to the potentates of India, sent to fill the emperor's menagerie. . . . Their gladiators, constantly recruited from men condemned to death and from prisoners taken in war, formed an effective army of fighters.

The body of gladiators was divided into pupils and instructors, who were assigned according to their physical aptitudes to the different "arms": the Samnites carried the shield . . . and sword . . . ; the Thracians protected themselves with a round buckler . . . and handled the dagger . . . ; the *murmillones* wore a helmet crowned with a sea fish; the *retiarii*, who were usually pitted against the *murmillones*, carried a net and a trident.

Like the games, the *munera* usually lasted from dawn to dusk, although sometimes . . . they were prolonged into the night. It was, therefore, all important to vary the fighting, and the gladiators were trained to fight on water in a *naumachia* as readily as on the firm arena of the amphitheatre. They were not, however, pitted against wild animals; such contests were reserved for the *bestiarii*.[16]

Writers and inscriptions on monuments tell of several types of animal contests or hunts (*venationes*). There were some relatively innocent ones

[14]Municipalities.

[15]Deputies.

[16]Fighters of wild beasts.

to break the monotony of massacre—tame animals doing incredible circus turns . . . : teams of panthers obediently drawing chariots; lions releasing from their jaws a live hare they had caught; tigers coming to lick the hand of the tamer who had just been lashing them; elephants gravely kneeling before the imperial box or tracing Latin phrases in the sand with their trunks. There were terrible spectacles, in which ferocious beasts fought duels to the death: bear against buffalo, buffalo against elephant, elephant against rhinoceros. There were disgusting ones in which the men, from the safe shelter of iron bars or from the height of the imperial box . . . let fly their arrows at animals roaring with baffled rage, and flooded the arena with the blood of butchery. Some were given a touch of beauty by living greenery planted in the arena which ennobled the courage and the skill of the fighters. They risked their lives, it is true, in battle with bulls, panthers and lions, leopards and tigers; but they were always armed with hunting spears and glowing firebrands, with bows, lances and daggers, and often accompanied by a pack of Scotch hounds, so that they were exposing themselves no more than the emperor himself in the hunts, which were in those days a kind of minor war. They made it a point of honour to redouble the danger by their daring, stunning the bear with their fists instead of their weapons, or blinding the lion by flinging over his head the folds of their cloak; or they would quicken the spectators' pleasure by waving a red cloth in front of the bull, as the Spanish toreadors still do, or by eluding his charge with deft feints and skilful ruses. Sometimes to escape the beast's attack they would scale a wall or leap onto a pole, slip into one of the partitioned turnstiles . . . which had been prepared beforehand in the arena, or hastily disappear into a spherical basket fitted with spikes which gave it the forbidding appearance of a porcupine. . . .

Such *venationes*, however, usually provided an added attraction to the main spectacle of gladiators. They were but a slight exaggeration of the stern reality of ancient hunting, and can hardly be held a reproach to the amphitheatre, for the Praetorian[17] cavalry sometimes took part in them as in military manoeuvres. What revolts us is the quantity of victims, the bath of animal blood: 5,000 beasts were killed in one day of the *munera* with which Titus inaugurated the Colosseum in 80 A.D.; 2,246 and 443 in two *munera* of Trajan. The extent of this carnage nauseates us today, but it served at least one practical purpose. Thanks to this large-scale slaughter the Caesars purged their states of wild beasts; the hippopotamus was driven out of Nubia, the lion out of Mesopotamia, the tiger from Hyrcania, and the elephant from North Africa. . . .

But the Roman Empire also dishonoured civilisation with all the forms of *hoplomachia* and with a variety of *venatio* as cowardly as it was cruel.

Hoplomachia was the gladiatorial combat proper. Sometimes the battle was a mimic one, fought with muffled weapons, as our fencing matches

---

[17]The Praetorians constituted the emperor's guard.

are staged with buttons on the foils. . . . These mock battles were only a foretaste of the *munus,* a sequence or simultaneous performance of serious duels in which the weapons were not padded nor the blows softened, and in which each gladiator could hope to escape death only by dealing it to his opponent. The night before, a lavish banquet, which was destined to be the last meal of many, united the combatants of the morrow. The public was admitted to view this *cena libera,*[18] and the curious circulated round the tables with unwholesome joy. Some of the guests brutalised or fatalistic, abandoned themselves to the pleasures of the moment and ate gluttonously. Others, anxious to increase their chances by taking thought for their health, resisted the temptations of the generous fare and ate with moderation. The most wretched, haunted by a presentiment of approaching death, their throats and bellies already paralysed by fear, gave way to lamentation, commended their families to the passers-by, and made their last will and testament.

On the following day the *munus* began with a parade. The gladiators, driven in carriages . . . to the Colosseum, alighted in front of the amphitheatre and marched round the arena in military array, dressed in chlamys[19] dyed purple and embroidered in gold. They walked nonchalantly, their hands swinging freely, followed by valets carrying their arms; and . . . they turned toward the emperor, their right hands extended in sign of homage, and addressed to him the justifiably melancholy salutation: "Hail, Emperor, those who are about to die salute thee! . . . " When the parade was over, the arms were examined . . . and blunt swords weeded out, so that the fatal business might be expedited. Then the weapons were distributed, and the duellists paired off by lot. Sometimes it was decided to pit against each other only gladiators of the same category, while at other times gladiators were to oppose each other with different arms: a Samnite against a Thracian; a *murmillo* against a *retiarius;* or, to add spice to the spectacle, such freak combinations as negro against negro, as in the *munus* with which Nero[20] honoured Tiridates, king of Armenia; dwarf against woman, as in Domitian's[21] *munus* in 90 A.D.

Then at the order of the president the series of duels opened, to the cacophonies of an orchestra, or rather a band, which combined flutes with strident trumpets, and horns with a hydraulic organ. The first pair of gladiators had scarcely come to grips before a fever, like that which reigned at the races, seized the amphitheatre. As at the Circus Maximus[22] the spectators panted with anxiety or hope, some for the Blues, others for the Greens, the spectators of the *munus* divided their prayers between the

[18]Free meal.

[19]A short mantle clasped at the shoulder.

[20]Emperor, 54–68 A.D.

[21]Emperor, 81–96 A.D.

[22]The major race track in Rome.

parmularii (men armed with small shields)... or the *scutarri* (men armed with large shields).... Bets... were exchanged...; and lest the result be somehow prearranged between the fighters, an instructor stood beside them ready to... excite their homicidal passion by crying "Strike!..."; "Slay!..."; "Burn him!..."; and, if necessary, to stimulate them by thrashing them with leather straps (*lora*) till the blood flowed. At every wound which the gladiators inflicted on each other, the public—trembling for its stakes—reacted with increasing excitement. If the opponent of their champion happened to totter, the gamblers could not restrain their delight and savagely counted the blows: "That's got him!..."; "Now he's got it!..."; and they thrilled with barbaric joy when he crumpled under a mortal thrust.

At once the attendants, disguised either as Charon[23] or as Hermes Psychopompos,[24] approached the prostrate form, assured themselves that he was dead by striking his forehead with a mallet, and waved to their assistants... to carry him out of the arena on a stretcher, while they themselves hastily turned over the blood-stained sand. Sometimes it happened that the combatants were so well matched that there was no decisive result; either the two duellists, equally skilful, equally robust, fell simultaneously or both remained standing.... The match was then declared a draw and the next pair was called. More often the loser, stunned or wounded, had not been mortally hit, but feeling unequal to continuing the struggle, laid down his arms, stretched himself on his back and raised his left arm in a mute appeal for quarter. In principle the right of granting this rested with the victor, and we can read the epitaph of a gladiator slain by an adversary whose life he had once spared in an earlier encounter. It professes to convey from the other world this fiercely practical advice to his successors: "Take warning by my fate. No quarter for the fallen, be he who he may!..." But the victor renounced his claim in the presence of the emperor, who often consulted the crowd before exercising the right thus ceded to him. When the conquered man was thought to have defended himself bravely, the spectators waved their handkerchiefs, raised their thumbs, and cried: "...Let him go!" If the emperor sympathised with their wishes and like them lifted his thumb, the loser was pardoned and sent living from the arena.... If, on the other hand, the witnesses decided that the victim had by his weakness deserved defeat, they turned their thumbs down, crying: "...Slay him!" And the emperor calmly passed the death sentence with inverted thumb....

The victor had, this time, escaped and he was rewarded on the spot. He received silver dishes laden with gold pieces and costly gifts, and taking these presents in his hands he ran across the arena amid the acclamations

[23]The ferryman in Greek mythology responsible for taking the dead across the river Styx.

[24]Hermes the messenger-god who leads souls to the underworld.

of the crowd. Of a sudden he tasted both wealth and glory. In popularity and riches this slave, this decadent citizen, this convicted criminal, now equalled the fashionable pantomimes and charioteers. At Rome as at Pompeii, where the *graffiti* retail his conquests, the butcher of the arena became the breaker of hearts: "decus puellarum, suspirium puellarum."[25] But neither his wealth nor his luck could save him. He usually had to risk his own life again and sacrifice other lives in new victories before he could win, not the palms which symbolised success, but the more coveted wooden sword, the *rudis*, which signified his liberation and was granted as a title of honour.

At the period which we have reached, the emperors inclined to cut short the period of service which delayed the liberation of the best duellists. Martial[26] praises the magnanimity of the invincible Domitian . . . because he had cried a halt to a fight between two gladiators who had reached a deadlock, and handed to both the *rudis* of liberty along with the palm of victory. . . .

There are therefore occasional gleams of humanity in this business of wholesale butchery. At first the gladiator often begged leave to decline the emperor's clemency; he had fallen so low morally that he preferred to resume his trade of slayer rather than renounce the luxurious life of his barracks, the thrill of danger, and the intoxication of victory. We possess the epitaph of such a one, Flamma by name, who, after bearing off the palm twenty-one times, had four times received the *rudis* and each time "signed on again." Later the *munera* developed to astounding proportions. I shall quote only the figures . . . which cover the period extending from the end of March, 108 A.D., through April, 113 A.D. There we find mention of two minor shows, one of 350 pairs of gladiators, the other of 202, while the major event was a *munus* lasting 117 days in which 4,941 pairs of gladiators took part. Even the assumption that Trajan granted the survivors their liberty *en bloc* does little to assuage the memory of a field strewn with corpses. Cicero[27] indeed assures us that although there may be other methods of teaching contempt for pain and death, there is assuredly none which speaks more eloquently to the eye than a *munus;* and later Pliny the Younger[28] contended that these massacres were essentially calculated to engender courage by showing how the love of glory and the desire to conquer could lodge even in the breast of criminals and slaves. These are specious excuses. The thousands of Romans who day after day, from morning until night, could take pleasure in this slaughter and not spare a tear for those whose sacrifice multiplied their stakes, were learning nothing but contempt for human life and dignity.

---

[25]"The women's prize, the one who makes them breathe heavily."

[26]Roman poet, c.40–104 A.D.

[27]Roman philosopher and republican statesman of the first century B.C.

[28]Statesman and civil servant, 61/2–113 A.D.

These feigned combats, moreover, were often made the cloak of sordid murders and ruthless executions. Rome and even the *municipia* retained until the end of the third century the practice of proclaiming . . . gladiatorial combats from which none might escape alive. No sooner had one of the duellists fallen than a substitute . . . was produced to fight the conqueror, until the entire body of combatants was exterminated. Then, too, there were moments in the normal full-day program at Rome when exceptional atrocities were committed. The *gladiatores meridiani,* whose account was squared at the noon pause, were recruited exclusively from robbers, murderers, and incendiaries, whose crimes had earned them the death of the amphitheatre . . . . The pitiable contingent of the doomed was driven into the arena. The first pair were brought forth, one man armed and one dressed simply in a tunic. The business of the first was to kill the second, which he never failed to do. After this feat he was disarmed and led out to confront a newcomer armed to the teeth, and so the inexorable butchery continued until the last head had rolled in the dust.

The morning massacre was even more hideous. Perhaps it was Augustus who unintentionally invented this spectacular punishment when he erected in the Forum a pillory which collapsed and dropped the victim, the bandit Selurus, into a cage of wild beasts. Later the idea was taken up and made general. Criminals of both sexes and all ages, who by reason of their villainy—real or supposed—and their humble status had been condemned *ad bestias,*[29] were dragged at dawn into the arena to be mauled by the wild animals loosed from the basement below. . . .

This was the kind of torture heroically undergone by the virgin Blandina in the amphitheatre at Lyons, by Perpetua and Felicita[30] in Carthage, and in the Eternal City itself by so many Christians, anonymous or canonised, of the Roman Church. In memory of these martyrs a cross now rises in the Colosseum in silent protest against the barbarism which cost so many of them their lives before the spirit of Christianity succeeded in abolishing it. . . .

. . . [T]he Roman people remain guilty of deriving a public joy from their capital executions by turning the Colosseum into a torture-chamber and a human-slaughter house.

We must, however, credit the flower of Rome with terror at the progress of this dread disease and more than one attempt to reduce its virulence.

Augustus . . . tried to acclimatise Greek games at Rome. These contests strengthened the body instead of destroying it, and included artistic as well as physical competitions. Both to commemorate his victory over Anthony and Cleopatra and to give thanks for it to Apollo, Augustus founded

---

[29]To the wild beasts.
[30]Christian martyrs.

the Actiaca, which were to be celebrated every fourth year both at Actium[31] and Rome. But by 16 A.D. the Actiaca are no longer recorded. Nero wished to revive them in his Neronia, which were to be periodic festivals comprising tests of physical endurance and competitions of poetry and song. The senators deigned to take part in the former; but in the latter none dared to dispute the crown with the emperor, who believed himself an unrivalled artist. Despite their august patronage, however, the Neronia fell quickly into abeyance, and it was Domitian who at length succeeded in endowing Rome with a lasting cycle of games in the Greek style. In 86 A.D. he instituted the *Agon Capitolinus*, whose prizes the emperor awarded alternately for foot races and for eloquence, for boxing and Latin poetry, for discus-throwing and Greek poetry, for javelin-casting and for music. He built the Circus Agonalis . . . especially for his sports; and for the more "spiritual" contests erected the Odeum. . . . In his reign the Greek games which his bounty maintained enjoyed an ephemeral popularity. . . . The games survived their founder, but though we have proof that they were celebrated in the fourth century and that the jurists never ceased to emphasise the high honour they deserved, they never seriously rivalled the *munera* in favour. For one thing the *Agon Capitolinus* recurred only once in four years. Furthermore, Domitian designed them to appeal to a select and limited public, for his Odeum provided only 10,600 *loca*[32] and his Circus Agonalis only 30,088 — say 5,000 and 15,000 seats respectively — so that the two together were less than half the size of the Amphitheatrum Flavium alone.

There is no denying the fact that the Greek games were never very popular. The crowd, addicted to the thrills of the Colosseum, looked on them as colourless and tame; and they enjoyed no greater favour among the upper classes, who professed to detect an exotic degeneracy and immorality in their nudism.

Pliny the Younger applauds the Senate's decision under Trajan to forbid the scandal of the gymnastic games at Vienne in Gallia Narbonensis and complacently quotes his colleague Junius Mauricus, . . . as saying, "and I would that they could be abolished in Rome, too!" for "these games have greatly infected the manners of the people of Vienne, as they have universally had the same effect among us." The incompatibility between the . . . Greek games and the brutality of gladiatorial combats was bound to be irreconcilable. It is significant that while the majority of provincial towns imitated Rome by building amphitheatres, whose ruins have been found in South Algeria and on the banks of the Euphrates, Greece herself fought tooth and nail against the contagion, and in Attica, at least, apparently succeeded. This one exception is a poor make-weight to the general infatuation. . . .

[31]Battle in 31 B.C. in which Augustus (then known as Octavian) defeated Anthony and Cleopatra.

[32]Places.

It seemed indeed that the *munus* was not to be eradicated. Good emperors, therefore, sought to humanise it. While Hadrian[33] forbade impressment of slaves into gladiatorial troupes, Trajan and Marcus Aurelius[34] exerted themselves to the utmost to extend the part played in their festivals by the mimic combats (*lusiones*), at the expense of the *munus* proper. On March 30, 108, Trajan finished a *lusio* which had lasted thirty days and involved 350 pairs of gladiators. Marcus Aurelius, obeying the dictates of his Stoic philosophy, exhausted his ingenuity in reducing the regulations and budgets of the *munera* and in this way lessening their importance, and whenever it fell to him to offer entertainment to the Roman plebs he substituted simple *lusiones*. But philosophy lost the round in this struggle against spectacles where, as Seneca phrased it, man drank the blood of man. . . .

After Marcus Aurelius, whose son Commodus[35] himself aspired to gladiatorial fame, the Romans, not contented with the discontinuation of *lusiones,* inclined to desert the theatre for the amphitheatre. From the second century on we find the theatre architects in the provinces, notably in Gaul and Macedonia, modifying their building plans to accommodate gladiatorial duels and *venationes*. At Rome the representation of sinister drama was transferred to the arena, and it became usual to play the most terrifying mimes at the Colosseum—*Laureolus,* who was crucified alive for the amusement of the public, *Mucius Scaevola,* who plunged his right hand into the burning coals of a brazier, and the *Death of Hercules,* whose hero in the last act writhed in the flames of his pyre. As the amphitheatre henceforth sufficed for the more lurid dramatic representations, no attempt was made to repair the ruined theatres. . . .

It might have been predicted that the *munera* would be everlasting and that nothing henceforward could stop their invading growth. But where Stoicism had failed the new religion was to succeed. The conquering Gospel taught the Romans no longer to tolerate the inveterate shame. Racing continued as long as the races of the circus were maintained, but the butcheries of the arena were stopped at the command of Christian emperors. On October 1, 326, Constantine decreed that condemnation *ad bestias* must be commuted to forced labour . . . , and dried up at one blow the principal source of recruitment for the gladiatorial schools. By the end of the fourth century gladiatorial shows had disappeared from the East. In 404 an edict of Honorius suppressed gladiatorial combats in the West. Roman Christianity thus blotted out the crime against humanity which under the pagan Caesars had disgraced the amphitheatre of the empire.

[33] Emperor, 117–138 A.D.

[34] Philosopher and emperor, 161–180 A.D.

[35] Emperor, 180–182 A.D.

Why Were the Early
Christians Persecuted?

G.E.M. DE STE. CROIX

*Advocates of brotherly love, humility, moral uprightness, and religious righteous-
ness, Christians were nevertheless persecuted, albeit sporadically, from the end of the
first to the fourth century. G.E.M. de Ste. Croix attempts to explain why. He looks
at the Roman government's attitudes toward Christians, the legal procedures under
which Christians could be tried and punished, the reasons why the pagan populace
abhorred Christians, and the views that educated Romans held of Christianity.*

*What was the government's role in persecuting Christians? To what extent
did emperors influence persecution? What leeway did provincial governors have
in determining whether or not to try Christians? Did the legal process encourage
persecution or did it function to prevent maltreatment of Christians? The role of
private as opposed to state prosecutors surely made persecution more difficult, for
the accuser himself could be liable if the court determined his charge to be without
foundation.*

*Many of the charges against Christians, such as cannibalism and incest, had
no basis in fact. Most often, Christians were simply charged with being Christians.
Some Christians renounced their faith, often only temporarily, yet others coura-
geously maintained it. Many publicly acknowledged their Christianity and thus committed religious suicide. Why were numerous Christians anxious to become martyrs? It is important to remember that, unlike others charged with capital offences,
Christians did not usually have to die; they could deny their religion and live. Thus
we cannot lay all the blame for persecution on the Romans; Christians bore much
responsibility for their fate. In addition, different Christian groups leveled charges
against one another that could only convince Romans that the evil things they had
heard about Christians must have been true. It must not be forgotten, too, that,
when the Roman Empire officially became Christian in the fourth century, Christians
began to persecute pagans.*

... The question I have taken as a title needs to be broken down in two
quite different ways. One is to distinguish between the general population
of the Graeco-Roman world and what I am going to call for convenience
"the government": I mean of course the emperor, the senate, the central officials and the provincial governors, the key figures for our purpose being
the emperor and even more the provincial governors. In this case we ask
first, "For what reasons did ordinary pagans demand persecution?", and
secondly, "Why did the government persecute?" The second way of divid-
ing up our general question is to distinguish the reasons which brought
about persecution from the purely legal basis of persecution — the juridical
principles and institutions invoked by those who had already made up
their minds to take action.

But let us not look at the persecutions entirely from the top, so to speak—from the point of view of the persecutors. Scholars who have dealt with this subject . . . have with few exceptions paid too little attention to . . . persecution as seen by the Christians—in a word, martyrdom, a concept which played a vitally important part in the life of the early Church.

It is convenient to divide the persecutions into three distinct phases. The first ends just before the great fire at Rome in 64; the second begins with the persecution which followed the fire and continues until 250; and the third opens with the persecution under Decius[1] in 250–1 and lasts until 313—or, if we take account of the anti-Christian activities of Licinius[2] in his later years, until the defeat of Licinius by Constantine[3] in 324. We know of no persecution by the Roman government until 64, and there was no general persecution until that of Decius. Between 64 and 250 there were only isolated, local persecutions; and even if the total number of victims was quite considerable (as I think it probably was), most individual outbreaks must usually have been quite brief. Even the general persecution of Decius lasted little more than a year, and the second general persecution, that of Valerian[4] in 257–9, less than three years. The third and last general persecution, by Diocletian[5] and his colleagues from 303 onwards (the so-called "Great Persecution"), continued for only about two years in the West, although it went on a good deal longer in the East. In the intervals between these general persecutions the situation . . . remained very much what it had been earlier, except that on the whole the position of the Church was distinctly better: there were several local persecutions, but there were also quite long periods during which the Christians enjoyed something like complete peace over most of the empire; and in addition the capacity of the Christian churches to own property was recognized, at least under some emperors . . . . [C]omplete toleration of Christianity was never officially proclaimed before the edict of Galerius[6] in 311.

The subject is a large one, and I cannot afford to spend time on the first phase of persecution (before 64), during which, in so far as it took place at all, persecution was on a small scale and came about mainly as a result of Jewish hostility, which tended to lead to disturbances. After the execution of Jesus, the organs of government come quite well out of it all: their general attitude is one of impartiality or indifference towards the religious squabbles between Jews and Christians. In consequence of riots provoked by Christian missionary preaching, action was sometimes taken by the officials of local communities. But any Christians who were

[1]Emperor, 249–251.

[2]Coemperor in 308, then emperor of the East, 313–324.

[3]Emperor, 310–337.

[4]Emperor, 253–259.

[5]Emperor, 284–305.

[6]Emperor, 305–311.

martyred . . . were victims of purely Jewish enmity, which would count for little outside Judaea itself. . . .

I do not intend to give a narrative, even in outline, of the second and third phases of persecution, which I shall mainly deal with together. The earliest stages of intervention on the part of the government, before about 112, are particularly obscure to us. We cannot be certain how and when the government began to take action; but . . . I believe it was in the persecution by Nero at Rome which followed the great fire in 64. . . . In order to kill the widely believed rumour that he himself was responsible for starting the fire, Nero falsely accused and savagely punished the Christians. First, those who admitted being Christians were prosecuted, and then, on information provided by them (doubtless under torture), a great multitude were convicted, not so much (according to Tacitus)[7] of the crime of incendiarism as because of their hatred of the human race. . . . The Christians were picked on as scapegoats, then, because they were already believed by the populace to be capable of horrid crimes, *flagitia:* that is worth noticing. (Had not the Empress Poppaea Sabina[8] been particularly sympathetic towards the Jews, they might well have been chosen as the most appropriate scapegoats.) And once the first batch of Nero's Christian victims had been condemned, whether on a charge of organised incendiarism or for a wider "complex of guilt", there would be nothing to prevent the magistrate conducting the trials . . . from condemning the rest of the charge familiar to us in the second century, of simply "being a Christian" — a status which now necessarily involved, by definition, membership of an anti-social and potentially criminal conspiracy.

I now want to begin examining the attitude of the government towards the persecution of the Christians. I propose to consider mainly the legal problems first, . . . and we shall then be in a very much better position to understand the reasons which prompted the government to persecute; although before we can finally clarify these, we shall have to consider the other side of our problem: the reasons for the hatred felt towards Christianity by the mass of pagans.

The legal problems, from which a certain number of non-legal issues can hardly be separated, may be grouped under three heads. First, what was the nature of the official charge or charges? Secondly, before whom, and according to what form of legal process, if any, were Christians tried? And thirdly, what was the legal foundation for the charges? . . .

I will deal with the first question now, and then the other two together.

First, then, the nature of the charges against the Christians. . . . [F]rom at least 112 onwards (perhaps, as we have seen, from 64) the normal charge against Christians was simply "being Christians": they are punished, that

[7]Roman historian, c.55–c.117.
[8]Wife of the Emperor Nero, d.65.

is to say, "for the Name".... Pliny[9] speaks of the Christians he had executed as "those who were charged before me *with being Christians*" ...,
and the only question he says he asked these confessors was whether they
admitted this charge..., and Trajan[10] in his reply speaks of "those who
had been charged before you *as Christians*" ..., and goes on to say that
anyone "who *denies he is a Christian*" ... and proves it "by offering prayers
to our gods" can go free. With the other evidence, that settles the matter.
Now the *delatores*[11] who first accused the Christians as such before Pliny
could not be sure... that Pliny would consent to take cognizance of the
matter at all, let alone inflict the death penalty. Since they thought it was
worth "trying it on", they evidently knew that in the past other officials
had been prepared to punish Christians as such. And in fact Pliny now did
so, although later on he had second thoughts and consulted the emperor,
saying he was doubtful on what charge and to what extent he should investigate and punish, and in particular whether he should take the age of
the accused into account, whether he should grant pardon to anyone who
was prepared to apostatize, and whether he should punish for the Name
alone or for the abominable crimes associated with being a Christian....
Trajan explicity refused to lay down any general or definite rules and was
very selective in his answers to Pliny's questions. In two passages which
do him great credit he instructs Pliny that Christians must not be sought
out..., and that anonymous denunciations are to be ignored, "for they
create the worst sort of precedent and are quite out of keeping with the
spirit of our age". Christians who are accused as such, in due form...,
and are convicted must be punished, but anyone who denies he is a Christian, and proves it "by offering prayers to our gods", is to receive "pardon
on the score of his repentance" and be set free.... Pliny could justifiably
take this to mean that punishment was to be for the Name alone.

... One often hears it said that the Christians were martyred "for refusing to worship the emperor". In fact, emperor-worship is a factor of
almost no independent importance in the persecution of the Christians.
It is true that among our records of martyrdoms emperor-worship does
crop up occasionally, but far more often it is a matter of sacrificing *to the
gods*—as a rule, not even specifically to "the gods *of the Romans*". And
when the cult act involved does concern the emperor, it is usually an oath
by his Genius... or a sacrifice to the gods on his behalf. Very characteristic is the statement of Vigellius Saturninus, proconsul of Africa in 180, to
the Scillitan martyrs:[12] "We too are religious, and our religion is simple,
and we swear by the Genius of our lord the emperor, and we pray for
his welfare, as you also ought to do." ... And there is ample evidence to

[9]Pliny (the Younger), statesman and civil servant, 61/2–113.

[10]Emperor, 98–117.

[11]Private prosecutors. Private prosecution was the norm in Rome; today, state prosecution is.

[12]Twelve Christian martyrs from Scillium in North Africa.

show that the situation remained substantially the same right through the third and early fourth centuries, even during the general persecutions.

I now turn to the nature of the judicial process against the Christians. . . .

The procedure against Christians was in every case that used for the vast majority of criminal trials under the Principate: *cognitio extra ordinem* (or *extraordinaria*),[13] which I shall discuss in a moment. Capital trials under this process in the provinces took place before the provincial governor and no one else. In Rome . . . none of the known cases was important enough to come directly before the emperor himself, or the senate, although in the early Principate appeals by Roman citizens first accused elsewhere may have gone to the emperor's court.

Now Roman law was surely the most impressive intellectual achievement of Roman civilization. But what Roman lawyers of today mean when they speak of Roman law is essentially private law, a large part of which is concerned with property rights, their definition and protection. . . . Large areas of Roman criminal and public law, however, were by contrast very unsatisfactory, and one of the worst of these blemishes was precisely *cognitio extra ordinem*, the procedure by which the large deficiencies of the *quaestio*[14] system (the *ordo iudiciorum publicorum*,[15] regulating the punishment of what may be called "statutory crimes"), which at least was subject to fairly strict rules, were supplemented by direct governmental intervention. . . . [T]he rather few offences dealt with by the *quaestio* system were essentially those of "high society and the governing personnel"; the "crimes of the common man"—theft and so forth—had largely to be dealt with *extra ordinem*, even at Rome. In making use of *cognitio extra ordinem* the magistrate concerned had a very wide discretion—even more so, of course, in criminal trials than in civil actions, just because of the relative vagueness of the criminal law. This discretion extended not only to fixing penalties, but even to deciding which cases the magistrate would recognize as criminal and which . . . he would refuse even to consider. The right of judicial *cognitio* (*iurisdictio*)[16] belonged to all provincial governors as part of their *imperium*.[17] In the criminal sphere it was almost unlimited, save in so far as the rights of Roman citizens . . . had to be respected, and in so far as a prosecution might be brought against the governor at Rome after his term of office was over. . . .

In a sense, the power to conduct a criminal *cognitio* was part of the power of *coercitio*[18] inherent in *imperium*; but it is quite wrong to conceive

[13]Extraordinary criminal procedure or jurisdiction.

[14]The ordinary criminal procedure.

[15]System of public judgments.

[16]Jurisdiction.

[17]Right to command, or full executive power.

[18]Coercion.

the Christians as being punished by pure *coercitio* in the narrower sense, summarily and without the exercise of proper *iurisdictio*: *coercitio* in that sense, exercised . . . in an informal manner, was limited to minor offences. I cannot help feeling that some of those who have persisted in speaking of the proceedings against the Christians as "police measures" have not fully realized that the trials in question were in no way summary proceedings by pure *coercitio* but proper legal trials, involving the exercise of *iurisdictio* in the fullest sense. . . .

Since our information comes almost entirely from Christian sources, interested in recording martyrdoms, the great majority of the trials of Christians we know about in detail end in conviction and a death sentence. But the very wide discretion exercised by the provincial governor might on occasion work in favour of accused Christians. The most significant evidence comes from Tertullian's[19] *Ad Scapulam*,[20] written probably in 212, where we hear that the very first proconsul to shed Christian blood in Africa was Vigellius Saturninus, who was in office as late as 180; and that a whole series of African proconsuls (after Saturninus, it seems) had gone out of their way to be friendly to accused Christians: one of them helped the Christians to conduct their case in such a way as to secure an acquittal . . . ; another acquitted an accused Christian outright, apparently on the ground that to convict him would cause a riot; yet another, reluctant at having to deal with such a case, released an accused Christian who consented under torture to apostatize, without actually making him sacrifice; and a fourth tore up the vexatious indictment of a Christian when his accuser failed to appear.

That shows how things might work in practice. A governor exercising *cognitio extraordinaria* in a criminal case was bound (for all practical purposes) only by those imperial *constitutiones*[21] and *mandata*[22] which were relevant in his particular area and were still in force. Unfortunately, official publication of imperial *constitutiones* seems to have been an extremely inefficient and haphazard process, and a conscientious governor might often find himself in great perplexity as to what the law was. . . .

Once Pliny's correspondence with Trajan had been "published" (no doubt by his friends, soon after 117, when he and Trajan were both dead), every educated Roman would be likely to know what instructions Trajan had given regarding the Christians; and thereafter any provincial governor might well feel that until official policy towards the Christians changed he had better follow the same procedure. But other governors, at any rate in other provinces, were not absolutely bound by this precedent. . . .

It is important to remember that the standard procedure in punishing Christians was "accusatory" and not "inquisitorial": a governor would

---

[19] Christian theologian, c.160–c.230.

[20] *To Scapula*.

[21] Constitutions.

[22] Instructions.

not normally take action until a formal denunciation (*delatio nominis*) was issued by a *delator*, a man who was prepared not merely to inform but actually to conduct the prosecution in person, and to take the risk of being himself arraigned on a charge of *calumnia*, malicious prosecution, if he failed to make out a sufficient case. Trajan . . . forbade the seeking out of Christians. This principle, however, could be and sometimes was disregarded. The best attested example comes from the savage persecution at Lyons and Vienne in 177, when the governor did order a search to be made for Christians. . . . It is wrong to say the governor here was acting "illegally", because of course he was not absolutely bound to follow Trajan's rescript to Pliny; but it looks as if the great majority of governors did follow it. On this occasion the governor actually condemned to the beasts, as a favour to the enraged populace, a Christian named Attalus, who was a Roman citizen, although the emperor had just given specific instructions to the governor that Christians who were Roman citizens should be beheaded. He was exceeding his instructions, certainly; but he could plead political necessity, and there is no reason to think he was taken to task by the emperor. . . .

This raises another point: the attitude of the emperor. Christian propaganda from at least the middle of the second century onwards tried to make out that it was only the "bad emperors" who persecuted, and that the "good emperors" protected the Christians; but there is no truth in this at all. . . . In reality, persecution went on automatically, if sporadically, whoever the emperor might be; and until the third century at any rate it is better not to think of persecutions primarily in terms of emperors. It was the provincial governor in each case who played the more significant role—and even his attitude might be less important than what I must call "public opinion". If the state of local feeling was such that no one particularly wanted to take upon himself the onus of prosecuting Christians, very few governors would have any desire to instigate a persecution. If, on the other hand, public opinion was inflamed against the Christians . . ., then delators would not be lacking, and Christians would be put on trial; and few governors would have any motive for resisting strong local feeling demonstrated in this perfectly permissible way, especially if some of the more influential men in the area were leading the agitation, as they often would be. Imperial instructions . . . given to provincial governors bade them take care to rid their provinces of "bad men" (*mali homines*). . . . Probably the main reason why some martyrdoms—perhaps many martyrdoms—took place was that they were thought to be necessary if the province were to be kept "pacata atque quieta".[23] Most governors were doubtless only too willing to take action against men who were strongly disapproved of by "all right-thinking people", and who tended to become the centre of disturbances. Everyone will remember how Pilate

---

[23]Settled and orderly.

yielded to the vociferous demands of the local notables and their followers for the crucifixion of Jesus. If a governor, indeed, refused to do what was expected of him in this way, not only would he become unpopular: the general indignation against the Christians would be only too likely to vent itself in riots and lynching, as we have evidence that it did on occasion; and once violence began, anything might happen.

Christians might also be suspect, as *mali homines,* in the eyes of some governors, because they worshipped a man who had admittedly been crucified by a governor of Judaea, as a political criminal, who thought of himself as "king of the Jews". Their loyalty to the state, whatever they might say, could well appear doubtful, if only because they refused even to swear an oath by the emperor's Genius. They were always talking about the imminent end of the world; and one of their books[24] spoke with bitter hatred of Rome, thinly disguised under the name of Babylon, and prophesied its utter ruin. And furthermore the secrecy of their rites might well seem a cover for political conspiracy, or at any rate anti-social behaviour. A governor who had such considerations in mind when trying Christians might even decide to find them guilty of *maiestas* (treason). . . . In any event, the factors I have just been mentioning would have less and less weight as time went on, and it became clear that Christians had no political objectives whatever and few particularly anti-social habits.

Sometimes a Christian who was in danger of being put on trial might be able to escape altogether by bribing the intending delator or the authorities. There is evidence that this was happening in Africa by the early third century at the latest: not merely individuals but whole churches had purchased immunity, to the disgust of Tertullian, who believed that during persecution Christians must stand their ground and neither take to flight nor buy themselves off. This rigorist attitude was only partly shared by the churches of the West, and in the East it seems to have been generally repudiated: flight or concealment during persecution was officially approved everywhere (except in so far as leading clergy might incur disapproval for deserting their flocks); but in the West, though apparently not in the East, the purchase of immunity, at any rate in a form which might give the impression of apostasy, was regarded as a sin, if not a particularly grave one. Our evidence comes mainly from Africa, Spain and Rome during the Decian persecution, when certificates of compliance with the imperial order to sacrifice to the gods were purchased wholesale by the less steadfast members of the Christian community.

Although we have not yet disposed of all the legal issues, we have at least reached a point from which we can see that the last of my three questions of a legal nature, "What was the legal foundation for the charges against the Christians?", has answered itself, because under the *cognitio*

[24] *Revelation.*

process no foundation was necessary, other than a prosecutor, a charge of Christianity, and a governor willing to punish on that charge. . . .

On the face of Pliny's letter the "obstinacy" of the Christians consisted merely in their threefold confession of Christianity, in face of a warning (after the first confession) that they would be punished for it. Further light is shed upon this "obstinacy" by some of the Passions of the martyrs, many of whom either repeat the standard formula, "Christianus sum",[25] in reply to all questions, or make legally irrelevant replies.

> If you will give me a quiet hearing, I will tell you the mystery of simplicity. . . . I do not recognize the empire of this world, but rather I serve that God whom no man sees or can see with these eyes. I have committed no theft; but if I buy anything, I pay the tax, because I recognize my Lord, the King of kings and Emperor of all peoples. . . . It is evil to advocate murder or the bearing of false witness.

These are the answers given to the proconsul of Africa by Speratus the Scillitan[26]—edifying, no doubt, but irritating to a judge and certainly giving an impression of other-worldly "pertinacity and inflexible obstinacy".

My next point concerns what I call "the sacrifice test", used by Pliny in order to give those who denied being Christians a chance to prove their sincerity. . . . The character of the sacrifice test changed when judicial torture, which until the second century had been used (except in very special circumstances) only on slaves, came to be regularly applied to all those members of the lower classes (the vast majority of the population of the empire) who became involved in criminal trials, whether they were Roman citizens or not. Once judicial torture had become a standard practice, the sacrifice test naturally tended to lose its original character as a privilege, and to become something which was enforced, usually with the aid of torture. But the essential aim was to make apostates, not martyrs. One could say without exaggeration that a governor who really wanted to execute Christians would be careful to avoid torturing them, lest they should apostatize and go free. For there is no doubt that with few exceptions an accused who was prepared to perform the prescribed cult acts was immediately released without punishment. Tertullian, of course, . . . makes much of this as evidence that the authorities did not really regard the Christians as criminals at all. "Others, who plead not guilty", he cries, "you torture to make them confess, the Christians alone to make them deny". This was perfectly true, and it must surely count as a lonely anomaly in the Roman legal system. The explanation is that the only punishable offense was *being* a Christian, up to the very moment sentence was pronounced, not *having been* one. I certainly know of no parallel to this in Roman criminal law. Tertullian ridicules the situation. What is the use

[25]"I am a Christian."

[26]One of the twelve from Scillium in North Africa martyred in 180.

of a forced and insincere denial, he asks scornfully. What is to prevent a Christian who has given such a denial and been acquitted from "laughing at your efforts, a Christian once more?"

I need not spend much time on the question of the supposed abominations (*flagitia*) with which the Christians were charged— . . . cannibalism and incest. It is hard to say how seriously these charges were taken by the government. The Christian Apologists of the second and early third centuries devote a good deal of attention to rebutting such accusations, which were evidently believed by the populace in both the eastern and the western part of the empire. After the first half of the third century, however, they seem to have died out. . . . The reproaches of *flagitia* seem to have been essentially appendages of some more real complaint. Unfortunately, these charges were given some colour by the fact that orthodox Christians and heretics tended to fling them at each other. . . .

. . . I want to take a brief glance at a long series of events which may have given pagans rather more ground for their active antagonism to Christianity than we tend to suppose: I refer to what I have called "voluntary martyrdom". Examination of it will require us to look at persecution, for once, mainly from the receiving end.

It is a significant fact . . . that a very large number of sources . . . show intrepid Christians going far beyond what their churches officially required of them, often indeed offering themselves up to the authorities of their own accord, and occasionally acting in a provocative manner, smashing images and so forth. After making a detailed study of the evidence for these "voluntary martyrs", I would claim that the part they played in the history of the persecutions was much more important than has yet been realized. It seems to me impossible to doubt that the prevalence of voluntary martyrdom was a factor which, for obvious reasons, both contributed to the outbreak of persecution and tended to intensify it when already in being. . . . The heads of the churches, sensibly enough, forbade voluntary martyrdom again and again, and were inclined to refuse to these zealots the very name of martyr. . . . Nevertheless, we do hear of an astonishingly large number of volunteers, most of whom, whatever the bishops might say, were given full honour as martyrs, the general body of the faithful apparently regarding them with great respect.

One of the most fascinating of the Passions of the Great Persecution is that of Euplus, who suffered at Catana in Sicily. It begins

> . . . [I]n 304, in the most famous city of Catana, in the court room, in front of the curtain, Euplus shouted out, "I wish to die, for I am a Christian". His excellency Calvisianus . . . said, "Come in, whoever shouted". And the Blessed Euplus entered the court room, bearing the immaculate Gospels—

and he achieved the end he had sought.

In the next year, 305, while a festival was being celebrated at Caesarea in Palestine, a false rumour began to spread that certain Christians would be given to the beasts as part of the joyful celebrations. While the governor was on his way to the amphitheatre, six young men suddenly presented themselves before him with their hands bound behind them, crying out that they were Christians and demanding to be thrown to the beasts with their brethren. . . . [T]he governor and his entire suite were reduced to a condition of no ordinary amazement. The young men were arrested and imprisoned, but instead of giving them to the beasts as they had demanded, the merciless pagan condemned them to a speedy death by decapitation.

These are but two of a large number of similar examples. Sometimes the fact that certain martyrs were volunteers, and were not sought out by the authorities, may alter our whole picture of a persecution. . . . The seeking out of Christians . . . , therefore, need not have been nearly as vigorous as we might otherwise have assumed from the evidently large number of victims.

The positive evidence for voluntary martyrdom begins . . . about 150. . . . But I should like to suggest . . . that in fact it is likely to have begun much earlier, and that the reason why we do not hear of it before the middle of the second century is simply that we have too little specific evidence of any sort about persecution or martyrdom before that time. Here the Jewish background of Christianity, above all the Jewish martyr-literature, is a very material factor. . . . We have examples of voluntary martyrdom on the part of Jews even before the Christian era, notably the incident in 4 B.C., . . . when two pious rabbis instigated their followers to cut down the golden eagle set up by Herod[27] over the great gate of the Temple: about forty men were executed, the rabbis and the actual perpetrators of the deed being burnt alive. Now the two most fervent works of Jewish martyr-literature, the Second and Fourth Books of Maccabees,[28] with their unrestrained sensationalism and gruesome descriptions of tortures, both formed part of the Septuagint, and must therefore have been well known to the early Church. . . .

We are in a position at last to attempt to answer the question confronting us, which, it will be remembered, is twofold: "Why did the government persecute?", and "Why did the mass of pagans often demand and initiate persecution?". I propose to take the second question first.

. . . It was not so much the positive beliefs and practices of the Christians which aroused pagan hostility, but above all the negative element in their religion: their total refusal to worship any god but their own. The monotheistic exclusiveness of the Christians was believed to alienate the

---

[27]Herod the Great, King of Judea, 40–4 B.C.

[28]Two books in the Old Testament in the Christian, but not in the Hebrew, Bible, named after a family that led Jewish resistance to Syrian rule in the second and first centuries B.C.

goodwill of the gods, to endanger what the Romans called the *pax deo-rum* (the right harmonious relationship between gods and men), and to be responsible for disasters which overtook the community. I shall call this exclusiveness, for convenience, by the name the Greeks gave to it, "athe-ism" . . . ; characteristically, the Latin writers refer to the same phenomenon by more concrete expressions having no philosophical overtones, such as "deos non colere" (not paying cult to the gods). . . .

Whatever view we may hold about the mentality of educated, upper-class intellectuals, we must admit that the great mass of the population of the Roman empire, in both East and West, were at least what we should call deeply superstitious; and I see not the least reason why we should deny them genuine religious feeling, provided we remember the essential differences between their kind of religion and that with which we are fa-miliar. By far the most important of these was that pagan religion was a matter of performing cult acts rather than of belief, or ethics. No positive and publicly enforceable obligation, however, rested upon any private in-dividual, whether a Roman citizen or not, or upon a common soldier, to participate in any particular acts of cult, although magistrates and sena-tors of Rome itself, and magistrates (and perhaps senators) of individual Greek and Roman towns, might be legally obliged to do so; and of course great social pressure might be brought to bear upon individuals who re-fused (on adopting Christianity or Judaism, for instance) to take part in family or other observances. No compulsion was necessary, because un-til the advent of Christianity no one ever had any reason for refusing to take part in the ceremonies which others observed—except of course the Jews, and they were a special case, a unique exception. Much as the Jews were detested by the bulk of the Roman governing class, as well as by many humbler Romans and Greeks, it was admitted (by the educated, at any rate) that their religious rites were ancestral, and very ancient. All men were expected piously to preserve the religious customs of their ancestors. And so even Tacitus, who strongly disliked Judaism, could say that the re-ligious rites of the Jews "have the recommendation of being ancient". The gods would forgive the inexplicable monotheism of the Jews, who were, so to speak, licensed atheists. The Jews of course would not sacrifice to the emperor or his gods, but they were quite willing, while the Temple still stood, to sacrifice to their own god for the well-being of the emperor. . . . Matters were very different with the Christians, who had . . . abandoned their ancestral religions. Gibbon[29] expressed the contrast perfectly when he wrote, "The Jews were people which followed, the Christians a sect which deserted, the religion of their fathers".

The Christians asserted openly either that the pagan gods did not exist at all or that they were malevolent demons. Not only did they themselves refuse to take part in pagan religious rites: they would not even recog-

[29]Edward Gibbon (1737–1794), English historian, author of *The History of the Decline and Fall of the Roman Empire.*

nize that others ought to do so. As a result, because a large part of Greek religion and the whole of the Roman state religion was very much a community affair, the mass of pagans were naturally apprehensive that the gods would vent their wrath at this dishonour not upon the Christians alone but upon the whole community; and when disasters did occur, they were only too likely to fasten the blame on to the Christians. That the Christians were indeed hated for precisely this reason above all others appears from many passages in the sources, from the mid-second century right down to the fifth. Tertullian sums it all up in a brilliant and famous sentence . . . : the pagans, he says, "suppose that the Christians are the cause of every public disaster, every misfortune that happens to the people. If the Tiber overflows or the Nile doesn't, if there is a drought or an earthquake, a famine or a pestilence, at once the cry goes up, 'The Christians to the lion'."

The essential point I want to make is that this superstitious feeling on the part of the pagans was due above all to the Christians' "atheism", their refusal to acknowledge the gods and give them their due by paying them cult. . . .

We must not confuse the kind of atheism charged against the Christians with philosophical scepticism. Tertullian pretends to be very indignant because philosophers are permitted openly to attack pagan superstitions, while Christians are not. "They openly demolish your gods and also attack your superstitions in their writings, and you applaud them for it", he exclaims. The vital difference was, of course, that the philosophers, whatever they might believe, and even write down for circulation among educated folk, would have been perfectly willing to perform any cult act required of them—and that was what mattered.

That the religious misbehaviour of certain individuals should be thought of by pagans as likely to bring unselective divine punishment may seem less strange to us when we remember that similar views were held by Jews and Christians. Orthodox Christians felt towards heretics much as pagans felt toward them. The martyred bishop Polycarp,[30] who (it was said) had actually known the Apostles personally, used to tell how the Apostle John,[31] entering the baths at Ephesus, rushed out again when he saw the heresiarch Cerinthus[32] inside, crying, "Away, lest the very baths collapse, for within is Cerinthus the enemy of the truth".

About the middle of the third century, however, the attitude of the general run of pagans towards the Christians begins to undergo a distinct change. Whereas until then the initiative in persecution seems to have come from below, from 250 onwards persecution comes from above, from the government, and is initiated by imperial edict, with little or no sign of persecuting zeal among the mass of pagans. The beginning of the change

[30]Saint, c.69–c.155.

[31]Saint and author of the fourth Gospel.

[32]Gnostic, flourished c.100.

seems to me to come with the Decian persecution. . . . The change has gone quite far by the time of the Great Persecution, when the majority of pagans . . . seem to be at least indifferent, some even sympathetic to the Christians, and few provincial governors display any enthusiasm for the task. . . . The reason for the change . . . is that Christianity had by now spread widely and lost its secretive character, and pagans had come to realize that Christians were not so different from themselves, and just as religious.

I have ignored minor reasons for popular dislike of the Christians; but no doubt some people might feel a grudge against them on simple economic grounds. . . .

Finally, we can try to analyse the attitude of the government. . . . [T]he great problem posed by Christianity, its exclusiveness, was something Rome had never encountered before—except under very different conditions, in the Jewish national religion.

I do not myself believe that there is a single solution to our problem. I believe that different members of the governing class may have been actuated by different motives, and I think that each one of us must decide for himself how much weight he would attach to each. I have already mentioned some minor factors, which may in some cases have played an important and even a decisive part: the need to pacify public opinion; and suspicion of the Christians as a conspiratorial body, or at least as undesirables, *mali homines*. . . . I believe that the main motives of the government, in the long run, were essentially religious in character, according to the ancient conception of religion. These religious motives appear in two rather different forms, which some people might prefer to call "superstitious" and "political" respectively, thereby avoiding the term "religious" altogether. Some of the governing class, in the third century at any rate (and I believe from the first), were undoubtedly inspired by the very motives I have described as characteristic of their subjects. Among the persecuting emperors, we must certainly place Galerius in this category, . . . and also Diocletian, who seems to have been a thoroughly religious man. . . . [E]ven in the third century, and to a far greater extent in the second, especially the early second, there may have been a significant number of members of the governing class who did not share the superstitious horror felt for the Christians by the masses. But even such people, I believe, were impelled to persecute—perhaps as vigorously as their less emancipated brethren— by motives I think we are justified in calling religious, in that their aim also was always primarily to break down the Christian refusal to worship the pagan gods, even if the basis from which they proceeded was different.

I want to stress two vital pieces of evidence which I do not see how we can explain away. First, there is the fact that except to a limited extent in the time of Valerian, and more seriously under Diocletian, what I have called the positive side of Christianity is never officially attacked: persecution did not extend to any aspect of the Christian religion other than its refusal to acknowledge other gods. No attempt was ever made, even in the general persecutions, to prohibit Christians from worshipping their own god in private, although Valerian and Diocletian (but not Decius) forbade them to assemble for common worship, and Diocletian also ordered the destruction of churches and the confiscation of sacred books and church property. As the deputy prefect of Egypt said to Bishop Dionysius of Alexandria in 257, "Who prevents you from worshipping your own god also, if he is a god, along with the natural gods?" And of course the sacrifice test continues to be used, and if the Christian complies with it he goes free, even in the general persecutions.

Secondly, there is what I believe to have been the complete immunity from persecution of most of the Gnostic sects. Some of these professed doctrines of a recognizably Christian character (heretical in varying degrees as they were) and called themselves Christians. Yet in Roman eyes there was evidently a fundamental difference between Gnostics and orthodox Christians, if Gnostics were not persecuted. Why? The reason can only be that the Gnostics did not think it necessary to be exclusive, like the orthodox, and refuse to pay outward respect to the pagan gods when the necessity arose. We are told by orthodox Christian sources that Basilides,[33] perhaps the most important of all the Gnostic heresiarchs, permitted his followers to eat meat which had been offered to idols, and in time of persecution "casually to deny the faith", doubtless by accepting the sacrifice test. It appears, then, that although the tenets of the Gnostics must have appeared to the Roman governing class to be very similar to those of the orthodox, the Gnostics escaped persecution precisely because they consented to take part in pagan religious ceremonies on demand, when the orthodox refused to do so.

What then was the attitude of the more enlightened pagans among the governing class? Why did they too persecute? . . .

. . . Religion, for such Romans, was above all the *ius divinum,* the body of state law relating to sacred matters, which preserved the *pax deorum*[34] by means of the appropriate ceremonial. It derived its great value . . . mainly from the fact that it rested upon the . . . force of ancestral tradition. . . . The Roman state religion contained nothing that was personal to the individual. And as for *rational* belief (or disbelief) in the gods—did it ever figure in the thoughts of Cicero[35] and his kind except when they were playing the Greek game of philosophical disputation? . . . These people had a deep emotional feeling for Roman religion, as the *ius divinum,* the "foundation of our state", an essential part of the whole Roman way of life. One can still hold this to be true, even if, taking perhaps an uncharitable view (as I would myself), one holds that quite a large part of that religion was above

---

[33]Gnostic theologian at Alexandria, second century.

[34]Peace of the gods.

[35]Roman orator and politician, 106–43 B.C.

all an instrument by which the governing class hoped to keep the reins of power in its own hands. . . .

. . . For Cicero's spiritual descendants of the early Principate,[36] Roman religion was part of the very stuff of Roman life and Roman greatness; and they were prepared to extend their protection also to the cults of the peoples of their empire, whose devotion to their ancestral religions seemed to their rulers only right and proper. Can we imagine that such men, however intellectually emancipated from the superstitions of the vulgar, would have had any compunction about executing the devotees of a new-fangled sect which threatened almost every element of Roman religion, and indeed of all the traditional cults conducted by the inhabitants of the Roman world? I would be prepared to speak of persecution so motivated as being conducted for religious reasons, though I realize that other people might prefer to use another word—political, perhaps.

I shall end by quoting what seems to me the most illuminating single text in all the ancient sources, for the understanding of the persecutions. Paternus, proconsul of Africa, is speaking to Cyprian[37] at his first trial in 257, and telling him what the emperors have just decreed. This, it is true, is a special edict, making it incumbent upon the Christian clergy, on pain of exile, to perform certain acts which ordinary folk would not normally be obliged to carry out; but what is enjoined is something any accused Christian might be ordered to perform, and this gives the text general significance. The decree is: . . . "Those who do not profess the Roman religion"—it is admitted that there are such people—"must not refuse to take part in Roman religious ceremonies".

[36]The Early Empire, 27 B.C.–180 A.D.
[37]Saint and martyr, c.200–258.

III

THE MIDDLE AGES

Covering the years roughly from 500 to 1500, the Middle Ages included a number of cultures and territories. Western civilization during this epoch was increasingly confined to western Europe, leaving the eastern Mediterranean to the expanding Islamic world. Opening with Germanic invasions of the western Roman Empire, the Middle Ages concluded with European invasions of exotic and distant lands as men crossed the oceans in the guise of explorers, soldiers, and missionaries in the fifteenth and sixteenth centuries to discover, fight, and convert the indigenous peoples.

Some historians further subdivide the medieval epoch into the early (500–1000), high (1000–1300), and late (1300–1500) Middle Ages. The early Middle Ages, often misnamed the Dark Ages, witnessed Germanic invasions, political fragmentation, a rural economy, small population, little international trade, and a decline in education, urbanization, and commercialization. Christianity spread throughout western Europe so completely that the entire Middle Ages is sometimes branded the Age of Faith or the Christian centuries. Following Charlemagne's reign (768–814), which saw administrative innovations and a small cultural flowering, invasions by the Vikings, Hungarians, and Saracens plunged Europe back into the chaotic conditions that recalled the collapse of Roman rule in the fifth and sixth centuries. But the ninth and tenth centuries also provided the final elements that defined rural life and the method of governance, feudalism.

The high Middle Ages was an era of relative prosperity that saw medieval civilization approach its zenith, marked perhaps by the prodigiously tall cathedrals built according to a new architectural and artistic style, the Gothic. The population expanded as a result of the surplus provided by improved agricultural techniques; towns and commerce grew; education (though highly limited in social scope) blossomed, first in cathedral schools and later in universities; and the slow accumulation of power in fewer hands offered a greater measure of political stability. Religion infused the economy, social order, politics, art, and mentality of the Middle Ages. The crusades exemplified the brash exuberance and confidence of this period. It took the unprecedented disasters of the fourteenth and fifteenth centuries to end this vibrant civilization, though there was certainly much continuity with succeeding centuries. A worsening climate, famines, economic depression, international warfare, peasant revolts, and the worst scourge in history—the Plague—made the later Middle Ages a bleak era in many ways. But this was also, in Italy, the age of the Renaissance, a cultural flowering that coincided with economic depression and severe population loss. Humanism (the major intellectual movement of the Renaissance), artistic innovation, and political experimentation made Italy arguably the most dynamic area in Europe at the end of the Middle Ages.

The selections that follow describe basic subjects in the social history of the Middle Ages: the nobility, the family, marriage, children, peasants, pollution, religion, social behavior, women, and crime. They show medieval societies to have been violent, intense, severe, patriarchal, and devoted to professed values and traditional modes of conduct from which nonetheless they often enthusiastically broke away. This was an energetic culture, difficult to categorize because of the substantial gap between people's ideals and the harsh reality of their daily life and behavior.

Rural Economy and Country Life in the Medieval West

GEORGES DUBY

Europe of the ninth and tenth centuries was a rural civilization, in which seasonal rhythms and patterns of cultivation determined the lifestyles of all, even the few who lived in small towns. In contrast, today less than twenty percent of the population in the Western world live in rural areas, large-scale mechanized agriculture is the norm, and farmers are linked to the outside world by television, automobiles, and package tours.

Georges Duby begins his study of medieval agricultural communities by describing peasant settlements. What did a village comprise? Beyond the living area and the fields were forests. How did medieval people use the forests? What type of food did peasants consume? How effectively did the agricultural technology of the time exploit the land? Put another way, what factors limited the production of more food?

For most of history, people have stood rather helpless before the inadequacies of their land, the unpredictability of the weather, and their own inability to influence their environment in a stable, effective way. Medieval peasants proved no exception. Their constant battle against the soil and climate, not to mention the parasitic aristocracy and clergy, gave them little food and much insecurity. In theory at least, the lords and clergy provided certain forms of security, but the reality was that the peasantry faced an epic struggle, with few material rewards.

One fact is outstanding: in the civilization of the ninth and tenth centuries the rural way of life was universal. Entire countries, like England and almost all the Germanic lands, were absolutely without towns. Elsewhere some towns existed: such as the few ancient Roman cities in the south which had not suffered complete dilapidation, or the new townships on trade routes which were making their appearance along the rivers leading to the northern seas. But except for some in Lombardy, these 'towns' appear as minute centres of population, each numbering at most a few hundred permanent inhabitants and deeply immersed in the life of the surrounding countryside. Indeed they could hardly be distinguished from it. Vineyards encircled them; fields penetrated their walls; they were full of cattle, barns and farm labourers. All their inhabitants from the very richest, bishops and even the king himself, to the few specialists, Jewish or Christian, who conducted long-distance trade, remained first and foremost countrymen whose whole life was dominated by the rhythm of the agricultural seasons, who depended for their existence on the produce of the soil, and who drew directly from it their entire worldly wealth. . . .

Another thing is also certain. It was a countryside created by man around a few fixed points of settlement. Western Europe was peopled by a stable peasantry rooted in its environment. Not that we should picture it as totally immobile. There was still room in rural life for nomadic movements. In high summer cartage and pastoral activities took many peasants to distant places, while others were occupied in gathering the wild products of the woodland, in hunting, in raiding their neighbours, and in some other activities that were necessary to acquire vital food supplies for survival. Other members of the rural population regularly participated in warlike adventures. However, most of these were only seasonal or part-time nomads. They spent most of their days on land which housed their families and formed part of organized village territories. They give the impression of belonging to villages.

Indeed the countryman's life was very rarely conducted in solitude. Dwelling houses appear to have been close together and very seldom isolated. Clusters of houses were usual. . . . [T]he village, whatever its size or shape, provided the normal background of human existence. In Saxon England, for instance, the village served as the basis for the levying and collection of taxes. Around these fixed points was laid out the pattern of the cultivated land, and particularly the network of trackways and paths, which appear in the landscape of today as the most tenacious relic of our ancient heritage, the reality which provides the starting point for archeological study of the village territory.

In western Europe, pioneer excavations are under way which will one day help us to know better what medieval rural dwellings were like. Already evidence exists which leads us to believe that, except in the Mediterranean coastal lands where building was in stone, men's habitations in the early, and even the not-so-early, Middle Ages were huts of wattle and daub, short-lived and destructible; even at the beginning of the thirteenth century an English peasant was found guilty of having destroyed the house of his neighbour by merely sawing through the central beam.

. . . [T]he land on which the village stood was subject to a particular legal status, different from that of the surrounding land, and enjoying customary privileges which made its boundaries unalterable. Legal historians have shown that the village was made up of contiguous parcels of land which most Carolingian documents describe by the word *mansus,* and which the peasant dialects of the earliest Middle Age called variously *meix, Hof, masure, toft.* . . . We understand by this an enclosure, solidly rooted to its site by a permanent barrier such as a palisade or a living hedge, carefully maintained, a protected asylum to which the entry was forbidden and the violation of which was punished by severe penalties: an island of refuge where the occupant was assumed to be the master and at whose threshold communal servitude and the demands of chiefs and lords stopped short. These enclosures provided a haven for possessions, cattle, stocks of food, and sleeping men, protected them against natural and supernatural dangers, and taken together, constituted the kernel of the village, and expressed in terms of land and territory the essence of a society of which the family was the nucleus. Furthermore, it is probable that occu-

1 of such a *manse* carried with it a place in the village community collective rights over the surrounding fields. By the same token new-rs remained dwellers in a secondary zone of habitations outside the sures. . . .

. . The soil which lay nearest to the house and to the stable was :ially rich and fertile. By proximity alone the site of peasant settlement zed itself: household waste and the domestic animals were sufficient tablish around the dwelling, precisely because it was immovable, :manent condition of fertility. Moreover, this land, because it was nveniently placed, could be repeatedly dug over. In no other spot l the natural state of the earth be so profoundly modified to meet the s of man; the constant manuring and digging created there an artificial ind raised on it a specialized and particular plant life. Thus each istic fence enclosed and protected a vegetable garden, . . . in other s a continually cultivated plot, where the ground was never left to and where in carefully protected conditions grew tender plants, the s and roots of the daily diet, hemp and the vine. These plots were iubtedly most productive and the atmosphere of garden care which cast over their surroundings did much to anchor the village to its

ieyond the encircling hedges, nature was also subject to a certain, if a not very rigorous, discipline. Without the need to tame her, men 1 win from nature a large part of their subsistence. River, marsh, for-nd thicket offered to whoever could take advantage of them, fish, e, honey and many other edible substances in generous measure. . . . re encouraged to believe that [the countryman] was as skilled in the)f the hunting spear, the net and the warrener's stick as he was with)lough. In 1180 when Alexander Neckham, an English teacher in the ols of Paris, wrote his treatise *Du Nom des Outils*,[1] he listed nets, lines, snares for trapping hares and deer amongst the ordinary tools of the ant household. It is certain that the thinly growing forest of the early dle Ages, with its numerous clearings, and its varied vegetation rang-from thick woodland to grassy glades, formed an essential background e domestic economy. Apart from the livelihood that it bestowed gen-sly on foodgatherer and hunter, it furnished the larger domestic ani-with their chief sources of nourishment. Sheep and cows grazed there war- and farm-horses were let loose in it. But above all else the woods e the domain of pigs. . . . Indeed over vast stretches of northern Europe ie ninth century bacon was an essential ingredient in the household iomy. Herds of swine yielding both meat and lard formed everywhere the mainstay of every farming system, large and small. . . . In fact agrar-ian archeology leads us to suppose that many villages and especially those in the north-west and north-east, in England, Frisia and Saxony, possessed

[1] *The Names of Tools.*

no cultivated lands, apart from the 'tofts'. And in the eleventh century we know of communities in the English fenlands, on the Wash and in the flooded valley of the Saône which lived solely by fishing.

However, because of man's customary eating habits the cultivation of the small plots around the dwelling houses and the quest for the gifts of nature were nearly everywhere allied to the efforts to farm more extensively. We know very little about the food of early medieval man in western Europe outside the monastic communities. . . . It is clear that at this period not only were men unable to feed themselves on what they found by chance, but they were driven to grow what custom decreed they should consume. . . . [T]he expansion of winegrowing in Gaul was a direct consequence of the social habits of the nobles, with whom it was a point of honour to drink and to offer their guests none but the best wine. But on a much humbler level also the whole system of agricultural production was organized to fulfil the social requirements which determined eating habits.

References in documents . . . reveal the universal acceptance of bread as a basic foodstuff, even in the least civilized regions of the Christian world. . . . Indeed, all the documents indicate that peas, vetches, beans — the leguminous plants — together with 'herbs' and 'roots', the ancestors of our garden vegetables (the hermits were praised for restricting their diet to these) and of course meat, a most desirable item of consumption from which the clergy ostentatiously abstained, comprised only the *companaticum*, the accompaniment to bread. It was the latter that was the mainstay of existence.

It is reasonably clear that bread was not baked solely from wheat, rye or spelt, but also from other, lesser, cereals, such as barley and even oats, which was eaten as much by humans as by animals. What is less easy to distinguish is in what measure these food grains were consumed in the form of porridge . . . or brewed into ale, the commonest beverage throughout north-western Europe. Ale had often the consistency of thick soup and so could be counted perhaps more as a food than a drink. Eleventh-century peasants had to grow cereals even when climatic conditions were not favourable. As arable fields had to be laid out around the villages, the least exposed and most easily worked sites had to be cleared for the purpose, in close proximity to habitations and in the midst of woods and pastures.

Here and there, in places where the climate allowed grapes to ripen, a few vines were planted for the masters on the most suitable and permanently enclosed plots. Meadows were confined to damper ground, and the hay, together with the grass and rushes which could be gathered in the marshes, provided winter fodder for the cattle. Nevertheless neither vines nor meadows covered more than a very limited part of the cultivated area since the cereal crop was the really important one, and almost the whole of the area given over to agricultural activity was reserved for its culture.

These fields had also to be protected against the depredations of animals, both domestic and wild. They can thus be visualized as separated from the uncultivated lands, which were open to pasture, by enclosures which in the country of the Franks seemed generally to have been temporary. In spring as soon as the new grass began to push up and the corn to sprout these mobile barriers made of wooden stakes . . . were erected and signs were put up forbidding shepherds to let their animals stray there. For a season therefore these strips seemed, like the cultivated 'tofts' of the village, to be the territory of individual owners. But after the harvest, signs and fences were removed, and the strips returned for a time to pastoral use, and were reincorporated into the larger areas where access to animals was free. To a greater or lesser extent then, according to the quantity of bread men were used to eating, the arable appeared as a limited and temporary extension of the cultivated 'toft' area and thus private property, at the expense of the wild area which was left to collective use.

Can we ever hope, even in the best documented regions, to plot the portion of village lands occupied by the arable fields? . . . What we know now suggests that this area was small everywhere and that a large space was being left to natural vegetation, the forest and pasture, whose presence 'had helped to form this combination of agriculture and animal husbandry which was the principal feature' of rural economy in the west. . . . This union indeed appears constant and fundamental throughout the Middle Ages. What we might describe as three concentric zones formed the picture . . . —the village enclosures, the *coûtures*, that is the arable, and finally surrounding all, a broad uncultivated belt. These were the three zones in which the effects of man's labour became less and less visible as the distance from the inhabited centre grew greater, but which were of equal importance to him as a means of subsistence.

Village communities thus found themselves hemmed in with no way of absorbing the increase in their birth rate. Periodic waves of mortality, such as those caused by military activity and, increasingly in the second half of the ninth and in the tenth centuries, raids of invaders, rather than any systematic clearing of the wastes and the resulting hiving off of colonists, relieved demographic pressure at intervals. Such a situation suggests a peasantry poorly equipped with efficient tools and incapable for this reason of taming the encircling wilderness.

Was the undoubted technical progress to which the diffusion of the water mill bears witness accompanied in Europe of the ninth and tenth centuries by the spread of ploughs with wheeled foreparts, by improvements in harness, and by the adoption of a more efficient ploughshare? This important problem of technique cannot be resolved, but it is reasonable to assume that even in the most favoured sectors of rural life, those of the great farming complexes described by inventories, men used feeble wooden implements. They found themselves ill-equipped to come to grips with nature and worked with their bare hands for a great part of the time.

The primitive technical equipment obviously restricted narrowly the individual's productive capacity. And this observation agrees completely with the impression gained from land settlement. Villages teemed with people whose efforts were needed to work the soil on the home fields, but they were situated in clearings separated by stretches of wild country because agricultural tools were not robust enough to overcome the obstacles of heavy, wet and thickly wooded land. Areas of natural vegetation adjoining the villages were of course actually necessary because the cultivation of cereals was so demanding of manpower that each rural community had to supplement its means of livelihood by making the most of the products of the wastelands—animal husbandry, hunting and foodgathering.

These limited portions of the village lands suitable for grain growing and therefore providing the village's main food supply . . . , or 'furlongs' to use the English term, were not given over wholly to food production every year. Unlike the cultivated 'tofts' whose soil, manured by the household waste and stable dung, could be cultivated without interruption, the fields demanded a periodic rest if fertility was not to be lost. Every spring a section of the arable was not sown; it remained open, unenclosed, available for pasture, in the same way as the wild area of wastes and commons. For an understanding of the productivity of the land and the manner in which it was able to support human life, we need to know the rhythm of the resting periods. What was the place of the fallow and what the place of spring-sown corn, oats and leguminous crops? How much land was devoted to autumn-sown corn, that is the bread grains—wheat, rye and spelt (the most widely grown grain in the Rhineland and north-west France), and lastly barley, which was in those days often a winter-sown crop? . . .

1. The description of harvest and sowing and, more often, that of dues in the form of grain exacted from peasant tenants proved that the fields of peasants as well as lords very frequently produced spring as well as winter corn and especially oats.

2. The arrangement of the ploughing services exacted from manorial dependants in the agricultural calendar shows that the cycle of ploughing was often divided into two sowing 'seasons', one in the winter . . . , and the other in the summer or the spring. . . .

3. Ploughing units on the great properties appear often in groups of three. . . . This arrangement leads us to think that cultivation was organized on a ternary rhythm. . . . By this arrangement, a third portion was prepared in May by a preliminary ploughing, and was turned over again by the plough in November before sowing; the following year after harvest the same fields were left throughout autumn and winter for the animals to graze on, and were then ploughed in Lent and sown with spring grain, after which they rested for a year. Thus at least a third of the agricultural area produced nothing, while another third produced bread grains and the last third the ingredients of porridge and soup.

I do not consider, however, that these indications are sufficient for us to conclude without further consideration that a regular three-year rotation was general, or even widespread. What argues against any such conclusion is that none of our examples is in southern Europe where climatic conditions, and above all early spring droughts, made March sowings somewhat hazardous, and also that our documents describe none but the great monastic or royal farms which were run in an unusually rational and even scientific manner....

... It is therefore safest to conjecture that there was considerable variation in the crop rotation in use. Man was forced to bow to the natural capacity of the soil because he was poorly prepared to alter it. We can imagine an infinite variety of systems in use ranging all the way from the strict three-course rotation to temporary cultivation based on burning where bits and pieces of land on the outer fringes of the village enclave would be tilled after the undergrowth had been burned, and continued to be cropped for years until fertility was exhausted. It is also probable that oats and other spring grains were often a supplementary crop taken from the fallow, and that such a system, even when the regular ploughings in winter and early spring... were adhered to, frequently lasted more than one year on the largest part of the available arable. It must be added that seed corn was sown very thinly.... The agricultural practice of those early days demanded not only plentiful manpower, but wide open spaces.

The insistent demands for long fallow periods, and the need to scatter the seed thinly arose at least partly because of mediocre ploughing implements which could not turn the ground over properly, but they were also due to the virtual absence of manure. It is true that animal husbandry was always complementary to agriculture and the draught oxen whose task was to plough the fields could also fertilize them with their dung. In reality the combination of arable with pasture was not close enough to enable animal manure to make much impression. Men who were so inadequately equipped with tools were forced to devote all their energies to producing their own food, and cattle had to take second place. A little fodder was harvested, but barely enough to keep those few beasts which had not been slaughtered in the autumn alive during the lean winter months when nature's offerings failed. But for the rest of the year the herds grazed alone in the open air on the land which was not enclosed. They must also have ranged over the fallow fields and in doing so deposited their manure on them; but the deposit was quite insufficient to maintain fertility. Scarce fodder meant restricted periods of stall-feeding, and the limited quantities of stable manure thus available were almost wholly devoured by the cultivated 'tofts' in the inner fertile belt of the village territory. No wonder areas of fallow had to be huge. And we can appreciate afresh the need of each family to dispose of as large a space for subsistence as possible which had to cover, besides pasture, an arable area much more extensive than the portion actually in use each year. Even so, despite the long resting periods, output remained extremely low.

. . . These elusive details allow at any rate one firm conclusion. Carried out with rudimentary equipment and in a generally unfavourable climate, the cultivation of cereal crops was at the mercy of the caprices of the weather. Even on the best equipped farms an excessively wet spring or summer could render the heavy toil in the fields totally unproductive. Despite an enormous expenditure of manpower and the disproportionate size of the village lands country folk could be racked with hunger. Obviously their main preoccupation was to survive through spring and early summer, that period of backbreaking toil. When the scraps of food remaining to them after the demands of their masters had been exhausted, the yearly nightmare of hand-to-mouth existence began, and the pangs of hunger had to be stilled by devouring garden herbs and forest berries and by begging bread at the gates of the rich. At such moments the threat of starvation overshadowed the whole village world.

The Life of the Nobility

MARC BLOCH

The nobility of twelfth-century Europe were rough, cruel, physical beings. In describing the life of medieval noblemen, Marc Bloch stresses their ferocity. The aristocracy loved war and fought for economic and political reasons. How did economic and political pressures subvert the culture of Christianity? Nobles killed with abandon other knights, the defenseless, and even prisoners; they robbed and mutilated. Why did the nobility so love war? Why did Christian virtues not dominate their lives? What were the qualities of the ideal knight? Even during periods of peace, knights fought in hunts and tournaments. How did those activities prepare knights for war?

If not yet well-behaved gentlemen, the nobility did at least subscribe to certain rules of courtesy that tempered their violence. How did courtly love influence the behavior of knights? By what processes did high-born ladies affect the nobility? From reading this selection, one can easily understand why churchmen and townspeople feared the nobility, unruly pests that they were.

'I love the gay Eastertide, which brings forth leaves and flowers; and I love the joyous songs of the birds, re-echoing through the copse. But also I love to see, amidst the meadows, tents and pavilions spread; and it gives me great joy to see, drawn up on the field, knights and horses in battle array; and it delights me when the scouts scatter people and herds in their path; and I love to see them followed by a great body of men-at-arms; and my heart is filled with gladness when I see strong castles besieged, and the stockades broken and overwhelmed, and the warriors on the bank, girt about by fosses, with a line of strong stakes, interlaced . . . . Maces, swords, helms of different hues, shields that will be riven and shattered as soon as the fight begins; and many vassals struck down together; and the horses of the dead and the wounded roving at random. And when battle is joined, let all men of good lineage think of naught but the breaking of heads and arms; for it is better to die than to be vanquished and live. I tell you, I find no such savour in food, or in wine, or in sleep, as in hearing the shout "On! On!" from both sides, and the neighing of steeds that have lost their riders, and the cries of "Help! Help!"; in seeing men great and small go down on the grass beyond the fosses; in seeing at last the dead, with the pennoned stumps of lances still in their sides.'

Thus sang, in the second half of the twelfth century, a troubadour who is probably to be identified with the petty nobleman from Périgord, Bertrand de Born. The accurate observation and the fine verve, in contrast with the insipidity of what is usually a more conventional type of poetry, are the marks of an uncommon talent. The sentiment, on the other hand, is in no way extraordinary; as is shown in many another piece from the same social world, in which it is expressed, no doubt with less gusto, but with equal spontaneity. In war . . . the noble loved first and foremost the display of physical strength, the strength of a splendid animal, deliberately maintained by constant exercises, begun in childhood. 'He who has stayed at school till the age of twelve,' says a German poet, repeating the old Carolingian[1] proverb, 'and never ridden a horse, is only fit to be a priest.' The interminable accounts of single combats which fill the epics are eloquent psychological documents. The reader of today, bored by their monotony, finds it difficult to believe that they could have afforded so much pleasure—as they clearly did—to those who listened to them in days of old; theirs was the attitude of the sedentary enthusiast to reports of sporting events. In works of imagination as well as in the chronicles, the portrait of the good knight emphasizes above all his athletic build: he is 'big-boned', 'large of limb', the body 'well-proportioned' and pitted with honourable scars; the shoulders are broad, and so is the 'fork'—as becomes a horseman. And since this strength must be sustained, the valiant knight is known for his mighty appetite. In the old *Chanson de Guillaume*,[2] so barbarous in its tone, listen to Dame Guibourc who, after having served at the great table of the castle of the young Girart, her husband's nephew, remarks to her spouse:

[1]From the period named after the Carolingian dynasty, which began in 751.
[2]*Song of William.*

...

By God! fair sire! he's of your line indeed,
Who thus devours a mighty haunch of boar
And drinks of wine a gallon at two gulps;
Pity the man on whom he wages war!

A supple and muscular body, however, it is almost superfluous to say, was not enough to make the ideal knight. To these qualities he must add courage as well. And it was also because it gave scope for the exercise of this virtue that war created such joy in the hearts of men for whom daring and the contempt for death were, in a sense, professional assets. It is true that this valour did not always prevent mad panics (we have seen examples of them in face of the Vikings), nor was it above resorting to crude stratagems. Nevertheless the knightly class knew how to fight— on this point, history agrees with legend. Its unquestionable heroism was nurtured by many elements: the simple physical reaction of a healthy human being; the rage of despair—it is when he feels himself 'wounded unto death' that the 'cautious' Oliver[3] strikes such terrible blows, in order 'to avenge himself all he could'; the devotion to a chief or, in the case of the holy war, to a cause; the passionate desire for glory, personal or collective; the fatalistic acquiescence in face of ineluctable destiny . . . finally, the hope of reward in another world, promised not only to him who died for his God, but also to him who died for his master.

Accustomed to danger, the knight found in war yet another attraction: it offered a remedy for boredom. For these men whose culture long remained rudimentary and who—apart from a few great barons and their counsellors—were seldom occupied by very heavy administrative cares, everyday life easily slipped into a grey monotony. Thus was born an appetite for diversions which, when one's native soil failed to afford the means to gratify it, sought satisfaction in distant lands. William the Conqueror,[4] bent on exacting due service from his vassals, said of one of them, whose fiefs he had just confiscated as a punishment for his having dared to depart for the crusade in Spain without permission: 'I do not believe it would be possible to find a better knight in arms; but he is unstable and extravagant, and he spends his time gadding about from place to place.' . . . The roving disposition was especially widespread among the French. The fact was that their own country did not offer them, as did half-Moslem Spain, or, to a less degree, Germany with its Slav frontier, an arena for conquests or swift forays; nor, like Germany again, the hardships and the pleasures of the great imperial expeditions. It is also probable that the knightly class was more numerous there than elsewhere, and therefore cramped for room. In France itself it has often been observed that Nor-

---

[3]In medieval romances, Oliver was one of the twelve peers of Charlemagne and the friend of Roland, hero of the *Song of Roland.*

[4]Duke of Normandy and King of England (1066–1087).

mandy was of all the provinces the richest in bold adventurers. Already the German Otto of Freising[5] spoke of the 'very restless race of the Normans'. Could it have been the legacy of Viking blood? Possibly. But it was above all the effect of the state of relative peace which, in that remarkably centralized principality, the dukes established at an early date; so that those who craved the opportunity for fighting had to seek it abroad. Flanders, where political conditions were not very different, furnished an almost equally large contingent of roving warriors.

These knights-errant[6] helped the native Christians in Spain to reconquer the northern part of the peninsula from Islam; they set up the Norman states in southern Italy; even before the First Crusade[7] they enlisted as mercenaries in the service of Byzantium and fought against its eastern foes; finally, they found in the conquest and defence of the Tomb of Christ their chosen field of action. Whether in Spain or in Syria, the holy war offered the dual attraction of an adventure and a work of piety. 'No need is there now to endure the monk's hard life in the strictest of the orders . . .' sang one of the troubadours; 'to accomplish honourable deeds and thereby at the same time to save oneself from hell—what more could one wish?' These migrations helped to maintain relations between societies separated from each other by great distances and sharp contrasts; they disseminated Western and especially French culture beyond its own frontiers . . . . At the same time the bloodletting thus practised abroad by the most turbulent groups in the West saved its civilization from being extinguished by guerilla warfare. The chroniclers were well aware that at the start of a crusade the people at home in the old countries always breathed more freely, because now they could once more enjoy a little peace.

Fighting, which was sometimes a legal obligation and frequently a pleasure, might also be required of the knight as a matter of honour: in the twelfth century, Périgord ran with blood because a certain lord thought that one of his noble neighbours looked like a blacksmith and had the bad taste to say so. But fighting was also, and perhaps above all, a source of profit—in fact, the nobleman's chief industry.

The lyrical effusions of Bertrand de Born have been mentioned above. He himself made no secret of the less creditable reasons which above all disposed him 'to find no pleasure in peace'. 'Why', he asks, 'do I want rich men to hate each other?' 'Because a rich man is much more noble, generous and affable in war than in peace.' And more crudely: 'We are going to have some fun. For the barons will make much of us . . . and if they want us to remain with them, they will give us *barbarins*' (i.e. coin of Limoges). And again: 'Trumpet, drums, flags and pennons, standards and horses white and black—that is what we shall shortly see. And it will be a happy day;

[5]c.1114/15–1158; Bishop of Freising, theologian, historian, and participant in the Second Crusade (1147–1148).

[6]Knights traveling in search of adventures.

[7]1095–1099.

for we shall seize the usurers' goods, and no more shall beasts of burden pass along the highways by day in complete safety; nor shall the burgess journey without fear, nor the merchant on his way to France; but the man who is full of courage shall be rich.' The poet belonged to that class of petty holders of fiefs, the 'vavasours'—he so described himself—for whom life in the ancestral manor-house lacked both gaiety and comforts. War made up for these deficiencies by stimulating the liberality of the great and providing prizes worth having.

The baron, of course, out of regard for his prestige as well as his interest, could not afford to be niggardly in the matter of presents, even towards vassals summoned to his side by the strictest conventions of feudal duty. If it was desired to retain them beyond the stipulated time, to take them farther or call on them more often than an increasingly rigorous custom appeared to permit, it was necessary to give them more. Finally, in face of the growing inadequacy of the vassal contingents, there was soon no army which could dispense with the assistance of that wandering body of warriors to whom adventure made so strong an appeal, provided that there was a prospect of gain as well as of mighty combats. Thus cynically, our Bertrand offered his services to the count of Poitiers: 'I can help you. I have already a shield at my neck and a helm on my head. . . . Nevertheless, how can I put myself in the field without money?'

But it was undoubtedly considered that the finest gift the chief could bestow was the right to a share of the plunder. This was also the principal profit which the knight who fought on his own account in little local wars expected from his efforts. It was a double prize, moreover: men and things. It is true that the Christian code no longer allowed captives to be reduced to slavery and at most permitted a few peasants or artisans to be forcibly removed from one place to another. But the ransoming of prisoners was a general practice. A ruler as firm and prudent as William the Conqueror might indeed never release alive the enemies who fell into his hands; but most warriors were not so far-sighted. The ransoming of prisoners occasionally had more dreadful consequences than the ancient practice of enslavement. The author of the *chanson*[8] of Girart de Roussillon, who certainly wrote from personal observation, tells us that in the evening after a battle Girart and his followers put to the sword all the humble prisoners and wounded, sparing only the 'owners of castles', who alone were in a position to buy their freedom with hard cash. As to plunder, it was traditionally so regular a source of profit that in the ages accustomed to written documents the legal texts treat it as a matter of course—on this point, the barbarian codes, at the beginning of the Middle Ages, and the thirteenth-century contracts of enlistment at the end, speak with the same voice. Heavy wagons followed the armies, for the purpose of collecting the spoils of war. Most serious of all, by a series of transitions

[8]Song.

almost unnoticed by the rather simple minds of the time, forms of violent action which were sometimes legitimate—requisitions indispensable to armies without commissariat, reprisals exacted against the enemy or his subjects—degenerated into pure brigandage, brutal and mean. Merchants were robbed on the highway; sheep, cheeses, chickens were stolen from pens and farmsteads. . . . The best of men contracted strange habits. William Marshal[9] was certainly a valiant knight. Nevertheless when, as a young and landless man travelling through France from tourney to tourney, he encountered on the road a monk who was running away with a girl of noble family and who candidly avowed his intention of putting out to usury the money he was carrying, William did not scruple to rob the poor devil of his cash, under the pretext of punishing him for his evil designs. One of his companions even reproached him for not having seized the horse as well.

Such practices reveal a signal indifference to human life and suffering. War in the feudal age was in no sense war in kid gloves. It was accompanied by actions which seem to us today anything but chivalrous; as for instance—a frequent occurrence, sometimes even in disregard of a solemn oath—the massacre or mutilation of garrisons which had held out 'too long'. It involved, as a natural concomitant, the devastation of the enemy's estates. Here and there a poet, like the author of *Huon of Bordeaux*, and later a pious king like St. Louis[10] protested in vain against this 'wasting' of the countryside which brought such appalling miseries upon the innocent. The epics, the German as well as the French, are faithful interpreters of real life, and they show us a whole succession of 'smoking' villages. 'There can be no real war without fire and blood,' said the plain-spoken Bertrand de Born.

In two passages exhibiting striking parallels, the poet of *Girart de Roussillon* and the anonymous biographer of the Emperor Henry IV[11] show us what the return of peace meant for the 'poor knights': the disdainful indifference of the great, who would have no more need of them; the importunities of money-lenders; the heavy plough-horse instead of the mettlesome charger; iron spurs instead of gold—in short an economic crisis as well as a disastrous loss of prestige. For the merchant and the peasant, on the contrary, peace meant that it was possible once again to work, to gain a livelihood—in short, to live. . . . [T]he knight, proud of his courage and skill, despised the unwarlike *(imbellis)* people—the villeins who in face of the armies scampered away 'like deer', and later on the townsmen, whose economic power seemed to him so much the more hateful in that it was obtained by means which were at once mysterious and directly opposed to his own activities. If the propensity to bloody deeds was prevalent everywhere—more than one abbot indeed met his death as the victim of

---

[9] Earl of Pembroke and regent of England in the early thirteenth century.

[10] Louis IX, King of France, 1226–1270.

[11] Holy Roman Emperor, 1056–1105.

a cloister feud—it was the conception of the necessity of war, as a source of honour and as a means of livelihood, that set apart the little group of 'noble' folk from the rest of society.

Favourite sport though it was, war had its dead seasons; but at these times the knightly class was distinguished from its neighbours by a manner of life which was essentially that of a nobility.

We should not think of this mode of existence as having invariably a rural setting. . . . It was only gradually and in consequence of a more pronounced differentiation of classes that knightly society, outside Italy and southern France, became almost entirely divorced from the urban populations properly so called. Although the noble certainly did not cease altogether to visit the town, he henceforth went there only occasionally, in pursuit of pleasure or for the exercise of certain functions. . . .

The manor-house usually stood in the midst of a cluster of dwellings, or nearby; sometimes there were several in the same village. The manor-house was sharply distinguished from the surrounding cottages . . . —not only because it was better built, but above all because it was almost invariably designed for defence. . . .

These edifices were generally of a very simple type. For a long time the most common, at least outside the Mediterranean regions, was the wooden tower. . . . Normally, a ditch was dug at the foot. Sometimes, at a little distance from the tower, there was a stockade or a rampart of beaten earth, surrounded in its turn by another ditch. . . . Tower and stockade frequently stood on a mound *(motte)*, sometimes natural, sometimes—at least in part—man-made. Its purpose was twofold: to confront the attackers with the obstacle of the slope and to gain a better view of the surrounding country. . . . It was the great men who first had recourse to stone as a building-material. . . . Before the completion of the great clearings, the forests seem to have been easier and less expensive to exploit than the quarries; and while masonry called for specialist workers, the tenants, a permanent source of compulsory labour, were almost all to some extent carpenters as well as wood-cutters. . . .

The favourite amusements of the nobility bore the imprint of a warlike temper.

First, there was hunting. . . . [I]t was more than a sport. The people of western Europe were not yet living in surroundings from which the menace of wild beasts had been finally removed. Moreover, at a time when the flesh of cattle, inadequately fed and of poor stock, furnished only indifferent meat, much venison was eaten, especially in the homes of the rich. . . .

Then there were the tournaments. . . . [T]he practice of these make-believe combats undoubtedly dates back to the remotest times. . . . The distinctive contribution of the feudal age was to evolve from these contests, whether military or popular, a type of mock battle at which prizes were generally offered, confined to mounted combatants equipped with knightly arms; and hence to create a distinctive class amusement, which the nobility found more exciting than any other.

Since these meetings, which could not be organized without considerable expense, usually took place on the occasion of the great 'courts' held from time to time by kings or barons, enthusiasts roamed the world from tournament to tournament. . . .

. . . Since the victor frequently took possession of the equipment and horses of the vanquished and sometimes even of his person, releasing him only on payment of a ransom, skill and strength were profitable assets. More than one jousting knight made a profession, and a very lucrative one, out of his skill in combat. Thus the love of arms inextricably combined the ingredients of 'joy' and the appetite for gain.

. . . The term which, from about the year 1100, commonly served to describe the sum of noble qualities was the characteristic word 'courtesy' (*courtoisie*). . . .

'We shall yet talk of this day in ladies' chambers,' said the count of Soissons, at the battle of Mansurah.[12] This remark . . . is characteristic of a society in which sophistication has made its appearance and, with it, the influence of women. The noblewoman had never been confined within her own secluded quarters. Surrounded with servants, she ruled her household, and she might also rule the fief—perhaps with a rod of iron. It was nevertheless reserved for the twelfth century to create the type of the cultivated great lady who holds a salon. This marks a profound change, when we consider the extraordinary coarseness of the attitude usually ascribed by the old epic poets to their heroes in their relations with women, even with queens—not stopping at the grossest insults, which the lady requites with blows. One can hear the guffaws of the audience. The courtly public had not lost their taste for this heavy humour; but they now allowed it only . . . at the expense of the peasants or the bourgeoisie. For courtesy was essentially an affair of class. The boudoir of the high-born lady and, more generally, the court, was henceforth the place where the knight sought to outshine and to eclipse his rivals not only by his reputation for great deeds of valour, but also by his regard for good manners and by his literary talents. . . .

Towards the pleasures of the flesh the attitude of the knightly class appears to have been frankly realistic. It was the attitude of the age as a whole. . . .

. . . The noble's marriage . . . was often an ordinary business transaction, and the houses of the nobility swarmed with bastards. . . .

The characteristic features of courtly love can be summarized fairly simply. It had nothing to do with marriage, or rather it was directly opposed to the legal state of marriage, since the beloved was as a rule a

---

[12]Battle in Egypt in 1249 where the Saracens defeated the French and captured their king, Louis IX.

married woman and the lover was never her husband. This love was often bestowed upon a lady of higher rank, but in any case it always involved a strong emphasis on the man's adoration of the woman. It professed to be an all-engrossing passion, constantly frustrated, easily jealous, and nourished by its own difficulties; but its stereotyped development early acquired something of a ritual character.... Finally, ... it was, ideally, a 'distant' love. It did not indeed reject carnal intercourse on principle, nor according to Andrew the Chaplain,[13] who discoursed on the subject, did it despise minor physical gratifications if obliged to renounce 'the ultimate solace'. But absence or obstacles, instead of destroying it, only enriched it with a poetic melancholy. If possession, always to be desired, was seen to be quite out of the question, the sentiment none the less endured as an exciting emotion and a poignant joy....

Still less, in spite of what has sometimes been said, was this code dependent on religious ideas.... [W]e must in fact recognize that it was directly opposed to them, although its adherents had no clear consciousness of this antithesis. It made the love of man and woman almost one of the cardinal virtues, and certainly the supreme form of pleasure. Above all, even when it renounced physical satisfaction, it sublimated—to the point of making it the be-all and end-all of existence—an emotional impulse derived essentially from those carnal appetites whose legitimacy Christianity only admits in order to curb them by marriage (profoundly despised by courtly love), in order to justify them by the propagation of the species (to which courtly love gave but little thought), and in order, finally, to confine them to a secondary plane of moral experience. It is not in the knightly lyrics that we can hope to find the authentic echo of the attitude of contemporary Christianity towards sexual relations. This is expressed, quite uncompromisingly, in that passage of the pious and clerical *Queste du Saint-Graal*[14] where Adam and Eve, before they lie together under the Tree to beget 'Abel the Just', beg the Lord to bring down upon them a great darkness to 'comfort' their shame....

Thus set apart by its power, by the nature of its wealth and its mode of life, by its very morals, the social class of nobles was toward the middle of the twelfth century quite ready to solidify into a legal and hereditary class. The ever more frequent use which from that time onwards seems to have been made of the word *gentilhomme*—man of good *gent* or lineage—to describe the members of this class is an indication of the growing importance attributed to qualities of birth. With the wide adoption of the ceremony of 'dubbing' or formal arming of the knight the legal class of nobility took definite shape.

[13] Andreas Capellanus, author of the twelfth-century treatise, *The Art of Courtly Love.*
[14] *Quest for the Holy Grail.*

Environment and Pollution

JEAN GIMPEL

Medieval people believed that God had made the world for man, who could therefore exploit nature as he wished. They viewed nature as spiritually instructive, as the "Book of God's Works" to complement the "Book of God's Words," but they had little appreciation for the beauties of nature. Our medieval ancestors viewed forests, waters, and animals as objects, good only to meet people's needs, though they did not countenance mindless destruction. Given these attitudes, waste and pollution developed. How did industrialization cause pollution in its varying forms? Jean Gimpel cites people who worried about the destruction of the environment, but they lamented only the increasing lack of materials to be exploited—they did not criticize the God-given right, for example, to clear forests. Their objections were purely practical. Did medieval civilization find any successful means to combat pollution?

Gimpel argues against those who date the industrialization of Europe from the late eighteenth and nineteenth centuries. He believes there was an industrial revolution in the Middle Ages. Also, he reminds us that the concerns we have today—such as those relating to pollution and the environment—have a long history; those worries are not especially new. Does he succeed in making the Middle Ages seem a bit modern (or modern times relatively medieval)? In the same way, he dispels any notion that care for personal hygiene is a recent development. The profusion of public and private baths speaks for a medieval sense of cleanliness. Why did those baths disappear in the late Middle Ages?

The industrialization of the Middle Ages played havoc with the environment of western Europe. Millions of acres of forests were destroyed to increase the area of arable and grazing land and to satisfy the ever greater demand for timber, the main raw material of the time. Not only was timber used as fuel for the hearths of private homes and for ovens, it was also in one way or another essential to practically every medieval industry. In the building industry wood was used to build timber-framed houses, water mills and windmills, bridges, and military installations such as fortresses and palisades. In the wine industry wood was used for making casks and vats. Ships were made of wood, as was all medieval machinery such as weavers' looms. Tanners needed the bark of the trees and so did the rope makers. The glass industry demolished the woods for fuel for its furnaces, and the iron industry needed charcoal for its forges. By 1300, forests in France covered only about 32 million acres—2 million acres less than they do today.

There is a remarkable document from 1140 which provides evidence of this onslaught on the medieval forests. Suger,[1] France's first great na-

[1] (1081–1151) Abbot of Saint-Denis as well as advisor to the king.

tionalist prime minister... wrote in one of his books of his difficulty in finding the 35-foot beams that he desperately needed as tie beams for the roof of the central nave of the Abbey of Saint-Denis, which he was having rebuilt. He had been told by all his master carpenters that it was absolutely impossible to find such large beams any longer in the area around Paris and that he would have to go far afield for that sort of timber. But Suger was not a man to take no for an answer:

> On a certain night, when I had returned from celebrating Matins, I began to think in bed that I myself should go through all the forests of these parts.... Quickly disposing of other duties and hurrying up in the early morning, we hastened with our carpenters, and with the measurements of the beams, to the forest called Iveline. When we traversed our possession in the Valley of Chevreuse we summoned... the keepers of our own forests as well as men who knew about the other woods, and questioned them under oath whether we would find there, no matter with how much trouble, any timbers of that measure. At this they smiled, or rather would have laughed at us if they had dared; they wondered whether we were quite ignorant of the fact that nothing of the kind could be found in the entire region.... We however— scorning whatever they might say—began, with the courage of our faith as it were, to search through the woods; and towards the first hour we found one timber adequate to the measure. Why say more? By the ninth hour or sooner, we had, through the thickets, the depths of the forest and the dense, thorny tangles, marked down twelve timbers (for so many were necessary) to the astonishment of all....

The Forest of Yvelines toward which he had "hastened" had once covered an immense area to the southwest of Paris. It now covers only 15,500 hectares (38,750 acres).

Suger must have ridden well over 50 kilometers that morning to reach his final destination....

... Richard Fitz Nigel, treasurer to the King of England, writing in the 1170s (a period when there seems to have been extensive clearing), shows clearly the concern felt at the time for forests cleared without the ground being prepared properly for agriculture. "If," he says, "woods are so severely cut that a man standing on the half-buried stump of an oak or other tree can see five other trees cut down about him, that is regarded as waste. Such an offense," he goes on to say, "even in a man's own woods, is regarded as so serious that even these men who are free of taxation because they sit at the king's exchequer must pay a money penalty all the heavier for their position."

Whatever Fitz Nigel's concerns, the fact remains that medieval man brought about the destruction of Europe's natural environment. He wasted its natural resources, and very soon felt the consequences of his destructive activities, the first of which was the considerable rise in the price of timber as a result of its increasing scarcity. At Douai, in northern France, in the thirteenth century wood had already become so scarce and expensive that families from the lower income groups could not afford to buy a wooden coffin for their dead. They had to rent one, and when the ceremony at the cemetery was over, the undertaker would open the coffin, throw the corpse into the earth, and bring back the coffin to use again.

Owing to the difficulty of finding suitable large timber, men looked for new technical solutions to building and construction problems. For example, in the famous sketchbook of Villard de Honnecourt, the thirteenth-century architect and engineer, who was working in the north of France not very far from Douai, there is a design for a bridge. The author of the drawing states proudly that it is built with short timber only twenty feet long: "How to make a bridge over water with twenty-foot timber." On another page is a drawing of a floor, under which is written: "How to work on a house or tower even if the timbers are too short." The lack of long beams had a considerable influence on the techniques of timber-framed building, and carpenters created a revolutionary timber-framed house with many shorter timbers.

A few figures from building accounts serve to show how quickly medieval man could destroy his environment. An average house built of wood needed some twelve oaks. In the middle of the fourteenth century, for the building operation at Windsor Castle, a whole wood was bought and all the trees felled—3,004 oaks. This was still not sufficient, for some ten years later 820 oaks were cut in Combe Park and 120 in Pamber Forest, bringing the total for this one castle up to 3,994 oaks. . . .

The building of thousands of furnaces in hundreds of medieval forests to satisfy the extensive demand for iron was a major cause of deforestation. Iron ore, unlike gold ore, is practically never found in its natural state except in meteorites, and it requires a special fuel to smelt and reduce it. From the very beginning, the fuel used was charcoal, the black porous residue of burned wood. This absolute reliance on charcoal made it essential for iron smelters up to the late eighteenth century to build their furnaces in the forests, where wood for the making of charcoal was directly at hand.

The extent of the damage caused by iron smelters to forests can be appreciated when one realizes that to obtain 50 kilograms of iron it was necessary at that time to reduce approximately 200 kilograms of iron ore with as much as 25 steres (25 cubic meters) of wood. It has been estimated that in forty days, one furnace could level the forest for a radius of 1 kilometer.

It is not surprising to hear that certain authorities took measures to halt or at least slow down the massacre of the forests. It was in their financial interest. . . . In the Dauphiné in 1315 the representatives of the Dauphin[2] were greatly alarmed at the widespread destruction of the woods of that

---

[2]Eldest son of the French king.

region. They formally accused the iron-producing factories of being directly responsible for this disaster and recommended that forcible measures should be taken to arrest the situation.

There were objections in 1255 when two limekilns in the Forest of Wellington consumed five hundred oaks in one year, and on the territory of Colmars in the Basses-Alpes water-powered saws were forbidden at the end of the thirteenth century. In 1205 exploitation of the woods belonging to the monks of Chelles in France was regulated, and in the same year the commune of Montaguloto in Italy required every citizen to plant ten trees annually.

In England, the royal forest, which covered quite an extensive area of the kingdom, was protected by the much-hated forest law (laid down to protect the hunting grounds of the Norman conquerors rather than for any ecological reasons). Nevertheless, encroachments were made regularly on the woodlands in the royal forests, and kings in financial difficulties had to accept vast disforestations. In 1190, the first year of Richard I's reign, the knights of Surrey offered him 200 marks[3] that "they might be quit of all things that belong to the forest from the water of Wey to Kent and from the street of Guildford southwards as far as Surrey stretches." In 1204 the men of Essex offered King John 500 marks and 5 palfreys for the disforestation of "the forest of Essex which is beyond the causeway between Colchester and Bishops Stortford." . . .

The decreasing availability of timber and the progressive rise in the price of wood led England to import timber from Scandinavia. The first fleet of ships loaded with Norwegian fir trees sailed into Grimsby harbor, on the east coast of England, in 1230. And in 1274, the master carpenter of Norwich Cathedral went to Hamburg to buy timber and boards. During this same period a substitute fuel for wood was found—coal.

Some of the great European coalfields of the nineteenth and twentieth centuries were first mined in the thirteenth century. . . .

As early as 1226, we find in London a Sea Coal Lane, also known as Lime Burners Lane. The lime-burning industry was one of the first to convert to the use of coal, along with the iron industry. Brewers, dyers, and others followed. In 1243 the first recorded victim of coal mining, Ralph, son of Roger Ulger, drowned in an open pit. At first coal was mined in shallow pits, usually 6 to 15 meters (20 to 50 feet) deep, but sometimes, as in the French coal mines of Boussagues in the Languedoc, there were already underground galleries. In Newcastle there were such extensive diggings around the city that it was dangerous to approach it by night, lest one fall and break one's neck in the open trenches. Here and in many other places, the medieval environment was already an industrial environment. . . .

With the burning of coal, western Europe began to face atmospheric pollution. The first person recorded to have suffered from medieval pollu-

---

[3]A money of account in medieval England.

tion was a Queen of England, Eleanor, who was driven from Nottingham Castle in 1257 by the unpleasant fumes of the sea coal burned in the industrial city below. Coal smoke was considered to be very detrimental to one's health, and up to the sixteenth century coal was generally used as a domestic fuel only by the poorer members of society, who could not afford to buy wood. Medieval coal extracted from the surface was of inferior quality, with more bitumen in it than the coal mined today. As it burned, it gave off a continuous cloud of choking, foul-smelling, noxious smoke. The only good domestic coal was that extracted from the coalfields bordering the Firth of Forth, which was burned by the Scottish kings, and the coal extracted at Aachen in Germany, which was used to make fires in the town hall and in the mayor's chambers.

By the last decades of the thirteenth century, London had the sad privilege of becoming the first city in the world to suffer man-made atmospheric pollution. In 1285 and 1288 complaints were recorded concerning the infection and corruption of the city's air by coal fumes from the limekilns. Commissioners of Inquiry were appointed, and in 1307 a royal proclamation was made in Southwark, Wapping, and East Smithfield forbidding the use of sea coal in kilns under pain of heavy forfeiture. . . .

The bad reputation of sea coal continued throughout the ages. In the fifteenth century Enea Sylvio Piccolomini, who later became Pope Pius II, wrote when visiting Scotland, "this kind of stone being impregnated with sulfur or some fatty matter is burned instead of wood, of which the country is destitute." Sea coal was still unpopular in the sixteenth century when the Venetian envoy Soranzo wrote an account of England in which he says: "In the north towards Scotland they find a certain sort of earth, almost mineral, which burns like charcoal and is extensively used by blacksmiths, and but for a bad odour which it leaves would be yet more employed as it gives great heat and costs but little." The London Company of Brewers offered in 1578 to burn wood instead of sea coal in the brew-houses nearest to the Palace of Westminster because its members understood that the Queen "findeth hersealfe greately greved and anoyed with the taste and smoke of the sea-cooles." . . .

While Londoners were choked with noisome fumes, tens of thousands of villagers throughout Europe were deafened by the din of the village forges. . . .

In the towns people suffered also from industrial water pollution. Two industries in particular were held responsible in the Middle Ages for polluting the rivers: the slaughtering and the tanning industries, especially tanning. Municipalities were always trying to move the butchers and the tanners downstream, outside the precincts of the town.

The slaughtering and quartering of livestock in the Middle Ages was generally done on the butcher's premises. A French parliamentary decree of September 7, 1366, compelled Paris butchers to do their slaughtering and cleaning alongside a running stream beyond the city. This decree was certainly necessary, as some 250,000 head of livestock were slaughtered each year in Paris. The author of the *Menagier de Paris*[4] worked out that 269,256 animals had been slaughtered in 1293: 188,522 sheep, 30,346 oxen, 19,604 calves, and 30,784 pigs. Quite enough to pollute the Seine.

The Paris authorities tried to limit the degree of this pollution not only by restricting the slaughtering of animals within the precincts of the city but also by imposing restrictions on the tanners, who dressed ox, cow, and calf hides, and the tawers, who dressed the skins of deer, sheep, and horses. "In 1395 the king's representative at the *Châtelet*[5] wanted to compel the tawers who were dressing their leather on the banks of the Seine, between the Grand-Pont and the Hotel du duc de Bourbon to move downstream, because industry corrupted the water of the riverside dwellers, both those lodging in the Louvre and those lodging in the Hôtel du duc de Bourbon."

Tanning polluted the river because it subjected the hides to a whole series of chemical operations requiring tannic acids or lime. Tawing used alum and oil. Dried blood, fat, surplus tissues, flesh impurities, and hair were continually washed away with the acids and the lime into the streams running through the cities. The water flowing from the tanneries was certainly unpalatable, and there were tanneries in every medieval city. . . .

Many local authorities took measures to combat the pollution of their cities, but in 1388 the English Parliament sitting in Cambridge passed the first nationwide antipollution act. It concerned not only the pollution of the air but also of the waters. It forbade throwing garbage into rivers or leaving it uncared for in the city. All garbage had to be carried away out of town. Otherwise, the law proclaimed, "the air . . . is greatly corrupt and infect and many Maladies and other intolerable Diseases do daily happen. . . . "

However effective these various antipollution measures were, medieval people usually preferred to rely on wells for drinking water. Sometimes they repaired the Roman aqueducts, which were often in a half-ruined state, and occasionally they built new ones. Sometimes they brought water considerable distances in underground conduits. Just about a century after the Norman Conquest, in 1167, the monks of the Cathedral Priory of Canterbury, who had obtained a grant of land containing the springs, installed a very elaborate and complete system of water supply. . . . The water was carried by an underground pipe and, after entering the city walls, flowed into a whole series of pipes. One pipe fed water to the infirmary hall; another went to the refectory, the scullery, and the kitchen; another carried water to the baker's house, the brewer's house, the guest hall, and the bathhouse; and a pipe ran into a tank beside the prior's chambers and fed his water tub. Waste from the water tub and

[4]*The Parisian Household.*
[5]Royal court and prison in Paris.

from the bathroom flowed into the main drain, flushing the rere-dorter or *necessarium.*[6]

Numerous documents of the period mention the existence of private and public baths as well as private and public toilets. If there was medieval pollution, there was also medieval hygiene. But the medieval pollution must have increased still more with the breaking down of medieval hygiene. The standards of hygiene in the twelfth and thirteenth centuries were relatively high, but progressively the authorities worried about the "permissiveness" they discovered in the many public baths, and the incidence of the Black Death certainly hardened this attitude. . . .

In the thirteenth century there were no less than thirty-two public baths in Paris, for men and women. According to the professional statutes . . . recorded in 1268 by the provost of Paris, Etienne Boileau, the owners of the bathhouses were allowed to ask two prices at the entrance: 2d. for a steam bath and 4d. for a bath in a tub. In the linen inventories of private houses, mention is sometimes made of a piece of linen to be laid on the bottom of the wooden tub as a protection against splinters. In the statutes, the owners of the bathhouses made a reservation for the future: if the price of wood or coal (another example of the use of coal in the Middle Ages) should go up, the prices of the steam and hot baths would be raised accordingly. The owners were to protect their establishments materially and morally by making sure that men such as lepers could not enter and that men with a bad reputation would be kept out. The bathhouse was not to be used as a house of prostitution or as a *bordel*. . . . (Interestingly, the medieval word in English for bathhouse was *stew*, which has come down to the English today as a synonym for brothel.) Miniatures of the period show that the bath was indeed a place where people gossiped, ate, and soaked socially, often with a companion of the opposite sex. . . . One entertained one's friends in one's *baignerie*,[7] generally situated near one's bedroom.

On the manuscript page where the provost of Paris had had transcribed the statutes of the bathhouse owners . . . a few lines were added at a later date which show that the authorities were getting increasingly worried about hygiene, or the way hygiene was put to use by lovers. From then on a bathhouse proprietor had to decide if he wanted to run a bathhouse for women or for men. He was not allowed to accommodate both sexes in the same establishment. The author of these lines went on to relate what happens when the bathhouses are mixed. "Shameful things. Men make a point of staying all night in the public baths and women at the break of day come in and through 'ignorance' find themselves in the men's rooms." This prudish attitude toward the growing permissiveness brought the bathhouses into financial difficulties, and they finally had to close one after another. . . . Hygiene thus disappeared from Western society, not to reappear for half a millennium.

[6]Toilet.

[7]Bath.

Medieval Children

DAVID HERLIHY

In this survey of children in the Middle Ages, David Herlihy emphasizes the complexity of the subject. There is first the problem of documentation. Children did not write about themselves and adults usually did not specifically detail their attitudes and behavior toward children. Herlihy thus has had recourse to many different types of source materials. What sources does he rely on in his discussion of children in classical society, among the barbarians, and, finally, in the Middle Ages? Second, Herlihy notes that the information available about medieval children can lead the historian to quite opposite conclusions, that the Middle Ages either maltreated offspring or took pleasure in their spirituality and goodness. Which conclusion does Herlihy adopt? Does the evidence support his interpretation?

What explains the different treatment of children in classical, barbarian, and medieval cultures? Instead of looking within the family for the causes of these changes, Herlihy usually points to outside influences, such as Christianity, and socioeconomic developments. Christian theologians disagreed on the basic nature of children, stressing their ties to original sin or their holy innocence. According to Herlihy, changing attitudes toward the baby Jesus reflected the way in which society viewed all children. Of course, the impact of theology and Christian art on the family is impossible to measure exactly—one wonders, for example, about peasant children, a subject Herlihy neglects in favor of urban social groups. Increasing commercialization and urbanization in the eleventh and twelfth centuries led to a new concern for children, one that was both practical and psychological. The establishment of schools and orphanages suggests that children received more attention and care. Pedagogues, both religious and lay, worried about children's education, health, and spiritual well-being. The result, says Herlihy, was an idealization of childhood in the Middle Ages, long before many historians place that development. Herlihy thus refutes those historians who argue that a concept of and an appreciation for childhood did not emerge until the sixteenth and seventeenth centuries.

. . . Many, perhaps most, children in most traditional societies did no more than come and go. And most never acquired, or were given, a voice which might have recorded and preserved their impressions concerning themselves, their parents, and the world they had recently discovered. Of all social groups which formed the societies of the past, children, seldom seen and rarely heard in the documents, remain for historians the most elusive, the most obscure.

The difficulties of interviewing the mute have doubtlessly obstructed and delayed a systematic investigation of the history of childhood. But today, at least, historians are aware of the commonplace assumption of psychologists, that childhood plays a critical role in the formation of the adult personality. Perhaps they are awakening to an even older wisdom, the recognition that society, in the way it rears its children, shapes itself. . . .

Today, the literature devoted to the history of children in various places and epochs may be described, rather like children themselves, as small but growing daily. It remains, however, difficult to discern within that literature a clear consensus, an acceptable hypothesis, concerning the broad trends of children's history, even within Western societies. To be sure, there is frequent allusion within these recent publications to a particular interpretation which, for want of a better name, we shall call the "theory of discovered childhood." The principal formulator of this interpretation, at least in its most recent form, has been the French social historian Philippe Ariès. In a book published in 1960, called in its English translation *Centuries of Childhood*, Ariès entitled the second chapter "the discovery of childhood." In it he affirmed that the Middle Ages of Western history did not recognize childhood as a distinct phase in life. Medieval people allegedly viewed and treated their children as imperfectly formed adults. Once the infant was weaned, medieval parents supposedly made no concessions to its special and changing psychological needs and took little satisfaction in the distinctive traits of the young personality. The corollary to this assumption is that, at some point in the development of Western society and civilization, the young years of life were at last discovered: childhood needed a Columbus.

Proclamations of the alleged discovery of childhood have become commonplace in the growing literature, but wide differences in interpretation still separate the authors. When, for example, was childhood first recognized? On this important question, Ariès himself is indefinite, even evasive, and seems to place the discovery over three or four hundred years, from the fifteenth to the eighteenth centuries. . . .

If historians of the modern world do not agree concerning the date of childhood's discovery, their colleagues, working in more remote periods, show signs of restiveness with Ariès' postulate, that medieval people did not distinguish children from adults. A number of scholars . . . have noted among the pedagogues, humanists, and even artists of fifteenth-century Italy a new orientation toward children, a new awareness of their problems, and an appreciation of their qualities. The fat and frolicksome babies, the *putti*, who cavort through many solemn paintings of the Italian Renaissance, leave little doubt that the artists of the epoch knew how to depict, and they or their patrons liked to contemplate, children. A still more radical departure from Ariès' views was proposed, in 1968, by the French medievalist Pierre Riché. Riché accepted Ariès' phrase, the "discovery of childhood," but radically changed his chronology. The initial explorers of childhood were, for Riché, the monastic pedagogues active in Western Europe between the sixth and eighth centuries. Their sensitivity toward the psychology of children allegedly transformed the harsh educational methods of classical antiquity and developed a new pedagogy which was finely attuned to the personality of the child-monk. Thus, over an extended period of time, from the early Middle Ages until the present, one or another author would have us believe that a consciousness of childhood was at last emerging.

The lessons that I would draw from this confusion of learned opinions are the following. Historians would be well advised to avoid such categoric and dubious claims, that people in certain periods failed to distinguish children from adults, that childhood really did lie beyond the pale of collective consciousness. Attitudes toward children have certainly shifted, as has the willingness on the part of society to invest substantially in their welfare or education. But to describe these changes, we need terms more refined than metaphors of ignorance and discovery. I would propose that we seek to evaluate, and on occasion even to measure, the psychological and economic investment which families and societies in the past were willing to make in their children. However, we ought also to recognize that alternative and even competitive sets of child-related values can coexist in the same society, perhaps even in the same household. Different social groups and classes expect different things from their children; so do different epochs, in accordance with prevailing economic, social, and demographic conditions. In examining the ways in which children were regarded and reared in the past, we should not expect either rigorous consistency across society or lineal progress over time.

In the current, lively efforts to reconstruct the history of children in Western civilization, the long period of the Middle Ages has a special importance. The medieval child represents a kind of primordial form, an "eo-pais," a "dawn child" as it were, against whom Western children of subsequent epochs must be measured if we are to appreciate the changes they have experienced. To be sure, the difficulties of observing medieval children cannot be discounted. Medieval documentation is usually sparse, often inconsistent, and always difficult. . . . We can hope to catch only fleeting glimpses of medieval children in their rush through, or out of, life. On the other hand, even glimpses may be enough to dispel some large misconceptions concerning medieval children and to aid us toward a sound reconstruction of the history of children in the Western world.

In surveying medieval children, it is first necessary to consider the two prior traditions which largely shaped the medieval appraisal of the very young—the classical and the barbarian. It is important also to reflect upon the influence exerted upon child rearing by a special component of the ancient Mediterranean heritage: the Christian church.

Classical society, or at least the elites within it, cultivated an impressive array of intellectual traditions, which were founded upon literacy and preserved over time through intensive, and expensive, educational methods. Classical civilization would be inconceivable in the absence of professional teachers, formal instruction, and numerous schools and academies.

But as social historians of antiquity now emphasize, the resources that supported ancient society were in truth scant. "The classical Mediterranean has always been a world on the edge of starvation," one historian has recently written, with much justice if perhaps some exaggeration. Scarce resources and the high costs of rearing children helped form certain distinctive policies regarding the young. The nations which comprised the Roman Empire, with the exception only of the Jews, refused to support deformed, unpromising, or supernumerary babies. In Roman practice, for example, the newborn baby was at once laid before the feet of him who held the *patria potestas*[1] over it, usually the natural father. Through a ritual gesture called *susceptio*, the holder of paternal authority might raise up the infant and receive it into his family and household. But he could also reject the baby and order its exposure. Infanticide, or the exposure of infants, was a common and accepted social practice in classical society, shocking perhaps to modern sensibilities but rational for these ancient peoples who were seeking to achieve goals with limited means.

Here however is a paradox. Widespread infanticide in ancient society does not imply disinterest in or neglect of those children elected for survival. On the contrary, to assure a good return on the precious means invested in them, they were subject to close and often cruel attention and to frequent beatings. St. Augustine[2] in his *Confessions* tells how his father, Patricius, and even his pious mother, Monica, urged him to high performance at school, "that I might get on in the world and excel in the handling of words, to gain honor among men and deceitful riches." "If I proved idle in learning," he says of his teachers, "I was soundly beaten. For this procedure seemed wise to our ancestors; and many, passing the same way in the days past, had built a sorrowful road, by which we too must go, with multiplication of grief and toil upon the sons of Adam." The memories which the men of antiquity preserved of their childhood were understandably bleak. "Who would not shudder," Augustine exclaims in the *City of God*, "if he were given the choice of eternal death or life again as a child? Who would not choose to die?"

The barbarian child grew up under quite different circumstances. Moreover, barbarian practices of child rearing seem to have been particularly influential in the society of early medieval Europe, between the fifth and eleventh centuries. This is not surprising. Early in the Middle Ages, the cities which had dominated society and culture in antiquity lost importance, the literate social elites of classical society all but disappeared, and their educational institutions and ideals went down amid the debacle of the Western empire. On the other hand, barbarian practices were easily preserved within, and congenial to, the semibarbarized society of the early medieval West.

[1]Paternal authority.

[2]Christian theologian, 354–430, and Bishop of Hippo in North Africa.

In a tract called *Germania*, written in A.D. 98, the Roman historian Tacitus has described for us the customs of the barbarian Germans, including their treatment of children. Tacitus, to be sure, likes to contrast barbarian virtues with Roman vices and doubtlessly exaggerates in his depictions of both, but his words are nonetheless worth our attention. The Germans, he claims, did not, like the Romans, kill their supernumerary children. Rather, the barbarians rejoiced in a numerous progeny. Moreover, the barbarian mother, unlike her Roman counterpart, nursed her own baby and did not hand it over for feeding to servants or a hired nurse. On the other hand, Tacitus notes, the barbarian parents paid little attention to their growing children. "In every household," he writes, "the children grow up naked and unkempt. . . . " "The lord and slave," he continues, "are in no way to be distinguished by the delicacy of their bringing up. They live among the same flocks, they lie on the same ground. . . . " Barbarian culture did not depend for its survival on the costly instruction of the young in complex skills and learned traditions; barbarian parents had no need to invest heavily in their children, either psychologically or materially. The cheap costs of child rearing precluded the adoption of infanticide as standard social policy but also reduced the attention which the growing child received from its parents. Only on the threshold of adulthood did the free German male re-establish close contacts with adult society. He typically joined the following of a mature warrior, accompanied him into battle, observed him, and gained some instruction in the arts of war, which, like the arts of rhetoric in the classical world, were the key to his social advance.

A casual attitude toward children seems embodied in the laws of the barbarian peoples—Franks, Lombards, Visigoths, Anglo-Saxons, and others—which were redacted into Latin largely between the sixth and the ninth centuries. The barbarian laws typically assigned to each member of society a sum of money—a fine, or wergeld—which would have to be paid to the relatives if he or she was injured or killed. The size of the wergeld thus provides a crude measure of social status or importance. One of the barbarian codes, the Visigothic, dating from the middle seventh century, gives a particularly detailed and instructive table of values which shows how the worth of a person varied according to age, sex, and status. A free male baby, in the first year of life, was assigned a wergeld of 60 solidi. Between age 1 and age 9, his social worth increased at an average rate of only 3.75 solidi per year, thus attaining the value of 90 solidi in the tenth year of life. Between ages 10 and 15, the rate of increase accelerated to 10 solidi per year; and between ages 15 and 20 it grew still more, to 30 solidi per year. In other words, the social worth of the free Visigothic male increased very slowly in the early years of childhood, accelerated in early adolescence, and grew most substantially in the years preceding full maturity. Considered mature at age 20, he enjoyed a wergeld of 300 solidi—five times the worth of the newborn male infant—and this he retained until age 50. In old age, his social worth declined, to 200 solidi between ages 50 and 65 and to 100 solidi from age 65 to death. The old man, beyond age 65, was worth the same as a child of ten years.

The contrast between the worth of the child and the worth of the adult is particularly striking in regard to women. Among the Visigoths, a female under age 15 was assigned only one-half the wergeld enjoyed by males—only 30 solidi during her first year of life. Her social worth, however, increased enormously when she entered the years of childbearing, between ages 15 and 40 in the Visigothic codes. Her wergeld then leaped to 250 solidi, nearly equal to the 300 solidi assigned to the male and eight times the value of the newborn baby girl. The sterile years of old age brought a reduction of the fine, first to 200 solidi, which she retained to age 60, and then to 100 solidi. In old age, she was assigned the same worth as the male. . . .

The low values assigned to children in these barbarian codes is puzzling. Did the lawgivers not realize that the supply of adults, including the especially valued childbearing women, was critically dependent on the protection of children? This obvious truth seemingly escaped the notice of the barbarian lawgivers; children, and their relation to society, did not loom large in their consciousness.

Apart from laws, one other source offers some insight into the treatment of children in the early Middle Ages: surveys of the population settled on particular estates and manors. These sporadic surveys have survived from the Carolingian period of medieval history, the late eighth and ninth centuries. The largest of them, redacted in the first quarter of the ninth century, lists nearly 2,000 families settled on the lands of the abbey of Saint-Germain-des-Prés near Paris. The survey gives no exact ages, but of 8,457 persons included in it, 3,327 are explicitly identified as *infantes*, or children. . . .

The proportion of known children within the population is very low— only 85 children for every 100 adults. Even if all those of uncertain age are considered *infantes*, the ratio then becomes 116 children for every 100 adults. This peasant population was either singularly barren or it was not bothering to report all its children. Moreover, the sexual composition of the population across these age categories is perplexing. Among the known adults, men and women appear in nearly equal numbers. But among the known children, there are 143 boys for every 100 girls—a male-to-female ratio of nearly three to two. Among those of uncertain age, the sex ratio is even higher. The high sex ratio among the known children may indicate widespread female infanticide, but if this were so, we should expect to find a similarly skewed ratio among the known adults. The death of numerous baby girls inevitably would affect over time the proportions of adult women in this presumably closed population. But the proportions of males and females among the known adults are reasonably balanced. The more likely explanation is that the monastic surveyors, or the peasants who reported to them, were negligent in counting children and were particularly deficient in reporting the presence of little girls in the households. As the barbarian legal codes suggest, children, and especially girls, became of substantial interest to society, and presumably to their families, only as they aged.

The low monetary worth assigned to the very young, and the shadowy presence of children in the statistical documents of the early Middle Ages, should not, however, imply that parents did not love their children. Tacitus notes that the barbarian mother usually nursed her own babies. Kinship ties were strongly emphasized in barbarian society, and these were surely cemented by affection. The German epic fragment the *Song of Hildebrand* takes as its principal theme the love which should unite father and son. The warrior Hildebrand flees into exile to live among the Huns, leaving "a babe at the breast in the bower of the bride." Then, after sixty years of wandering, he confronts his son as his enemy on the field of battle. He recognizes his offspring and tries to avoid combat; he offers the young warrior gold and, as the poet tells us, his love besides. . . . If classical methods of child rearing can be called cruel but closely attentive, the barbarian child grew up within an atmosphere of affectionate neglect.

The Christian church also powerfully influenced the treatment of children in many complex ways. Christianity, like Judaism before it, unequivocally condemned infanticide or the exposure of infants. To be sure, infanticide and exposure remained common social practices in Western Europe across the entire length of the Middle Ages. Church councils, penitentials, sermons, and secular legal codes yield abundant and repeated references to those crimes. As late as the fifteenth century, if we are to believe the great popular preachers of the period, the streams and cesspools of Europe echoed with the cries of abandoned babies. But medieval infanticide still shows one great difference from the comparable practice in the ancient world. Our sources consistently attribute the practice to two motivations: the shame of seduced and abandoned women, who wished to conceal illegitimate births, and poverty—the inability of the mother, and often of both parents, to support an additional mouth. The killing or abandonment of babies in medieval society was the characteristic resort of the fallen, the poor, the desperate. In the ancient world, infanticide had been accepted practice, even among the social elites.

Christian teachings also informed and softened attitudes toward children. Christian scriptures held out several examples of children who enjoyed or earned God's special favor: in the Old Testament, the young Samuel and the young Daniel; in the New, the Holy Innocents and the Christ child himself. According to the evangelists, Jesus himself welcomed the company of children, and he instructed his disciples in the famous words: "Unless you become as little children, you will never enter the Kingdom of Heaven."

This partiality toward children evoked many echoes among patristic[3] and medieval writers. In a poem attributed to St. Clement of Alexandria,[4] Christ is called the "king of children." Pope Leo the Great[5] writes . . . "Christ loves childhood, for it is the teacher of humility, the rule of innocence, the model of sweetness." . . .

A favorable appraisal of childhood is also apparent in the monastic culture of the early Middle Ages. Western monasteries, from the sixth century, accepted as oblates to the monastic life children who were hardly more than toddlers, and the leaders of the monastic movement gave much attention to the proper methods of rearing and instructing these miniature monks. In his famous rule, St. Benedict of Nursia insisted that the advice of the children be sought in important matters, "for often the Lord reveals to the young what should be done." St. Columban[6] in the seventh century, and the Venerable Bede[7] in the eighth, praised four qualities of the monastic child: he does not persist in anger; he does not bear a grudge; he takes no delight in the beauty of women; and he expresses what he truly believes.

But alongside this positive assessment of the very young, Christian tradition supported a much harsher appraisal of the nature of the child. In Christian belief, the dire results of Adam's fall were visited upon all his descendants. All persons, when they entered the world, bore the stain of original sin and with it concupiscence, an irrepressible appetite for evil. Moreover, if God had predestined some persons to salvation and some to damnation, his judgments touched even the very young, even those who died before they knew their eternal options. The father of the Church who most forcefully and effectively explored the implications of predestination for children was again St. Augustine. Voluminous in his writings, clear in his logic, and ruthless in his conclusions, Augustine finally decided, after some early doubts, that the baby who died without baptism was damned to eternal fires. There were heaven and hell and no place in-between. "If you admit that the little one cannot enter heaven," he argued, "then you concede that he will be in everlasting fire."

This cruel judgment of the great African theologian contrasts with the milder views of the Eastern fathers, who affirmed that unbaptized children suffer only the loss of the vision of God. The behavior of Augustine's God seems to mimic the posture of the Roman paterfamilias, who was similarly arbitrary and ruthless in the judgment of his own babies, who elected some for life and cast out others into the exterior darkness. And no one in his family dared question his decisions. . . .

[3]Referring to the fathers, or theologians, of the early Christian Church.

[4]Greek Christian theologian, c.150–c.215.

[5]440–461.

[6]Irish monk and missionary, c.543–615.

[7]English monk, historian, and saint, c.673–735.

Augustine was, moreover, impressed by the early dominion which evil establishes over the growing child. The suckling infant cries unreasonably for nourishment, wails and throws tantrums, and strikes with feeble but malicious blows those who care for him. "The innocence of children," Augustine concludes, "is in the helplessness of their bodies, rather than any quality of soul." ...

The suppression of concupiscence thus becomes a central goal of Augustine's educational philosophy and justifies hard and frequent punishments inflicted on the child. While rejecting the values of pagan antiquity, he adheres to the classical methods of education. Augustine prepared the way for retaining under Christian auspices that "sorrowful road" of schooling which he, as a child at school, had so much hated.

Medieval society thus inherited and sustained a mix of sometimes inconsistent attitudes toward children. The social historian, by playing upon one or another of these attitudes, by judiciously screening his sources, could easily color as he pleases the history of medieval children. He could compile a list of the atrocities committed against them, dwell upon their neglect, or celebrate medieval views of the child's innocence and holiness. One must, however, strive to paint a more balanced picture, and for this we obviously need some means of testing the experiences of the medieval child. The tests we shall use here are two: the social investment, the wealth and resources which medieval society was apparently willing to invest in children; and the psychological investment, the attention they claimed and received from their elders. The thesis of this essay, simply stated, is that both the social and psychological investments in children were growing substantially from approximately the eleventh and twelfth centuries, through to the end of the Middle Ages, and doubtlessly beyond.

The basic economic and social changes which affected medieval society during this period seem to have required a heightened investment in children. From about the year 1000, the medieval community was growing in numbers and complexity. Commercial exchange intensified, and a vigorous urban life was reborn in the West. Even the shocking reduction in population size, coming with the plagues, famines, and wars of the fourteenth century, did not undo the importance of the commercial economy or of the towns and the urban classes dependent upon it. Medieval society, once a simple association of warriors, priests, and peasants, came to include such numerous and varied social types as merchants, lawyers, notaries, accountants, clerks, and artisans. A new world was born, based on the cultivation and preservation of specialized, sophisticated skills.

The emergence of specialized roles within society required in turn a social commitment to the training of children in the corresponding skills. Earlier educational reforms—notably those achieved under Charlemagne[8]— had largely affected monks and, in less measure, clerics; they had little

[8]Carolingian Emperor, 768–814.

impact on the lay world. One novelty of the new medieval pedagogy, as it is developed from the twelfth century, is the attention now given to the training of laymen. Many writers now comment on the need and value of mastering a trade from early youth. Boys . . . should be taught a trade "as soon as possible." . . . "Men from childhood," Thomas Aquinas[9] observes, "apply themselves to those offices and skills in which they will spend their lives. . . . This is altogether necessary. To the extent that something is difficult, so much the more must a man grow accustomed to it from childhood."

Later in the thirteenth century, Raymond Lull,[10] one of the most learned men of the epoch, compares society to a wheel upon which men ride ceaselessly, up and down, gaining and losing status; the force which drives the wheel is education, in particular the mastery of a marketable skill. Through the exercise of a trade, a man earns money, gains status, and ultimately enters the ranks of the rich. Frequently, however, he becomes arrogant in his new status, and he neglects to train his children in a trade. His unskilled offspring inevitably ride the wheel on its downward swing. And so the world turns. A marketable skill offers the only certain riches and the only security. . . .

One hundred and fifty years later, the Florentine Dominican Giovanni Dominici voices exactly the same sentiments. Neither wealth nor inherited status offers security. Only a marketable skill can assure that children "will not be forced, as are many, to beg, to steal, to enter household service, or to do demeaning things." . . .

Although statistics largely elude us, there can be little doubt that medieval society was making substantial investments in education from the twelfth century. . . . The chronicler Giovanni Villani[11] gives us some rare figures on the schools functioning at Florence in the 1330s. The children, both boys and girls, who were attending the grammar schools of the city, presumably between 6 and 12 years of age, numbered between eight and ten thousand. From what we know of the population of the city, better than one out of two school-aged children were receiving formal instruction in reading. Florentine girls received no more formal instruction after grammar school, but of the boys, between 1,000 and 1,200 went on to six secondary schools, where they learned how to calculate on the abacus, in evident preparation for a business career. Another 550 to 600 attended four "large schools" where they studied "Latin and logic," the necessary preparation for entry into the universities and, eventually, for a career in law, medicine, or the Church. Florence, it might be argued, was hardly a typical medieval community. Still, the social investment that Florentines were making in the training of their children was substantial.

[9]Saint and theologian, c.1225–1274.
[10]Missionary and philosopher, c.1223–c.1315.
[11]Florentine, d.1348.

Another indicator of social investment in children is the number of orphanages or hospitals devoted to their care, and here the change across the Middle Ages is particularly impressive. The care of the abandoned or orphaned child was a traditional obligation of Christian charity, but it did not lead to the foundation and support of specialized orphanages until late in the Middle Ages. The oldest European orphanage of which we have notice was founded at Milan in 787, but we know nothing at all concerning its subsequent history or that of other orphanages sporadically mentioned in the early sources. The great hospital orders of the medieval Church, which sprang up from the twelfth century, cared for orphans and foundlings, but none initially chose that charity as its special mission.

The history of hospitals in the city of Florence gives striking illustration of a new concern for abandoned babies which emerged in Europe during the last two centuries of the Middle Ages. In his detailed description of his native city, written in the 1330s, Villani boasts that Florence contained thirty hospitals with more than a thousand beds. But the beds were intended for the "poor and infrm," and he mentions no special hospital for foundlings. A century later, probably in the 1420s, another chronicler, Gregorio Dati,[12] . . . composed another description of the marvels of Florence. By then the city contained no fewer than three hospitals which received foundlings and supported them until an age when the girls could marry and the boys could be instructed in a trade. . . .

Even a rapid survey of the foundling hospitals of Europe shows a similar pattern. Bologna seems not to have had an orphanage until 1459, and Pavia not until 1449. At Paris, the first specialized hospital for children, Saint-Esprit en Grèves, was founded in 1363, but according to its charter it was supposed to receive only orphans of legitimate birth. Care of foundlings, it was feared, might encourage sexual license among adults. But the hospital in practice seems to have accepted abandoned babies, and several similar institutions were established in French cities in the fifteenth century.

This new concern for the survival of children, even foundlings, seems readily explicable. Amid the ravages of epidemics, the sheer numbers of orphans must have multiplied in society. Moreover, the plagues carried off the very young in disproportionate numbers. Parents feared for the survival of their lineages and their communities. . . . The frequent creation of foundling hospitals and orphanages indicates that society as a whole shared this concern and was willing to invest in the survival of its young, even orphans and foundlings.

The medieval social investment in children thus seems to have grown from the twelfth century and to have passed through two phases: the first one, beginning from the twelfth century, largely involved a commitment, on the part of the urban communities, to the child's education and training;

---

[12]Florentine writer, businessman, and statesman, 1362–1435.

the second, from the late fourteenth century, reflected a concern for the child's survival and health under difficult hygienic conditions.

This social investment also presumes an equivalent psychological investment, as well as a heightened attention paid to the child and his development. This is evident, for example, in the rich tradition of pedagogical literature intended for a lay audience, which again dates from the twelfth century. One of the earliest authors to provide a comprehensive regimen of child care was Vincent of Beauvais, who died in 1264. . . . [H]e gives advice on the delivery of the baby; its care in the first hours, days, and months of life; nursing and weaning; the care of older children; and their formal education. Later in the century, Raymond Lull . . . is similarly comprehensive, including passages not only on formal schooling but also on the care and nourishment of the child. "For every man," he explains, "must hold his child dear." . . . The learning of the scholars seems to have spread widely, even among the humble social classes.

These medieval pedagogues also developed a rudimentary but real psychology of children. Vincent of Beauvais recommends that the child who does not readily learn must be beaten, but he warns against the psychological damage which excessive severity may cause. "Children's minds," he explains, "break down under excessive severity of correction; they despair, and worry, and finally they hate. And this is the most injurious; where everything is feared, nothing is attempted." A few teachers . . . wanted to prohibit all corporal punishment at school. For them physical discipline was "contrary to nature"; it "induced servility and sowed resentment, which in later years might make the student hate the teacher and forget his lesson."

The teacher—and on this all writers agree—should be temperate in the use of force, and he should also observe the child, in order to identify his talents and capacities. For not all children are alike, and natural differences must be recognized and developed. Raymond Lull affirms that nature is more capable of rearing the child than the child's mother. The Florentine Giovanni Dominici stresses the necessity of choosing the proper profession for the child. Society, he notes, requires all sorts of occupations and skills, ranging from farmers to carpenters, to bankers, merchants, priests, and "a thousand others." . . .

To read these writers is inevitably to form the impression that medieval people, or some of them at least, were deeply concerned about children. Indeed, Jean Gerson[13] expressly condemns his contemporaries, who, in his opinion, were excessively involved with their children's survival and success. In order to gain for them "the honors and pomp of this world," parents, he alleges, were expending "all their care and attention; they sleep neither day nor night and often become very miserly." In investing in their children, they neglected charitable works and the good of their own souls. . . .

[13]French theologian, 1363–1429.

Medieval society, increasingly dependent upon the cultivation of sophisticated skills, had to invest in a supporting pedagogy; when later threatened by child-killing plagues, it had to show concern for the survival of the very young. But the medieval involvement with children cannot be totally described in these functional terms. Even as they were developing an effective pedagogy, medieval people were re-evaluating the place of childhood among the periods of life.

One indication of a new sympathy toward childhood is the revision in theological opinion concerning the salvation of the babies who died without baptism. Up until the twelfth century, the leading theologians of the Western church . . . reiterated the weighty opinion of St. Augustine, that such infants were surely damned. In the twelfth century, Peter Abelard and Peter Lombard, perhaps the two most influential theologians of the epoch, reversed the condemnation of unbaptized babies to eternal fires. A thorough examination of the question, however, awaited the work of Thomas Aquinas, the first to use in a technical theological sense the term *limbus puerorum*, the "limbo of children." The unbaptized baby, he taught, suffered only the deprivation of the Beatific Vision.[14] . . .

Aquinas' mild judgment on babies dead without baptism became the accepted teaching of the medieval Church. Only one prominent theologian in the late Middle Ages, Gregory of Rimini,[15] resisted it, and he came to be known as the *tortor puerorum*, the "torturer of children."

No less remarkable is the emergence, from the twelfth century, of a widespread devotion to the Child Jesus. The texts from the early Middle Ages which treat of the Christ Child . . . present Christ as a miniature wonder worker, who miraculously corrects Joseph's mistakes in carpentry, tames lions, divides rivers, and even strikes dead a teacher who dared reprimand him in class. All-knowing and all-powerful, he is the negation of the helpless, charming child. A new picture of the Child Jesus emerges, initially under Cistercian auspices, in the twelfth century. For example, between 1153 and 1157 the English Cistercian Aelred of Rievaulx composed a meditation, "Jesus at the Age of Twelve." Aelred expatiates on the joy which the presence of the young Christ brought to his elders and companions: " . . . the grace of heaven shone from that most beautiful face with such charm as to make everyone look at it, listen to him, and be moved to affection. . . . Old men kiss him, young men embrace him, boys wait upon him. . . . Each of them, I think, declares in his inmost heart: 'Let him kiss me with the kiss of his mouth.' " . . .

Doubtlessly, the special characteristics of Cistercian monasticism were influential here. Like other reformed orders of the twelfth century, the Cistercians no longer admitted oblates, the boys placed in the monastery at tender ages, who grew up in the cloister with no experience of secu-

[14]The immediate vision of God in Heaven
[15]d.1358.

lar life. The typical Cistercians . . . were raised within a natural family, and many were familiar with the emotions of family life. Grown men when they entered the monastery, they carried with them a distinct mentality—a mentality formed in the secular world and open to secular values. Many doubtlessly had considered and some had pursued other careers before electing the monastic life; they presumably had reflected upon the emotional and spiritual rewards of the married state and the state of parenthood. While fleeing from the world, they still sought in their religious experiences analogues to secular and familial emotions. . . . In celebrating the joys of contemplating a perfect child, they find in their religious experience an analogue to the love and satisfaction which parents feel in observing their growing children. The Cistercian cult of the Child Jesus suggests, in other words, that lay persons, too, were finding the contemplation of children emotionally rewarding.

In the thirteenth century, devotion to the Child Jesus spread well beyond the restricted circle of Cistercian monasticism. St. Francis of Assisi,[16] according to the *Legenda Gregorii*[17] set up for the first time a Christmas crèche, so that the faithful might more easily envision the tenderness and humility of the new-born Jesus. St. Francis, the most popular saint of the late Middle Ages, was thus responsible, at least in legend, for one of the most popular devotional practices still associated with Christmas. . . .

This cult of the Christ Child implies an idealization of childhood itself. "O sweet and sacred childhood," another Cistercian . . . writes of the early years of Christ, "which brought back man's true innocence, by which men of every age can return to blessed childhood and be conformed to you, not in physical weakness but in humility of heart and holiness of life."

How are we to explain this celebration of "sweet and sacred childhood"? It closely resembles other religious movements which acquire extraordinary appeal from the twelfth century—the cults of poverty, of Christian simplicity, and of the apostolic life. These "movements of cultural primitivism" . . . point to a deepening psychological discontent with the demands of the new commercial economy. The inhabitants of towns in particular, living by trade, were forced into careers of getting and spending, in constant pursuit of what Augustine had called "deceitful riches." The psychological tensions inherent in the urban professions and the dubious value of the proferred material rewards seem to have generated a nostalgic longing for alternate systems of existence, for freedom from material concerns, for the simple Christian life as it was supposedly lived in the apostolic age. Another model for an alternate existence, the exact opposite of the tension-ridden urban experience, was the real or imagined life of the child, who was at once humble and content, poor and pure, joyous and giving joy.

[16]Founder of the Franciscans, c.1182–1226.

[17]*Legends by Gregory.*

The simple piety of childhood remained an ideal of religious reformers for the duration of the Middle Ages. At their close, both Girolamo Savonarola[18] in the south of Europe and Desiderius Erasmus[19] in the north urged their readers to look to pious children if they would find true models of the Christian life. . . .

Moreover, the medieval cult of childhood extends beyond religious movements and informs secular attitudes as well. . . . Later in the Middle Ages, a Florentine citizen and merchant . . . , reflecting on his own life, calls childhood "nature's most pleasant age." In his *Praise of Folly*, Erasmus avers that the simplicity and unpretentiousness of childhood make it the happiest time of life. "Who does not know," Folly asks her audience, "that childhood is the happiest age and the most pleasant for all? What is there about children that makes us kiss and hug them and cuddle them as we do, so that even an enemy would help them, unless it is this charm of folly?" Clearly, we have come far from Augustine's opinion, that men would prefer eternal death to life again as a child.

The history of medieval children is as complex as the history of any social group, and even more elusive. This essay has attempted to describe in broad outline the cultural attitudes which influenced the experiences of medieval children, as well as the large social trends which touched their lives. The central movements which, in this reconstruction, affected their fate were the social and economic changes widely evident across Europe from the twelfth century, most especially the rise of a commercialized economy and the proliferation of special skills within society; and the worsening health conditions of the late Middle Ages, from the second half of the fourteenth century. The growth of a commercialized economy made essential an attentive pedagogy which could provide society with adequately trained adults. And the deteriorating conditions of hygiene across the late Middle Ages heightened the concern for, and investment in, the health and survival of the very young. Paradoxically, too, the growing complexities of social life engendered not truly a discovery but an idealization of childhood: the affirmation of the sentimental belief that childhood is, as Erasmus maintains, a blessed time and the happiest moment of human existence. . . .

[18]Dominican reformer who ruled Florence from 1494 to 1498.
[19]Dutch humanist, c.1466–1536.

Fast, Feast, and Flesh:
The Religious Significance
of Food to Medieval Women

CAROLINE WALKER BYNUM

In this bold essay, Caroline Walker Bynum explores the religious significance of food for medieval women, a subject she believes scholars have ignored in favor of sex and money. Bynum argues that food as a religious symbol was vitally important to medieval people, who wrote often about eating, gluttony, and fasting and related them to God, sin, and salvation. Her evidence comes from the experience of holy women, some of whom became saints, and all of whom were revered by a society disposed to admire severe asceticism. How did male saints compare to female saints in the Middle Ages? What qualities were each sex likely to have?

These holy women usually performed miracles while abstaining from all food save the holy eucharist. They fasted on communion wafers and, as Bynum illustrates through the life of Lidwina of Schiedam, suffered greatly. The stories of her shedding skin, bones, and intestines; her illness; and her desire to take upon herself the suffering of others—all this seems preposterous to a more materialistic twentieth-century culture. Modern medical and psychological categories such as anorexia do not recapture the intense religiosity of the high and late Middle Ages. These holy women did not have a universal psychological ailment; their behavior reflected historical theological doctrines and the position of women in society. What assumptions in medieval theology and culture associated women with food? How did women use food to control themselves and their world? What cultural explanation does Bynum offer in arguing that food was more significant to women than to men?

How did the clergy, exclusively male, feel about the exploits of holy women? These women, supposedly of a lower order of creation than men, taught the dominant sex much through their fasts from worldly food and their feasts of holy food. Of course, priests alone had the miracle-working power to change ordinary bread into the body of Jesus, the only food that could sustain many holy women. Yet Lidwina's eucharistic visions and hunger, as Bynum shows, involved her in conflict with the clergy. Were Lidwina and other saintly women submissive as women were supposed to be? How did the association of submissiveness and weakness with women relate to society's conception of Jesus, of flesh, and of food?

. . . Scholars have recently devoted much attention to the spirituality of the thirteenth, fourteenth, and fifteenth centuries. In studying late medieval spirituality they have concentrated on the ideals of chastity and poverty— that is, on the renunciation, for religious reasons, of sex and family, money and property. It may be, however, that modern scholarship has focused so tenaciously on sex and money because sex and money are such crucial symbols and sources of power in our own culture. Whatever the motives, modern scholars have ignored a religious symbol that had tremendous

163

force in the lives of medieval Christians. They have ignored the religious significance of food. Yet, when we look at what medieval people themselves wrote, we find that they often spoke of gluttony as the major form of lust, of fasting as the most painful renunciation, and of eating as the most basic and literal way of encountering God. Theologians and spiritual directors from the early church to the sixteenth century reminded penitents that sin had entered the world when Eve ate the forbidden fruit and that salvation comes when Christians eat their God in the ritual of the communion table.

In the Europe of the late thirteenth and fourteenth centuries, famine was on the increase again, after several centuries of agricultural growth and relative plenty. Vicious stories of food hoarding, of cannibalism, of infanticide, or of ill adolescents left to die when they could no longer do agricultural labor sometimes survive in the sources, suggesting a world in which hunger and even starvation were not uncommon experiences. The possibility of overeating and of giving away food to the unfortunate was a mark of privilege, of aristocratic or patrician status—a particularly visible form of what we call conspicuous consumption, what medieval people called magnanimity or largesse. Small wonder then that gorging and vomiting, luxuriating in food until food and body were almost synonymous, became in folk literature an image of unbridled sensual pleasure; that magic vessels which forever brim over with food and drink were staples of European folktales; that one of the most common charities enjoined on religious orders was to feed the poor and ill; or that sharing one's own meager food with a stranger (who might turn out to be an angel, a fairy, or Christ himself) was, in hagiography and folk story alike, a standard indication of heroic or saintly generosity. Small wonder too that voluntary starvation, deliberate and extreme renunciation of food and drink, seemed to medieval people the most basic asceticism, requiring the kind of courage and holy foolishness that marked the saints.

Food was not only a fundamental material concern to medieval people; food practices—fasting and feasting—were at the very heart of the Christian tradition. A Christian in the thirteenth and fourteenth centuries was required by church law to fast on certain days and to receive communion at least once a year. Thus the behavior that defined a Christian was food-related behavior. . . .

Food was, moreover, a central metaphor and symbol in Christian poetry, devotional literature, and theology because a meal (the eucharist) was the central Christian ritual, the most direct way of encountering God. And we should note that this meal was a frugal repast, not a banquet but simply the two basic food stuffs of the Mediterranean world: bread and wine. Although older Mediterranean traditions of religious feasting did come, in a peripheral way, into Christianity, indeed lasting right through the Middle Ages in various kinds of carnival, the central religious meal was reception of the two basic supports of human life. Indeed Christians believed it *was* human life. Already hundreds of years before transubstantiation was defined as doctrine, most Christians thought that they quite literally ate Christ's body and blood in the sacrament. . . .

Thus food, as practice and as symbol, was crucial in medieval spirituality. But in the period from 1200 to 1500 it was more prominent in the piety of women than in that of men. . . . Recent work . . . demonstrates that, although women were only about 18 percent of those canonized or revered as saints between 1000 and 1700, they were 30 percent of those in whose lives extreme austerities were a central aspect of holiness and over 50 percent of those in whose lives illness (often brought on by fasting and other penitential practices) was the major factor in reputation for sanctity. In addition, . . . most males who were revered for fasting fit into one model of sanctity—the hermit saint (usually a layman)—and this was hardly the most popular male model, whereas fasting characterized female saints generally. Between late antiquity and the fifteenth century there are at least thirty cases of women who were reputed to eat nothing at all except the eucharist, but I have been able to find only one or possibly two male examples of such behavior before the well-publicized fifteenth-century case of the hermit Nicholas of Flüe.[1] Moreover, miracles in which food is miraculously multiplied are told at least as frequently of women as of men, and giving away food is so common a theme in the lives of holy women that it is very difficult to find a story in which this particular charitable activity does not occur. The story of a woman's basket of bread for the poor turning into roses when her husband (or father) protests her almsgiving was attached by hagiographers to at least five different women saints.

If we look specifically at practices connected with Christianity's holy meal, we find that eucharistic visions and miracles occurred far more frequently to women, particularly certain types of miracles in which the quality of the eucharist as food is underlined. It is far more common, for example, for the wafer to turn into honey or meat in the mouth of a woman. Miracles in which an unconsecrated host is vomited out or in which the recipient can tell by tasting the wafer that the priest who consecrated it is immoral happen almost exclusively to women. Of fifty-five people from the later Middle Ages who supposedly received the holy food directly from Christ's hand in a vision, forty-five are women. In contrast, the only two types of eucharistic miracle that occur primarily to men are miracles that underline not the fact that the wafer is food but the power of the priest. Moreover, when we study medieval miracles, we note that miraculous abstinence and extravagant eucharistic visions tend to occur together and are frequently accompanied by miraculous bodily changes. Such changes are found almost exclusively in women. Miraculous elongation of parts of the body, the appearance on the body of marks imitating the various

[1] Swiss saint, 1417–1487.

wounds of Christ (called stigmata), and the exuding of wondrous fluids (which smell sweet and heal and sometimes *are* food—for example, manna or milk) are usually female miracles.

If we consider a different kind of evidence—the *exempla* or moral tales that preachers used to educate their audiences, both monastic and lay—we find that, according to Frederic Tubach's index [*Index Exemplerum: A Handbook of Religious Tales* (Helsinki 1969)], only about 10 percent of such stories are about women. But when we look at those stories that treat specifically fasting, abstinence, and reception of the eucharist, 30 to 50 percent are about women. The only type of religious literature in which food is more frequently associated with men is the genre of satires on monastic life, in which there is some suggestion that monks are more prone to greed. But this pattern probably reflects the fact that monasteries for men were in general wealthier than women's houses and therefore more capable of mounting elaborate banquets and tempting palates with delicacies.

Taken together, this evidence demonstrates two things. First, food practices were more central in women's piety than in men's. Second, both men and women associated food—especially fasting and the eucharist—with women. There are, however, a number of problems with this sort of evidence. In addition to the obvious problems of the paucity of material and of the nature of hagiographical accounts . . . —there is the problem inherent in quantifying data. In order to count phenomena the historian must divide them up, put them into categories. Yet the most telling argument for the prominence of food in women's spirituality is the way in which food motifs interweave in women's lives and writings until even phenomena not normally thought of as eating, feeding, or fasting seem to become food-related. In other words, food becomes such a pervasive concern that it provides both a literary and a psychological unity to the woman's way of seeing the world. And this cannot be demonstrated by statistics. Let me therefore tell in some detail one of the many stories from the later Middle Ages in which food becomes a leitmotif of stunning complexity and power. It is the story of Lidwina of the town of Schiedam in the Netherlands, who died in 1433 at the age of 53.

Several hagiographical accounts of Lidwina exist, incorporating information provided by her confessors; moreover, the town officials of Schiedam, who had her watched for three months, promulgated a testimonial that suggests that Lidwina's miraculous abstinence attracted more public attention than any other aspect of her life. The document solemnly attests to her complete lack of food and sleep and to the sweet odor given off by the bits of skin she supposedly shed.

The accounts of Lidwina's life suggest that there may have been early conflict between mother and daughter. When her terrible illness put a burden on her family's resources and patience, it took a miracle to convince her mother of her sanctity. One of the few incidents that survives from her childhood shows her mother annoyed with her childish dawdling. Lidwina was required to carry food to her brothers at school, and on the way home she slipped into church to say a prayer to the Virgin. The incident shows how girlish piety could provide a respite from household tasks—in this case, as in so many cases, the task of feeding men. We also learn that Lidwina was upset to discover that she was pretty, that she threatened to pray for a deformity when plans were broached for her marriage, and that, after an illness at age fifteen, she grew weak and did not want to get up from her sickbed. The accounts thus suggest that she may have been cultivating illness—perhaps even rejecting food—before the skating accident some weeks later that produced severe internal injuries. In any event, Lidwina never recovered from her fall on the ice. Her hagiographers report that she was paralyzed except for her left hand. She burned with fever and vomited convulsively. Her body putrified so that great pieces fell off. From mouth, ears, and nose, she poured blood. And she stopped eating.

Lidwina's hagiographers go into considerable detail about her abstinence. At first she supposedly ate a little piece of apple each day, although bread dipped into liquid caused her much pain. Then she reduced her intake to a bit of date and watered wine flavored with spices and sugar; later she survived on watered wine alone—only half a pint a week—and she preferred it when the water came from the river and was contaminated with salt from the tides. When she ceased to take any solid food, she also ceased to sleep. And finally she ceased to swallow anything at all. Although Lidwina's biographers present her abstinence as evidence of saintliness, she was suspected by some during her lifetime of being possessed by a devil instead; she herself appears to have claimed that her fasting was natural. When people accused her of hypocrisy, she replied that it is no sin to eat and therefore no glory to be incapable of eating.

Fasting and illness were thus a single phenomenon to Lidwina. And since she perceived them as redemptive suffering, she urged both on others. We are told that a certain Gerard from Cologne, at her urging, became a hermit and lived in a tree, fed only on manna sent from God. We are also told that Lidwina prayed for her twelve-year-old nephew to be afflicted with an illness so that he would be reminded of God's mercy. Not surprisingly, the illness itself then came from miraculous feeding. The nephew became sick by drinking several drops from a pitcher of unnaturally sweet beer on a table by Lidwina's bedside.

Like the bodies of many other women saints, Lidwina's body was closed to ordinary intake and excreting but produced extraordinary effluvia. The authenticating document from the town officials of Schiedam testifies that her body shed skin, bones, and even portions of intestines, which her parents kept in a vase; and these gave off a sweet odor until Lidwina, worried by the gossip that they excited, insisted that her mother bury them. Moreover, Lidwina's effluvia cured others. A man in England sent for her wash water to cure his ill leg. The sweet smell from her left hand led one of her confessors to confess his own sins. And Lidwina actually nursed others in an act that she herself explicitly saw as a parallel to the Virgin's nursing of Christ.

One Christmas season, so all her biographers tell us, a certain widow Catherine, who took care of her, had a vision that Lidwina's breasts would fill with milk, like Mary's, on the night of the Nativity. When she told Lidwina, Lidwina warned her to prepare herself. Then Lidwina saw a vision of Mary surrounded by a host of female virgins; and the breasts of Mary and of all the company filled with milk, which poured out from their open tunics, filling the sky. When Catherine entered Lidwina's room, Lidwina rubbed her own breast and the milk came out, and Catherine drank three times and was satisfied (nor did she want any corporeal food for many days thereafter). . . .

Lidwina also fed others by charity and by food multiplication miracles. Although she herself did not eat, she charged the widow Catherine to buy fine fish and make fragrant sauces and give these to the poor. The meat and fish she gave as alms sometimes, by a miracle, went much further than anyone had expected. She gave water and wine and money for beer to an epileptic burning with thirst; she sent a whole pork shoulder to a poor man's family; she regularly sent food to poor or sick children, forcing her servants to spend or use for others money or food she would not herself consume. When she shared the wine in her bedside jug with others it seemed inexhaustible. So pleased was God with her charity that he sent her a vision of a heavenly banquet, and the food she had given away was on the table.

Lidwina clearly felt that her suffering was service—that it was one with Christ's suffering and that it therefore substituted for the suffering of others, both their bodily ills and their time in purgatory. Indeed her body quite literally became Christ's macerated and saving flesh, for, like many other female saints, she received stigmata (or so one—but only one—of her hagiographers claims). . . . Her hagiographers state that the fevers she suffered almost daily from 1421 until her death were suffered in order to release souls in purgatory. And we see this notion of substitution reflected quite clearly in the story of a very evil man, in whose stead Lidwina made confession; she then took upon herself his punishment, to the increment of her own bodily anguish. We see substitution of another kind in the story of Lidwina taking over the toothache of a woman who wailed outside her door.

Thus, in Lidwina's story, fasting, illness, suffering, and feeding fuse together. Lidwina becomes the food she rejects. Her body, closed to ordinary intake and excretion but spilling over in milk and sweet putrefaction, becomes the sustenance and the cure—both earthly and heavenly—of her followers. But holy eating is a theme in her story as well. The eucharist is at the core of Lidwina's devotion. During her pathetic final years, when she had almost ceased to swallow, she received frequent communion (indeed as often as every two days). Her biographers claim that, during this period, only the holy food kept her alive. But much of her life was plagued by conflict with the local clergy over her eucharistic visions and hunger. One incident in particular shows not only the centrality of Christ's body as food in Lidwina's spirituality but also the way in which a woman's craving for the host, although it kept her under the control of the clergy, could seem to that same clergy a threat, both because it criticized their behavior and because, if thwarted, it could bypass their power.

Once an angel came to Lidwina and warned her that the priest would, the next day, bring her an unconsecrated host to test her. When the priest came and pretended to adore the host, Lidwina vomited it out and said that she could easily tell our Lord's body from unconsecrated bread. But the priest swore that the host was consecrated and returned, angry, to the church. Lidwina then languished for a long time, craving communion but unable to receive it. About three and a half months later, Christ appeared to her, first as a baby, then as a bleeding and suffering youth. Angels appeared, bearing the instruments of the passion, and (according to one account) rays from Christ's wounded body pierced Lidwina with stigmata. When she subsequently asked for a sign, a host hovered over Christ's head and a napkin descended onto her bed, containing a miraculous host, which remained and was seen by many people for days after. The priest returned and ordered Lidwina to keep quiet about the miracle but finally agreed, at her insistence, to feed her the miraculous host as communion. Lidwina was convinced that it was truly Christ because she, who was usually stifled by food, ate this bread without pain. The next day the priest preached in church that Lidwina was deluded and that her host was a fraud of the devil. But, he claimed, Christ was present in the bread he offered because it was consecrated with all the majesty of the priesthood. Lidwina protested his interpretation of her host, but she agreed to accept a consecrated wafer from him and to pray for his sins. Subsequently the priest claimed that he had cured Lidwina from possession by the devil, while Lidwina's supporters called her host a miracle. Although Lidwina's hagiographers do not give full details, they claim that the bishop came to investigate the matter, that he blessed the napkin for the service of the altar, and that the priest henceforth gave Lidwina the sacrament without tests or resistance.

As this story worked its way out, its theme was not subversive of clerical authority. The conflict began, after all, because Lidwina wanted a consecrated host, and it resulted in her receiving frequent communion, in humility and piety. According to one of her hagiographers, the moral of the story is that the faithful can always substitute "spiritual communion" (i.e., meditation) if the actual host is not given. But the story had radical implications as well. It suggested that Jesus might come directly to the faithful if priests were negligent or skeptical, that a priest's word might not be authoritative on the difference between demonic possession and sanctity, that visionary women might test priests. Other stories in Lidwina's life had similar implications. She forbade a sinning priest to celebrate mass; she read the heart of another priest and learned of his adultery. Her visions of souls in purgatory especially concerned priests, and she substituted her sufferings for theirs. One Ash Wednesday an angel came to bring ashes for her forehead before the priest arrived. Even if Lidwina did not reject the clergy, she sometimes quietly bypassed or judged them.

Lidwina focused her love of God on the eucharist. In receiving it, in vision and in communion, she became one with the body on the cross. Eating her God, she received his wounds and offered her suffering for the salvation of the world. Denying herself ordinary food, she sent that food to others, and her body gave milk to nurse her friends. Food is the basic theme in Lidwina's story: self as food and God as food. For Lidwina, therefore, eating and not-eating were finally one theme. To fast, that is, to deny oneself earthly food, and yet to eat the broken body of Christ—both acts were to suffer. And to suffer was to save and to be saved.

Lidwina did not write herself, but some pious women did. And many of these women not only lived lives in which miraculous abstinence, charitable feeding of others, wondrous bodily changes, and eucharistic devotion were central; they also elaborated in prose and poetry a spirituality in which hungering, feeding, and eating were central metaphors for suffering, for service, and for encounter with God. For example, the great Italian theorist of purgatory, Catherine of Genoa (d. 1510)—whose extreme abstinence began in response to an unhappy marriage and who eventually persuaded her husband to join her in a life of continence and charitable feeding of the poor and sick—said that the annihilation of ordinary food by a devouring body is the best metaphor for the annihilation of the soul by God in mystical ecstasy. She also wrote that, although no simile can adequately convey the joy in God that is the goal of all souls, nonetheless the image that comes most readily to mind is to describe God as the only bread available in a world of the starving. Another Italian Catherine, Catherine of Siena (d. 1380), in whose saintly reputation fasting, food miracles, eucharistic devotion, and (invisible) stigmata were central, regularly chose to describe Christian duty as "eating at the table of the cross the food of the honor of God and the salvation of souls." To Catherine, "to eat" and "to hunger" have the same fundamental meaning, for one eats but is never full, desires but is never satiated. "Eating" and "hungering" are active, not passive, images. They stress pain more than joy. They mean most basically to suffer and to serve—to suffer because in hunger one joins with Christ's suffering on the cross; to serve because to hunger is to expiate the sins of the world. Catherine wrote:

> And then the soul becomes drunk. And after it . . . has reached the place [of the teaching of the crucified Christ] and drunk to the full, it tastes the food of

patience, the odor of virtue, and such a desire to bear the cross that it does not seem that it could ever be satiated. . . . And then the soul becomes like a drunken man; the more he drinks the more he wants to drink; the more it bears the cross the more it wants to bear it. And the pains are its refreshment and the tears which it has shed for the memory of the blood are its drink. And the sighs are its food.

. . . To the stories and writings of Lidwina and the two Catherines—with their insistent and complex food motifs—I could add dozens of others. Among the most obvious examples would be the beguine Mary of Oignies (d. 1213) from the Low Countries, the princess Elisabeth of Hungary (d. 1231), the famous reformer of French and Flemish religious houses Colette of Corbie (d. 1447), and the thirteenth-century poets Hadewijch and Mechtild of Magdeburg. But if we look closely at the lives and writings of those men from the period whose spirituality is in general closest to women's and who were deeply influenced by women—for example, Francis of Assisi[2] in Italy, Henry Suso[3] and Johann Tauler[4] in the Rhineland, Jan van Ruysbroeck[5] of Flanders, or the English hermit Richard Rolle[6]—we find that even to these men food asceticism is not the central ascetic practice. Nor are food metaphors central in their poetry and prose. Food then is much more important to women than to men as a religious symbol. The question is why?

Modern scholars who have noticed the phenomena I have just described have sometimes suggested in an offhand way that miraculous abstinence and eucharistic frenzy are simply "eating disorders." The implication of such remarks is usually that food disorders are characteristic of women rather than men, perhaps for biological reasons, and that these medieval eating disorders are different from nineteenth- and twentieth-century ones only because medieval people "theologized" what we today "medicalize." While I cannot deal here with all the implications of such analysis, I want to point to two problems with it. First, the evidence we have indicates that extended abstinence was almost exclusively a male phenomenon in early Christianity and a female phenomenon in the high Middle Ages. The cause of such a distribution of cases cannot be primarily biological. Second, medieval people did not treat all refusal to eat as a sign of holiness. They sometimes treated it as demonic possession, but they sometimes also treated it as illness. Interestingly enough, some of the holy women whose fasting was taken as miraculous (for example, Colette of Corbie) functioned as healers of ordinary individuals, both male and female, who could not eat. Thus, for most of the Middle Ages, it was only

[2]Founder of the Franciscans, c.1182–1226.

[3]German mystic, c.1295–1336.

[4]German mystic, c.1300–1361.

[5]Flemish mystic, 1293–1381.

[6]Mystic, c.1300–1349.

in the case of some unusually devout women that not-eating was both supposedly total and religiously significant. Such behavior must have a cultural explanation.

On one level, the cultural explanation is obvious. Food was important to women religiously because it was important socially. In medieval Europe (as in many countries today) women were associated with food preparation and distribution *rather than* food consumption. The culture suggested that women cook and serve, men eat. Chronicle accounts of medieval banquets, for example, indicate that the sexes were often segregated and that women were sometimes relegated to watching from the balconies while gorgeous foods were rolled out to please the eyes as well as the palates of men. Indeed men were rather afraid of women's control of food. Canon lawyers suggested, in the codes they drew up, that a major danger posed by women was their manipulation of male virility by charms and potions added to food. Moreover, food was not merely *a* resource women controlled; it was *the* resource women controlled. Economic resources were controlled by husbands, fathers, uncles, or brothers. In an obvious sense, therefore, fasting and charitable food distribution (and their miraculous counterparts) were natural religious activities for women. In fasting and charity women renounced and distributed the one resource that was theirs. Several scholars have pointed out that late twelfth- and early thirteenth-century women who wished to follow the new ideal of poverty and begging . . . were simply not permitted either by their families or by religious authorities to do so. They substituted fasting for other ways of stripping the self of support. Indeed a thirteenth-century hagiographer commented explicitly that one holy woman gave up food because she had nothing else to give up. Between the thirteenth and fifteenth centuries, many devout laywomen who resided in the homes of fathers or spouses were able to renounce the world in the midst of abundance because they did not eat or drink the food that was paid for by family wealth. Moreover, women's almsgiving and abstinence appeared culturally acceptable forms of asceticism because what women ordinarily did, as housewives, mothers, or mistresses of great castles, was to prepare and serve food rather than to eat it.

The issue of control is, however, more basic than this analysis suggests. Food-related behavior was central to women socially and religiously not only because food was a resource women controlled but also because, by means of food, women controlled themselves and their world.

First and most obviously, women controlled their bodies by fasting. Although a negative or dualist concept of body does not seem to have been the most fundamental notion of body to either women or men, some sense that body was to be disciplined, defeated, occasionally even destroyed, in order to release or protect spirit is present in women's piety. Some holy women seem to have developed an extravagant fear of any bodily contact. Clare of Montefalco (d. 1308), for example, said she would rather spend days in hell than be touched by a man. Lutgard of Aywières[7] panicked at an abbot's insistence on giving her the kiss of peace, and Jesus had to interpose his hand in a vision so that she was not reached by the abbot's lips. She even asked to have her own gift of healing by touch taken away. Christina of Stommeln (d. 1312), who fell into a latrine while in a trance, was furious at the laybrothers who rescued her because they touched her in order to do so.

Many women were profoundly fearful of the sensations of their bodies, especially hunger and thirst. Mary of Oignies, for example, was so afraid of taking pleasure in food that Christ had to make her unable to taste. From the late twelfth century comes a sad story of a dreadfully sick girl named Alpaïs who sent away the few morsels of pork given her to suck, because she feared that any enjoyment of eating might mushroom madly into gluttony or lust. Women like Ida of Louvain (d. perhaps 1300), Elsbeth Achler of Reute (d. 1420), Catherine of Genoa, or Columba of Rieti (d. 1501), who sometimes snatched up food and ate without knowing what they were doing, focused their hunger on the eucharist partly because it was an acceptable object of craving and partly because it was a self-limiting food. Some of women's asceticism was clearly directed toward destroying bodily needs, before which women felt vulnerable.

Some fasting may have had as a goal other sorts of bodily control. There is some suggestion in the accounts of hagiographers that fasting women were admired for suppressing excretory functions. Several biographers comment with approval that holy women who do not eat cease also to excrete, and several point out explicitly that the menstruation of saintly women ceases. Medieval theology—profoundly ambivalent about body as physicality—was ambivalent about menstruation also, seeing it both as the polluting "curse of Eve" and as a natural function that, like all natural functions, was redeemed in the humanity of Christ. Theologians even debated whether or not the Virgin Mary menstruated. But natural philosophers and theologians were aware that, in fact, fasting suppresses menstruation....

Moreover, in controlling eating and hunger, medieval women were also explicitly controlling sexuality. Ever since Tertullian[8] and Jerome,[9] male writers had warned religious women that food was dangerous because it excited lust. Although there is reason to suspect that male biographers exaggerated women's sexual temptations, some women themselves connected food abstinence with chastity and greed with sexual desire.

Women's heightened reaction to food, however, controlled far more than their physicality. It also controlled their social environment. As the story of Lidwina of Schiedam makes clear, women often coerced both fam-

[7]Benedictine nun and mystic, 1182–1246.
[8]Christian theologian, c.160–c.230.
[9]Christian theologian and translator of the Bible, c.347–420.

ilies and religious authorities through fasting and through feeding. To an aristocratic or rising merchant family of late medieval Europe, the self-starvation of a daughter or spouse could be deeply perplexing and humiliating. It could therefore be an effective means of manipulating, educating, or converting family members. In one of the most charming passages of Margery Kempe's[10] autobiography, for example, Christ and Margery consult together about her asceticism and decide that, although she wishes to practice both food abstention and sexual continence, she should perhaps offer to trade one behavior for the other. Her husband, who had married Margery in an effort to rise socially in the town of Lynn and who was obviously ashamed of her queer penitential clothes and food practices, finally agreed to grant her sexual abstinence in private if she would return to normal cooking and eating in front of the neighbors. Catherine of Siena's sister, Bonaventura, and the Italian saint Rita of Cascia (d. 1456) both reacted to profligate young husbands by wasting away and managed thereby to tame disorderly male behavior. Columba of Rieti and Catherine of Siena expressed what was clearly adolescent conflict with their mothers and riveted family attention on their every move by their refusal to eat. Since fasting so successfully manipulated and embarrassed families, it is not surprising that self-starvation often originated or escalated at puberty, the moment at which families usually began negotiations for husbands for their daughters. Both Catherine and Columba, for example, established themselves as unpromising marital material by their extreme food and sleep deprivation, their frenetic giving away of paternal resources, and their compulsive service of family members in what were not necessarily welcome ways. (Catherine insisted on doing the family laundry in the middle of the night.)

Fasting was not only a useful weapon in the battle of adolescent girls to change their families' plans for them. It also provided for both wives and daughters an excuse for neglecting food preparation and family responsibilities. . . . Margaret of Cortona[11] refused to cook for her illegitimate son (about whom she felt agonizing ambivalence) because, she said, it would distract her from prayer.

Moreover, women clearly both influenced and rejected their families' values by food distribution. Ida of Louvain, Catherine of Siena, and Elisabeth of Hungary, each in her own way, expressed distaste for family wealth and coopted the entire household into Christian charity by giving away family resources, sometimes surreptitiously or even at night. Elisabeth, who gave away her husband's property, refused to eat any food except that paid for by her own dowry because the wealth of her husband's family came, she said, from exploiting the poor.

---

[10]Mystic and author of the first autobiography in English, c.1373–c.1433.

[11]Italian saint, c.1247–1297.

Food-related behavior—charity, fasting, eucharistic devotion, and miracles—manipulated religious authorities as well. Women's eucharistic miracles—especially the ability to identify unconsecrated hosts or unchaste priests—functioned to expose and castigate clerical corruption. The Viennese woman Agnes Blannbekin,[12] knowing that her priest was not chaste, prayed that he be deprived of the host, which then flew away from him and into her own mouth. Margaret of Cortona saw the hands of an unchaste priest turn black when he held the host. Saints' lives and chronicles contain many stories, like that told of Lidwina of Schiedam, of women who vomited out unconsecrated wafers, sometimes to the considerable discomfiture of local authorities.

The intimate and direct relationship that holy women claimed to the eucharist was often a way of bypassing ecclesiastical control. Late medieval confessors and theologians attempted to inculcate awe as well as craving for the eucharist; and women not only received ambiguous advice about frequent communion, they were also sometimes barred from receiving it at exactly the point at which their fasting and hunger reached fever pitch. In such circumstances many women simply received in vision what the celebrant or confessor withheld. Imelda Lambertini,[13] denied communion because she was too young, and Ida of Léau,[14] denied because she was subject to "fits," were given the host by Christ. And some women received, again in visions, either Christ's blood, which they were regularly denied because of their lay status, or the power to consecrate and distribute, which they were denied because of their gender. Angela of Foligno[15] and Mechtild of Hackeborn[16] were each in a vision given the chalice to distribute. Catherine of Siena received blood in her mouth when she ate the wafer.

It is thus apparent that women's concentration on food enabled them to control and manipulate both their bodies and their environment. We must not underestimate the effectiveness of such manipulation in a world where it was often extraordinarily difficult for women to avoid marriage or to choose a religious vocation. But such a conclusion concentrates on the function of fasting and feasting, and function is not meaning. Food did not "mean" to medieval women the control it provided. It is time, finally, to consider explicitly what it meant.

As the behavior of Lidwina of Schiedam or the theological insights of Catherine of Siena suggest, fasting, eating, and feeding all meant suffering, and suffering meant redemption. These complex meanings were embedded in and engendered by the theological doctrine of the Incarnation.

[12]Nun, d.1315.

[13]Italian, 1322–1333.

[14]Belgian mystic, d. c.1260.

[15]Italian Franciscan tertiary of the late thirteenth century (d.1309).

[16]German nun (d.1298 or 1299) of the convent of Helfta.

Late medieval theology . . . located the saving moment of Christian history less in Christ's resurrection than in his crucifixion. Although some ambivalence about physicality, some sharp and agonized dualism, was present, no other period in the history of Christian spirituality has placed so positive a value on Christ's humanity as physicality. Fasting was thus flight not so much *from* as *into* physicality. Communion was consuming—i.e., becoming—a God who saved the world through physical, human agony. Food to medieval women meant flesh and suffering and, through suffering, salvation: salvation of self and salvation of neighbor. Although all thirteenth and fourteenth-century Christians emphasized Christ as suffering and Christ's suffering body as food, women were especially drawn to such a devotional emphasis. The reason seems to lie in the way in which late medieval culture understood "the female."

Drawing on traditions that went back even before the origins of Christianity, both men and women in the later Middle Ages argued that "woman is to man as matter is to spirit." Thus "woman" or "the feminine" was seen as symbolizing the physical part of human nature, whereas man symbolized the spiritual or rational. Male theologians and biographers of women frequently used this idea to comment on female weakness. They also inverted the image and saw "woman" as not merely below but also above reason. Thus they somewhat sentimentally saw Mary's love for souls and her mercy toward even the wicked as an apotheosis of female unreason and weakness, and they frequently used female images to describe themselves in their dependence on God. Women writers, equally aware of the male/female dichotomy, saw it somewhat differently. They tended to use the notion of "the female" as "flesh" to associate Christ's humanity with "the female" and therefore to suggest that women imitate Christ through physicality.

Women theologians saw "woman" as the symbol of humanity, where humanity was understood as including bodiliness. To the twelfth-century prophet, Elisabeth of Schönau,[17] the humanity of Christ appeared in a vision as a female virgin. To Hildegard of Bingen (d. 1179), "woman" was the symbol of humankind, fallen in Eve, restored in Mary and church. She stated explicitly: "Man signifies the divinity of the Son of God and woman his humanity." Moreover, to a number of women writers, Mary was the source and container of Christ's physicality; the flesh Christ put on was in some sense female, because it was his mother's. Indeed whatever physiological theory of reproduction a medieval theologian held, Christ (who had no human father) had to be seen as taking his physicality from his mother. Mechtild of Magdeburg went further and implied that Mary was a kind of preexistent humanity of Christ as the Logos[18] was his preexis-

---

[17] German mystic and Benedictine nun, 1129–1164.

[18] In Christian theology, the Word—that is, Christ as God.

tent divinity. Marguerite of Oingt,[19] like Hildegard of Bingen, wrote that Mary was the *tunica humanitatis*, the clothing of humanity, that Christ puts on. And to Julian Norwich,[20] God himself was a mother exactly in that of our humanity in its full physicality was not merely loved and saved but even given being by and from him. . . . Although male writers were apt to see God's motherhood in his nursing and loving rather than in the fact of creation, they too associated the flesh of Christ with Mary and therefore with woman.

Not only did medieval people associate humanity as body with woman; they also associated woman's body with food. Woman was food because breast milk was the human being's first nourishment—the one food essential for survival. Late medieval culture was extraordinarily concerned with milk as symbol. Writers and artists were fond of the theme, borrowed from antiquity, of lactation offered to a father or other adult male as an act of filial piety. The cult of the Virgin's milk was one of the most extensive cults in late medieval Europe. A favorite motif in art was the lactating Virgin. Even the bodies of evil women were seen as food. Witches were supposed to have queer marks on their bodies (sort of supernumerary breasts) from which they nursed incubi.[21]

Quite naturally, male and female writers used nursing imagery in somewhat different ways. Men were more likely to use images of being nursed, women metaphors of nursing. Thus when male writers spoke of God's motherhood, they focused more narrowly on the soul being nursed at Christ's breast, whereas women were apt to associate mothering with punishing, educating, or giving birth as well. Most visions of drinking from the breast of Mary were received by men. In contrast, women (like Lidwina) often identified with Mary as she nursed Jesus or received visions of taking the Christchild to their own breasts. Both men and women, however, drank from the breast of Christ, in vision and image. Both men and women wove together—from Pauline references to milk and meat and from the rich breast and food images of the Song of Songs—a complex sense of Christ's blood as the nourishment and intoxication of the soul. Both men and women therefore saw the body on the cross, which in dying fed the world, as in some sense female. Again, physiological theory reinforced image. For, to medieval natural philosophers, breast milk was transmuted blood, and a human mother (like the pelican that also symbolized Christ) fed her children from the fluid of life that coursed through her veins.

Since Christ's body itself was a body that nursed the hungry, both men and women naturally assimilated the ordinary female body to it. A

---

[19]French nun, d.1310.

[20]English mystic, c.1342–1413, sometimes called Dame Juliana.

[21]Demons who have sexual intercourse with sleeping women.

number of stories are told of female saints who exuded holy fluid from breasts or fingertips, either during life or after death. These fluids often cured the sick. The union of mouth to mouth, which many women gained with Christ, became also a way of feeding. Lutgard's saliva cured the ill; Lukardis of Oberweimar (d. 1309) blew the eucharist into another nun's mouth; Colette of Corbie regularly cured others with crumbs she chewed. Indeed one suspects that stigmata—so overwhelmingly a female phenomenon—appeared on women's bodies because they (like the marks on the bodies of witches and the wounds in the body of Christ) were not merely wounds but also breasts.

Thus many assumptions in the theology and the culture of late medieval Europe associated woman with flesh and with food. But the same theology also taught that the redemption of all humanity lay in the fact that Christ was flesh and food. A God who fed his children from his own body, a God whose humanity *was* his children's humanity, was a God with whom women found it easy to identify. In mystical ecstasy as in communion, women ate and became a God who was food and flesh. And in eating a God whose flesh was holy food, women both transcended and became more fully the flesh and the food their own bodies were.

Eucharist and mystical union were, for women, both reversals and continuations of all the culture saw them to be. In one sense, the roles of priest and lay recipient reversed normal social roles. The priest became the food preparer, the generator and server of food. The woman recipient ate a holy food she did not exude or prepare. Woman's jubilant, vision-inducing, inebriated eating of God was the opposite of the ordinary female acts of food preparation or of bearing and nursing children. But in another and, I think, deeper sense, the eating was not a reversal at all. Women became, in mystical eating, a fuller version of the food and the flesh they were assumed by their culture to be. In union with Christ, woman became a fully fleshly and feeding self—at one with the generative suffering of God.

Symbol does not determine behavior. Women's imitation of Christ, their assimilation to the suffering and feeding body on the cross, was not uniform. Although most religious women seem to have understood their devotional practice as in some sense serving as well as suffering, they acted in very different ways. Some, like Catherine of Genoa and Elisabeth of Hungary, expressed their piety in feeding and caring for the poor. Some . . . lay rapt in mystical contemplation as their own bodies decayed in disease or in self-induced starvation that was offered for the salvation of others. Many, like Lidwina of Schiedam and Catherine of Siena, did both. Some of these women are, to our modern eyes, pathological and pathetic. Others seem to us, as they did to their contemporaries, magnificent. But they all dealt, in feast and fast, with certain fundamental realities for which all cultures must find symbols—the realities of suffering and the realities of service and generativity.

Vendetta and Civil Disorder in 'Late Medieval Ghent

DAVID NICHOLAS

Faced with plague, warfare, and economic depression, fourteenth-century cities were hotbeds of social antagonisms and daily violence. Ghent, the greatest city of Flanders, in present-day Belgium, provides a case study for an understanding of late medieval criminality, the underside of urban life.

Unlike most historians who have studied revolts and discontent in medieval cities, David Nicholas eschews class struggle as the source of medieval troubles with law and order and instead focuses on family life. He offers a cogent argument that family relationships explain the proliferation of feuds and thus of beatings, mutilations, and homicides. Moreover, the families involved included not only the nuclear unit of parents and children, but also grandparents, uncles, and cousins—not to mention the dozens of clients, retainers who wore the colors of and bore arms for the wealthy families that plagued Ghent with their violent and bloody ways.

The family was the only unit that could provide adequate protection against personal attack in Ghent. When it came to homicide, the city government sought to arbitrate rather than to punish. We are far from the modern notion that the state bears the primary responsibility for the protection of its citizens. Fourteenth-century Ghent had a relatively weak government but a strong family structure, rather than the opposite situation in existence today.

What exactly did the government of Ghent do to curb violence? How did the principle of collective responsibility serve to restrain family members from committing crimes and to resolve feuds already begun? What notions of honor and morality contributed to the bloodletting that often characterized interfamily relations? How did the blood price function? How does Philip van Artevelde's scheme of revenge illustrate the familial and urban ethos of late medieval Ghent?

Western Europe underwent a social and economic upheaval in the late Middle Ages. In the late thirteenth or early fourteenth century, population virtually everywhere reached levels that could only be supported with difficulty. Death rates were high even before the famines and plagues that visited Europe with numbing regularity began about 1310; beginning with the "Black Death" of 1348–1349, mortality became catastrophic. Faced with shrinking markets, the occupational guilds in the cities began restricting the entry of persons who were not kinspeople of masters [fully trained and enfranchised members of the organization]. The cities were filled with unskilled workers, many of them recent immigrants, who could not join guilds and were unable to find steady work.

The classic situation of the rich getting richer while the poor got poorer is found in virtually all major cities. There was a dramatic increase in the extent of unemployment and poor relief. Most towns began providing assistance to churches, hospitals, orphanages, and parish organizations for poor relief in the fourteenth century. Yet the virtually constant threat of war and the fiscal demands of the territorial princes forced city governments to spend such enormous amounts of money on fortifications and weaponry that their domestic spending was severely limited. Much of what they did spend went into pageantry and building.

It thus comes as no surprise to learn that most late medieval cities were extremely violent and dangerous places. Studies of such diverse places as Siena, Venice, Florence, Oxford, and Paris have shown a desensitizing succession of street wars, gang rapes, individual sexual assaults, and fights that could erupt for anything from a misinterpreted stare to a personal insult. A brawl began at Ghent when one young man, accompanied by a band of his friends, called mockingly to the leader of another group across the square "Tra la la la la, Parijs [the man's family name] has a long cock."

Most historians have interpreted this urban violence as a reflection of class struggle: the unemployed fought the employed, and poorer crafts fought wealthy guilds for political power. But recent studies of family bonds have shown that economic rivalries were supplemented virtually everywhere, and in some places were actually less important as causes of violence than powerful families and their clienteles. An offense to any member of the family, including affines [in-laws] in most cities, could lead to bloodshed and vendettas that could involve non-combatants on both sides and might last for many years. Family alliances created a maze of patronage and influence from which few could escape.

Flanders, the most densely urbanized part of northwestern Europe, offers a particularly instructive example of late medieval urban problems. The Flemish cities based their prosperity on manufacturing luxurious woolen textiles, but they had to import most of their food from France and the finer wools for their cloth from England. In addition, the counts of Flanders were Frenchmen who were often at odds with their subjects, most of whom spoke a dialect of Dutch. As political hostilities deepened in the thirteenth century between Flanders' major suppliers, France and England, the Flemish textile industry began to decline, and parties formed in the major cities.

Ghent, the metropolis of Flanders, was the second largest (after Paris) city of northern Europe in the fourteenth century. Its records provide a superb case study of the vital importance of the vendetta in exacerbating urban violence. It had a population of perhaps 80,000 around 1300 but had declined to 30,000 by 1390 after a century of plagues, foreign and civil wars, and decline of its textile industry. The city was racked by the feuds of powerful extended families that the government had little power to curb. The city was governed by two councils of thirteen members who were chosen after 1360 on the basis of guild affiliation. One council functioned as Justices of the Peace. The Justices held mass trial days several times a year where uncontested cases of slander and petty violence involving minimal bloodshed were judged and punished. The Justices sent the miscreants on pilgrimages and awarded personal damages in most of these cases, usually acting on the basis of the prior rulings of arbitrators who had been agreed upon by the parties. Between 1350 and 1379, the Justices handled an average of 151 cases a year, but the problem of crime was worsening: the average in the 1370s was 185, and by 1370 the population of Ghent was only about three-fifths of its level of 1350. Fewer people were responsible for more violent deeds.

For a population the size of Ghent's, these figures are not large, but the convictions at the trial days of the Justices of the Peace are only a part of the larger pattern of violent behavior. The aldermen, who constituted the higher of the two councils, tried criminal cases in which the facts were disputed, but the records of these actions have not survived. The prince, the count of Flanders, also appointed a bailiff to assist the aldermen in keeping order. He had a miniscule staff, consisting of a deputy bailiff and four sergeants. By the fourteenth century the only arrests that the bailiff could make on his own authority were in cases of thieves caught in the act, homicide, and assault so serious that it might eventually result in a death. For all other crimes, he could make arrests only in the presence of the aldermen. He could put citizens on trial only before the aldermen, who had the right to release any culprit whom he had arrested.

Thus the bailiff of Ghent handled mainly cases involving transients and citizens whom the town fathers did not care to protect. The bailiff had jurisdiction outside the city as well as within the walls, but even there he could not try people of Ghent unless the aldermen agreed. In 1373 the bailiff of Eeklo, a small town northwest of Ghent, reported that "several burghers of Ghent, together with others who were not burghers, came into Eeklo and hit and slashed at Henry de Ketelboetere's house during the day. On this account the bailiff conducted an inquest with the aldermen to have justice for the misdeed." The culprits apparently went unpunished. The next year the victimized men of Eeklo retaliated against them. This attack was handled by arbitration at Ghent, to the considerable advantage of the Ghent citizens.

Although the bailiff and the town government had some quarrels over jurisdiction, relations between them were generally correct. The bailiffs had to render trimesterly accounts to the counts, and these include the emoluments of justice. Between 1373 and 1378, when complete records survive, they handled an average of 158 cases a year that in principle should have been heard by the aldermen, but most of these actions did not come to formal trial. Rather, the bailiffs exacted a fine, called "composition," before they would release suspects whom they thought that the aldermen would not convict, and they were brazen enough to state this as their reason. In 1373 the bailiff of Ghent released a man whose guilt was undeniable because "he thought he would not get anything through the court, so he made peace for lack of a better alternative."

In addition to functioning as judges in formal trials, both the Justices and the aldermen could act as arbitrators whenever the parties to a legal action agreed to it. More often, private citizens, usually members of the families of the two protagonists, served as arbitrators. The aldermen could try homicide cases. The Justices of the Peace could not, but they had the duty of arranging arbitration between sets of kindred who wanted to avoid having one of their number go to trial. The city's constitution of 1191 made homicide a capital offense, but there was no *ex officio* prosecution: someone had to press charges before the aldermen would intervene and hold a formal trial. Thus most homicides in Ghent were settled by private arrangements between extended families, rather than in trials. In modern terms, such cases were torts rather than crimes. Between 1350 and 1380 the deaths of 725 persons were atoned by arbitration, an annual average of twenty-four per year. Most of these were cases in which multiple homicides and other acts of original and retaliatory bloodletting were settled as part of a general peace settlement between "kinsmen and friends."

How did this state of affairs come about? Why did the magistrates not intervene directly more often, despite the limitation of the law of 1191, forcing the parties into trials? How did the extended families gain such power? For what ends did they exercise it? The answers to these questions will reveal the forces of order in Ghent negotiating a delicate course between the Scylla of chaos and the Charybdis of savagery.[1]

First, the rivalry between the English and French parties in Flanders contributed to but did not cause this dangerous situation. Matters reached a crisis in the struggles between the Flemish count Guy of Dampierre (ruled 1278–1305) and his feudal overlord, King Philip IV (1285–1314) of France, who hoped to annex Flanders. Parties called "Claws" (for the lion on the Flemish counts' coat of arms) and "Lilies" for the French fleur-de-lys formed in the Flemish cities. Although most aristocratic families were Lilies, some became Claws, usually because their rivals within the ruling group were not.

A particularly flagrant example of a feud that assumed political overtones after beginning as a family struggle racked Ghent between 1294 and 1306. Two ancient lineages, the Borluuts and the van Sint Baafs, were already enemies when John Borluut the younger answered a verbal slight by striking a kinsman of Matthew van Sint Baafs, the rival patriarch. His act broke the existing truce between their families, and the aldermen exiled him. Before he left, he took a gang at night to the abbey village of Saint Bavo, where his rivals had property and clients, and butchered several people in a fight in which the Borluut forces outnumbered their rivals by at least three to one. While in exile, he remained in touch with his ally, Peter de Visschere, brother of the abbot of St. Peter's, the great rival of Saint

---

[1]In Greek mythology, Scylla was a sea monster and Charybdis a whirlpool. They assumed positions on opposite sides of the straits of Messina, and sailors who tried to avoid the one fell victim to the other. (Author's note.)

Bavo. Alerting each other to movements of enemies, the pair engineered several more homicides and mutilations by stealth. In one of these cases, a servant of the van Sint Baafs had his hands and feet hacked off before expiring from his injuries. Peter de Visschere was finally killed during a brief truce in 1296 by a van Sint Baaf ally, in a brawl that erupted when the men of both sides came to a funeral with knives concealed under their coats. Borluut then returned in disguise and used the shelter of St. Peter's abbey to avenge his friend by murdering two more people, one by a knife thrust in the back.

The personal feud between the van Sint Baafs and Borluuts corresponded to a political stance: the Borluuts were Claws, while the van Sint Baafs, who were more closely associated with the older patrician ruling element of Ghent, were Lilies. When Count Guy in 1297 ordered the Lily patricians arrested, the van Sint Baafs had to flee the city. They returned in 1300, when French troops occupied Flanders and installed Lily governments in the cities. The French were in serious trouble elsewhere in Flanders by the spring of 1302, but they held out at Ghent. When Courtrai, a town south of Ghent, joined the Claws, John Borluut came there from exile and sent word that men of Ghent who wanted to fight against the French invasion could join him. The government of Ghent did not send the city militia to fight at the battle at Courtrai, where a crushing defeat was administered to the French on July 11, 1302, but Borluut's contingent of guildsmen and Claw patricians did so. The Lily regime at Ghent was quickly ended, and Borluut was acclaimed as a hero. He was the first but not the last mass murderer who has become a hero of the Ghent working classes through the sheer accident that his pursuit of family goals forced him to seek allies with the guildsmen who were outside the governing elite.

When the Lilies were again repatriated in 1305, the van Sint Baafs returned to Ghent. The son of the murdered bailiff of 1296, now an adult and taught to seek revenge, stalked John Borluut. He failed in two attempts on his life but finally knifed him as he left a drinking bout at the town hall in December 1305. By this time the families were ready to hold a peace conference. The result of the nine homicides and countless mutilations and injuries was twenty-seven pilgrimages and damage assessments that nearly cancelled out between the sides.

Several protagonists in the Borluut–van Sint Baafs feud served on the town council and used their positions in the government to further their families' interests. Yet there is considerable evidence that however readily the magistrates would rush to the defense of one of their own relatives, most of them saw in principle the need to contain family violence. The endemic disorder in Ghent was not caused by an abdication of responsibility, but rather by legal limitations on the magistrates' power and by an ethic that saw bloodletting to avenge family injuries not as a mere right, but as a moral obligation.

The vendetta was thus as alive in Flanders in 1360 as it had been in 960. Although no formal *wergeld* scales [blood price listed in Germanic law codes to compensate the homicide victim's kindred] survive this late, an enormous sum was paid to the males of the clan for their slaughtered brother. Homicide, as an affair of honor, did not involve women as principals and only rarely as victims. The most important determinant of the blood price was clearly the wealth or social standing of the deceased; there is no evidence that the status of the killer had anything to do with setting the blood price. The penalties for violence perpetrated during truce were more severe than those where no formal peace existed between the families. They might be imposed by the aldermen rather than the antagonists.

But the countless feuds show that atonement for homicide, indeed of any injury in which blood was drawn, was the sacred duty of every kindred, not the town government. The aldermen never accepted a homicide case until the parties had tried private mediation. Litigants had the right to refuse the aldermen's arbitration, and the magistrates only intervened when private arbitrators had failed to reach a verdict. The aldermen would record any agreement acceptable to both feuding parties. So minimal was respect for public authority that when one party took another to court, and the legal action resulted in the latter's execution, the former was obligated to offer his kinsmen a blood price, just as if he had been killed in a street fight. When enough blood had been shed to exhaust their energies, the senior males of the families concerned arranged settlements by which injuries on both sides might be cancelled out, more serious injuries paid for by a fee, and homicides handled by pilgrimages and always a blood price. These reconciliations involved not individuals, but entire families, all of whom were brought into the peace terms and were required to post bond guaranteeing that they would abide by the terms of the settlement.

The blood price was divided among the family members according to a fixed formula, but the mechanics of division caused some brotherly friction. Half of the blood price went to the closest surviving male blood relative of the deceased party, preferably his oldest brother. He in turn had the obligation of avenging his brother's death by, if he wished to satisfy all demands of honor, killing his brother's murderer. Failing that, he should kill one of his relatives, or at the very least demand as high a blood price as the market would bear. After expenses of reaching the settlement were deducted, the rest of the money was divided into shares for the other blood kin. Support of the widow and orphans was in principle the duty of her father or brothers. It was not to come from the blood price, and exceptions to this were entirely at the discretion of the decedent's male relatives.

A few well documented cases illustrate the pride and arrogance of the prominent men of Ghent. In 1358 Soy van der Dorent, who was leasing a farm at Vurste, near Ghent, from John van der Zickelen, one of the richest men of the city, was assaulted by a youth who was acting on orders of van der Zickelen's personal enemies. John van der Zickelen, not the injured farmer who was part of his clientele, took matters into his own hands. After waiting in vain for several months for an atonement to be offered, he sent formal notice to the culprit and his patron, Cornelius van Prendale. The next Sunday Cornelius' brother was given lethal wounds from the van der Zickelens. To prevent further violence, the parish priest of Vurste arranged an arbitrated settlement in which John van der Zickelen not only forced the van Prendales to pay for Soy van der Dorent's injuries, but also obliged Cornelius van Prendale himself to atone John's own killing of Cornelius' brother. That noble spirit in turn gave it to the parish priest of Vurste to support the dead man's orphan. The Justices of the Peace at Ghent recorded this settlement on the same day when it was reached.

No moral or legal stigma was attached to any deed that was paid for. Few would ally with a family enemy; yet Philip van Artevelde, who as we shall see had a maniacally strong consciousness of family responsibility, served in the government of Ghent in 1382 alongside John van Merlaer, who had killed Philip's brother James in 1370. Since van Merlaer had paid the blood price rather than paying with his own life, he had satisfied his debt to the van Arteveldes.

The principle of compensating all injuries regardless of fault or motive was followed to the letter. When the victim of an assault injured his assailant by defending himself, he had to pay for the person's damages. In 1355 a butcher's son admitted that he had entered a house "saying that he had been fighting and drinking all week and had paid for all that, and he was now ready for more and would pay for that too." They did indeed pay enormous sums that would have ruined persons who lacked their wealth. This fray, in which he was joined by three other youths of prominent families, cost one innocent man his life and left the homeowner with life threatening wounds and his wife and son with less serious injuries. Despite the clear culpability of the invaders, the homeowner had to pay one of them 9 lb. parisis, which was roughly what a continuously employed master carpenter would earn in a month and a half, to compensate him for the injuries that he sustained during the assault. There was thus open season on human flesh. Indeed, there is surprisingly little evidence of persons defaulting blood prices for homicide or damage assessments. Most of the bloodletting was done by persons of property who saw nothing wrong with what they were doing but rather considered it a mark of honor.

Wives and widows and their blood kin were expected to pay half the blood prices, while the perpetrator and his relatives paid the other half, and this in turn simply multiplied exponentially the number of persons involved in family-related violence. When an individual was unable to pay the blood price, his relatives were expected as a matter of honor to help him. Although this obligation was usually not legally enforceable, very few family members legally excused themselves from liability in homicide atonements. Since relatives could be injured or killed by the enemies of any of their kinspeople, even if they had no knowledge of what was going on, it was very risky to remove oneself from the warmth of the family circle. The attitude that the kindred should help was sanctioned by the aldermen. In a case of 1370, they noted that the killer "can hardly do this [pay the blood price] without the help and grace of his kinsmen and friends." The magistrates thus suggested pointedly that they help him "insofar as kin or friends help their kinsman and should do it out of grace, to the extent that you would want help or assistance from your kinsman, which we promise you in equal or even greater measure."

Although the Justices normally would not force innocent relatives to help with blood prices, arbitrators frequently did, and the Justices recorded their verdicts and enforced them. This was true even when the other relatives had urged the malefactor to modify his behavior. In 1369, one Henry van Heedevelde had collected a 10 lb. groot [the pound groot was worth twelve times the pound parisis] damage settlement from Arnold van der Borch. Then, contrary to his two brothers' advice, he resumed hostilities, and eventually he and his family became liable for 25 lb. 10s. groot [roughly what a continuously employed master carpenter would earn in four years] for another death and injury. Henry's personal liability, however, was only for the 10 lb. that he had collected for his own injuries. He successfully sued his brothers to pay everything over this from their own property. Henry had no obligation to repay them; they probably lost more money from his bad behavior than he did.

No tactic was too odious to use on one's enemies. Numerous homicides involved large groups ambushing an isolated person or two. Tempers were hot, and while some insults were visited with immediate retribution in the view of a crowd, others were the result of premeditation and stealth: the back stab, the tracking of an antagonist until he got into a place where his own clan could not protect him or where the city government could not enforce its regulations. Children and non-combatants were fair game. Persons with the same family name as an enemy were forced to swear in the presence of the magistrates that there was no blood relationship or face immediate extinction. Gangs that might include scores of persons roamed the streets. Some families had their own uniforms or colors by which their retainers could be recognized. Several cases in the Borluut–van Sint Baafs feud show that servants were particularly vulnerable; they were considered part of the clan and thus were subject to retribution that really was aimed at the patriarch. Servants were often ordered into enemy territory in the city or the surrounding abbey villages where the family leaders had sense enough not to go. Of course, since they were part of the household, their own masters would avenge their injuries.

Ghent was an armed camp. The rural areas near the city were not exempt from its violence. In 1373 a brewer of Ghent was seriously injured by other men of Ghent in a tavern in a nearby town, despite the fact that he had taken the precaution of wearing an iron helmet while he dined. Although statutes forbade the inhabitants to carry deadly weapons, and the bailiff regularly fined a few people for infractions, several cases show that it was expected that everyone would have weapons on his person. In 1365, one fistfight led to retaliation with a knife; the fray escalated to a battleaxe, whose victim then chased his victim with an iron morning star [a heavy iron ball studded with spikes and attached to a chain, from which it could be flailed]. The aldermen simply set personal damages for the knife and battleaxe injuries, but drew the line at the morning star, which "is not an honorable man's weapon, but rather it is forbidden among all decent people," and set its user on a pilgrimage. Most cases even of assault in which no deadly weapon is involved specify a beating "with the fist and its contents."

To combat this chaos, the city government of Ghent had an official personnel of only about 150 persons in the fourteenth century, although the extensive use of arbitrators, and the fact that many cases were handled in guild courts that have left no records, make the picture somewhat less bleak. All persons in an official capacity, from the aldermen to the city messengers, could make arrests. Yet, except when there was open revolt in the city, the government maintained only seventeen full-time police officers during the 1360s and 1370s. Their task was complicated by the total absence of a notion that violence was anything other than completely ethical. Cases survive showing that contracts to commit premeditated murder were enforceable in the very courts that were supposed to be trying to quell the violence. Even more cases show that while named individuals are legally responsible for deeds of violence, the damages that are owed to their victims would be paid openly for them by their patron, most often a prominent man of the city.

The problem of peacekeeping was exacerbated by the persistence of enclaves outside the jurisdiction of the city government, notably the two great abbey villages of Saints Peter and Bavo, where malefactors such as John Borluut's ally Peter de Visschere could take refuge. Even within the city fugitives and exiles could take shelter in the churches and adjacent cemeteries, for the city government generally respected the right of asylum that prohibited secular powers from functioning on ecclesiastical immunities.

Even when cases reached the magistrates, they often imposed punishments that were more symbolic than deterrent. Imprisonment was rarely used as a punishment for crime. As was generally true in medieval Europe, the town prison of Ghent was used mainly for debtors and for persons who were being detained awaiting trial. Only the bailiff could impose blood justice, which involved penalties of death or loss of a limb, ear, or the nose; when the aldermen convicted someone of a capital crime, they had to have the bailiff execute him. Perhaps for this reason and also because arbitration was possible for any misdeed except treason, few mutilations are mentioned, and the bailiff rarely executed as many as ten persons per year, and many of these were for heresy or witchcraft. At the mass trial days, the Justices usually sent the person considered primarily responsible for a fight on a pilgrimage, usually to a nearby shrine, but would order his victim to compensate the assailant for his injuries. This meant that the victim often suffered greater financial loss than the instigator.

Pilgrimages to more distant places, of course, amounted to a temporary exile. The problem with exile was that while the city government could banish a convicted felon from Flanders, it had no means of enforcing this judgement outside the town. Thus even the suburbs of the city were havens for persons banished by the aldermen. As exiles, however, they could be summarily dispatched by anyone catching them; in practice, this meant that their personal enemies, whose grievances had led to the banishment in the first place, had open season on them. The exiles were accordingly desperate enough to do anything. Some of them lived openly on their rural estates, and some homicide atonements specifically forbid a guilty man's wife to send him provisions during his exile. The smaller towns around Ghent resented the power of the metropolis, which was often used to their political or economic disadvantage, and many of them gave haven to exiles from Ghent. The municipal accounts of Ghent record numerous armed expeditions to dislodge exiles from Ghent from the small towns.

Evidence is ambiguous about the extent of family solidarity during the numerous political upheavals of the later fourteenth century in Ghent, but there can be no doubt that political and personal rivalries fed each other. The careers of James and Philip van Artevelde, the legendary father and son who became captains of Ghent and to this day are considered heroes of both nationalist and socialist movements in Flanders, afford a chilling example of the political impact of the vendetta. James van Artevelde became chief captain of Ghent in 1338 in the emergency caused by Flanders being caught in the middle between France and England in the opening stages of the Hundred Years War. He maintained his position virtually unchallenged until early 1343, when he survived a coup attempt led by people who felt that the English alliance into which he had led the city was catastrophic. The new government of Ghent that took office on August 15, 1344 contained several men who had no objection to the English alliance—indeed, they adhered to it after van Artevelde's death—but were van Artevelde's personal enemies who disliked him for playing the prince as ruler of Ghent and in fact the rest of Flanders. Van Artevelde was deposed from his captaincy in late March 1345, but he continued to perform diplomatic missions for the city government. In the last week of his life, he was negotiating with the English when he was summoned home into a trap by the captain John de Scouteete. When van Artevelde returned to Ghent on the evening of July 17, 1345, he was ambushed and killed at his home. One source says that he was given the death stroke by an anonymous "maker [restorer] of old shoes," evidently a disgruntled neighbor, in the alley behind his house as he tried to escape the mob. James van Artevelde was killed by personal enemies, not as an act of policy.

When peace was restored in 1349, van Artevelde's sons were exiled. They evidently knew that John de Scouteete had been involved in enticing their father back to Ghent. In 1361, just after they were repatriated, the oldest, John, killed John de Scouteete; although de Scouteete had living relatives, they demanded no blood price, evidently feeling that the homicide had been a consequence of John de Scouteete's official duties and that their kinsman had compromised himself with the van Arteveldes.

The van Arteveldes of the second generation thus seem at first to have thought that their father's death had been avenged. This did not stop them from getting into other feuds. James van Artevelde the younger was killed in 1370 by his family's neighbors at the polder village of Weert, a village along the Scheldt where James the elder had owned land. The killers in turn were bound in a tangled kinship net with the van Arteveldes' political opponents in Ghent. The leaders of the killers were the de Mey and van Merlaer families, who were related to one another and to other van Artevelde enemies in Ghent. The principal assassin was Walter de Mey, but John, son of Walter van Merlaer, was also responsible. His mother was Catherine Parijs, a kinswoman of uncertain degree of Simon Parijs, a dyer who had been dean of the "small guilds" [the fifty-nine locally based trades that had individual guild organizations but a common overdean] of Ghent in 1345 and had been implicated with John de Scouteete in James van Artevelde the elder's death. Before her marriage, Catherine had had a liaison with another prominent Ghent burgess, Gilbert son of Baldwin de Grutere.

John van Artevelde died in 1365. James the younger then assumed control of his father's economic interests in rural Flanders and eventually was killed by persons who had family ties to his father's enemies in the city. After James' death in 1370, only one van Artevelde son was left: Philip, who was much younger than his brothers. But Philip was now the oldest son, and the duty of avenging any wrongs done to the family thus descended on him. But as far as any of the van Arteveldes then knew, the scores had been settled: the death of John de Scouteete had avenged James the elder, and payment of the blood price by the de Meys and van Merlaers avenged James the younger.

On December 27, 1381, when Ghent was in a civil war against most of the rest of Flanders, Philip van Artevelde, who had never held public office before, was suddenly made commissioner in charge of handling property confiscated from fugitives. Contemporary chroniclers tell us that the recollection of his father's heroic role in Ghent's earlier struggle led to his elevation. On January 24, 1382, he was made chief of five captains, as his father had been. His first week in office was memorable. On January 26, he participated in a mob scene in which Simon Bette, the first alderman, the equivalent of the mayor of Ghent, was killed. Bette's family had not been implicated in the killing of James van Artevelde the elder, but they had been his political opponents. In 1379, when the war broke out, Bette had been First Justice of the Peace. He and Gilbert son of Gilbert de Grutere, who was first alderman at that time, banished two men who seem to have been van Artevelde partisans, on the spurious grounds that they had led an unauthorized attack on the city of Oudenaarde, south of Ghent.

On January 30 Philip van Artevelde enticed this Gilbert de Grutere, by then dean of the "small guilds," into an assembly, read a list of particulars accusing him of treason, and stabbed him on the spot. Some de Gruteres had been openly hostile to Philip's father's regime in the 1340s, but the family was bitterly split on personal grounds even then between the sons of Baldwin and those of Gilbert de Grutere. Philip van Artevelde had reason to dislike both branches: for Baldwin de Grutere fathered an illegitimate child by Catherine Parijs, who later gave birth to John van Merlaer, the killer of James van Artevelde the younger; while Gilbert was a political ally of the shippers, who by 1382 wanted peace with the count, while van Artevelde and the weavers who supported him wanted to continue the war.

During his same first week in power, Philip van Artevelde ordered three other men decapitated. Two of them were enemies of John van Merlaer, killer of James van Artevelde but now Philip's ally. On February 21, he murdered James Soyssone, the dean of the butchers' guild. Like the de Gruteres, the Soyssone family was bitterly split. James' branch was hostile to the van Arteveldes, although the other was not. Political affiliation in Ghent in early 1382 thus was a confused maelstrom. Disagreements within families caused different branches to choose opposite sides.

Philip van Artevelde's fury was directed both at persons who opposed his assumption of power in Ghent in early 1382 and against those with whom his family had grievances and specifically those whose ancestors had been implicated in his father's death. Which motive was uppermost in his mind in given cases is sometimes hard to determine. It seems likely, however, that the killings that we have mentioned to this point were not connected to the death of James the elder. Philip knew the Bettes, de Gruteres, and Soyssones personally. None of his documented actions before he became captain suggests that he thought that anyone other than John de Scouteete had been implicated in his father's assassination. He may have heard rumors; but as a youngest son—he was only five when his father died—he could have known little. If he had, he could have taken action on that knowledge; for as we have seen, eldest sons, and Philip van Artevelde had been that since 1370, had a solemn obligation to avenge killings with killings. But when Philip entered the city government in late 1381, he suddenly gained access not only to the records that we now use, but to much more detailed material that is now lost.

Contemporary writers make statements about his homicides in the month after Gilbert de Grutere's death that are sometimes dismissed as wild exaggerations. Philip van Artevelde was certainly in a position to use the forces of the city to accomplish private vengeance. The official accounts of the city mention payment of 2 francs "to Pete, Philip van Artevelde's executioner, for a sword" and of 12 pence "when he cut off ears." The historian Sir John Froissart (c. 1337–1410), who was usually well informed about affairs in Flanders, claimed that Philip had twelve persons beheaded in his presence because "some said" that they had been involved in his father's death.

But the death of James van Artevelde the elder was now thirty-seven years in the past. No one who was directly involved in his death in 1345 was still alive in 1382. The obvious answer to this riddle is that Philip van Artevelde considered the oldest sons of the men involved to bear the taint of their fathers' blood. We have seen that a restorer of old shoes had allegedly given the death stroke to James the elder. Professions often became family names at this time, and the city account mentions that Philip had one "Dennis de Scoemakere," whose name means "shoemaker," brought into his presence, although we are not told directly that the man was executed. Some families whose members felt themselves compromised evidently foresaw the van Artevelde restoration before it occurred and took the precaution of leaving the city. Clearly they suspected the action that he might take if he ever came to power, and with reason; others, who did not move fast enough, did not escape him. The elder son of the alderman of 1345, Francis Sloeve, was evidently killed; his younger brother had left Ghent earlier. The son of the town receiver of 1345, Peter Stocman, was murdered. Nicholas uten Dale, the son of the first Justice of the Peace of 1345, was killed. The clearest case is Lievin van Waes, an alderman of 1345. His older son and namesake, Lievin, left Ghent soon after March 24, 1382. On April 16, his younger brother Peter, who clearly was not considered liable for his father's deeds, bought Lievin's confiscated property from the city. Lievin van Waes was back in Ghent by August 1383, after van Artevelde's death but two years before the war against the count ended. He did not leave because he was opposed to the rebellion against the Flemish count, but because he feared the van Artevelde restoration. We have no way of estimating the number of other persons who left the city from fear of van Artevelde; the cases that we can document are chillingly revealing.

James and Philip van Artevelde have been acclaimed by posterity as democrats, men who had the welfare of the common people at heart, were popular figures, and who brought the guildsmen into power. Contemporary sources, however, inform us that although Philip van Artevelde's rebellion terrified the nobles and helped provoke revolts in some cities of northern France, half the population of Ghent opposed him. Although the city was in a civil war, had little food, no significant allies in Flanders—in contrast to the situation of the 1340s, Bruges and Ypres opposed Ghent now—and was being blockaded by the count's troops, Philip van Artevelde undertook no economic or diplomatic initiatives to relieve this situation until late March 1382 and no military initiatives until May. He had been too busy paying off his family's scores. The last of his homicides and most of the property seizures had been accomplished by February 21. Only when this man of honor had laid to rest the shade of his unavenged and thus dishonored father could he be bothered with the affairs of his afflicted city.

Family antagonisms were not the only causes of civil discord in late medieval Ghent, but they were involved as at least an aggravating element in virtually all breakdowns of public order. Political allegiances, personal enmities and amities, neighborhood solidarities, and occupational guilds were all important social and economic bonds, but they were relative and as transitory as human life itself. Reasonable men might differ about political or ideological issues, but the family was an absolute. To spill kinsmen's blood was to tarnish the family's honor, a sacrilege and shame requiring divine retribution consummated by the shedding of expiatory gore on the altar of vengeance. The males of medieval Ghent cared nothing for the rule of human law; their values were fixed on the holy, transcendent imperative of redemptive bloodshed.

BIBLIOGRAPHY

This essay is derived from information in Andrée Holsters, "Moord en politiek tijdens de Gentse opstand 1379-1385," *Handelingen der Maatschappij voor Geschiedenis en Oudheidkunde te Gent*, n.s. 37 (1983): 89–111; David Nicholas, "Crime and Punishment in Fourteenth-Century Ghent," *Revue Belge de Philologie et d'Histoire*, 48 (1970): 289–334, 1141–76; Nicholas, *The Domestic Life of a Medieval City: Women, Children, and the Family in Fourteenth-Century Ghent*. Lincoln: University of Nebraska Press, 1985; Nicholas, *The Metamorphosis of a Medieval City: Ghent in the Age of the Arteveldes, 1302–1390*. Lincoln: University of Nebraska Press; Leiden: E. J. Brill, 1987; Nicholas, "The Marriage and the Meat Hall: Ghent/Eeklo, 1373–75," *Medieval Prosopography* 10 (1989): 22–52; Nicholas, "The Governance of Fourteenth-Century Ghent." In *Law, Custom, and the Social Fabric in Medieval Europe: Essays in Honor of Bryce Lyon*. Edited, with an Appreciation, by Bernard S. Bachrach and David Nicholas. Kalamazoo, Michigan: Medieval Institute Publications, 1991: 235–260. The section on the Borluut-van Sint Baafs feud is based on Wim Blockman, *Een middeleeuwse vendetta. Gent 1300*. Houten: De Han, 1987. That on the van Artevelde family is based on David Nicholas, *The van Arteveldes of Ghent: The Varieties of Vendetta and the Hero in History*. Ithaca and London: Cornell University Press; Leiden: E. J. Brill, 1988.

The Development of
the Concept of Civilité

NORBERT ELIAS

The treatise by the Christian humanist Erasmus of Rotterdam, On Civility in Children *(1530), is the starting point for Norbert Elias in his analysis of manners. Erasmus wrote to instruct Europeans on their table manners and on control of bodily functions in public. What does Elias mean by the concept* civilité *and the term "civilizing process"? Why is Erasmus's treatise so important? What does his investigation of various areas of human conduct say about the notion of shame in the Middle Ages and in the sixteenth century?*

The contrast between the behavior of medieval people at table and the conduct Erasmus advocated is stark, yet a person today might still feel embarrassed by the discussion of the proverbial "three winds": burping, sneezing, and farting. Why did Erasmus stress outward bodily propriety? In the Middle Ages, what was socially acceptable behavior when eating? What was the "threshold of delicacy"? Of course, proper behavior was different for the nobility than for the peasantry, as the attempt was to define manners according to social rank. Part of the difference was owing to the abundance of the aristocratic table. How, for example, did changes in utensils affect table manners? How might these changes in table manners relate to other contemporaneous changes for the aristocracy in education, economic and political activities, literary and artistic tastes?

. . . The concept of *civilité* acquired its meaning for Western society at a time when chivalrous society and the unity of the Catholic church were disintegrating. It is the incarnation of a society which, as a specific stage in the formation of Western manners or "civilization," was no less important than the feudal society before it. The concept of *civilité*, too, is an expression and symbol of a social formation embracing the most diverse nationalities, in which, as in the Church, a common language is spoken, first Italian and then increasingly French. These languages take over the function earlier performed by Latin. They manifest the unity of Europe, and at the same time the new social formation which forms its backbone, court society. The situation, the self-image, and the characteristics of this society find expression in the concept of *civilité*.

The concept of *civilité* received the specific stamp and function under discussion here in the second quarter of the sixteenth century. Its individual starting point can be exactly determined. It owes the specific meaning adopted by society to a short treatise by Erasmus of Rotterdam, *De civilitate morum puerilium* (On civility in children), which appeared in 1530. This work clearly treated a theme that was ripe for discussion. It immediately achieved an enormous circulation, going through edition after edition. Even within Erasmus's lifetime—that is, in the first six years after its publication—it was reprinted more than thirty times. In all, more than 130 editions may be counted, 13 of them as late as the eighteenth century. The multitude of translations, imitations, and sequels is almost without limit. . . .

. . . And a whole genre of books, directly or indirectly influenced by Erasmus's treatise, appeared under the title *Civilité* or *Civilité puérile.*[1] . . .

Here, as so often in the history of words, and as was to happen later in the evolution of the concept *civilité* into *civilisation*, an individual was the instigator. By his treatise, Erasmus gave new sharpness and impetus to the long-established and commonplace word *civilitas.*[2] Wittingly or not, he obviously expressed in it something that met a social need of the time. The concept *civilitas* was henceforth fixed in the consciousness of people with the special sense it received from his treatise. And corresponding words were developed in the various popular languages: the French *civilité*, the English "civility," the Italian *civiltà*, and the German *Zivilität*. . . .

Erasmus's book is about something very simple: the behavior of people in society—above all, but not solely, "outward bodily propriety." It is dedicated to a noble boy, a prince's son, and written for the instruction of boys. . . . [T]he treatise points to attitudes that we have lost, that some among us would perhaps call "barbaric" or "uncivilized." It speaks of many things that have in the meantime become unspeakable, and of many others that are now taken for granted. . . .

Bodily carriage, gestures, dress, facial expressions—this "outward" behavior with which the treatise concerns itself is the expression of the inner, the whole man. Erasmus knows this and on occasion states it explicitly: "Although this outward bodily propriety proceeds from a well-composed mind, nevertheless we sometimes find that, for want of instruction, such grace is lacking in excellent and learned men."

There should be no snot on the nostrils, he says somewhat later. A peasant wipes his nose on his cap and coat, a sausage maker on his arm and elbow. It does not show much more propriety to use one's hand and then wipe it on one's clothing. It is more decent to take up the snot in a cloth, preferably while turning away. If when blowing the nose with two fingers something falls to the ground, it must be immediately trodden away with the foot. The same applies to spittle.

With the same infinite care and matter-of-factness with which these things are said—the mere mention of which shocks the "civilized" man of a later stage with a different affective molding—we are told how one ought to sit or greet. Gestures are described that have become strange to us, e.g., standing on one leg. . . .

The more one immerses oneself in the little treatise, the clearer becomes this picture of a society with modes of behavior in some respects

[1]Childish civility.
[2]Civility.

related to ours, and in many ways remote. We see people seated at table. . . . The goblet and the well-cleaned knife on the right, on the left the bread. That is how the table is laid. Most people carry a knife, hence the precept to keep it clean. Forks scarcely exist, or at most for taking meat from the dish. Knives and spoons are very often used communally. There is not always a special implement for everyone: if you are offered something liquid, says Erasmus, taste it and return the spoon after you have wiped it.

When dishes of meat are brought in, usually everyone cuts himself a piece, takes it in his hand, and puts it on his plate if there are plates, otherwise on a thick slice of bread. . . .

. . . Some put their hands into the dishes when they are scarcely seated, says Erasmus. Wolves or gluttons do that. Do not be the first to take from a dish that is brought in. Leave dipping your fingers into the broth to the peasants. Do not poke around in the dish but take the first piece that presents itself. And just as it shows a want of forbearance to search the whole dish with one's hand . . . neither is it very polite to turn the dish round so that a better piece comes to you. What you cannot take with your hands, take on your *quadra*.[3] . . .

. . . Paintings of table scenes from this or earlier times always offer the same spectacle, unfamiliar to us, that is indicated by Erasmus's treatise. The table is sometimes covered with rich cloths, sometimes not, but always there is little on it: drinking vessels, saltcellar, knives, spoons, that is all. Sometimes we see the slices of bread, the *quadrae*, that in French are called *tranchoir* or *tailloir*. Everyone, from the king and queen to the peasant and his wife, eats with the hands. In the upper class there are more refined forms of this. One ought to wash one's hands before a meal, says Erasmus. But there is as yet no soap for this purpose. Usually the guest holds out his hands, and a page pours water over them. The water is sometimes slightly scented with chamomile or rosemary. In good society one does not put both hands into the dish. It is most refined to use only three fingers of the hand. This is one of the marks of distinction between the upper and lower classes.

The fingers become greasy. . . . It is not polite to lick them or wipe them on one's coat. Often you offer others your glass, or all drink from a communal tankard. Erasmus admonishes: "Wipe your mouth beforehand." You may want to offer someone you like some of the meat you are eating. "Refrain from that," says Erasmus, "it is not very decorous to offer something half-eaten to another." And he says further: "To dip bread you have bitten into the sauce is to behave like a peasant, and it shows little elegance to remove chewed food from the mouth and put it back on the *quadra*. If you cannot swallow a piece of food, turn round discreetly and throw it somewhere."

[3]Plate or slice of bread.

Then he says again: "It is good if conversation interrupts the meal from time to time. Some people eat and drink without stopping, not because they are hungry or thirsty, but because they can control their movements in no other way. They have to scratch their heads, poke their teeth, gesticulate with their hands, or play with a knife, or they can't help coughing, snorting, and spitting. All this really comes from a rustic embarrassment and looks like a form of madness."

But it is also necessary, and possible, for Erasmus to say: Do not expose without necessity "the parts to which Nature has attached modesty." Some prescribe, he says, that boys should "retain the wind by compressing the belly." But you can contract an illness that way. And in another place: . . . (Fools who value civility more than health repress natural sounds.) Do not be afraid of vomiting if you must; "for it is not vomiting but holding the vomit in your throat that is foul."

With great care Erasmus marks out in his treatise the whole range of human conduct, the chief situations of social and convivial life. He speaks with the same matter-of-factness of the most elementary as of the subtlest questions of human intercourse. In the first chapter he treats "the seemly and unseemly condition of the whole body," in the second "bodily culture," in the third "manners at holy places," in the fourth banquets, in the fifth meetings, in the sixth amusement, and in the seventh the bedchamber. This is the range of questions in the discussion of which Erasmus gave new impetus to the concept of *civilitas*.

. . . The unconcerned frankness with which Erasmus and his time could discuss all areas of human conduct is lost to us. Much of what he says oversteps our threshold of delicacy.

But precisely this is one of the problems to be considered here. In tracing the transformation of the concepts by which different societies have tried to express themselves, in following back the concept of civilization to its ancestor *civilité*, one finds oneself suddenly on the track of the civilizing process itself, of the actual change in behavior that took place in the West. That it is embarrassing for us to speak or even hear of much that Erasmus discusses is one of the symptoms of this civilizing process. The greater or lesser discomfort we feel toward people who discuss or mention their bodily functions more openly, who conceal and restrain these functions less than we do, is one of the dominant feelings expressed in the judgment "barbaric" or "uncivilized." Such, then, is the nature of "barbarism and its discontents" or, in more precise and less evaluative terms, the discontent with the different structure of affects, the different standard of repugnance which is still to be found today in many societies which we term "uncivilized," the standard of repugnance which preceded our own and is its precondition. The question arises as to how and why Western society actually moved from one standard to the other, how it was "civilized." In considering this process of civilization, we cannot avoid arousing feelings of discomfort and embarrassment. It is valuable to be aware of them. It is necessary, at least while considering this process, to attempt to suspend all the feelings of embarrassment and superiority, all the value judgments and criticism associated with the concepts "civilization" or "uncivilized." Our kind of behavior has grown out of that which we call uncivilized. But these concepts grasp the actual change too statically and coarsely. In reality, our terms "civilized" and "uncivilized" do not constitute an antithesis of the kind that exists between "good" and "bad," but represent stages in a development which, moreover, is still continuing. It might well happen that our stage of civilization, our behavior, will arouse in our descendants feelings of embarrassment similar to those we sometimes feel concerning the behavior of our ancestors. Social behavior and the expression of emotions passed from a form and a standard which was not a beginning, which could not in any absolute and undifferentiated sense be designated "uncivilized," to our own, which we denote by the word "civilized." And to understand the latter we must go back in time to that from which it emerged. The "civilization" which we are accustomed to regard as a possession that comes to us apparently ready-made, without our asking how we actually came to possess it, is a process or part of a process in which we are ourselves involved. . . .

. . . What came before Erasmus? Was he the first to concern himself with such matters?

By no means. Similar questions occupied the men of the Middle Ages, of Greco-Roman antiquity, and doubtless also of the related, preceding "civilizations." . . .

The Middle Ages have left us an abundance of information on what was considered socially acceptable behavior. Here, too, precepts on conduct while eating had a special importance. Eating and drinking then occupied a far more central position in social life than today, when they provide—frequently, not always—rather the framework and introduction for conversation and conviviality. . . .

The standard of "good behavior" in the Middle Ages is, like all later standards, represented by a quite definite concept. Through it the secular upper class of the Middle Ages, or at least some of its leading groups, gave expression to their self-image, to what, in their own estimation, made them exceptional. The concept epitomizing aristocratic self-consciousness and socially acceptable behavior appeared in French as *courtoisie*, in English "courtesy," in Italian *cortezia*, along with other related terms, often in divergent forms. . . . All these concepts refer quite directly (and far more overtly than later ones with the same function) to a particular place in society. They say: That is how people behave at court. . . .

. . . What emerges as typical behavior, as the pervasive character of its precepts?

Something, in the first place, that in comparison to later times might be called its simplicity, its naïvté. There are, as in all societies where the emotions are expressed more violently and directly, fewer psychological nuances and complexities in the general stock of ideas. There are friend and foe, desire and aversion, good and bad people.

> You should follow honorable men and vent your wrath on the wicked.

. . . .

> When your companions anger you, my son, see that you are not so hot-tempered that you regret it afterward.

In eating, too, everything is simpler, impulses and inclinations are less restrained:

> A man of refinement should not slurp with his spoon when in company; this is the way people at court behave who often indulge in unrefined conduct.

. . . Noble, courteous behavior is constantly contrasted to "coarse manners," the conduct of peasants.

> Some people bite a slice and then dunk it in the dish in a coarse way; refined people reject such bad manners.

If you have taken a bite from the bread, do not dip it in the common dish again. Peasants may do that, not "fine people."

> A number of people gnaw a bone and then put it back in the dish—this is a serious offense.

Do not throw gnawed bones back into the communal dish. From other accounts we know that it was customary to drop them on the floor. Another precept reads:

> A man who clears his throat when he eats and one who blows his nose in the tablecloth are both ill-bred, I assure you.

Here is another:

> If a man wipes his nose on his hand at table because he knows no better, then he is a fool, believe me.

To use the hand to wipe one's nose was a matter of course. Handkerchiefs did not yet exist. But at table certain care should be exercised; and one should on no account blow one's nose into the tablecloth. Avoid lip-smacking and snorting, eaters are further instructed:

If a man snorts like a seal when he eats, as some people do, and smacks his chops like a Bavarian yokel, he has given up all good breeding.

If you have to scratch yourself, do not do so with your bare hand but use your coat:

Do not scrape your throat with your bare hand while eating; but if you have to, do it politely with your coat.

Everyone used his hands to take food from the common dish. For this reason one was not to touch one's ears, nose, or eyes:

It is not decent to poke your fingers into your ears or eyes, as some people do, or to pick your nose while eating. These three habits are bad.

Hands must be washed before meals:

I hear that some eat unwashed (if it is true, it is a bad sign). May their fingers be palsied!

... If you have no towel, ... do not wipe your hands on your coat but let the air dry them. Or:

Take care that, whatever your need, you do not flush with embarrassment.

Nor is it good manners to loosen one's belt at table.

All this is said to adults, not only to children. To our minds these are very elementary precepts to be given to upper-class people, more elementary in many respects than what, at the present stage of behavior, is generally accepted as the norm in rural-peasant strata. . . .

This is, if it may so be called, the standard eating technique during the Middle Ages, which corresponds to a very particular standard of human relationships and structure of feeling. Within this standard there is . . . an abundance of modifications and nuances. If people of different rank are eating at the same time, the person of higher rank is given precedence when washing hands, for example, or when taking from the dish. The forms of utensils vary considerably in the course of centuries. There are fashions, but also a very definite trend that persists through the fluctuations of fashion. The secular upper class, for example, indulges in extraordinary luxury at table. It is not a poverty of utensils that maintains the standard, it is quite simply that nothing else is needed. To eat in this fashion is taken for granted. It suits these people. But it also suits them to make visible their wealth and rank by the opulence of their utensils and table decoration. At the rich tables of the thirteenth century the spoons are of gold, crystal, coral, ophite. It is occasionally mentioned that during Lent knives with ebony handles are used, at Easter knives with ivory handles, and inlaid knives at Whitsun. The soupspoons are round and rather flat to begin with, so that one is forced when using them to open one's mouth wide. From the fourteenth century onward, soupspoons take on an oval form. . . .

. . . From the sixteenth century on, at least among the upper classes, the fork comes into use as an eating instrument, arriving by way of Italy first in France and then in England and Germany, after having served for a time only for taking solid foods from the dish. Henri III[4] brought it to France, probably from Venice. His courtiers were not a little derided for this "affected" manner of eating, and at first they were not very adept in the use of the instrument: at least it was said that half the food fell off the fork as it traveled from plate to mouth. As late as the seventeenth century the fork was still essentially a luxury article of the upper class, usually made of gold or silver. What we take entirely for granted, because we have been adapted and conditioned to this social standard from earliest childhood, had first to be slowly and laboriously acquired and developed by society as a whole. . . .

However, the attitude that has just been described toward the "innovation" of the fork shows one thing with special clarity. People who ate together in the way customary in the Middle Ages, taking meat with their fingers from the same dish, wine from the same goblet, soup from the same pot or the same plate, with all the other peculiarities of which examples have been . . . given—such people stood in a different relationship to one another than we do. . . . Their affects were conditioned to forms of relationship and conduct which, by today's standard of conditioning, are embarrassing or at least unattractive. What was lacking in this *courtois* world, or at least had not been developed to the same degree, was the invisible wall of affects which seems now to rise between one human body and another, repelling and separating, the wall which is often perceptible today at the mere approach of something that has been in contact with the mouth or hands of someone else, and which manifests itself as embarrassment at the mere sight of many bodily functions of others, and often at their mere mention, or as a feeling of shame when one's own functions are exposed to the gaze of others, and by no means only then.

[4]King of France, 1574–1589.

The Family in Renaissance Italy

DAVID HERLIHY

During the fourteenth and fifteenth centuries, a cultural flowering known as the Renaissance took place in Italy. David Herlihy studies primarily Florence, the center of the Renaissance and a leading city in Europe, in order to understand the nature of the family in Renaissance Italy. He finds that three factors—demography, environment, and wealth—affected the long-term development of the family.

Population trends, especially after the Black Death, shifted during the Renaissance. How did those changes influence the size of households and the number of servants? Note that Herlihy is very careful to make comparisons whenever possible between urban and rural families. In other words, environment influenced the structure of the family and the functions it performed. Families in cities differed from their counterparts in the countryside, not only in size, but also in the establishment of new families, remarriage, and the very functions the family performed. Wealth likewise shaped the family in determining whom to marry, household size, and age at marriage. What does Herlihy mean when he argues that demography, environment, and wealth led to a crisis of the Renaissance family?

Herlihy next discusses the composition of the Italian household, particularly in regard to marriage and children. Age at marriage seems to provide much information about family structure. Why was there such a disparity in Florence between the age of first marriage for women and for men? Why did the situation differ in rural areas? Why did some men and women remain unmarried? What was their fate? Why did some women prefer to remain widows rather than remarry? How did marriage patterns affect the prevalence of prostitution and homosexuality? Children were very important to the Renaissance family, though the relationship between mother and child was unlike that between father and child. The fathers cared for their children's future, especially their sons', often leaving some posthumous instructions specifying their upbringing. Mothers, closer in age to their offspring and tending to survive their husbands, influenced their children in areas of special concern to women. In this way, Herlihy believes that the character of the Renaissance was determined considerably by female education of the young. Thus he accords singular importance to the family and holds its peculiar structure responsible in large part for the cultural awakening of the Renaissance.

. . . Sociologists and historians once assumed that the typical family in traditional Europe (that is, in Europe before the Industrial Revolution) was large, stable and extended, in the sense that it included other relatives besides the direct descendants and ascendants of the head and his wife. The sources of Renaissance Italy rather show that there is no such thing as a traditional family, or, in different terms, a family with unchanging characteristics. The family in ca. 1400 was perceptibly different from what it had been in ca. 1300, and was to be different again in the sixteenth century. Moreover, the rural family varied in marked respects from the city household, and the poor—can this be surprising?—lived differently from the rich. How precisely did the times, location and wealth affect the Renaissance household?

In Italy as everywhere in Europe, the population between the thirteenth and the sixteenth centuries experienced powerful, even violent, fluctuations. These directly affected the households in their average size and internal structure. The history of population movements in late medieval and Renaissance Italy may be divided into four periods, with distinctive characteristics: (1) stability in numbers at very high levels, from some point in the thirteenth century until ca. 1340; (2) violent contraction, from ca. 1340 to ca. 1410, to which the terrible Black Death of 1348 made a major but not exclusive contribution; (3) stability at very low levels, from approximately 1410 to 1460; (4) renewed expansion, which brought the Italian population to another peak in the middle sixteenth century.

To judge from Tuscan evidence, the population in our second period (ca. 1340 to ca. 1410) fell by approximately two-thirds. A city of probably 120,000 persons in 1338, Florence itself counted less than 40,000 in 1427. In some remote areas of Tuscany, such as the countryside of San Gimignano, losses over the same period surpassed 70 percent. The region of San Gimignano was in fact more densely settled in the thirteenth century than it is today.

It is difficult for a modern reader even to grasp the dimensions of these losses; for every three persons living in ca. 1300, there was only one to be found alive in ca. 1410, in many if not most Italian regions. And the population, stable at low levels from approximately 1410, shows no signs of vigorous growth until after 1460. The subsequent expansion of the late fifteenth and early sixteenth centuries was particularly notable on the fertile plain of the Po river in Northern Italy and in the Veneto (the region of Venice). Verona, near Venice, for example, had fewer than 15,000 inhabitants in 1425, but reached 42,000 by 1502, nearly tripling in size. Venice itself reached approximately 170,000 persons by 1563; it was not to reach that size again until the twentieth century. Rome and Naples were also gaining rapidly in population. Florence too was growing, but at a moderate rate. In 1562 Florence counted slightly fewer than 60,000 inhabitants, which made the city only a third larger than it had been in 1427. Florence, in sum, even in this period of growth, was losing relative position among the major cities of Italy.

Inevitably, the collapse in population, subsequent stability, then growth affected the average size of the households. At Prato, for example, a small region and city 20 miles west of Florence, the average size of the rural household was 5.6 persons in 1298, and only 5 in 1427. Within the city of Prato, average household size similarly fell from 4.1 persons in 1298 to only 3.7 in 1427. By the late fourteenth and fifteenth centuries, the urban household widely across northern Italy was extremely small: 3.8 persons per household at Florence in 1427; 3.6 at Pistoia in the same year; 3.5 at Bologna in 1395; and 3.7 at Verona in 1425.

The acute population fall and the ensuing period of demographic stability at low levels (to ca. 1460) also affected the internal structure of the households. The demographic catastrophes, especially the plagues and famines, left within the community large numbers of incomplete or truncated households—those which lacked a married couple and included only widowers, widows, bachelors or orphaned children. At Florence in 1427, the most common of all household types found within the city counted only a single person; these one-member households represented some 20 percent of all urban households. The numerous, small, severely truncated and biologically inactive families (in the sense that they could produce no children) may be regarded as the social debris, which the devastating plagues and famines of the epoch left in their wake.

The renewed demographic expansion from about 1460 in turn affected average size and the internal structure of the household. Average household size at Verona, only 3.7 persons in 1425, reached 5.2 persons only thirty years later, in 1456, and was 5.9 persons in 1502. Within the city of Florence, average household size gained from 3.8 persons in 1427 to 4.8 persons in 1458 to 5.2 persons in 1480, and reached 5.7 members in 1552. Within the Florentine countryside, average household size similarly grew from 4.8 persons in 1427, to 5.3 in 1470, to 5.8 in 1552.

Several factors explain this increase in average household size in both city and countryside, during this period of demographic growth after 1460. As the plague and famine lost their virulence, the numbers of very small, highly truncated and biologically inactive families diminished within the community. Families were also producing larger numbers of children (perhaps we should say, of surviving children). Paradoxically, however, the large households of the late fifteenth and sixteenth centuries also indicate an effort to slow the rate of population growth. In a rapidly growing community, average household size tends to remain relatively low, as sons and daughters leave the paternal home at an early age to marry, and the community contains many young, hence small, families. But no community can allow its population to grow without limit, and in traditional society the principal means of slowing or stopping growth was to prevent young persons from marrying, or marrying young. These young persons remained in their parents' house for long periods, thus increasing average household size. Many of them, especially males, remained unmarried even after the death of their parents, living as bachelors in households headed by an older, married brother. Within the city of Florence, for example, in 1427 some 17.1 percent of the households included a brother or sister of the household head, but 26.1 percent did so in 1480. We have no exact figures from the sixteenth century, but the percentage was doubtlessly even larger. The Florentine household, in other words, was much more laterally extended in the sixteenth century than it had been in 1427. The effort to slow or stop population growth, more than the growth itself, accounts for the larger size and more complex structure of the Italian household in the late fifteenth and sixteenth centuries.

Another factor which contributed to these shifts in average household size was the changing servant population. The drastic fall in the population in the late fourteenth century made labor scarce and forced wages upward, and this meant that households before 1460 could afford to support comparatively few servants. At Verona in 1425, for example, some 7 percent of the urban population were employed as household servants. After 1460, as the population once more was growing, wages tended to decline, and households could afford to support larger numbers of retainers. By 1502 at Verona, servants constituted 12.3 percent of the urban population. The numbers of servants grew especially large in the city of Florence, where, by 1552, 16.7 percent of the urban population were employed in household service; nearly half the urban households (42 percent) had at least one domestic, and one Florentine citizen employed no fewer than 57 servants. This growth in the number of servants has great social and cultural importance. It meant that the Italian urban family of some means could live with considerably greater comfort and elegance in ca. 1500—during the height of the Renaissance—than had been possible a hundred years before.

By the sixteenth century, the typical Italian household was large in size and complex in structure; it included numerous children, servants, and lateral relatives of the head. Sociologists and historians used to consider this extended household characteristic of traditional European society. Today, we can discern that this type of household was characteristic only of particular periods and circumstances in the varied history of the Italian family.

The location of the household, its surroundings or environment, also exerted a powerful influence upon its internal structure. Unlike the long-term demographic trend, this factor exerted a largely uniform influence over time. In most periods and places, the rural household was larger than its urban counterpart. At Prato in 1298, the average household size was 5.6 in rural areas and 4.1 in the city; at Florence in 1427, the comparable figures are 4.8 in the countryside and 3.8 in the city. However, the changes we have already considered—particularly the great growth in the number of servants, which was more characteristic of the cities than of rural areas—tended to reduce these contrasts in the sixteenth century. In 1552, the average size of the urban household at Florence was 5.7 persons; it was 5.8 in the countryside.

Average household size, however, reveals very little about the internal character of the family. No matter what their relative size, the households of the countryside remained fundamentally different from those of the city. Perhaps the most evident contrast was this: almost invariably, the rural household contained at least one married couple; households headed by a bachelor, widow, widower or orphans were rarely found in rural areas. In the cities, on the other hand, bachelors and widows frequently appeared at the head of households at all periods. Households which lacked sexually active partners were therefore common in the city, but rare in the countryside. So also, the number of children supported in urban households tended to be below the number found in rural homes. . . .

These contrasts point to fundamental differences in the functions of the family in the countryside and the city. In the countryside, the family fulfilled both biological and economic functions: the procreation and rearing of children, and the maintenance of a productive enterprise, the family farm. In Italy, as everywhere in medieval Europe, a peasant economy dominated the countryside. In the peasant economy, the basic unit of labor was not so much the individual but the family. A single man or woman did not have the capacity to work an entire farm, but needed the help of a spouse and eventually children. The young peasant who wished to secure his own economic independence consequently had to marry. For the same reason, if a peasant or his wife were widowed, he or she tended to remarry quickly, unless a young married couple was already present in the household, for the farm could be successfully worked only through family labor. In rural areas there were consequently very few truncated households, that is, those which did not contain at least one married couple. The rural environment encouraged marriage, not only for biological but for economic reasons. Conversely, those residents of the countryside who did not wish to marry or remarry were strongly drawn to the cities.

Within the cities, the family of course continued to perform its biological functions of rearing children, but its economic functions were very different. The young man seeking to make his fortune in most urban trades or professions often found a wife more of a burden than a help. He frequently had to serve long years at low pay as an apprentice. He had to accumulate diligently his earnings and profits; capital alone permitted him one day to pursue his trade in his own right and name. Such a man could not usually contemplate marriage until his mature years, when he was economically established; even then, the urban family was not cemented, as was the rural household, by close participation in a common economic enterprise.

The urban environment, in other words, tended to be hostile to the formation of new households, and added little to their inner strength. Moreover, at the death of a spouse, his or her partner was not under the same pressures to remarry, as was the rural widower or widow who needed help in farming. Urban communities consequently contained far greater numbers of adult bachelors and widows than could be found in the rural villages. The urban environment was often hostile to the very survival of lineages. Both inside and outside of Italy, the city frequently proved to be the graveyard of family lines. . . .

The third factor which strongly influenced the character of the household was wealth or social position, but this influence was exerted in complex ways. In some respects, wealth reinforced the environmental influences reviewed above. Thus, in the cities, rich young men tended to approach marriage even more cautiously than their poorer neighbors. Marriage among the wealthy involved the conveyance of substantial sums of money through the dowry. Marriage also called for the sealing of family alliances, which affected the political and social position of all parties involved. The high stakes associated with marriage frequently led the wealthy young man (or his family) to search long for a suitable bride, and to protract the negotiations when she was found. Marriage, in other words, was not lightly regarded, or hastily contracted, among the rich. Moreover, if death should dissolve the marriage, the surviving partner, particularly the widow, usually controlled enough wealth in her own name to resist pressures to remarry. Bachelors and widows were therefore especially numerous among the wealthy. The poorer families of the city, in approaching marriage, had less reason for caution and restraint.

In the countryside, on the other hand, the wealthy peasant usually owned a large farm, which could only be worked with the aid of a wife and family. The rich inhabitant of the city looked upon marriage in the light of future advantages—the dowry and the family connections it would bring him; the substantial peasant needed family labor to make himself rich in harvests as well as land. Among the rural rich there were consequently few families headed by a bachelor or widow. Poorer inhabitants of the countryside—peasants who possessed less than an entire farm and who worked primarily as agricultural laborers—were less eager to take a wife, who, with children, might excessively tax already scant resources. Wealth, in sum, facilitated marriage in rural areas, while obstructing it within the city.

We must note, however, that there are important exceptions to the rule we have just enounced. In Tuscany, and widely in central Italy, there existed large numbers of sharecroppers, called *mezzadri*, who leased and worked entire farms in return for half the harvest. The owner of the farm provided his *mezzadro* with most of the capital he needed—cattle, tools, seed, fertilizer and the like. With few possessions of his own, the sharecropper usually appeared in the tax rolls as very poor, but he still required a wife and family to help him in his labors. In other words, the need to recruit a family of workers, rather than wealth itself, was the critical factor in encouraging marriages among the peasants.

Besides reinforcing environmental influences, wealth had another effect upon households, which was common to both cities and countryside. In both environments, almost invariably, rich households tended to be larger than poor households. And they were more abundantly supplied with all types of members: they supported relatively more children, more servants and more lateral relatives of the head. For example, if we consider only those households in the city of Florence in 1427 with a male head between age 43 and 47, the average size for the richer half of the urban households was 6.16 persons; it was 4.57 among the poorer half. In rural areas too, and in other periods, wealth exerted a similar, strong influence upon the size and complexity of households. It was as if the family head of the Renaissance, in both city and countryside, equipped himself with as large a household as his resources could reasonably support.

The marked influence of wealth upon household size had some paradoxical effects. Considerations of property . . . prompted rich young men in the city to marry late, and some did not marry at all; but once married, the rich were prolific in producing children. . . . The urban poor were far less hesitant in entering marriage, but the poor urban family was also far less successful than the rich in rearing children. Probably the children of the deprived fell victim, in greater relative numbers than the children of the privileged, to the rampant diseases of the age. Poor parents certainly had strong reasons for exercising restraint in procreating children, and they probably limited the number of their offspring in other ways—through primitive methods of birth control and through the abandonment of babies they could not support. In the countryside, on the other hand, wealth tended to encourage both early marriage and high fertility among those who married.

Our consideration of these three factors—the long-term demographic trend, environment and wealth—which strongly influenced the Renaissance family brings us to the following conclusion. The huge losses and slow recovery in the population in the late Middle Ages precipitated a major crisis within the Italian household, as it did in many other social institutions. Frequent deaths undermined the durability and stability of the basic familial relations—between husband and wife, and parents and children. High mortalities threatened the very survival of numerous family lines. The crisis was especially acute within the city, the environment of which was already basically hostile to the formation of households and to their cohesiveness. . . .

This grave crisis did, however, increase awareness of the family and its problems. Writers of the age were led to examine, and at times to idealize, familial relationships and the roles which father, mother and children played within the household. They sought to determine when young men should marry, how brides should be chosen, and how children should be trained, in order to assure the happiness and especially the survival of the family. . . .

Against this background, we can now look in more detail at the Renaissance household. Specifically, we shall examine what sociologists call the "developmental cycle" of the household—how it was formed through marriage, grew primarily through births, and was dissolved or transformed through deaths.

Perhaps the most distinctive feature of the Renaissance marriage was the great age difference which separated the groom from his bride. At

Florence in 1427-28, in 55 marriages reported in the *Catasto*,[1] the average age difference between the bride and groom was 13.6 years. Demographers can also estimate age of first marriage from the proportions of the population remaining single at the various age levels, through somewhat complicated calculations we need not rehearse here. By this method, the average age of first marriage for women in the city of Florence in 1427 can be estimated at 17.9 years; for men it is 29.9 years.

In this, the city of Florence presents an extreme example of a common pattern. In the Florentine countryside in 1427, the estimated age of first marriage for women, based on the proportions remaining single, was 18.3 years, and for men 25.6 years. The age difference between the spouses, 7.3 years, was less than in the city, but still considerable. In the city of Verona in 1425, the age difference was also smaller—7 years—but still extended.

The three factors of environment, wealth and long-term demographic trend affected the formation of new households and inevitably therefore the age of first marriage. However, the age of first marriage for men was far more sensitive to all these influences than the marriage age for women. The typical bride was never much older than 20 years, and was usually much younger. The age of first marriage for men varied over a much wider range of years, from 25 to 35 and at times perhaps to 40. According to a Florentine domestic chronicler writing in the early 1400's, Giovanni Morelli, his male ancestors in the thirteenth century were prone to postpone their first marriage until age 40. . . . In the period before the devastating plagues,[2] when the mean duration of life was relatively extended, men would be forced to wait long before they would be allowed to marry. The medieval community had already reached extraordinary size in the thirteenth century and could ill support continued, rapid growth.

It is at all events certain that the great plagues and famines of the fourteenth century lowered the average age at which men first entered marriage. Thus, in 1427 in the city of Florence, the average age of first marriage for men was approximately 30 years, which compared to Morelli's estimate of 40 years for the thirteenth century. Subsequently, as the plagues grew less virulent, and lives became longer, the age of first marriage for men again moved upward. In 1458, for example, the estimated age of first marriage for Florentine men was 30.5 years, and it was 31.4 years in 1480.

The age of first marriage for women moved upward and downward in the same direction as that of men, but, as we have mentioned, over a shorter range of years. (The estimated age of first marriage for Florentine women was 17.9 years in 1427, 19.5 in 1458 and 20.8 in 1480.) The reasons for this relative inelasticity in marriage age for women seem to have been preeminently cultural: Italian grooms of the Renaissance, under almost all

---

[1]1427 census in Florence.
[2]That is, before 1348.

circumstances, no matter what their own age, preferred brides no older than 20.

So also, between city and countryside, the differences in age of first marriage for men (29.9 and 25.6 years respectively in 1427) were much greater than the differences in age of first marriage for women (17.9 and 18.3 years respectively). Women were slightly older at first marriage in rural areas, perhaps because the agricultural labors they were to perform required physical maturity. Again within the city, the richest Florentine males in 1427, from households with an assessment of over 400 florins, entered marriage for the first time at an estimated age of 31.2 years; their poorest neighbors, from households with no taxable assets, were considerably younger at first marriage—only 27.8 years. But rich girls and poor girls married for the first time at nearly the same ages—17.9 and 18.4 years respectively. Rich girls tended to be slightly younger, perhaps because their worried fathers wanted to settle their fate as quickly as possible. But almost all Florentine brides, in every corner of society, were remarkably young, at least by modern standards.

We should further note that in those segments of society where men married late (that is, in the towns, and particularly among the wealthy) many men, perhaps 10 percent, did not marry at all, but remained as bachelors, usually in the households of married relatives. On the other hand, girls who did not marry either entered domestic service—an option not open to girls from well-to-do households—or joined a religious order. There were almost no lay spinsters in urban society, apart from servants.

How does this pattern of marriage compare with modern practices? Sociologists now identify what they call a "west European marriage pattern," which is apparently found in no other, non-Western society. This pattern is distinguished by late marriages for both men and women, and by the presence in the population of many adult men and women who do not marry at all. How "modern" were the men and women of the Renaissance? Clearly, within the cities, male behavior already corresponded closely to this modern pattern; men married late and some did not marry at all, especially among the wealthy. The women of the Renaissance, on the other hand, even within the cities, were far from modern in their marital behavior; they married young and those who did not marry rarely remained in the lay world. Renaissance Italy, in other words, was not the birthplace of the modern marriage pattern, at least not for women.

The long span of years, which separated the groom from his bride, had distinctive effects upon both the character of the Renaissance household and upon the larger society. The young girl had little voice in selecting her mate, and usually no competence to choose. The first weeks of marriage must have been traumatic for these child brides. . . . But the position and status of these young matrons thereafter improved, for several reasons. The husbands were older, occupied men; many were already past the prime of their years. The brides, themselves only reaching maturity, rapidly assumed chief responsibility for the management of their households. . . . For many women, ultimate liberation would come with the deaths of their much older husbands. At the death of the husband, the dowry returned to the widow; the large sum of money which had taxed her family's resources at her marriage now could make her a woman of means, independent enough to resist a second marriage if she did not want it. As a widow with some property, she was free from male domination in a way she had never been as a child and a wife. The years of childhood, of service as a wife, were hard but often abbreviated for the lady of the Renaissance; and time worked in her favor.

Within the larger society, especially within the cities, the tendency for males to postpone marriage meant that the community would contain large numbers of unattached young men, who were denied legitimate sexual outlets for as long as two decades after puberty. Erotic tensions thus ran high within the city, and the situation inevitably promoted both prostitution and sodomy, for which the Renaissance cities enjoyed a merited reputation. The typical triad of many contemporary stories and dramas—the aged husband, beautiful young wife, and clever young man intent on seducing her—reflects a common domestic situation. These restless young men, uninhibited by responsibilities for a wife and family, were also quick to participate in the factional and family feuds and battles which were frequent occurrences in Renaissance social history. . . .

Delayed marriage for men inevitably affected the treatment and the fate of girls. Because of high mortalities and the inevitable shrinking of the age pyramid, there were fewer eligible and willing grooms, at approximately age 30, than prospective brides, girls between 15 and 20. The girls, or rather their families, had to enter a desperate competition for grooms, and this drove up the value of dowries to ruinous levels. . . . Since prospective brides outnumbered available grooms, many girls had no statistical chance of finding a husband. For most of them, there would be no alternative but the convent. A great saint of the fifteenth century, Bernardino of Siena, once described these unhappy girls, placed in convents because they were too poor, too homely, or too unhealthy to be married, as the "scum and vomit of the world."

The acts by which the marriage was contracted were several. The formal engagement usually involved the redaction of a notarial contract, which stipulated when the marriage should occur and how the dowry should be paid. The promise of marriage would often be repeated solemnly in church. On the wedding day, the bride and groom would often attend a special Mass, at which they received the Church's blessing. But that blessing, or even the presence of a priest, was not required for a legitimate marriage until the Council of Trent[3] in the sixteenth century made

[3]Church council, 1545–1563.

it obligatory for Catholics. The central act in the wedding ceremony was a procession, in which the groom led his bride from her father's house to his own. Through this public display, society recognized that this man and this woman would henceforth live together as husband and wife. The groom then usually gave as lavish a feast as his resources would allow, which sometimes lasted for days.

... Given the character of the marriage, the typical baby was received by a very young mother and a much older father. Within the city of Florence in 1427, the mean age of motherhood was approximately 26.5 years...; the mean age of fatherhood was 39.8 years. The age differences between mothers and fathers were again, less extreme in the countryside or in other Italian towns, but still must be considered extended.

The great differences in the average ages of fathers and mothers affected the atmosphere of the home and the training of children The mature, if not aged, fathers would have difficulty communicating with their children, and many would not live to see their children reach adulthood. One reason the male heads of family placed moral exhortations in their *ricordi*[4] is that they feared that they would not survive long enough to give much advice ... to the younger generation.

This distinctive situation placed the wife and mother in a critical position between the old generation of fathers and the children. Much younger and more vigorous than her husband, usually destined for longer and more intimate contact with her children, she became a prime mediator in passing on social values from old to young. Understandably, many of the educational tracts, which proliferate in Italy from the early fifteenth century, are directed at women. One of the first of them, Dominici's *Governance and Care of the Family*, ... beautifully describes both what Florentine mothers did, and what the author, a Dominican friar, wished them to do. Mothers, according to the friar, spent the days pampering and playing with their young children, fondling and licking them, spoiling them with beautiful toys, dressing them in elegant clothes, and teaching them how to sing and dance. An effeminizing influence seems evident here, which was not balanced by a strong masculine presence within the home. The friar recommends that the mothers rather impart spiritual values to their children; in telling them how to do this, he shows the new fifteenth-century awareness of the psychology of children. The home should contain a play altar, at which the young could act out the liturgy, and pictures of Christ and St. John represented as playful children, to whom real children will feel immediate rapport. Clearly, Dominici did not regard the child simply as a miniature adult, without a mind and psychology of his own.

Two conclusions seem appropriate here. The Renaissance household, with an aged, occupied and often absent husband and a young wife, was not ideally equipped to give balanced training to its children. But this de-

[4]Diaries.

ficiency seems to have increased the concern for the proper education of children. . . . [W]omen continued to dominate the training of young children, and inevitably they inculcated in them qualities which they admired—a taste for refined manners and elegant dress, and a high esthetic sensibility. In the sixteenth century, a character in the *Book of the Courtier*, by Baldassare Castiglione, then the most popular handbook of good manners, attributes all gracious exercises—music, dancing and poetry—to the influence of women. The gentleman of the Renaissance was fashioned to the tastes of women; so also was much of the culture of the age.

Births also helped shape the total society. Here, an important factor was the differences in relative fertility among the various segments of the community. The rural population, as we have mentioned, tended to be more prolific than the urban, and the rich, while slow to marry, still reproduced themselves more successfully than the poor. Differences in fertility rates inevitably generated flows of people from some parts of society to others. Thus, differential fertility between city and countryside assured that there would be constant immigration from rural areas into the towns. . . . This immigration had important social effects. It appears to have been selective, as the city especially attracted the skilled and the highly motivated. At Florence, many of the cultural leaders of the Renaissance . . . were of rural or small-town origins. The urban need for people promoted the careers of these gifted men. On the other hand, by introducing them into a milieu which made their own reproduction difficult, immigration also tended over the long run to extirpate the lines of creative individuals. It was not an unmixed blessing.

Within the cities, the wealthier families, in spite of the male reluctance to enter marriage, still tended to produce more children than the poor. Many of these children would be placed in convents or enter careers in the Church, but some would face a difficult decision. Either they would have to accept a social position lower than their parents, or they would have to seek to make their fortunes outside of their native city, even outside of Italy. . . . Many were forced therefore to wander through the world in search of fortune. Demographic pressures, in other words, required that even the sons of the wealthy adopt an entrepreneurial stance. This helps explain the ambitions and high energy of the Florentines and other Italians, and the prominence they achieved all over Europe, in many fields, in the Renaissance period.

The final event in the history of a marriage was death, and we can deal with death more briefly, as we have already referred to its central role in the social history of the epoch. Death was everywhere present during the Renaissance, and the ravages it perpetrated were at the root of the crisis of the family, which was most severe in the late fourteenth and early fifteenth centuries. Here, we shall note only the distinctive reactions of the surviving partner in a marriage to the death of a spouse.

For reasons already discussed, in the countryside it was typical for both widows and widowers quickly to remarry, if they were of suitable age. But in the city, the behavior of widowed men and women was quite different. The urban widower, who as a young man had usually waited long before entering his first marriage, quickly sought out a new wife. The widow, on the other hand, who as a young girl had been rushed into wedlock, delayed remarriage, and many widows did not remarry at all. The cities of the Renaissance consequently contained numerous male bachelors and widows, but very few spinsters and widowers. The mature male, who once had married, found it difficult to live without the continuing companionship of a woman. But the woman, after she had lost a husband, felt little compulsion to remarry. . . .

IV

EARLY MODERN EUROPE

In one sense, history is the solving of problems. Two of the classic problems have been the difficulty of defining "modern" and, following from that, the difficulty of determining when the modern world began. Wrangling over these problems persists, with little agreement. The Italians of the Renaissance were the first to broach the subject, seeing themselves, with no little immodesty, as the first modern people, more closely akin to the ancient world than to their immediate ancestors, whom they called Gothic and barbaric. Renaissance Italy saw the centuries after the fall of Roman civilization as the Middle Ages, a period between the classical world of Greece and Rome and fifteenth-century Italy. In the nineteenth century, historians began a debate over whether Renaissance Italy was modern, protomodern, or perhaps still essentially medieval. The debate continues today, part of the larger problem of periodization. Are there periods in history, or do historians arbitrarily classify certain centuries as periods, distinct eras?

As a way out of the dilemma, the term "early modern Europe" has come frequently to be favored, possibly because its chronological boundaries are so nebulous that historians can include within it very different cultures. Sometimes the early modern period in Europe refers to 1400–1789, thus encompassing Renaissance Italy, or 1500–1789, omitting both the Renaissance and the French Revolution. On the other hand, all categories of early modern Europe contain the sixteenth and seventeenth centuries, the period that the following selections describe.

These were the centuries when Italian humanism spread beyond the Alps, becoming Northern or Christian humanism. This is the era of the Protestant Reformation, Catholic Counter-Reformation, European exploration overseas, and the beginnings of political absolutism. It is the age of Michelangelo, Cervantes, Shakespeare, and Milton. But this was also a premodern society, characterized by tradition, relative immobility, and privilege. This society was still predominantly rural, though urban centers increased in size. Capitalism likewise grew, though this was surely not its heyday. Monarchy remained the political ideal and reality, though there were some calls for socialist or republican governments. The religion was Christian, though Christianity changed dramatically. In sum, the early modern era in Europe was a period of the confluence of old and new, a period of rapid change in some areas, but not a period of desire for or expectation of change, as the modern Western world is. Some historians refer to this as an age of crisis, because so much was called into question and so many institutions, beliefs, and conventions were shaken.

The following selections show dramatically a life that could be described in the words of the English philosopher, Thomas Hobbes, as "poor, nasty, brutish, and short." Condemned to hunger and cold, wracked by diseases, intensely religious if not fanatical, often violent, subject to increasing supervision by church and state, sixteenth- and seventeenth-century Europeans could, moreover, expect a lifespan less than half that of ours today.

The Early History of Syphilis: A Reappraisal

ALFRED W. CROSBY, JR.

Too often historians have described the voyages of Columbus and their aftermath in terms of how Europeans affected the Americas through exploration and settlement. In his important book, The Columbian Exchange. Biological and Cultural Consequences of 1492, *Alfred W. Crosby, Jr., offers a more balanced perspective by showing that the opening up of the Western Hemisphere affected life—human, animal, and plant—on both sides of the Atlantic. Although the balance sheet is mixed, Crosby believes that the bad outnumbered the good. Thus, maize, manioc, and potatoes increased the amount of food, improved the diet, and so led to a rise in the population of Europe. On the other hand, smallpox and measles decimated the American Indians, and the Spaniards began the breakdown of ecological stability in the New World.*

In this selection, Crosby discusses syphilis, the New World's revenge on the Old World. Against those who argue that syphilis had been present in Europe before Columbus, Crosby maintains that it first came to Europe in the 1490s. What arguments does the author make to support this claim? How did syphilis spread in Europe once it had arrived? In other words, what groups of people were primarily responsible for infecting others with that loathsome disease?

What exactly did syphilis do to people physically? Crosby stresses that the disease changed over time. How did people cope with it? What cures were available? Syphilis affected social relations even as it infected bodies. How did the relations of men and women—how did love-making—change as a result of this new virus? Bedeviled by herpes and AIDS, our own age might seem analogous to the sixteenth century.

The New World gave much in return for what it received from the Old World. In the writings of Desiderius Erasmus,[1] one can find mention of nearly every significant figure, event, crusade, fad, folly, and misery of the decades around 1500. Of all the miseries visited upon Europe in his lifetime, Erasmus judged few more horrible than the French disease, or syphilis. He reckoned no malady more contagious, more terrible for its victims, or more difficult to cure . . . or more fashionable! . . .

The men and women of Erasmus's generation were the first Europeans to know syphilis or so they said, at least. The pox, as the English called it, had struck like a thunderbolt in the very last years of the fifteenth century. But unlike most diseases that appear with such abruptness, it did not fill up the graveyards and then go away, to come again some other day or perhaps never. Syphilis settled down and became a permanent factor in human existence.

[1]Dutch humanist, c.1466–1536.

Syphilis has a special fascination for the historian because, of all mankind's most important maladies, it is the most uniquely "historical." The beginnings of most diseases lie beyond man's earliest rememberings. Syphilis, on the other hand, has a beginning. Many men, since the last decade of the fifteenth century, have insisted that they knew almost exactly when syphilis appeared on the world stage, and even where it came from. "In the yere of Chryst 1493 or there aboute," wrote Ulrich von Hutten,[2] one of Erasmus's correspondents, "this most foule and most grevous dysease beganne to sprede amonge the people." Another contemporary, Ruy Dáz de Isla,[3] agreed that 1493 was the year and went on to say that "the disease had its origin and birth from always in the island which is now named Española."[4] Columbus had brought it back, along with samples of maize and other American curiosities.

. . . In fact, the matter of the origin of syphilis is doubtlessly the most controversial subject in all medical historiography. . . .

Until the most recent decades there were only two widely accepted views of the provenance of syphilis: the Columbian theory and its antithesis, which stated that syphilis was present in the Old World long before 1493. Now the Unitarian theory has appeared, which postulates that venereal syphilis is but one syndrome of a multi-faceted world-wide disease, treponematosis. But before we examine this newest challenge to the veracity of Ulrich von Hutten and Dáz de Isla and the other Columbians, let us deal with the older argument: was venereal syphilis present on both sides of the Atlantic in 1492 or only on the American?

The documentary evidence for the Old World seems clear. No unequivocal description of syphilis in any pre-Columbian literature of the Old World has ever been discovered. . . .

The physicians, surgeons, and laymen of the Old World who wrote about venereal syphilis in the sixteenth century recorded, with few exceptions, that it was a new malady; and we have no reason to believe they were all mistaken. . . . Spaniards, Germans, Italians, Egyptians, Persians, Indians, Chinese, and Japanese . . . agreed that they had never seen the pox before. It is very unlikely that they were all mistaken on the same subject at the same time.

. . . The variety of names given it and the fact that they almost always indicate that it was thought of as a foreign import are strong evidence for its newness. Italians called it the French disease, which proved to be the most popular title; the French called it the disease of Naples; the English called it the French disease, the Bordeaux disease, or the Spanish disease; Poles called it the German disease; Russians called it the Polish disease; and so on. Middle Easterners called it the European pustules; Indians called it

[2]German humanist, 1488–1523.
[3]Sixteenth-century writer of medical books.
[4]Currently Hispaniola, divided between Haiti and the Dominican Republic.

the disease of the Franks (western Europeans). Chinese called it the ulcer of Canton, that port being their chief point of contact with the west. The Japanese called it Tang sore, Tang referring to China; or, more to the point, the disease of the Portuguese. . . . [I]t was not until the nineteenth century that . . . "syphilis," minted in the 1520s, became standard throughout the world.

Another indication of the abrupt appearance of the pox is the malignancy of the disease in the years immediately after its initial recognition in Europe. The classic course of a new disease is rapid spread and extreme virulence, followed by a lessening of the malady's deadliness. The most susceptible members of the human population are eliminated by death, as are the most virulent strains of the germ, in that they kill off their hosts before transmission to other hosts occurs. The records of the late fifteenth and early sixteenth centuries are full of lamentations on the rapid spread of syphilis and the horrible effects of the malady, which often occurred within a short time after the initial infection: widespread rashes and ulcers, often extending into the mouth and throat; severe fevers and bone pains; and often early death. The latter is a very rare phenomenon in the initial stages of the disease today, and most who do die of syphilis have resisted the disease successfully for many years. Ulrich von Hutten's description of syphilis in the first years after its appearance indicates a marked contrast between its nature then and its "mildness" today:

> There were byles, sharpe, and standing out, hauying the similitude and quantite of acornes, from which came so foule humours, and so great stenche, that who so ever ones smelled it, thought hym selfe to be enfect. The colour of these pusshes [pustules] was derke grene, and the slight therof was more grevous unto the pacient then the peyne it selfe: and yet their peynes were as thoughe they hadde lyen in fire.

. . . The most convincing of all evidence for the abrupt arrival of the French disease in the Old World in approximately 1500 is the physical remains, the bones of the long dead. No one has ever unearthed pre-Columbian bones in the Old World which display unequivocal signs of syphilitic damage. . . .

Several anti-Columbian theorists have brushed aside all the above arguments by hypothesizing that syphilis had existed in the Old World prior to the 1490s, but in a *mild* form. Then, in the 1490s the causative organism mutated into the deadly *Treponema pallidum*, and syphilis began to affect the deep body structures and became a killer. This hypothesis cannot be disproved and it comfortably fits all the facts, but it cannot be proved, either. . . .

Where did syphilis come from? If it came from America, then we may be nearly certain that it came in 1493 or shortly after. Let us consider the physical evidence first. Is there a contrast here between the Old and New

Worlds? The answer becomes more and more unequivocally affirmative as the archeologists and paleopathologists disinter from American soil an increasing number of pre-Columbian human bones displaying what is almost surely syphilitic damage. . . .

The documentary evidence for the Columbian provenance of venereal syphilis is obviously shaky. We cannot say, moreover, that the evidence provided by the paleopathologists is utterly decisive, but when the two are combined—when archivists and gravediggers join hands to claim that America is the homeland of *Treponema pallidum*—it becomes very difficult to reject the Columbian theory. . . .

Is venereal syphilis a separate and distinct disease, once endemic to only one part of the world, or is it merely a syndrome of a disease which has always been worldwide, but happens to have different symptoms and names in different areas? Those who accept the Unitarian theory, as it is called, claim that that which is called syphilis, when transmitted venereally, is really the same malady as the nonvenereal illnesses called yaws in the tropics, bejel in the Middle East, pinta in Central America, irkinja in Australia, and so on. The manner in which this ubiquitous disease, named "treponematosis" by the Unitarians, manifests itself in man is somewhat different in different areas, because of climatic and cultural differences, but it is all one disease. If this is true, then all the squabble about deformation of forehead bones here and not there, ulcers on the sex organs now and not then, and on and on, is completely irrelevant. As E. H. Hudson, the foremost champion of the Unitarian theory, puts it, "Since treponematosis was globally distributed in prehistoric times, it . . . is idle to speak of Columbus' sailors bringing syphilis to a syphilis-free Europe in 1493." . . .

In fact, such is the paucity of evidence from the fifteenth and sixteenth centuries that the Unitarian theory is no more satisfactory than the Columbian. We simply do not know much, and may never know much about the world distribution of the treponemas in the 1490s. . . .

There are only two things of which we can be sure. One, the only pre-Columbian bones clearly displaying the lesions of treponematosis or one of that family of disease are American. . . . Two, several contemporaries did record the return of venereal syphilis with Columbus. . . .

The Columbian theory is still viable. Even if it is unequivocally proved that all the treponematoses are one, the Columbians can simply claim that treponematosis was exclusively American in 1492. There is no unquestionable evidence that any of the treponematoses existed in the Old World in 1492. . . .

It is not impossible that the organisms causing treponematosis arrived from America in the 1490s in mild or deadly form, and, breeding in the entirely new and very salubrious environment of European, Asian, and African bodies, evolved into both venereal and nonvenereal syphilis and yaws. If this is true, then Columbus ranks as a villain with the serpent of the Garden of Eden.

A less presumptuous theory is that the treponematoses were one single disease many thousands of years ago. Then, as man changed his environment and habits, and especially when he crossed the Bering Straits into the isolation of the Americas, the differing ecological conditions produced different types of treponematosis and, in time, closely related but different diseases. . . .

. . . It seems logical to believe that if deadly diseases crossed the Atlantic from east to west, then there must have also been a similar countercurrent. The most likely candidate for the role of America's answer to the Old World's smallpox is venereal syphilis. The theory of the origin of the treponematoses offered in this chapter squares with all Darwin tells us about evolution, and allows the American Indians and Columbus the dubious honor of incubating and transporting venereal syphilis. It is this hypothesis which, in the current state of medical and historical research, seems to hold the most promise as a vehicle for future inquiry and speculation.

Having finished with the polemics of syphilis, let us turn to the first century of its recorded history. By the fifteenth century, treponematosis had evolved into several related maladies in the desert-isolated jungles, isolated plateaus, different islands, and continents of the world. Then came one of the greatest technological advances: European innovations in shipbuilding, seamanship and navigation. . . . A great mixing of peoples, cultural influences, and diseases began.

The various treponematoses spread out from their hearthlands, mixing and changing under new ecological conditions in a way that will probably always confound medical historians. The evidence that comes down to us from that time is sparse and confused. . . .

Europeans drew the world together by means of ocean voyages. . . . The epidemiology of syphilis has a special characteristic: it is usually transmitted by sexual contact and spreads when a society's or a group's allegiance to marital fidelity fails. Sailors, by the nature of their profession, are men without women, and therefore men of many women. If we may assume that the nature of sailors in the sixteenth century was not radically different than in the twentieth, then we can imagine no group of the former century more perfectly suited for guaranteeing that venereal syphilis would have worldwide distribution. . . . European sailors carried it to every continent but Antartica and Australia before Columbus was in his grave.

Venereal syphilis arrived in Barcelona in 1493, according to Diáz de Isla, but we have no other news of it in Spain for several years. Why? First, because of the paucity of documentation. Second, because syphilis spreads by venereal contact, and not by touch, breath, or insect vectors, as do the traditional epidemic diseases of smallpox, typhus, plague, and so on. In a stable society its spread will be steady but not extremely fast. . . . Imagine 1,000 people, one of whom is syphilitic. He infects two others, who infect two others each, in turn. The number of the diseased goes up steadily: 1, 2, 4, 8, 16, 32, and so on. In the early stages the disease's advance is rapid, but the victims are few and below the threshold of society's attention. The disease's spread does not accelerate, it is passed on from one to another no more rapidly than before, but 32 becomes 64, 64 leads to 128, 128 is suddenly 256—and society abruptly decides that its existence is threatened by epidemic, long after the initial arrival of syphilis.

Venereal syphilis will only spread with the rapidity of plague or typhus when a society is in such chaos that sexual morality breaks down. Such a sad state of affairs is usually the product of war. Women are without protection or food, and have only their bodies to sell. The men of the armies have a monopoly of force, most of the wealth and food—and no women.

The first recorded epidemic of syphilis took place in Italy in the mid-1490s. In 1494 Charles VIII of France,[5] in pursuit of his claims to the throne of Naples, crossed the Alps into Italy with an army of about 50,000 soldiers of French, Italian, Swiss, German, and other origins. The campaign was not one marked by full-scale battles, but the army, trailing its column of the usual camp followers, engaged in the usual practices of rape and sack anyway. The Neapolitans, retreating toward their city, laid the countryside to waste. Charles, once ensconced in Naples, discovered that the Italians, appalled by his success, were putting aside their personal conflicts and forming a coalition against him. Ferdinand[6] and Isabella,[7] anxious to prevent the establishment of French hegemony in Italy, were sending Spanish troops. Charles packed his bags and marched back to France, and the whole process of battle, rape, and sack was repeated in reverse.

Syphilis, hitherto spreading slowly and quietly across Europe, flared into epidemic in Italy during this invasion, just as the epidemiology of the malady would lead one to expect. It is probable that there was also a rapid spread of typhus, another traditional camp follower. It was in Italy that the truth of Voltaire's[8] epigram was first demonstrated: "Depend upon it, when 30,000 men engage in pitched battle against an equal number of the enemy, about 20,000 on each side have the pox."

Charles arrived back at Lyon in November 1495, where he disbanded his army; and its members, with billions of treponemas in their blood streams, scattered back to their homes in a dozen lands or off to new

---

[5]King of France, 1483–1498.

[6]Ferdinand V, the Catholic King of Castille and Léon (1474–1504, ruling jointly with his wife, Isabella I). As Ferdinand II, King of Aragon (1479–1516) and as Ferdinand III, King of Naples (1504–1516).

[7]Isabella I, the Catholic Queen of Castile and Léon (1474–1504), Queen of Aragon (1479–1504), and wife of Ferdinand V.

[8]French author, 1694–1778.

wars. With the dispersal of that army, the lightning advance of syphilis across Europe and the rest of the Old World became inevitable.

Syphilis had already appeared in Germany by the summer of 1495, for in August Emperor Maximilian[9] of the Holy Roman Empire issued a mandate at Worms calling it the "evil pocks" and blaming it on the sin of blasphemy. In the same year Swiss and Frenchmen recorded its arrival with horror. The pox reached Holland and England no later than 1496. Greece knew it in the same year, and Hungary and Russia in 1499. . . .

The epidemic rolled on into Africa, where "If any Barbarie be infected with the disease commonly called the Frenche pox, they die thereof for the most part, and are seldom cured"; and appeared in the Middle East as early as 1498, with a similar result. The Portuguese, among the earliest to receive the infection, probably carried it farthest, around the Cape of Good Hope. It appeared in India in 1498 and sped on ahead of the Portuguese to Canton by 1505. In a decade it advanced from the Caribbean to the China Sea, at once a tribute to man's nautical genius and social idiocy.

We are lucky in our attempt to trace the early history of syphilis in that shame was not attached to the disease at the beginning. . . . As if to illustrate the frankness of the age, Ulrich von Hutten, the great humanist, wrote a gruesomely detailed tract on his own sufferings, gratuitously mentioning that his father had the same disease, and dedicated the whole to a cardinal! . . .

The plentiful documentation enables the venerologist of an antiquarian bent to trace not only the history of the epidemic but the history of its remedies and of the character of the disease itself. The best analysis of the latter is by Jean Astruc.[10] . . . He breaks down the early history into five stages.

1. 1494–1516. In this period the first sign of the disease in a patient was small genital ulcers, followed by a widespread rash of various character . . . As the disease spread through the victim's body, palate, uvula, jaw, and tonsils were often destroyed. Large gummy tumors were common, and the victim suffered agonizing pains in muscles and nerves, especially at night. General physical deterioration followed and often culminated in early death.

2. During the period 1516 to 1526 two new symptoms were added to the syphilis syndrome: bone inflammation, characterized by severe pain and eventual corruption of the bone and marrow; and the appearance in some sufferers of hard genital pustules, resembling warts or corns.

3. A general abatement of the malignancy of the disease marked the period 1526 to 1540. The number of pustules per sufferer decreased, and we hear more of gummy tumors. Inflamed swelling of the lymph gland in the groin became common. Loss of hair and teeth became common, but this may have been caused by mercury poisoning, mercury having been used as a remedy.

[9]1493–1519.

[10]Eighteenth-century venerologist.

4. From 1540 to 1560 the diminution of the more spectacular symptoms of the malady continued. Gonorrhea, which by this time and for centuries afterward was confused with syphilis, became "the most common, if not perpetual symptom" in the early states of syphilis.

5. Between 1560 and 1610 the deadliness of the malady continued to decline, and only one new symptom was added: noise in the ears.

By the seventeenth century syphilis was as we know it today: a very dangerous infection, but not one that could be called explosive in the nature of its attack on the victim. . . .

If one wished to create a disease to encourage the proliferation of quacks and quack remedies, one could do no better than syphilis; and this was particularly true in the sixteenth century. The disease was new and no traditional remedies for it existed. Its symptoms were hideous, persuading sufferers to try any and all cures. Syphilis is a malady characterized by periods of remission and latency . . . and so if the quack does not kill with his cure, he can often claim success—for a time, at least. The quacks cured by searing the pustules with hot irons, and prescribed an unbelievable assortment of medicines to swallow and to apply, the latter including even boiled ants' nest, along with the ants. . . .

The two most popular remedies for syphilis in the sixteenth century were mercury and guaiacum. The first came into use very soon after the appearance of the pox, both in Europe and Asia. . . . [I]t proved to be the only generally effective means of arresting syphilis for the next four hundred years. Before the middle of the sixteenth century, mercury was being rubbed on, applied to the body in plasters and swallowed in pills.

Unfortunately, mercury was overused, and in many cases the cure was successful but the patient died of it. The humoral theory of disease, which dominated European thinking at the time, taught that illness came as the result of an imbalance among the four humors. Syphilis could be cured if the body could be obliged to bleed, defecate, sweat out, and spit out the excess of the offending humor: phlegm, in this case. The most obvious symptom of mercury poisoning is the constant dribbling of saliva, even to the amount of several pints a day. What, thought the sixteenth-century physician, could be more desirable? The body is purging itself of that which is making it sick. Out came the offending excess, often along with gums, teeth, and assorted interior fragments of the body. . . .

. . . Many other remedies were tried in its place—China root, sassafras, sarsaparilla, and so on—but only one displaced mercury as the cure, if only for a time. This was guaiacum, a decoction of the wood of a tree of the West Indies, which became the most popular panacea of the 1520s. The wood had much to recommend it. It came from America, as did the disease; and this is, of course, the way a thoughtful God would arrange things. It was a very impressive wood, extremely hard and so heavy that "the leaste pece of its caste into water, synketh streyght to the bottom," which indicated that it must have additional miraculous properties. A decoction of it caused the patient to perspire freely, a very desirable effect, according to humoral theory. . . .

The prevalence of syphilis and the wood's effectiveness not only against it but also against "goute in the feete, the stone, palsey, lepre, dropsy, fallying evyll, and other diseases," drove its price to dizzy heights. Like a poor man's soup bone, the sawdust of guaiacum was boiled up again and again for those not lucky enough or wealthy enough to buy the first decoction. Counterfeit guaiacum flooded the market and pieces of the wood were hung in churches to be prayed to by the most impecunious syphilitics. . . .

. . . Murmurs, soon rising to shouts, of the wood's ineffectiveness began to be voiced in the 1530s. . . . The fad of the Holy Wood from the New World returned a few generations later, and the use of it never quite died out—it was not removed from the British Pharmacopoeia until 1932—but its reputation as *the cure* had evaporated. Europe returned to China root, sassafras, prayer, and, especially, mercury. . . .

. . . In an age in which the Pope had to rescind an order expelling all prostitutes from Rome because of the loss of public revenue that resulted, the new venereal disease inevitably spread to every cranny of Europe and became, like smallpox or consumption, one of the permanently resident killers. The English doctor, William Clowes, stated in the 1580s that one out of every two he had treated in the House of St. Bartholomew had been syphilitic, and that "except the people of this land do speedily repent their most ungodly life and leave this odious sin, it cannot be but the whole land will shortly be poisoned with this most noisome sickness."

However, *Treponema pallidum* brought some good in its train, though those who benefited from it were few. Physicians, surgeons and quacks found a source of wealth in the pox. . . .

. . . When man is both helpless and foolish in the presence of horror, as is often the case in matters pertaining to venereal disease, he finds solace in jokes. There was a great deal of joking about the French disease in the sixteenth century. . . .

Erasmus mentions syphilis a number of times. In one of his *Colloquies* he announces to the world that "unless you're a good dicer, an infamous whoremonger, a heavy drinker, a reckless spendthrift, a wastrel and heavily in debt, decorated with the French pox, hardly anyone will believe you're a knight." . . .

To most, however, the pox was no subject for laughter, but an unmitigated disaster. It was no respecter of rank, and thus had a direct and dismal effect on political and church history . . . Two dynasties whose members were not noted for monogamous behavior died out in that age, the House of Valois[11] and the House of Tudor.[12] As usual, little can be proved,

[11] Royal dynasty in France, 1328–1589.
[12] Royal dynasty in England, 1485–1603.

but the inability of queens to give birth to living children makes one suspect that syphilis played a role in the demise of these families, and thus in the political turmoil of their realms. There is little doubt that Francis I,[13] famous for having "lost all save life and honor" in the battle of Pavia, lost both in the end to the pox. And there is little doubt that one and possibly two of the husbands of Mary Queen of Scots,[14] and, therefore, possibly the woman herself, had the disease. . . .

The pox's full impact, however, can never be measured if we restrict ourselves to economics, literature, politics, and religion. *Treponema pallidum* was chiefly a social villain, one of the most evil of the whole age of Erasmus, Shakespeare, and Francis I. The fear of infection tended to erode the bonds of respect and trust that bound men and women together. The prostitute's chance of Christian forgiveness faded. "If I were judge," roared Luther,[15] "I would have such venemous syphilitic whores broken on the wheel and flayed because one cannot estimate the harm such filthy whores do to young men." And those less obviously offensive suffered, also, from the terror engendered by the new plague. The sick and the stranger found closed doors where once they had found hospitality. Friendships were altered by a new coolness, as men began in some degree to limit their contacts with any who might conceivably have been touched by the pox.

We find little bits of information indicating the change. Public baths went out of style, for it was widely realized that many as innocent of promiscuity as newborn babes had contracted the French disease in such places. The use of the common drinking cup fell out of style. The kiss, a customary gesture of affection between friends as well as lovers, came under suspicion. . . .

What was the effect of syphilis on general human contact? Consider that one of the crimes—false or no—of which Cardinal Woolsey[16] was accused in his arraignment before Parliament in 1529 was that he, "knowing himself to have the foul and contagious disease of the great pox . . . came daily to your grace [Henry VIII],[17] rowning in your ear, and blowing upon your most noble grace with his perilous and infectious breath, to the marvellous danger of your highness." . . .

It is obvious that in no area did syphilis wreak more havoc than in relations between men and women. No civilization has ever satisfactorily solved the problem of sex. Even if there were no such thing as venereal disease, the sex relationship would still produce distrust, fear, and pain, as well as confidence, love, and comfort. Add to the normal emotional

[13]King of France, 1515–1547.

[14]Mary Stuart, Queen of Scotland, 1542–1567.

[15]Martin Luther, German Protestant reformer, 1483–1546.

[16]Lord Chancellor of England, 1515–1529.

[17]King of England, 1509–1547.

difficulties of the sex relationship not just the possibility of the pains of gonorrhea but the danger of a horrible and often fatal disease, syphilis. Where there must be trust, there must now also be suspicion. Where there must be a surrender of self, there must now also be a shrewd consideration of future health. . . .

Gabriello Falloppio, in his book of syphilis, *De Morbo Gallico*[18] (1564), suggested that after sexual intercourse a man should carefully wash and dry his genitals. The age of the canny lover had arrived.

[18] *Of the French Disease.*

"Lost Women" in Early Modern Seville: The Politics of Prostitution

MARY ELIZABETH PERRY

In the sixteenth and for the first half of the seventeenth century, Spain was militarily the strongest country in Europe. Spain fought the Turks, the French, and championed resurgent Catholicism against nascent Protestantism. Spaniards circumnavigated the world, explored distant lands, and conquered entire empires in the New World. This was Spain's "Golden Age," a period not only of political and military glory but also of brilliance in literature and art. Yet rapid socioeconomic developments during these centuries produced, in Seville at least, a golden age of prostitution.

Several topics are raised here, including the causes of prostitution, the role of the city government, and the relationship between religion and prostitution. Why in a country obsessed with religious purity—the monarchy had expelled Moslems and Jews and the Inquisition strove mightily to ensure religious orthodoxy—did prostitution so flourish in Seville? What changes specifically resulted in an increase in the numbers of prostitutes in early modern Seville? How did social and economic changes affect women in their traditional roles as nuns, wives, and workers? Why did women become prostitutes?

The city government chose not to attempt to eradicate prostitution. In fact, city fathers encouraged and regulated it. Why? How did regulations support and abet the practice of prostitution? Why were the occupations of actress, streethawker, and practitioner of folk medicine of such concern to the city government?

Perry emphasizes that morality was much on the minds of the urban elite as they sought to use prostitution to preserve public order and right behavior. What were the links between prostitution, morality, and the social order? How did the powerful female symbols of the Virgin Mary, the "Painted Prostitute," and Mary Magdalene underscore the double standard between men and women and between the reality of life and the image of Christian society? Why did the city fathers see brothels as essential pillars to upholding a Christian morality and a Christian social order? What position did the Catholic Church take regarding prostitution?

In the sixteenth century a new sexually transmitted disease, syphilis, became epidemic. How did the appearance and spread of syphilis influence the world of prostitution in Seville? Prostitutes could always be shunned and feared for moral contagion; now males looked upon them as carriers of a dreadful and incomprehensible disease. Moreover, prostitutes practiced contraception, abortion, and unlicensed medicine. Despite these illicit patterns of behavior, the city government still regulated prostitution and wished no end to it. Why? Was it a matter of economics, the money to be made in various ways from prostitutes? Or did political reasons predominate in the minds of the urban elite as they watched over the practice of prostitution?

Perry concludes by saying that the "lost women" of Seville "were not lost at all." What does she mean by this?

To city fathers in early modern Seville, prostitutes were "lost women." The euphemism suggests that prostitutes were outcasts, completely outside the culture of the city. Historical evidence argues just the opposite, however, for it presents a picture of prostitutes who were an integral part of their community.

Seville offers an exciting social arena for examining prostitution in the early modern period. Thousands of people poured into the city after 1503 when the Crown of Castile placed in this inland seaport its agency to control colonization and trade with the newly discovered Americas. Seville quickly became a boom town, its streets teeming with the thousands who came to seek their fortunes. Archival documents describe many of these people and the city's attempts to control them. These sources show that the alliance of churchmen and nobles who ruled Seville reeled under the impact of rapid socioeconomic changes. Desperately trying to preserve its position, this oligarchy consciously used legislation and existing institutions to buttress the existing social order. City fathers seized upon prostitution as a commercial prop, an agency to reinforce lines of authority, and a symbol of evil. They pointed to prostitutes as diseased, disgusting, and parasitical. They used prostitution to unite the community in their support against such evil, and they used it to justify the extension of their governmental powers.

Although historical sources provide rich descriptions of city regulation of prostitution, they contain little evidence of the numbers, ages, or social backgrounds of prostitutes in the city. Actual voices of prostitutes are heard only rarely in these sources, and then most often in the picaresque novels, plays, and ballads that they themselves did not write. For the most part, the literature, acts, medical treatises, social surveys, memoirs, and church and city documents of Seville present an official view of prostitution.

Despite these limitations, a study of "lost women" in Seville can broaden our understanding of prostitution. First, it describes sixteenth- and seventeenth-century women in a commercially active city and suggests that changes in this period disrupted traditional roles and promoted prostitution as a livelihood. Second, it demonstrates that prostitution was not only acceptable in the society of this city; it was even a pillar of the moral system that buttressed the existing social order. Finally, it suggests that any consideration of prostitution must examine its political implications, for evidence from Seville argues that prostitution thrived because it was politically useful to the ruling class.

For centuries women in Seville had found many ways to survive. As wives or nuns, many had depended for a livelihood on husbands or convents. Others worked in crafts and industry, streethawking and retail, domestic service, folk medicine, inns, and drama. Widows owned and operated the shops and dramatic companies that they had inherited. Some women were kept as concubines by the wealthier men of the community, and others earned a living as prostitutes on the streets or in the public brothels. In the early modern period, several factors combined to disrupt traditional roles of women and promote prostitution as a livelihood.

Seville thrived in the first half of the sixteenth century. Many people found instant wealth in the rich trade with the Americas, and even more benefited from the "price revolution," a sharp increase in prices that stemmed from the influx of precious metals from the Americas and the demographic increases of this period. Nobles enriched their own families through marriage to young women of wealthy merchant families. One merchant was so eager to buy noble status that he gave to the nobleman who married his daughter a dowry of two hundred forty thousand ducats, a sum greater than an unskilled worker would make in a thousand years. Families with large land holdings married into other landholding families in order to consolidate the large blocs of land that were increasingly profitable for olive and vine cultivation.

Not everyone in Seville profited from the economic boom, however. A decline in local industry accompanied the great success of commerce, for merchants found it more profitable to ship to the Americas foreign-made products rather than locally produced merchandise. Local products were often more expensive because many wages were higher in Seville where the "price revolution" made its first impact. Some local producers failed to keep up with the improving quality and techniques of production used abroad. Seville's silk industry, for example, fell behind the French silk weavers who were able to produce in quantity the more fashionable fabrics. Convents that sustained themselves by the silk-weaving of their nuns suffered so much from foreign competition that the crown prohibited foreign-made silks in 1621, declaring that foreign producers had caused many convents to lose their livelihood. By the middle of the seventeenth century, an official of the silk masters' guild reported that of the city's three thousand silk looms, only sixty were in use. While the fortunes of merchants continued to increase, textile workers found less and less work.

Agricultural producers were also affected by this boom. The opening of markets in the New World and the increased prices of the "price revolution" encouraged larger scale agricultural production, much of it devoted to olive and vine cultivation. The government set price ceilings on wheat in an attempt to keep bread at a reasonable price, but this policy encouraged agricultural producers to turn from wheat production to olives and vines, which were more profitable in both foreign and domestic markets. Spain's wars abroad closed some foreign markets to Spanish agricultural products and increased taxes so that small agricultural producers found it increasingly difficult to pay the rising costs of production as well as the heavy taxes. By the end of the sixteenth century, viceroys reported to the crown that one-half to two-thirds of the land that had once been cultivated had been abandoned. The wealthy agricultural producers absorbed more land and prospered, but the small producers left the land to find jobs in the cities or seek their fortunes in the New World.

Government monetary policy further increased economic distress. As the crown removed precious metals from coins to enrich the royal treasury, vellon, a mixture of copper and silver, replaced gold and silver. During the first half of the seventeenth century, the government restamped or revalued coins on seven separate occasions in Seville. Monetary speculation flourished, but real purchasing power fell. While wages increased in early modern Seville, they couldn't keep up with rising prices and monetary devaluation.

These economic changes disrupted the usual roles of women of the city. Convents, for example, offered fewer women a livelihood. Fathers had traditionally placed their daughters in convents when they lacked enough money for a suitable marriage dowry. . . .

Most convents also required a dowry, although a small amount. In some cases, the Archbishopric provided dowries so that poor girls could enter a religious order. One convent, the Monastery of the Sweet Name of Jesus, had been founded especially for reformed prostitutes, and it depended on city charity rather than dowries from its members. In 1581 this convent reported that it was the home for more than one hundred women and asked the city for more alms to support its nuns, novitiates, and lay sisters.

As prices rose and money fell in value, many convents had to increase the amount of dowry required from its members. Others simply fell into poverty. The Convent of Santa María la Real in Seville reported in 1597 that its building was in danger of collapse and its poverty was so great that it could feed its one hundred and twenty members on only three days of the week. Nuns were particularly hurt by the devaluation of money because they had few ways to augment their incomes. Unlike monks, nuns could not earn fees for preaching, burying the dead, or saying Masses. In addition, they were prohibited from begging door-to-door for food.

Lacking a dowry for either marriage or convent, some women lived together in "congregations" as *beatas* (holy women). Usually widows and young unmarried women, they often lived in a house next to the parish church and considered the parish priest their director. They supported themselves by the work of their hands and by income from any property they owned, but they were generally very poor. Some priests disapproved of this spontaneous form of religious community life and tried to impose on *beatas* the control of the regular clergy.

Marriage became less likely for women in the lower income groups. In his Third Discourse, the *tratadista* (economic theorist) Martínez de Mata[1] recognized the problems resulting because marriage was discouraged for young men with no livelihood. He blamed foreign competition for taking away the jobs of many Spaniards and causing small farmers, textile workers, and artisan-producers to become vagabonds. The women who could have married them in better economic circumstances remained single and perished from hunger.

Wives were more frequently abandoned in the early modern period. Many underemployed and unemployed husbands abandoned wives and children to seek their fortunes in the Indies, a pattern noted repeatedly by the priests who surveyed the poor of the city in 1667. Rural laborers left their families and miserable existence on the land, hoping to find a better life in the cities, the army, or the Indies. Foreigners married women of Seville so they could enjoy certain economic and political priveleges in the city, only to leave their wives and return to their homelands when they had earned some money. Although statistics of abandoned women are not available, this appears to have been a general pattern throughout the early modern period. The Venetian ambassador to Spain reported in 1525 that so many men had left Seville for the New World that "the city was left in the hands of women," and one hundred and fifty years later this same problem was noted in the 1667 survey of the poor.

Emigration, of course, was open to women as well as men, but it was regulated by the crown. A royal letter of 1604 complained that more than six hundred women had sailed from Seville for New Spain, although only fifty of them had been licensed. Women who emigrated had to have recommendations for a royal license or some money to buy passage as nonlicensed emigrants. They also had to have a certain venturesome spirit.

One emigrant in 1603 was . . . Catalina de Crusa. A nun in Vizcaya, she had run away from her convent and arrived in Seville in 1603. Disguising herself as a young man, she went to the New World where she worked

---

[1]Francesco Martínez de Mata penned many memorials in the 1650s on the problem of Spain's decline.

for twenty years and became a second lieutenant. A monk who knew her there said she had a string of mules in Vera Cruz that she used to bring in merchandise brought by the Spanish fleet to Mexico. Acquaintances in New Spain knew her as a young man, too tall for a woman, but lacking the stature and bearing of an arrogant youth. Her face was neither ugly nor beautiful, distinguished by shiny black wide-open eyes and a little fuzz above her upper lip. She wore her hair short like a man's, and carried a sword very well. Her step was light and elegant. Only her hands appeared rather feminine.

Catalina might have taken her secret to the grave, but in 1624 she was accused of killing a man. To save herself from the gallows, she declared that the court could not hang her because she was a woman and a nun. In great amazement, the local authorities sent her back to Spain where the king gave her five hundred ducats and the formal title of second lieutenant. She became a popular hero, treated as an awesome sensation. In 1630 the king granted her a license to dress as a man. . . .

Obviously, Catalina was an exception. For most women emigration was neither available as a means of escape nor as a catapult to fame. Marriage was favored in this society not only as a livelihood, but also as an institution to impose authority over young girls and prevent them from "losing themselves." The basic law of Castile declared that one reason for marriage was "to avoid quarrels, homicides, insolence, violence, and many other very wrongful acts which would take place on account of women if marriage did not exist." Because marriage appeared to be so crucial to social order, many benefactors provided charitable dowries so that poor girls could marry. . . .

Marriage was not always a formal arrangement in Seville, and many people took partners with neither dowry nor occupation. Poor people accepted these temporary alliances with practical cynicism, an attitude apparent in the following verse from a popular ballad:

> *A husband by night*
> *is a well-known threat:*
> *Don't believe any promises,*
> *Trust only what you can touch.*

While the men realized the inconvenience of heading a regular household, the women held no illusions about marriage.

Women who were unable to depend upon a husband for bread and shelter found their own wages increasingly inadequate and irregular. When the fleet for New Spain prepared to sail, seamstresses and silk workers worked night and day trying to fill merchants' orders. After the fleet sailed, however, demand fell off dramatically, and little money came in. Widows and women without husbands lived together to cut expenses and support one another as they tried to augment their small incomes. A report on charitable works in the city during the 1670s described the great number of widows and single women who had no other income but what they could earn with the labor of their hands. It estimated that each woman could earn only one *real* a day, while bread cost five *reales*. Unemployment, underemployment, and inadequate wages pushed many women into prostitution. For them, prostitution was a part-time occupation that could supplement their very meager incomes.

The economic and social dislocations of early modern Seville encouraged the exploitation of every possible means to survive. Traditional informal social controls no longer restrained exploitation in neighborhoods teeming with newcomers who soon moved away. Thousands of children and youths without parents appeared in Seville, overwhelming the few institutions that could provide food and shelter. People took in orphans and used them to beg money or get customers for both female and male prostitutes. Young women fortunate enough to find a job were considered fair prey by their employers.

In his report on the royal prison of Seville, the lawyer Cristóbal de Chaves described a typical pattern for young female servants. Ana was seduced by Juan de Molina, the son of her master. He gave her lessons every day in how to be a successful prostitute, and he placed her in a brothel. . . . On the days that she did not take in much money, he beat her, for he wanted the money for gambling. He taught her how to call out and get clients, and he showed her many tricks for getting money from them.

Juan developed a system to prevent Ana from cheating on him. He watched from an alleyway outside the brothel and carefully counted her clients, placing a pebble in the hood of his cape for each one. Since he had made her agree to charge each client a set price, he could easily tell if she were holding back any of her earnings by consulting the pebbles in his hood when she gave him the money.

Ana finally talked with another prostitute about her problems, and Juan was soon arrested. Sentenced to the galleys for ten years, he tried to keep his hold over her. He wrote to her from prison, reminding her that she was his "thing." He drew a picture for her that showed him, the former master, now a galley slave in chains with a chain leading from him to the hands of a woman he entitled "Ana." Between the two figures he drew a heart pierced by two arrows. The heart, he wrote, was Juan's, and the arrows were Ana's. Chaves did not indicate whether Juan and Ana saw the irony in the reversal of their roles.

Many people tried to maintain control over prostitutes who provided them with money, but others simply "pawned" women to the city brothels for a single lump sum. Fathers, brothers, boyfriends, or husbands sold women into brothels for ten or twenty ducats. A 1621 city ordinance reforming the administration of city brothels expressly prohibited the pawning of a woman to a brothel by a person to whom she owed a debt, even though she might agree to this arrangement. No woman, it asserted, should be sold into the brothels nor kept there to pay off a debt.

City regulations of this period encouraged prostitution because they made it more difficult for women to earn a living in other occupations. Streethawking, for example, was banned by city officials who suspected, with some justification, that streethawking was a cover for prostitutes and vagabonds. However, their attempts to ban street selling cut off the livelihood of many people who then turned to prostitution in earnest. One woman agreed to leave prostitution in 1572 if she could regain her place for selling fruit, which a public official had taken from her. Bartolomé Murillo, who painted saints and street people in seventeenth-century Seville, depicted streethawkers as quiet, rather serious young women trying to earn a living. City fathers, however, saw them as noisy, brazen price-gougers who threatened the peace of the city and their control of it.

The livelihood of another group of women was cut off by regulations on dramatic productions. Under pressure from clerics, Philip II[2] prohibited all dramatic performances in 1598. Two years later the crown directed a group of theologians to draw up conditions for dramatic performances in Spain. Among other conditions, the theologians insisted that no women should be permitted to act in dramatic productions because "such public activity especially provokes a woman to boldness. . . ." A royal council agreed to the conditions, except that it allowed women to continue in dramatic companies so long as they were accompanied by husbands or fathers. With the licensing and limitations of dramatic companies, the reduction in the numbers of religious festivals, and the prohibition of certain dances in religious festivals, fortunes waned for actresses, dancers, and singers.

Sumptuary laws[3] were passed in the sixteenth and seventeenth centuries to prevent rich people from parading their wealth. Although they were aimed at the newly rich merchants and shippers who liked to dress and behave as nobles, the real victims of these laws were women workers. Prohibitions against silk and brocade fabrics reduced the jobs available for women in the silk industry and embroidery shops, while limitation of the numbers of domestic servants meant that fewer women could earn a living as servants.

The Inquisition's campaign against heresy brought many folk practitioners and sorcerers to any unhappy end. The Holy Office[4] was not opposed to superstition so much as it wanted to control all uses of superstition. During the early modern period it increased its prosecution of

[2]King of Spain, 1556–1598.

[3]Sumptuary laws regulated and restrained personal extravagance, especially in dress and servants.

[4]Another term for the Inquisition.

women who challenged its monopoly. For example, a woman who was hanged in 1581 for practicing witchcraft and abortion was a Moor. As a member of this rival religious group, she had challenged the Church's attempts to monopolize truth. In 1624, a twenty-two-year-old woman was burned in an *auto de fe*[5] because she claimed to have the power of knowing the future. She might have escaped notice by the Inquisition if she had been older and had quietly plied her occult gifts as a neighborhood *sabia* (wise woman). The Inquisition dealt very cautiously with madness, and it often treated people accused of witchcraft as lunatics or senile eccentrics who should be only mildly punished. Insanity could be used by the Church as a weapon to discredit its competitors, but the Church did allow it to remain as a protective shield for folk practitioners who continued their traditional profession as "María la loca"[6] or "Ana la fantastica."[7]

The practice of medicine became more tightly controlled during this period, and uneducated female practitioners suffered especially. A royal decree of 1593 required all medical practitioners to be licensed, and it prohibited women from having or dispensing medicines. In 1629 the mayor of Seville formally required that all midwives, as well as all other people practicing medicine, be examined and licensed by him within fifteen days. Noncomplying practitioners were subject to a fine of ten thousand *maravedís*. Since most midwives and folk practitioners were older women, their inability to obtain a license did not necessarily mean that they became prostitutes. However, it is very likely that they increasingly turned to the subsidiary occupations of prostitution, becoming procuresses, street bawds, and false "abbesses" who kept houses of prostitution.

Prostitution flourished in this city not only because it provided a livelihood for women who had few alternatives, but also because it was a commercial enterprise that supported a vast network of pimps, procuresses, property-owners, innkeepers, and renters of little rooms and secondhand clothing. Underworld people regarded prostitution as a business, referring to brothels as *aduanas* (customs houses) or *cambios* (exchanges). They called prostitutes *pelotas,* a word that usually means a ball or toy, but a word that underworld people also used for a bag of money. Some women saw prostitution as their only means for survival, while others willingly entered prostitution as commercial entrepreneurs. Whether women became prostitutes under duress, unable to find another livelihood and shake themselves free of an exploiting "friend," or whether they voluntarily chose this profession as offering the best livelihood in the city, the socioeconomic changes in early modern Seville disrupted traditional roles for women and encouraged increasing numbers to turn to prostitution.

[5]"Act of faith," a public ceremony that, after a procession, Mass, and sermon, included the reading of the sentences. The Inquisition turned those sentenced for heresy over to the secular authority. The heretics were then burned at the stake.

[6]Mad Mary.

[7]Crazy Ann.

One reason that Seville's social order survived the serious economic disruptions of this period was that city fathers used a widely accepted system of morality to preserve the hierarchy of authority. Prostitution itself was an integral part of the city's moral system. The connection between prostitution, morality, and social order is clearly evident in the three most popular female symbols of this period.

The Holy Virgin was elevated in the early seventeenth century through the doctrine of the Immaculate Conception[8] and stylized into the beautiful image still carried in the Holy Week processions of present-day Seville. Forever girl-like, forever grieving, with diamond teardrops on her cheeks and a dagger thrust into her breast, her head slightly bowed by the weight of a golden crown, she held out her hands for the cares and sorrows of the world.

The Virgin was a pillar of the moral order of the city. Young girls who were taught to emulate her example of chastity and modesty would be less likely to defy parental authority and run off with the wild young men of the streets. With their eyes on the Virgin, women who entered convents had a beautiful image of perfection through chastity and obedience. For married women, the Virgin also symbolized chastity and submission to authority; but in addition, she represented a curiously asexual and influential motherhood. As mother, the Virgin epitomized women who were "the pivot, the fulcrum, the hub of the social relations of many, many people." Women could thus feel elevated, content with their social roles, and inspired to obedience. They would be chaste and modest, restricting sex to marriage and never endangering the social order or the system of property inheritance.

Men were considered to be much more active sexually than women, and this required another female symbol, the Painted Prostitute. Where women who emulated the Virgin were elevated above the weakness of the flesh, men were naturally expected to succumb to it, to seek sex outside marriage. If men lacked prostitutes to absorb their lust, who knew what would happen to an innocent woman walking along the street on a proper errand? The problem was to distinguish respectable women from those who served men's baser needs.

The Painted Prostitute represented depraved, sensual, commercial woman. Condemned for advertising herself in dress and manner, she was nevertheless required by law to wear a yellow hood so that she could be distinguished from the respectable women of the city. In distinction to the well-kept courtesan or flirtatious matron, she was often hungry and ill-dressed. She usually walked the city streets, unable to afford a sedan-chair or carriage. Sex to her was primarily a means of survival. She held out her hands like the Virgin, but she sought money rather than grieving

---

[8]The Roman Catholic dogma holding that the Virgin Mary, from the moment of her conception, was free of original sin.

hearts. She epitomized the unnatural, painting herself and publicizing her promiscuity. When syphilis appeared in Seville in the sixteenth century, she was blamed for spreading that disfiguring, often fatal, disease. This symbol, too, was a pillar of the moral order, for the Painted Prostitute permitted the existence of a double standard for women and men and provided a clear example of how respectable women should not behave.

Occasionally, however, the example of the Painted Prostitute was not completely negative. Orphanage administrators and priests who tried to reform prostitutes understood that the examples of experienced pimps and prostitutes were as infectious as any diseases they might carry. The Jesuits[9] established a little house as a temporary haven for converted prostitutes, and they carefully separated those young women from the older "women of the world" who wanted to procure for them and make money from them. The Jesuits' temporary home did not solve the problem, however, and city officials continued to worry that converted prostitutes could still "infect" young girls with their examples. One administrator of a girls' orphanage wrote to the city council complaining about the city's practice of placing converted prostitutes in his institution. It was easier, he argued, for young orphan girls to follow the bad examples of these women than any good examples they might present.

Mary Magdalene, the converted prostitute in the stories of Jesus, was the third major female symbol of early modern Seville. Many clergymen taught that prostitution was an evil from which prostitutes and the entire city could be saved. They preached fervently to the prostitutes on the feast days of Mary Magdalene, and they gloried in counting their conversions. This symbol reinforced both their faith in converting sinners and their belief that extramarital, "commercial" sex was evil. In their view, unregulated sex threatened both social order and individual salvation.

A cult had grown up around the seductive figure of Mary Magdalene in the seventeenth century, perhaps a reaction to the puritanical tendencies of the sixteenth-century Counter Reformation. Mary Magdalene represented the delicious combination of sex and religion. Murillo[10] painted her as a voluptuous young woman gazing heavenward. Her expression suggests the rapture of earthy sexual delights as well as spiritual transport. She avoids looking the observer boldly in the eye, for she is an appropriately modest, but sensual, "bride of Christ." One explanation for her popularity is that she represented the love-goddess, Venus. Under the guise of pious devotion to a Church-approved saint, many people continued to venerate an ancient and traditional folk-goddess who covered sex with a cloak of religion.

The symbols of Virgin, Prostitute, and Mary Magdalene were as useful to city fathers as they were popular with all city residents. Through

[9]Members of the Society of Jesus, a Roman Catholic religious order established in 1540.

[10]Bartolomé Esteban Murillo (1618–1682), Spanish painter and founder of the Academy of Seville.

these symbols, city fathers demonstrated their authority to define good and evil. The image of the Holy Virgin sanctified political events and provided a single visible personification of good that was understood by the entire community. On the other hand, the Painted Prostitute personified sex outside marriage, sex without the responsibility of children and home, sex with the threat of disease. When unregulated sex threatened their society, they could point to the lessons of the Virgin, the Prostitute, and Mary Magdalene, which taught very clearly that women should be safely enveloped in a convent or marriage, obedient, chaste, and modestly accepting their places in the social hierarchy.

Some city fathers may have preferred to rely only on the Virgin to support their moral order, but the Painted Prostitute and Mary Magdalene appeared to be necessary corollaries. A social order acknowledging sexuality in men could not survive if men had to treat all women as the Virgin. Elevating women through this symbol seemed to require that they also be degraded to the status of prostitute. Sexuality in women was permitted only if it were the acknowledged evil of prostitution or the converted religious ecstasy of Mary Magdalene. Ironically, this moral system depended as much on symbols of evil as on symbols of perfection.

Francisco Farfan, a sixteenth-century cleric of Spain, recognized this upside-down morality of prostitution. In his treatise on avoiding the sins of fornication, Farfan presented an argument for the moral practicality of prostitution. He declared that the brothel was necessary to a society just as a latrine was needed in a house:

> The brothel in the city, then, is like the stable or latrine for the house. Because just as the city keeps itself clean by providing a separate place where filth and dung are gathered, etc., so, neither less nor more, assuming the dissolution of the flesh, acts the brothel: where the filth and ugliness of the flesh are gathered like the garbage and dung of the city.

To Farfan, the prohibition of prostitution was a greater evil than prostitution itself because a society without brothels encouraged homosexuality, incest, the propositioning of innocent women, and an increased number of people living together in sin. Farfan recognized the weakness of the flesh and believed that the only way to deal with it was to divert human behavior away from moral sins. In order to avoid moral sin, he argued, behavior must be controlled. Prostitution could support the moral order, but only if it were closely regulated.

City fathers had long tried to control prostitution in Seville, but many nonlicensed prostitutes pursued their trade outside the confines of city-regulated brothels. These "lost women" were not lost at all geographically, for everyone in the city knew where to find them. Prostitutes gathered in several areas along the river bank, close to the port where many prospective clients entered the city. Prostitution also thrived in the poorer parts of the city that grew up along its margins and just outside its walls, such as the extramural parish of San Bernardo. Rents were undoubtedly lower in the marginal areas of the city and prostitutes could afford a room or a little shack. Since police power was less likely to invade the little alleyways on the edges of town, innkeepers here were probably less conscientious about keeping prostitutes out of their rooms. The 1568 syphilis epidemic in the city was called *"el contagio de San Gil"*[11] because it first broke out in San Gil, another parish bordering on the city's walls. Hospitals for victims of this epidemic were set up outside the city walls in the parish of San Bernardo.

Fear of disease is the major reason that the city government increased its efforts to regulate prostitution and limit it to the medically inspected, city-licensed brothels. Plagues passed from port to port in the early modern period and ravaged city populations. They posed a political threat as well as a very real physical danger, for the city in the throes of an epidemic was noted for neither law nor order. The machinery of local government frequently fell into paralysis and many officials died or disappeared. On the other hand, rumors of an epidemic so frightened city residents that they were willing for their local governments to greatly expand regulations. City fathers in Seville extended their powers when disease threatened, particularly over prostitutes who were commonly suspected of passing on plagues. Clients of prostitutes, after all, often entered the city from a ship that had arrived in port, and prostitutes could easily contract any diseases they carried and pass them on into the city. Prostitutes were more susceptible to illness, too, if they were the poorer women who were undernourished and used secondhand clothing and bedding that frequently carried disease.

Syphilis arrived in Seville in the sixteenth century, bringing death and disfigurement to thousands and frightening the city government to redouble its efforts to regulate prostitution. The city council appointed medical inspectors to examine prostitutes and recommend action against this disease. One doctor warned that the city's health was endangered by the bad condition of lettuce and deer's tongue (a plant) that were being sold in the city brothels as remedies for syphilis. A surgeon reported in 1572 that infected prostitutes dismissed from the city brothels were spreading their infection as they plied their trade in other parts of the city. He urged that Seville not merely discharge sick prostitutes from brothels, but also deliver them to hospitals for treatment. In the early seventeenth century, the administrator of city brothels countered clergymen's proposals to close the public brothels. He argued that this action would not end prostitution, but merely deregulate it and damage the health and well-being of the city. If prostitutes were not confined to city-licensed and medically inspected brothels, he said, they would scatter throughout the city, free to spread disease and provoke quarrels and murders.

[11] The disease of San Gil.

Seville lacked hospital space, however, to confine all its syphilitic prostitutes. Several hospitals would not accept people with any contagious disease. In the last part of the sixteenth century the *Hospital de San Cosme y San Damian* was known as *"las Bubas"* because it was designated to treat syphilitics, or those with pustules (*bubas*) resulting from *"la mal frances."*[12] Unfortunately, this hospital had only forty beds, and only twelve were for infected women. Patients here were treated for thirty days with . . . a medicinal water made with bark.

Most treatments for syphilis were ineffective, and it became a sixteenth-century successor to leprosy. It flourished despite city attempts to detect and isolate infected people. When Pedro de León[13] began working with the people in the city brothels in the late sixteenth century, he found many who were ill. He described the illness as "hideous," causing great pain and many pustules. Many times it resulted in death. He also reported that a number of young boys frequented the brothels. The 1621 ordinances to reform the ancient regulations on prostitution in the city prohibited the city brothels from admitting boys under the age of fourteen, adding that many "boys of a tender age" had become infected in the brothels. The infected prostitute released from city-licensed brothels could continue her trade as long as she was able to, but when her infection became so obvious that she could no longer get clients, she was as likely to die from starvation as from infection.

It is not surprising that the little houses of a brothel were sometimes called *"boticas,"* a word also used for pharmacies or little shops. Prostitutes were traditionally suspected of using potions, herbs, ointments, and pessaries as contraceptives. In the sixteenth century they also began to use herbal preparations to treat syphilis infections, and it has been suggested that men first used contraceptive sheaths in brothels as a means to prevent venereal infection. Prostitutes and procuresses knew many other forms of contraception. They prepared pessaries and ointments from herbs and dung. They made amulets, such as a seed of sorrel enclosed in a cloth bag, which was believed to prevent conception as long as it was carried on the left arm. They mixed alum and the yellow pulp of pomegranate to make vaginal pessaries, and they practiced some numerical magic, such as jumping backwards seven or nine times after coitus to prevent conception. Prostitutes were closely associated with the practice of abortion as well, and they and their older female companions also prepared aphrodisiacs. The brothel as pharmacy represented the evil of illicit sex supported by an unlicensed folk medicine that bordered on magic. It challenged both the Church's claim to monopolize magic and the city's presumption to license doctors. Thus the brothel called even more urgently for close regulation, for churchmen and city officials feared folk customs that flourished independently of their control.

[12]The French disease, as the Spanish called syphilis.
[13]Spanish Jesuit known for his missionary work among the common people.

Concern with increasing public disorder also pushed city fathers into more energetic regulation of prostitution. The growing numbers of ships sailing between Seville and the New World brought increased numbers of soldiers and sailors to the city in the sixteenth and seventeenth centuries. Fights over women often ended in huge street brawls. Confining prostitutes to city-licensed brothels could prevent many quarrels, fights, and crimes. It could also get rid of the swarms of streetwalkers and children or false beggars who acted as procurers.

Closely related to the desire to keep public order was the desire to protect property. When a captain wrote the city council to complain that ships in the port were being robbed and damaged, he asserted that men were robbing the ships in order to give money to the "bad women" who lived in little houses in the area of the port. Other residents complained of property damaged in the brawls that began over women.

Confining prostitutes in licensed brothels prevented some property damage, and it also protected the interests of those who owned the property used as the city brothels. . . . [P]roperty used as city-licensed brothels in the last part of the sixteenth century was owned by city officials and religious corporations, including the Cathedral council. These owners leased the property to private individuals, who then rented it to various prostitutes. In 1571, owners of the houses used by the city brothel included a *veinticuatro* (one of the city's oligarchy of nobles, originally twenty-four), an official of the *Santa Hermandad* (a national law enforcement association promoted by the crown), and an *alguazil de los veynte* (one of the twenty sheriffs with major law enforcement responsibilities). In 1604 the houses of the city brothel were rented by the sheriff, Francisco Vélez, who collected a daily rent of one and one-half *reales* from each prostitute. . . .

The city government's proprietary interest in the licensed brothels is evident in the time and money it spent administering, inspecting, and repairing them. The city government appointed *"padres,"*[14] or administrators of the city-licensed brothels. In the last part of the sixteenth century, there were three *padres,* each the head of a separate house licensed by the city. The 1621 ordinances limited the number of *padres* to two and required that they swear to uphold the laws of the city. These ordinances also prohibited the *padres* from renting clothing or bedding to prostitutes and from accepting "pawned" women in the brothels, two prohibitions that were also contained in a set of 1570 royal ordinances.

Brothel administrators often requested that the city repair walls and gates that seemed to crumble rapidly in the dampness of the river air and the harshness of their use. In 1590, for example, one *padre* reported to the city council that the gate for the brothel had been destroyed, allowing ruffians to mistreat the prostitutes, destroy the little houses of the brothel, and steal doors and other materials. Other *padres* invited the city council to

[14]Fathers. The word was used also for priests.

send a deputation to visit the brothel and see for themselves that repairs were necessary.

City officials inspected the brothels not only to maintain the value of their real estate, but also to preserve the value of the human property contained in their brothels. Three officials accompanied the canon of the Church of San Salvador on July 22, 1620, when he visited the brothels to preach to the prostitutes and try to convert them. Immediately after the visit, the officials announced that they would bring a doctor to examine the prostitutes. They fined one *padre* twelve *reales* for receiving an unlicensed prostitute into the brothel, and she was ordered to leave under penalty of one hundred lashes. Another prostitute was ordered to leave the brothel because she appeared ill and could infect the others. A third prostitute was ordered to leave because of her age; she had been in the brothel too long. Evidently, city officials were as concerned to have attractive prostitutes in their brothels as they were to prevent epidemics of syphilis.

Prostitution made sound business sense not only to the procurers and owners of brothels, but also to the charitable benefactors who were unable to provide every poor girl of the city with a dowry or a job. As demands for charity increased in the last part of the sixteenth century, many city fathers concluded that practicality outweighed morality in the question of prostitution. They saw that it was an evil, but they agreed that it was better to accept it and regulate it than to forbid it and send converted prostitutes to seek a nonexistent livelihood. Even the optimistic and diligent Pedro de León, who worked so hard to convert women from prostitution, admitted the difficulty of finding husbands, parents, or jobs for converted prostitutes. The 1667 survey of the poor in Seville is filled with the names of young women of marriageable age unable to marry because they were too poor, unable to find work, and doomed to die from starvation. City fathers who owned brothels could thus argue that these brothels benefited the entire community because they provided a livelihood for otherwise destitute women. It is not surprising, then, that the city council listened sympathetically to a *padre* of a brothel when he complained bitterly about "strange clergymen" and pious laymen . . . who were driving women away from city-licensed brothels. To most city fathers, prostitution was not only thinkable; it was practical.

"Lost women" were not lost at all in early modern Seville. They lived within the specific social and economic conditions of their city, and prostitution was one response to these conditions. More than lost, they were used. Prostitution was commercially profitable for city fathers as well as street people. It reinforced the authority of the ruling class over unmarried women, folk-practitioners, sailors, youths, and quick-fisted dandies. Prostitution was even a form of public assistance, providing jobs for women who would otherwise starve. It strengthened moral attitudes that supported the city's hierarchy of authority, and it permitted the city oligarchy to demonstrate its authority to define and confine evil. Under the guise of public health and public order, it extended the powers of city government. If prostitution was a symptom of social disease, it was also an example of social adaptation. In Seville prostitution helped to preserve the existing social order. It became a useful, practical political tool.

Nuns, Wives, and Mothers: Women and the Reformation in Germany

MERRY WIESNER

In a famous essay, a historian argued that there had been no Renaissance for women. That is, examined from the perspective of gender, the cultural flowering in the fourteenth and fifteenth centuries celebrated as the Italian Renaissance in fact scarcely affected the daily lives of women. Humanism, artistic innovations, and political experimentation did not improve the status of women in law, in the home, or in the workplace. In fact it has been argued that the condition of women may even have worsened during the Renaissance. Merry Wiesner takes a similar approach to the Protestant Reformation of the sixteenth century by examining how that religious movement influenced German women. She finds that—unlike the Italian Renaissance—the German Reformation made an appreciable difference to women.

Nevertheless, on the eve of and during the Protestant Reformation, German society placed social and political restrictions on women. What were these impediments that closed possible avenues of advancement to women? Moving beyond these hindrances, Wiesner sketches neatly the impact of religious change on women according to their status in three categories: as members of female religious orders, as single and married, and as workers. Within these broad typologies, there existed different groups. It is imperative to distinguish how the religious change from Catholic to Protestant marked the lives of these various groups.

First and most clearly, the Protestants closed convents. What happened to the nuns and lay sisters who now had to fend for themselves in the larger world? What might have happened when nuns refused to renounce their cloistered lives?

Second, the Reformation altered the lives of other women, single or married. How did the Protestant reformers get their ideas across to women, many of whom could not read? What were the reformers' ideas about women? How did the reformers view marriage and the relationship of wife and husband? Were women any less subordinate in the Protestant religions than in Catholicism? How did the reformers see single women?

One thorny problem in a society that looked upon religious toleration as an evil was marriages in which each spouse belonged to a different religion. What was a Protestant wife to do when her husband, to whom she owed obedience, was Catholic?

There is a difference, to be sure, between the ideas of Protestant theologians on the nature of women, their proper place, and their duties, on the one hand, and the translation of those ideas into actual practice, on the other hand. What laws did Protestant states pass that modified the behavior of women in marriage and in religion?

Wiesner rightly stresses that women reacted to the Reformation; they were not just acted upon. How did women have an impact on the religious developments sweeping Germany? To what extent did it make a difference if a woman was an aristocrat or a commoner? In what areas of religious change could women make themselves known? Did males welcome the efforts of women to further the cause of the Reformation? How did Protestant ideas and Protestant wives sway marriages?

Third, Wiesner scrutinizes the Reformation's impact on working women. How did new religious practices affect women in various occupations?

Could one conclude that overall the Reformation was beneficial to women? Did the Reformation improve the status or situation of any groups of women?

It is in many ways anachronistic even to use the word "Germany" when discussing the sixteenth century. At that time, modern-day Germany was politically part of the Holy Roman Empire, a loose confederation of several hundred states, ranging from tiny knightships through free imperial cities to large territorial states. These states theoretically owed obedience to an elected emperor, but in reality they were quite independent and often pursued policies in opposition to the emperor. Indeed, the political diversity and lack of a strong central authority were extremely important to the early success of the Protestant Reformation in Germany. Had Luther been a Frenchman or a Spaniard, his voice would probably have been quickly silenced by the powerful monarchs in those countries.

Because of this diversity, studies of the Reformation in Germany are often limited to one particular area or one particular type of government, such as the free imperial cities. This limited focus is useful when looking at the impact of the Reformation on men, for male participation and leadership in religious change varied depending on whether a territory was ruled by a city council, a nobleman, or a bishop. Male leadership in the Reformation often came from university teachers, so the presence or absence of a university in an area was also an important factor.

When exploring the impact of religious change on women, however, these political and institutional factors are not as important. Except for a few noblewomen who ruled territories while their sons were still minors, women had no formal political voice in any territory of the empire. They did not vote or serve on city councils, and even abbesses were under the direct control of a male church official. Women could not attend universities, and thus did not come into contact with religious ideas through formal theological training. Their role in the Reformation was not so determined by what may be called "public" factors—political structures, educational institutions—as was that of men.

Women's role in the Reformation and the impact of religious change on them did vary throughout Germany, but that variation was largely determined by what might be termed "personal" factors—a woman's status as a nun or laywoman, her marital status, her social and economic class, her occupation. Many of these factors, particularly social and economic class, were also important in determining men's responses to religious change, but they were often secondary to political factors whereas for women they were of prime importance.

The Protestant and Catholic reformers recognized this. Although they generally spoke about and to women as an undifferentiated group and proposed the same ideals of behavior for all women, when the reformers did address distinct groups of women they distinguished them by marital or clerical status. Nuns, single women, mothers, wives, and widows all got special attention in the same way that special treatises were directed to male princes and members of city councils—men set apart from others by their public, political role.

It is important to keep in mind that although a woman's religious actions were largely determined by her personal status, they were not regarded as a private matter, even if they took place within the confines of her own household. No one in the sixteenth century regarded religion or the family as private, as that term is used today. One's inner relationship with God was perhaps a private matter (though even that is arguable), but one's outward religious practices were a matter of great concern for political authorities. Both Protestants and Catholics saw the family as the cornerstone of society, the cornerstone on which all other institutions were constructed, and every political authority meddled in family and domestic concerns. Thus a woman's choice to serve her family meat on Friday or attend the funeral of a friend whose religion was unacceptable was not to be overlooked or regarded as trivial.

Although "personal" is not the same as "private" in Reformation Germany, grouping women by their personal status is still the best way to analyze their role in religious change. This essay thus follows "personal" lines of division and begins with an exploration of the impact of the Reformation on nuns, Beguines,[1] and other female religious. It then looks at single and married women, including a special group of married women, the wives of the Protestant reformers. Although the reformers did not have a special message for noblewomen, the situation of these women warrants separate consideration because their religious choices had the greatest effect on the course of the Reformation. The essay concludes with a discussion of several groups of working women whose labor was directly or indirectly affected by religious change.

Women in convents, both cloistered nuns and lay sisters, and other female religious, were the first to confront the Protestant Reformation.

[1]Roman Catholic lay sisterhoods.

In areas becoming Protestant religious change meant both the closing of their houses and a negation of the value and worth of the life they had been living. The Protestant reformers encouraged nuns and sisters to leave their houses and marry, with harsh words concerning the level of morality in the convents, comparing it to that in brothels. Some convents accepted the Protestant message and willingly gave up their houses and land to city and territorial authorities. The nuns renounced their vows, and those who were able to find husbands married, while the others returned to their families or found ways to support themselves on their own. Others did not accept the new religion but recognized the realities of political power and gave up their holdings; these women often continued living together after the Reformation, trying to remain as a religious community, though they often had to rely on their families for support. In some cases the nuns were given a pension. There is no record, however, of what happened to most of these women. Former priests and monks could become pastors in the new Protestant churches, but former nuns had no place in the new church structure.

Many convents, particularly those with high standards of learning and morality and whose members were noblewomen or women from wealthy patrician families, fought the religious change. A good example of this is the St. Clara convent in Nuremberg, whose nuns were all from wealthy Nuremberg families and whose reputation for learning had spread throughout Germany. The abbess at the time of the Reformation was Charitas Pirckheimer, a sister of the humanist Willibald Pirckheimer and herself an accomplished Latinist. In 1525, the Nuremberg city council ordered all the cloisters to close; four of the six male houses in the city dissolved themselves immediately, but both female houses refused. The council first sent official representatives to try to persuade the nuns and then began a program of intimidation. The women, denied confessors and Catholic communion, were forced to hear Protestant sermons four times a week; their servants had difficulty buying food; people threatened to burn the convent, threw stones over the walls, and sang profane songs when they heard the nuns singing. Charitas noted in her memoirs that women often led the attacks and were the most bitter opponents of the nuns. Three families physically dragged their daughters out of the convent, a scene of crying and wailing witnessed by many Nurembergers. The council questioned each nun separately to see if she had any complaints, hoping to find some who would leave voluntarily, and finally confiscated all of the convent's land. None of these measures was successful, and the council eventually left the convent alone, although it forbade the taking in of new novices. The last nun died in 1590.

Charitas' firmness and the loyalty of the nuns to her were perhaps extraordinary, but other abbesses also publicly defended their faith. Elizabeth Gottgabs, the abbess of Oberwesel convent, published a tract against the Lutherans in 1550. Although she denigrated her own work as that of a "poor woman," she hardly held back in her language when evaluating the reformers: "The new evangelical preachers have tried to plug our ears with their abominable uproar . . . our gracious God will not tolerate their foolishness any longer." . . .

Nuns who chose to leave convents occasionally published works explaining their actions as well. Martha Elizabeth Zitterin published her letters to her mother explaining why she had left the convent at Erfurt; these were republished five times by Protestant authorities in Jena, who never mentioned that the author herself later decided to return to the convent. Even if the former nuns did not publish their stories, these accounts often became part of Protestant hagiography, particularly if the women had left the convent surreptitiously or had been threatened. Katherine von Bora and eight other nuns were smuggled out of their convent at night after they had secretly made contact with Luther. The fact that this occurred on Easter and that they left in a wagon of herring barrels added drama to the story, and Katherine's later marriage to Luther assured that it would be retold many times.

The Jesuits[2] and other leaders of the Catholic Reformation took the opposite position from the Protestants on the value of celibacy, encouraging young women to disobey their parents and enter convents to escape arranged marriages. Although they did not encourage married women to leave their husbands, the Jesuits followed the pre-Reformation tradition in urging husbands to let their wives enter convents if they wished.

The Counter-Reformation church wanted all female religious strictly cloistered, however, and provided no orders for women who wanted to carry out an active apostolate; there was no female equivalent of the Jesuits. The church also pressured Beguines, Franciscan tertiaries,[3] and other sisters who had always moved about somewhat freely or worked out in the community to adopt strict rules of cloister and place themselves under the direct control of a bishop. The women concerned did not always submit meekly, however. The Beguines in Münster, for example, refused to follow the advice of their confessors, who wanted to reform the beguinage and turn it into a cloistered house of Poor Clares.[4] The women, most of whom were members of the city's elite families, appealed to the city council for help in defending their civil rights and traditional liberties. The council appealed to the archbishop of Cologne, the cardinals, and eventually the pope, and, though the women were eventually cloistered, they were allowed to retain certain of their traditional practices. In some ways, the women were caught in the middle of a power struggle between the archbishop and the city council, but they were still able to appeal to

[2]Members of the Society of Jesus, a Roman Catholic religious order established in 1540.

[3]A group of lay women attached to the Franciscan order, a Roman Catholic religious order founded in 1209.

[4]An order of Franciscan nuns.

the city's pride in its traditional privileges to argue for their own liberties and privileges. Perhaps the fact that they had not been cloistered kept them aware of the realities and symbols of political power.

Of course most of the women in sixteenth-century Germany were not nuns or other female religious but laywomen who lived in families. Their first contact with the Reformation was often shared with the male members of their families. They heard the new teachings proclaimed from a city pulpit, read or looked at broadsides attacking the pope, and listened to traveling preachers attacking celibacy and the monasteries.

The reformers communicated their ideas to women in a variety of ways. Women who could read German might have read Luther's two marriage treatises or any number of Protestant marriage manuals, the first of which was published in Augsburg in 1522. They could have read tracts against celibacy by many reformers, which varied widely in their level of vituperation and criticism of convent life. Both Protestant and Catholic authors wrote books of commonplaces and examples, which contained numerous references to proper and improper female conduct attributed to classical authors, the church fathers, and more recent commentators.

The vast majority of women could not read but received the message orally and visually. Sermons, particularly marriage sermons but also regular Sunday sermons, emphasized the benefits of marriage and the proper roles of husband and wife. Sermons at women's funerals stressed their piety, devotion to family, and trust in God through great trials and tribulations and set up models for other women to follow. Vernacular dramas about marriage replaced pre-Reformation plays about virgin martyrs suffering death rather than losing their virginity. Woodcuts depicted pious married women (their marital status was clear because married women wore their hair covered) listening to sermons or reading the Bible. Protestant pamphlets portrayed the pope with the whore of Babylon, which communicated a message about both the pope and about women. Catholic pamphlets showed Luther as a lustful glutton, driven only by his sexual and bodily needs. Popular stories about Luther's home life and harsh attitudes toward female virginity circulated by word of mouth. . . .

The Protestant reformers did not break sharply with tradition in their ideas about women. For both Luther and Calvin, women were created by God and could be saved through faith; spiritually women and men were equal. In every other respect, however, women were to be subordinate to men. Women's subjection was inherent in their very being and was present from creation—in this the reformers agreed with Aristotle[5] and the classical tradition. It was made more brutal and harsh, however, because of Eve's responsibility for the Fall—in this Luther and Calvin[6]

[5] Greek philosopher, 384–322 B.C.

[6] John Calvin (1509–1564), French Protestant theologian, founder of Calvinism and religious leader of Geneva.

agreed with patristic[7] tradition and with their scholastic and humanist predecessors.

There appears to be some novelty in their rejection of Catholic teachings on the merits of celibacy and championing of marriage as the proper state for all individuals. Though they disagreed on so much else, all Protestant reformers agreed on this point; the clauses discussing marriage in the various Protestant confessions show more similarities than do any other main articles of doctrine or discipline. Even this emphasis on marriage was not that new, however. Civic and Christian humanists also thought that "God had established marriage and family life as the best means for providing spiritual and moral discipline in this world," and they "emphasized marriage and the family as the basic social and economic unit which provided the paradigm for all social relations."

The Protestant exhortation to marry was directed to both sexes, but particularly to women, for whom marriage and motherhood were a vocation as well as a living arrangement. Marriage was a woman's highest calling, the way she could fulfill God's will: in Luther's harsh words, "Let them bear children to death; they are created for that." Unmarried women were suspect, both because they were fighting their natural sex drive, which everyone in the sixteenth century believed to be much stronger than men's, and because they were upsetting the divinely imposed order, which made woman subject to man. Even a woman as prominent and respected as Margaretha Blarer, the sister of Ambrosius Blarer, a reformer in Constance, was criticized for her decision to remain unmarried. Martin Bucer[8] accused her of being "masterless," to which she answered, "Those who have Christ for a master are not masterless." Her brother defended her decision by pointing out that she was very close to his family and took care of the poor and plague victims "as a mother."

The combination of women's spiritual equality, female subordination, and the idealization of marriage proved problematic for the reformers, for they were faced with the issue of women who converted while their husbands did not. What was to take precedence, the woman's religious convictions or her duty of obedience? Luther and Calvin were clear on this. Wives were to obey their husbands, even if they were not Christians; in Calvin's words, a woman "should not desert the partner who is hostile." Marriage was a woman's "calling," her natural state, and she was to serve God through this calling.

Wives received a particularly ambiguous message from the radical reformers. . . . Some radical groups allowed believers to leave their unbelieving spouses, but women who did so were expected to remarry quickly and thus come under the control of a male believer. The most radical Anabaptists were fascinated by Old Testament polygamy and accepted the statement in Revelations that the Last Judgment would only come if there were

---

[7]Referring to the fathers, or theologians, of the early Christian Church.

[8]German Protestant reformer, 1491–1551.

144,000 "saints" in the world; they actually enforced polygamy for a short time at Münster, though the required number of saints were never born. In practical terms, Anabaptist women were equal only in martyrdom.

Although the leaders of the Counter Reformation continued to view celibacy as a state preferable to matrimony, they realized that most women in Germany would marry and began to publish their own marriage manuals to counter those published by Protestants. The ideal wives and mothers they described were, however, no different than those of the Protestants; both wanted women to be "chaste, silent, and obedient."

The ideas of the reformers did not stay simply within the realm of theory but led to political and institutional changes. Some of these changes were the direct results of Protestant doctrine, and some of them had unintended, though not unforeseeable, consequences. . . .

Every Protestant territory passed a marriage ordinance that stressed wifely obedience and proper Christian virtues and set up a new court or broadened the jurisdiction of an existing court to handle marriage and morals cases which had previously been handled by church courts. They also passed sumptuary laws that regulated weddings and baptisms, thereby trying to make these ceremonies more purely Christian by limiting the number of guests and prohibiting profane activities such as dancing and singing. Though such laws were never completely successful, the tone of these two ceremonies, which marked the two perhaps most important events in a woman's life, became much less exuberant. Religious processions, such as Corpus Christi[9] parades, which had included both men and women, and in which even a city's prostitutes took part, were prohibited. The public processions that remained were generally those of guild masters and journeymen, at which women were onlookers only. Women's participation in rituals such as funerals was limited, for Protestant leaders wanted neither professional mourners nor relatives to take part in extravagant wailing and crying. Lay female confraternities, which had provided emotional and economic assistance for their members and charity for the needy, were also forbidden, and no similar all-female groups replaced them.

The Protestant reformers attempted to do away with the veneration of Mary and the saints. This affected both men and women, because some of the strongest adherents of the cult of the Virgin had been men. For women, the loss of St. Anne, Mary's mother, was particularly hard, for she was a patron saint of pregnant women; now they were instructed to pray during labor and childbirth to Christ, a celibate male, rather than to a woman who had also been a mother. The Protestant martyrs replaced the saints to some degree, at least as models worthy of emulation, but they

---

[9]A Roman Catholic festival instituted in the thirteenth century to honor the Blessed Sacrament (the body of Jesus).

were not to be prayed to and they did not give their names to any days of the year. The Protestant Reformation not only downplayed women's public ceremonial role; it also stripped the calendar of celebrations honoring women and ended the power female saints and their relics were believed to have over people's lives. Women who remained Catholic still had female saints to pray to, but the number of new female saints during the Counter Reformation was far fewer than the number of new male saints, for two important avenues to sanctity, missionary and pastoral work, were closed to women.

Because of the importance Protestant reformers placed on Bible-reading in the vernacular, many of them advocated opening schools for girls as well as boys. The number of such schools which opened was far fewer than the reformers had originally hoped, and Luther in particular also muted his call for mass education after the turmoil of the Peasants' War.[10] The girls' schools that were opened stressed morality and decorum; in the words of the Memmingen school ordinance from 1587, the best female pupil was one noted for her "great diligence and application in learning her catechism, modesty, obedience, and excellent penmanship." These schools taught sewing as well as reading and singing, and religious instruction was often limited to memorizing the catechism.

Along with these changes that related directly to Protestant doctrine, the Reformation brought with it an extended period of war and destruction in which individuals and families were forced to move frequently from one place to another. Women whose husbands were exiled for religious reasons might also have been forced to leave. Their houses and goods were usually confiscated whether they left town or not. If allowed to stay, they often had to support a family and were still held suspect by neighbors and authorities. A woman whose husband was away fighting could go years without hearing from him and never be allowed to marry again if there was some suspicion he might still be alive.

Women were not simply passive recipients of the Reformation and the ideas and changes it brought but indeed responded to them actively. Swept up by the enthusiasm of the first years of the Reformation, single and married women often stepped beyond what were considered acceptable roles for women. Taking literally Luther's idea of a priesthood of all believers, women as well as uneducated men began to preach and challenge religious authorities. In 1524 in Nuremberg, the city council took action against a certain Frau Voglin, who had set herself up in the hospital church and was preaching. In a discussion after a Sunday sermon by a Lutheran-leaning prior, a woman in Augsburg spoke to a bishop's representative who had been sent to hear the sermon and called the bishop a brothel manager because he had a large annual income from concubinage

---

[10]Uprisings in central and southwest Germany, 1524–1525, inspired by the Reformation leaders' defiance of authority.

fees. Several women in Zwickau, inspired by the preaching of Thomas Müntzer,[11] also began to preach in 1521.

All of these actions were viewed with alarm by civic authorities, who even objected to women's getting together to discuss religion. In their view, female preachers clearly disobeyed the Pauline injunction against women speaking in church and moved perilously close to claiming an official religious role. In 1529, the Zwickau city council banished several of the women who had gathered together and preached. In the same year, the Memmingen city council forbade maids to discuss religion while drawing water at neighborhood wells. No German government forbade women outright to read the Bible, as Henry VIII[12] of England did in 1543, but the authorities did attempt to prevent them from discussing it publicly.

After 1530, women's public witnessing of faith was more likely to be prophesying than preaching. In many ways, female prophets were much less threatening than female preachers, for the former had biblical parallels, clear biblical justification, and no permanent official function. Ursula Jost and Barbara Rebstock in Strasbourg began to have visions and revelations concerning the end of the world. When Melchior Hoffman, the Spiritualist, came to Strasbourg, they convinced him he was the prophet Elijah born again and thus one of the signs of the impending Apocalypse. He published seventy-two of Ursula's revelations, advising all Christians to read them. They were written in the style of Old Testament prophecy and became popular in the Rhineland and Netherlands. Several other female Anabaptists also had visions that were spread by word of mouth and as broadsides or small pamphlets. Though these women were illiterate, their visions were full of biblical references, which indicates that, like Lollard[13] women in England, they had memorized much of the Bible. Female prophecy was accepted in most radical sects, for they emphasized direct revelation and downplayed theological training. That these sects were small and loosely structured was also important for the continued acceptance of female revelation; in Münster, the one place where Anabaptism became the state religion, female prophecy was suppressed.

Not all female visionaries were radicals, however. Mysticism and ecstatic visions remained an acceptable path to God for Catholic women and increased in popularity in Germany after the works of Saint Theresa[14] were translated and her ideas became known. Even Lutheran women reported miracles and visions. Catherine Binder, for example, asserted that her speech had been restored after seven years when a pastor gave her a

---

[11] Radical religious leader who led a peasant rebellion in 1524–1525.

[12] Ruled 1509–1547.

[13] Lollard was originally a name given to followers of the fourteenth-century English reformer, John Wycliffe. Later the name was applied to any English religious dissenter in the fifteenth century.

[14] Spanish nun and mystic, 1515–1582.

copy of the Lutheran Catechism. The Lutheran clergy were suspicious of such events, but did not reject them out of hand.

With the advent of the religious wars, female prophets began to see visions of war and destruction and to make political, as well as religious and eschatological, predictions. Susanna Rugerin had been driven far from her home by imperial armies and began to see an angel who revealed visions of Gustavus Adolphus.[15] The visions of Juliana von Duchnik were even more dramatic. In 1628 she brought a warning from God to Duke Wallenstein, a commander of imperial troops, telling him to leave his estate because God would no longer protect him. Though Wallenstein's wife was very upset, his supporters joked about it, commenting that the emperor got letters from only the pope, while Wallenstein got them directly from God. Von Duchnik published this and other of her visions the following year and in 1634 returned to Wallenstein's camp warning him that she had seen a vision of him trying to climb a ladder into heaven; the ladder collapsed, and he fell to earth with blood and poison pouring out of his heart. Though Wallenstein himself continued to dismiss her predictions, others around him took her seriously. Her visions in this case proved accurate, for Wallenstein was assassinated less than a month later. In general, female prophets were taken no less seriously than their male counterparts.

The most dramatic public affirmation of faith a woman could make was martyrdom. Most of the female martyrs in Germany were Anabaptists, and the law granted women no special treatment, except for occasionally delaying execution if they were pregnant. Women were more likely to be drowned than beheaded, for it was thought they would faint at the sight of the executioner's sword and make his job more difficult. Some of them were aware that this reduced the impact of their deaths and wanted a more public form of execution. A good indication of the high degree of religious understanding among many Anabaptist women comes from their interrogations. They could easily discuss the nature of Christ, the doctrine of the Real Presence, and baptism, quoting extensively from the Bible. As a woman known simply as Claesken put it, "Although I am a simple person before men, I am not unwise in the knowledge of the Lord." Her interrogators were particularly upset because she had converted many people: they commented, "Your condemnation will be greater than your husband's because you can read and have misled him."

Although most of the women who published religious works during the Reformation were either nuns or noblewomen, a few middle-class women wrote hymns, religious poetry, and some polemics. Ursula Weide published a pamphlet against the abbot of Pegau, denouncing his support of celibacy. The earliest Protestant hymnals include several works by women, often verse renditions of the Psalms or Gospels. Justitia Sanger,

---

[15]Protestant king of Sweden who defeated the Catholic imperial forces in Germany during the Thirty Years' War (1618–1648).

a blind woman from Braunschweig, published a commentary on ninety-six Psalms in 1593, dedicating it to King Frederick II of Denmark. Female hymn-writing became even more common in the seventeenth century when the language of hymns shifted from aggressive and martial to emotional and pious; it was more acceptable for a woman to write of being washed in the blood of the Lamb than of strapping on the armor of God. Not all female religious poetry from the seventeenth century was meekly pious, however. Anna Oven Hoyer was driven from place to place during the Thirty Years' War, finally finding refuge in Sweden. She praised David Joris and Caspar von Schwenkfeld[16] in her writings, which she published without submitting them for clerical approval. Some of them, including her "Spiritual Conversation between a Mother and Child about True Christianity," were later burned as heretical. In this dialogue she attacked the Lutheran clergy for laxness, greed, pride, and trust in worldly learning and largely blamed them for the horrors of the Thirty Years' War.

Seventeenth-century women often wrote religious poems, hymns, and prose meditations for private purposes as well as for publication. They wrote to celebrate weddings, baptisms, and birthdays, to console friends, to praise deceased relatives, to instruct and provide examples for their children. If a woman's works were published while she was still alive, they included profuse apologies about her unworthiness and presumption. Many such works were published posthumously by husbands or fathers and include a note from these men that writing never distracted the author from her domestic tasks but was done only in her spare time. Unfortunately, similar works by sixteenth-century German women are rare. Thus, to examine the religious convictions of the majority of women who did not preach, prophesy, publish, or become martyrs, we must look at their actions within the context of their domestic and community life.

Married women whose religious convictions matched those of their husbands often shared equally in the results of those convictions. If these convictions conflicted with local authorities and the men were banished for religious reasons, their wives were expected to follow them. Because house and goods were generally confiscated, the wives had no choice in the matter anyway. Women whose husbands were in hiding, fighting religious wars, or assisting Protestant churches elsewhere supported the family and covered for their husbands, often sending them supplies as well. Wealthy women set up endowments for pastors and teachers and provided scholarships for students at Protestant, and later Jesuit, universities.

Many married women also responded to the Protestant call to make the home, in the words of the humanist Urbanus Rhegius, "a seminary for the church." They carried out what might best be called domestic missionary activity, praying and reciting the catechism with their children and

[16]German mystic and radical Protestant reformer, 1489–1561.

servants. Those who were literate might read some vernacular religious literature, and, because reading was done aloud in the sixteenth century, this was also a group activity. What they could read was limited by the level of their reading ability, the money available to buy books, and the effectiveness of the city censors at keeping out unwanted or questionable material. Women overcame some of the limitations on their reading material by paying for translations, thus continuing a tradition begun before the invention of the printing press. The frequency of widowhood in the sixteenth century meant that women often carried religious ideas, and the pamphlets and books that contained them, to new households when they remarried, and a few men actually admitted to having been converted by their wives. The role of women as domestic missionaries was recognized more clearly by Catholics and English Protestants than it was by continental Protestants, who were obsessed with wifely obedience. Richard Hooker,[17] a theorist for the Anglican church, commented that the Puritans made special efforts to convert women because they were "diligent in drawing away their husbands, children, servants, friends, and allies the same way." Jesuits encouraged the students at their seminaries to urge their mothers to return to confession and begin Catholic practices in the home; in this way, an indifferent or even Lutheran father might be brought back into the fold.

There are several spectacular examples among noble families of women whose quiet pressure eventually led to their husbands' conversions and certainly many among common people that are not recorded. But what about a married woman whose efforts failed? What could a woman do whose religious convictions differed from those of her husband? In some areas, the couple simply lived together as adherents of different religions. The records for Bamberg, for example, show that in 1595 about 25 percent of the households were mixed marriages, with one spouse Catholic and the other Lutheran. Among the members of the city council the proportion was even higher—43 percent had spouses of a different religion, so this was not something which simply went unnoticed by authorities. Bamberg was one of the few cities in Germany which allowed two religions to worship freely; therefore, mixed marriages may have been only a local phenomenon. This, however, has not yet been investigated in other areas.

Continued cohabitation was more acceptable if the husband was of a religion considered acceptable in the area. In 1631, for example, the Strasbourg city council considered whether citizens should lose their citizenship if they married Calvinists. It decided that a man would not "because he can probably draw his spouse away from her false religion, and bring her on to the correct path." He would have to pay a fine, though, for "bringing an unacceptable person into the city." A woman who married a Calvinist

---

[17]1554–1600, author of the *Laws of Ecclesiastical Polity* (1594).

would lose her citizenship, however, "because she would let herself easily be led into error in religion by her husband, and led astray."

As a final resort, a married woman could leave her husband (and perhaps family) and move to an area where the religion agreed with her own. This was extremely difficult for women who were not wealthy, and most of the recorded cases involve noblewomen with independent incomes and sympathetic fathers. Even if a woman might gather enough resources to support herself, she was not always welcome, despite the strength of her religious convictions, for she had violated that most basic of norms, wifely obedience. Protestant city councils were suspicious of any woman who asked to be admitted to citizenship independently and questioned her intensely about her marital status. Catholic cities such as Munich were more concerned about whether the woman who wanted to immigrate had always been a good Catholic than whether or not she was married, particularly if she wished to enter a convent.

Exceptions were always made for wives of Anabaptists. A tailor's wife in Nuremberg was allowed to stay in the city and keep her house as long as she recanted her Anabaptist beliefs and stayed away from all other Anabaptists, including her husband, who had been banished. After the siege of Münster, Anabaptist women and children began to drift back into the city and were allowed to reside there if they abjured Anabaptism and swore an oath of allegiance to the bishop. Both Protestant and Catholic authorities viewed Anabaptism as a heresy and a crime so horrible it broke the most essential human bonds.

It was somewhat easier for unmarried women and widows to leave a territory for religious reasons, and in many cases persecution or war forced them out. A widow wrote to the Nuremberg city council after the city had turned Lutheran that she wanted to move there "because of the respect and love she has for the word of God, which is preached here [that is, Nuremberg] truly and purely"; after a long discussion, the council allowed her to move into the city. But women still had greater difficulties than men being accepted as residents in any city. Wealthier widows had to pay the normal citizenship fee and find male sponsors, both of which were difficult for women, who generally did not command as many financial resources or have as many contacts as men of their class. Because of this, and because innkeepers were forbidden to take in any woman traveling alone, no matter what her age or class, women's cities of refuge were often limited to those in which they had relatives.

Women who worked to support themselves generally had to make special supplications to city councils to be allowed to stay and work. Since they had not been trained in a guild in the city, the council often overrode guild objections in permitting them to make or sell small items to support themselves and was more likely to grant a woman's request if she was seen as particularly needy or if her story was especially pathetic. A woman whose husband had been killed in the Thirty Years' War asked permission in 1632 to live in Strasbourg and bake pretzels; this was granted to her and several others despite the objections of the bakers because, in the council's words, "all of the supplicants are poor people, that are particularly hard-pressed in these difficult times." Another woman was allowed to make tonic and elixirs in Strasbourg after a city pastor assured the council that "she is a pious and godly woman who left everything to follow the true word of God."

One of the most dramatic changes brought about by the Protestant Reformation was the replacement of celibate priests by married pastors with wives and families. Many of the wives of the early reformers had themselves been nuns, and they were crossing one of society's most rigid borders by marrying, becoming brides of men rather than brides of Christ. During the first few years of the Reformation, they were still likened to priests' concubines in the public mind and had to create a respectable role for themselves. They were often living demonstrations of their husbands' convictions and were expected to be models of wifely obedience and Christian charity; the reformers had particularly harsh words for pastors who could not control their wives. Pastors' wives were frequently asked to be godmothers and thereby could be "important agents in the diffusion of evangelical domesticity from the household of the clergy to the rest of the population." But they also had to bring the child a gift appropriate to its social standing from the meager pastoral treasury. The demands on pastors' wives were often exacerbated by their husbands' lack of concern for material matters. Often former priests or monks, these men had never before worried about an income and continued to leave such things in God's (or actually their wives') hands.

Pastors' wives opened up their homes to students and refugees, providing them with food, shelter and medical care. This meant buying provisions, brewing beer, hiring servants, growing fruits and vegetables, and gathering herbs for a household that could expand overnight from ten to eighty. Katherine von Bora purchased and ran an orchard, personally overseeing the care of apple and pear trees and selling the fruit to provide income for the household. She occasionally took part in the theological discussions that went on after dinner in the Luther household and was teased by her husband for her intellectual interests; he called her "Professor Katie." . . .

Other pastors' wives assisted in running city hospitals, orphanages, and infirmaries, sometimes at the suggestion of their husbands and sometimes on their own initiative. Katherine Zell, the wife of Matthias Zell[18] and a tireless worker for the Reformation in Strasbourg, inspected the local hospital and was appalled by what she found there. She demanded the hospital master be replaced because he served the patients putrid, fatty

---

[18]Katherine (c.1497–1562) and Matthias Zell (1477–1548) were Protestant reformers at Strasbourg.

meat, "does not know the name of Christ," and mumbled the table grace "so you can't tell if it's a prayer or a fart." Wealthy women set up endowments for pastors and teachers and provided scholarships for students at Protestant, and later Jesuit, universities.

Neither the Protestant nor the Catholic reformers differentiated between noblewomen and commoners in their public advice to women; noblewomen, too, were to be "chaste, silent, and obedient." Privately, however, they recognized that such women often held a great deal of power and made special attempts to win them over. Luther corresponded regularly with a number of prominent noblewomen, and Calvin was even more assiduous at "courting ladies in high places."

Noblewomen, both married and ummarried, religious and lay, had the most opportunity to express their religious convictions, and the consequences of their actions were more far-reaching than those of most women. Prominent noblewomen who left convents could create quite a sensation, particularly if, like Ursula of Münsterberg, they wrote a justification of why they had left and if their actions put them in opposition to their families. Disagreements between husband and wife over matters of religion could lead to the wife being exiled, as in the case of Elisabeth of Brandenburg. They could also lead to mutual toleration, however, as they did for Elisabeth's daughter, also named Elisabeth, who married Eric, the duke of Brunswick-Calenburg. She became a Lutheran while her husband remained a Catholic, to which his comment was: "My wife does not interfere with and molest us in our faith, and therefore we will leave her undisturbed and unmolested in hers." After his death, she became regent and introduced the Reformation into Brunswick. . . . Several other female rulers also promoted independently the Reformation in their territories, while others convinced their husbands to do so. Later in the century noble wives and widows were also influential in opening up territories to the Jesuits.

Most of these women were following paths of action that had been laid out by male rulers and had little consciousness of themselves as women carrying out a reformation. Others as well judged their actions on the basis of their inherited status and power, for, despite John Knox's[19] bitter fulminations against "the monstrous regiment of women," female rulers were not regarded as unusual in the sixteenth century. Only if a noblewoman ventured beyond summoning and protecting a male reformer or signing church ordinances to commenting publicly on matters of theology was she open to criticism as a woman going beyond what was acceptable.

The best known example of such a noblewoman was Argula von Grumbach, who wrote to the faculty of the University of Ingolstadt in 1523 protesting the university's treatment of a young teacher accused of Lutheran leanings. She explained her reasons: "I am not unacquainted

[19]c.1505–1572, leader of the Protestant Reformation in Scotland.

with the word of Paul that women should be silent in Church [1 Tim. 1:2] but, when no man will or can speak, I am driven by the word of the Lord when he said, 'He who confesses me on earth, him will I confess, and he who denies me, him will I deny' [Matt. 10, Luke 9] and I take comfort in the words of the prophet Isaiah [3:12, but not exact], I will send you children to be your princes and women to be your rulers."

She also wrote to the duke of Bavaria, her overlord, about the matter. Neither the university nor the duke bothered to reply but instead ordered her husband or male relatives to control her and deprived her husband of an official position and its income as a show of displeasure. Instead of having the desired effect, these actions led her to write to the city council at Ingolstadt and to both Luther and Frederick the Wise of Saxony to request a hearing at the upcoming imperial diet at Nuremberg. Her letters were published without her knowledge, provoking a student at Ingolstadt to write an anonymous satirical poem telling her to stick to spinning and hinting that she was interested in the young teacher because she was sexually frustrated. She answered with a long poem that was both satirical and serious, calling the student a coward for writing anonymously and giving numerous biblical examples of women called on to give witness. This ended her public career. . . . Though she died in obscurity, her story was widely known and frequently reprinted as part of Lutheran books of witnesses and martyrs.

In the case of Argula von Grumbach, her sex was clearly more important than her noble status. Political authorities would not have ignored a man of similar status who was in contact with major reformers. Grumbach exhibited a strong sense of herself as a woman in her writings, even before her detractors dwelled on that point alone. Despite the extraordinary nature of her actions, she did not see herself as in any way unusual, commenting in her letter to the Ingolstadt city council that "if I die, a hundred women will write to you, for there are many who are more learned and adept than I am." She recognized that her religious training, which began with the German Bible her father gave her when she was ten, was shared by many other literate women and expected them to respond in the same way she did, proclaiming "the word of God as a member of the Christian church."

Like noblewomen, women engaged in various occupations did not receive any special message from the reformers. Even Luther's harsh diatribe against the prostitutes of Wittenberg was addressed to the university students who used their services. This is because in the sixteenth century, women who carried out a certain occupation were rarely thought of as a group. A woman's work identity was generally tied to her family identity.

This can best be explained with an example. For a man to become a baker, he apprenticed himself to a master baker for a certain number of years, then spent several more years as a journeyman, and finally might be allowed to make his masterpiece—a loaf of bread or a fancy cake—open his own shop, marry, and hire his own apprentices and journeymen. He was then a full-fledged member of the bakers' guild, took part in parades, festivals, and celebrations with his guild brothers, lit candles at the guild altar in Catholic cities, and perhaps participated in city government as a guild representative. He was thus a baker his entire life and had a strong sense of work identity.

For a woman to become a baker, she had to marry a baker. She was not allowed to participate in the apprenticeship system, though she could do everything in the shop her husband could. If he died, she might carry on the shop a short time as a widow, but, if she was young enough, she generally married again and took on whatever her new husband's occupation was. She had no voice in guild decisionmaking and took no part in guild festivals, though she may have actually baked more than her husband. Changes in her status were not determined by her own level of training but by changes in her marital or family status. Thus, although in terms of actual work she was as much a baker as her husband, she, and her society, viewed her as a baker's wife. Her status as wife was what was important in the eyes of sixteenth-century society, and, as we have seen, many treatises and laws were directed to wives.

Although female occupations were not directly singled out in religious theory, several were directly affected by changes in religious practices. The demand for votive candles, which were often made and sold by women, dropped dramatically, and these women were forced to find other means of support. The demand for fish declined somewhat, creating difficulties for female fishmongers, although traditional eating habits did not change immediately when fast days were no longer required. Municipal brothels were closed in the sixteenth century, a change often linked with the Protestant Reformation. This occurred in Catholic cities as well, however, and may be more closely linked with general concerns for public order and morality and obsession with women's sexuality than with any specific religion.

Charitable institutions were secularized and centralized, a process which had begun before the Reformation and was speeded up in the sixteenth century in both Protestant and Catholic territories. Many of the smaller charities were houses set up for elderly indigent women who lived off the original endowment and small fees they received for mourning or preparing bodies for burial. They had in many cases elected one of their number as head of the house but were now moved into large hospitals under the direction of a city official. The women who worked in these hospitals as cooks, nurses, maids, and cleaning women now became city, rather than church, employees. Outwardly their conditions of employment changed little, but the Protestant deemphasis on good works may have changed their conception of the value of their work, particularly given their minimal salaries and abysmal working conditions.

Midwives had long performed emergency baptisms if they or the parents believed the child would not live. This created few problems before the Reformation because Catholic doctrine taught that if there was some question about the regularity of this baptism and the child lived, the infant could be rebaptized "on the condition" it had not been baptized properly the first time; conditional baptism was also performed on foundlings. This assured the parents that their child had been baptized correctly while avoiding the snare of rebaptism, which was a crime in the Holy Roman Empire. In 1531, however, Luther rejected all baptisms "on condition" if it was known any baptism had already been carried out and called for a normal baptism in the case of foundlings. By 1540, most Lutheran areas were no longer baptizing "on condition," and those persons who still supported the practice were occasionally branded Anabaptists. This made it extremely important that midwives and other laypeople knew how to conduct correctly an emergency baptism.

Midwives were thus examined, along with pastors, church workers, and teachers, in the visitations conducted by pastors and city leaders in many cities, and "shocking irregularities" in baptismal practice were occasionally discovered. In one story, perhaps apocryphal, a pastor found one midwife confident in her reply that, yes, she certainly baptized infants in the name of the Holy Trinity—Caspar, Melchior, Balthazar! During the course of the sixteenth century, most Protestant cities included a long section on emergency baptisms in their general baptismal ordinance and even gave copies of this special section to the city's midwives. They also began to require midwives to report all illegitimate children and asked them to question any unmarried mother about who the father of the child was. If she refused to reveal his identity, midwives were to question her "when the pains of labor are greatest," for her resistance would probably be lowest at that point.

In areas of Germany where Anabaptism flourished, Anabaptist midwives were charged with claiming they had baptized babies when they really had not, so that a regular church baptism would not be required. In other areas the opposite seems to have been the case. Baptism was an important social occasion and a chance for the flaunting of wealth and social position, and parents paid the midwife to conveniently forget she had baptized a child so that the normal church ceremony could be carried out.

Despite the tremendous diversity of female experience in Germany during the Reformation, two factors are constant. First, a woman's ability to respond to the Reformation and the avenues her responses could take were determined more by her gender than by any other factor. The reformers—Catholic and Protestant, magisterial and radical—all agreed on the proper avenues for female response to their ideas. The responses judged acceptable were domestic, personal, and familial—prayer, meditation, teaching the catechism to children, singing or writing hymns, entering or leaving a convent. Public responses, either those presented publicly or those which concerned dogma or the church as a public institution, shocked and outraged authorities, even if they agreed with the ideas being expressed. A woman who backed the "wrong" religion was never as harshly criticized as a man; this was seen as simply evidence of her irrational and weak nature. One who supported the "right" religion too vigorously and vocally, however, might be censured by her male compatriots for "too much enthusiasm" and overstepping the bounds of proper female decorum. Thus, whatever a woman's status or class, her responses were judged according to both religious and sexual ideology. Since women of all classes heard this message from pamphlet and pulpit and felt its implications in laws and ordinances, it is not at all surprising that most of them accepted it.

Second, most women experienced the Reformation as individuals. Other than nuns in convents, women were not a distinct social class, economic category, or occupational group; thus, they had no opportunity for group action. They passed religious ideas along the networks of their family, friends, and neighbors, but these networks had no official voice in a society that was divided according to male groups. A woman who challenged her husband or other male authorities in matters of religion was challenging basic assumptions about gender roles, and doing this alone, with no official group to support her. Even women who reformed territories did so as individual rulers. Men, on the other hand, were preached to as members of groups and responded collectively. They combined with other men in city councils, guilds, consistories, cathedral chapters, university faculties, and many other bodies to effect or halt religious change. Their own individual religious ideas were affirmed by others, whether or not they were ultimately successful in establishing the religious system they desired.

The strongest female protest against the Reformation in Germany came from the convents, where women were used to expressing themselves on religious matters and thinking of themselves as members of a spiritual group. Thus, although the Protestant reformers did champion a woman's role as wife and mother by closing the convents and forbidding female lay confraternities, they cut off women's opportunities for expressing their spirituality in an all-female context. Catholic women could still enter convents, but those convents were increasingly cut off from society. By the mid-seventeenth century, religion for all women in Germany, whether lay or clerical, had become much more closely tied to a household.

Sexual Politics and Religious Reform in the Witch Craze

JOSEPH KLAITS

During the European witch craze or witch hunt, which lasted from approximately 1450 to 1650, perhaps 100,000 people were executed by burning, strangulation, or hanging. Fifty thousand died in the slaughter in Germany alone. Countless others were exiled or sentenced to prison, often after having been tortured. Some were even acquitted and returned to their community to be treated as outcasts.

In the last twenty years, the witch craze has interested a number of historians, whose research has added greatly to our knowledge of the alleged witches and those who persecuted them. But much is still not clear. For example, why did the craze begin during the Renaissance and Scientific Revolution, supposed periods of intellectual advance? Certainly the belief in witches was not new, yet the so-called medieval "Dark Ages" witnessed no hunt for witches. Some scholars locate the origins of the craze in folklore, theology, heresy, and changes in the law. Some look to the practice of ceremonial magic among socially prominent individuals or to the development of a fictitious stereotype of a small, secret sect of night-flying witches who met regularly and, with the aid of the devil, engaged in ritual murder, cannibalism, incest, and other antihuman activities, and strove to destroy Christian society.

The reasons for the rather sudden end of the craze in the mid-seventeenth century are not clear, either. The overwhelming majority of Europeans continued to believe in the reality of the devil and witches long after courts ceased prosecuting for witchcraft. Did judges experience a crisis of conscience, unsure of their ability to determine if the person before them was a witch? Did the Scientific Revolution's conception of a universe operating through natural law convince those in control of the mechanisms of persecution that Satan's personal intervention would contradict the regularity of nature and was therefore impossible? Or did the fires of the great witch hunt run their course, with Europeans suffering burnout, exhaustion from the constant fear of witches and from each individual's fear that someday she, too, might be accused? Possibly the decline of religious intensity in post-Reformation Europe could explain the diminished concern with Satan.

In this selection, Joseph Klaits discusses first of all the relationship of sexuality to the stereotype of the witch. Why was witchcraft primarily a woman's crime? (During this era, more women were killed for witchcraft than for all other capital crimes put together.) What were the sexual elements in the idea of the witches' sabbat? Who was the typical witch and what characteristics did she have? Does Klaits's emphasis on the role of sexuality in the craze help to explain why approximately 80 percent of those accused as witches were women? Why, then, were males accused at all?

Second, Klaits stresses the importance of spiritual reform as a cause of the increased persecution of witches. How does he argue that the reformers of both the Protestant Reformation and the Catholic Counter Reformation share responsibility for stoking the fires of the witch craze? How did the war on popular religion by the elite and the subsequent "Christianization" of Europe contribute to the hunt for witches?

Klaits sees misogyny (woman-hating) as a significant part of the Christian tradition and argues, furthermore, that Christian misogyny increased during the sixteenth and seventeenth centuries. What sexual and misogynistic prejudices influenced judges to prosecute witches?

Finally, Klaits links the misogyny of witch hunters to the movements for religious reform. Why does he believe that spiritual reform combined with this new emphasis on sexuality helps explain the intensity of the witch craze?

Why did the number of witch trials in Western Europe increase greatly after about 1550? Why did the crime of witchcraft, familiar for centuries, suddenly appear so much more menacing that thousands of trials unfolded between 1550 and 1700, whereas only a few hundred seem to have occurred earlier? . . .

. . . My thesis is that changes in sexual attitudes can help explain both the metamorphosing definitions of witchcraft and the role of reforming religious ideologies in creating the environment in which witch hunting flourished.

Consider first, by way of review, the stages of evolution in the concept of witchcraft. . . . [T]he meaning of witchcraft changed around the turn of the fifteenth century. Before 1375 or so, witchcraft almost always meant sorcery, i.e., maleficent magic. In the early trials of this period, the crime was defined as harm inflicted on a victim by such magical means as spells or potions. Making an image of the victim and then breaking off a leg to cause a neighbor's lameness or inducing reciprocated affection by administering a charmed drink—these were the typical offenses of fourteenth-century witch trials. Usually in these early trials there was no mention of the devil or demons. When a demon did appear, it was generally as the servant of the witch, who had invoked demonic aid to accomplish evil magic.

After 1375, and especially during the last two-thirds of the fifteenth century, a new definition of witchcraft emerged. In some clerical treatises and torture-elicited confessions, witchcraft was pictured as a combination of traditional sorcery and a novel diabolism. The witch was no longer merely a worker of malefice. She was also a servant of the devil. Clerics explained a witch's supernatural powers as the manifestation of abilities granted her by Satan, a point of view that conformed well with Aristotelian views of causation. It seemed implausible to these writers and judges that witches could do their mischief without demonic assistance, and they cast the witch as worshiper of the devil. This new definition of the crime of witchcraft overlay the older one of the witch as sorcerer. . . . [I]n the initial stage of a trial, when one villager accused another, only sorcery was attributed to the witch. But, when elite authorities intervened, they introduced the issue of devil worship into the proceedings. By the 1480s, when the classic witch-hunting treatise, the *Malleus Maleficarum*,[1] was first published, the image of the witch as evildoing devil worshiper was firmly established in elite consciousness.

An analysis of Europe's witch craze can begin either at the top of society or at the bottom. One may choose to emphasize changes in the outlook of the educated elites, both clerical and secular. Or one can stress the role of popular agitation for witch trials. But these mirror-image interpretive frameworks need not be regarded as mutually exclusive. It seems entirely reasonable to expect that the witch craze, like most other complex historical episodes, cannot be explained in accord with a single theoretical model, no matter how thoughtful or sophisticated. Instead, this book argues that witch-hunting impulses both trickled down from society's leaders and rose upward on a tide of popular anxieties.

Moreover, the cultural distance between elites and populace was not at all fixed. Especially in the later stages of the witch craze, ideas and practices characteristic of society's upper echelons had penetrated deeply into village life. Thus, higher and lower cultures should be regarded not as separate compartments but as overlapping categories with many points of contact. Witch hunting was one of the most dramatic areas of overlap. In the witch trials, members of the elites and ordinary folk found a common cause.

This [selection] discusses the impulses for witch trials that came from the educated and the politically powerful. It dwells on the concerns of the elites with spiritual reform in general and sexual reform in particular. The intention here is to show the impact that changing values among the educated had on ordinary folk, who were at the receiving end of reforming religious evangelism and made up the great majority of witches and their accusers. . . .

. . . After 1550, most European witch trials were of criminals who were said to be not only Satan's worshipers but his sexual slaves as well. Occasionally in the fifteenth century we read in learned treatises of witches who engage in perverse sexual practices. It was only during the witch craze itself, however, that the charge of sexual abuse became a normal component of a witchcraft indictment. As in the case of the introduction of devil worship in the fifteenth century, charges of sexual trespassing were introduced from above. They appear only rarely in the initial accusations but were raised by prosecutors predisposed to see the witch as a sex offender. A preoccupation with the sexual side of witchcraft is the feature that most clearly differentiates the witch stereotype of the sixteenth and seventeenth centuries from the earlier era of small-scale witch hunting.

The ways in which people dealt with sexual matters had an enormous impact on witch trials. The witch craze often has been described as one

---

[1] *The Hammer of Witches* (1486), written by Heinrich Kramer and Jakob Sprenger.

of the most terrible instances of man's inhumanity to man. But more accurate is a formulation by gender, not genus: witch trials exemplify men's
inhumanity to women. The sexually powerful and menacing witch figure
was nearly always portrayed as a female. For example, the authors of the
Malleus Maleficarum were convinced that the great majority of witches were
women. And, like a self-fulfilling diagnosis, women comprised the overwhelming bulk of the accused during the witch craze. Evidence from about
7,500 witch trials in diverse regions of Europe and North America during
the sixteenth and seventeenth centuries shows that nearly 80 percent of
accused witches were female, and, in parts of England, Switzerland, and
what is now Belgium, women accounted for over nine out of ten victims.
This disproportion was far greater than in earlier witchcraft trials, when
men had comprised close to half of the accused. Further, these numbers
understate the predominance of women, because many of the accused
men were implicated solely due to their connection with female suspects.
Thus, in the English county of Essex, where only twenty-three of 291 accused witches were men, eleven were either husbands of an accused witch
or were jointly indicted with one.

Everywhere, witchcraft was a woman's crime. Those who advocated
witch trials saw nothing remarkable in this sexual imbalance. It conformed
perfectly with the dominant notions of female inferiority, while it con-
firmed the legitimacy of woman-hatred with each new case. A circular
process of great force, the dynamics of the witch trials were one expression
of deep-seated misogyny in early modern times. Indeed, this [selection]
will argue that the witch trials were symptomatic of a dramatic rise in fear
and hatred of women during the era of the Reformation.

To illustrate the centrality of sexual imagery in the picture of the witch
during the peak period of witch hunting, consider one of the most influential descriptions of a supposed witches' sabbat. This account comes
from Pierre de Lancre, counselor in the Parlement[2] of Bordeaux and prosecutor, under King Henry IV's[3] commission, of hundreds of female witch
suspects in the predominantly Basque region of the Labourd in south-
western France. In 1609, de Lancre sent more than eighty women to the
stake in one of the largest of the French witch hunts. Three years later,
he published his *Tableau de l'inconstance des mauvais anges et démons.*[4] This
is a lengthy work describing the evil deeds of the Basque witches, and
prominently featured in it is an extended report on the witches' sabbat.

De Lancre portrayed the sabbat as a lurid affair attended by numerous
witches who flew in from considerable distances on broomsticks, shov-
els, spits, or a variety of domestic animals. Some sabbats were attended
by as many as twelve thousand witches, though most meetings were of

---

[2] A sovereign judicial court.
[3] King of France, 1589–1610.
[4] *Description of the Inconstancy of Evil Angels and Demons.*

more manageable scale. The devil might appear to his congregants as a three-horned goat, a huge bronze bull, or a serpent, but, whatever his guise, de Lancre's informers rarely failed to mention his large penis and scaly testicles. A festive air prevailed, reminiscent of a wedding or court celebration. Generally, the proceedings began with the witches kissing their master's rear. Then each witch reported malefice she had carried out since the last sabbat. Those with nothing to report were whipped. The business meeting concluded, a work session followed, during which the women industriously concocted poisons and ointments out of black bread and the rendered fat of murdered infants. Having built up an appetite, they next banqueted on babies' limbs and toads, foods variously reviewed as succulent or awful-tasting. Then the devil presided over a parody of the Mass. Finally, the social hour: the naked witches danced lasciviously, back to back, until the dancing turned into a sexual orgy that continued to the dawn. Incest and homosexual intercourse were encouraged. Often the devil would climax the proceedings by copulating—painfully, it was generally reported—with every man, woman, and child in attendance, as mothers yielded to Satan before their daughters' eyes and initiated them into sexual service to the diabolical master. . . .

Such was de Lancre's account of the sabbat, boiled down from his two hundred pages of detailed description. In this portrayal the sexual elements are of course very prominent. The powerfully sexual nature of the dominant imagery begins with the broomstick ride, continues with exciting whippings, the fascinating close-up look at devilishly huge sexual organs, the baby-eating (possibly sublimated incest or infanticide?), and, finally, the frenzied orgy itself.

The important place of the sabbat in de Lancre's book and in other demonological works of the late sixteenth and early seventeenth centuries is all the more striking when we note that the witches' sabbat was not a prominent feature in earlier formulations of the witch stereotype. The sabbat does not appear, for example, in the *Malleus Maleficarum*, the most widely circulated demonological treatise of the fifteenth century, and it is encountered infrequently before 1500. Earlier, the image of the witch was that of a rather isolated individual. Witches might get together in small groups to stir their cauldrons, . . . but, until the era of the Reformation, few writers thought in terms of large prayer meetings devoted to the adoration of Satan. The *Malleus*, like other early demonological works, had discussed witches' ability to "tie the knot" and cause impotence. It also pictured witches as the sexual partners of demons in human form. In later witch-hunting treatises, sexual overtones became the leading theme of demonological imagery, and the sabbat emerged as the central focus of the witch hunters' fantasies. Not only de Lancre but nearly every continental demonologist of the era of the witch craze laid great stress on the sabbat as the occasion for witches to express their perverse sexuality.

Along similar lines, witch-hunting judges regularly warned that a sure sign of witchcraft was the presence on a woman's body of the so-called devil's mark. This was an insensible spot or anesthetic scar with which Satan branded a woman (like a slave) when initiating her into witchcraft. Related to this idea, though somewhat less common, was the belief that the witch had an extra nipple through which to suckle her familiar or incubus.[5] Any wart, mole, or other skin growth on the accused's body might be identified as a devil's mark or witch's tit. Since the devil would of course do his best to hide the evidence of his servant's fidelity, it was deemed necessary to conduct a thorough, formal search. In practice, this meant stripping and shaving the accused's entire body before meticulously examining and pricking every part of her. Such inspections were usually conducted by physicians or surgeons, but sometimes by midwives or other women, before an all-male audience. In Scotland, witch pricking was the specialty of men who made a profession of the search for the devil's mark. There, as in some other places, it was common for suspects to undergo repeated examinations until a devil's mark was discovered. The devil's mark was unknown in popular beliefs about witchcraft, and even early demonologists like the authors of the *Malleus* had never heard of it. After 1560, however, the search for the mark became an ordinary feature of witchcraft investigations, particularly in Protestant lands, where strong emphasis was placed on the witch's pact with the devil.

In the republic of Geneva, this ceremony of stripping and probing took place regularly in the more than two hundred recorded trials of women for witchcraft, although failure to find a devil's mark on the accused often sufficed to save her from a death sentence in Genevan courts. The Genevan judges' unusually high standards of proof were condemned by commentators of the time, who no doubt would have been even more critical had they known that only about one-fifth of the republic's accused witches wound up at the stake. This was one of the lowest execution ratios anywhere in Europe. Genevan witch suspects, however, were typical of their counterparts elsewhere in their preponderantly rural origins. About half of Geneva's accused witches were peasants from the city's rural dependencies, even though these hamlets accounted for only about 20 percent of the republic's total population. That an urban, reformed patriciate regularly subjected country women to the rape-like humiliation of the search for the devil's mark is an indicator of elite suspicions about rural sexual habits and of the dehumanizing consequences that such suspicions could produce, even among relatively careful and lenient judges.

Another sign of the authorities' preconceptions about female sexuality was their association of the devil's mark with women's genitals. Demonological experts warned judges that women often bore the devil's mark on their "shameful parts," "on the breasts or private parts." As a seventeenth-

---

[5] A male demon who had intercourse with a woman.

century handbook for English justices of the peace pointed out, because "these the Devil's Marks . . . be often in women's secretest Parts, they therefore require diligent and careful Search." One witch suspect in the Swiss canton of Fribourg contemptuously chided her judges for their naivete about female anatomy. After the prosecutors discovered what they took to be a devil's mark on her genitals, Ernni Vuffiod informed them that "if this was a sign of witchcraft, many women would be witches." The same part of the female body received careful attention from judges at the Salem witch trials. The women examiners employed by the courts reported that they found on three suspects "a preternatural excrescence of flesh between the pudendum and the anus, much like teats, and not usual in women." A Scottish witch always was searched with similar thoroughness to discover "marks . . . between her thys and her body." . . .

By about 1560, the witch stereotype had taken on all its menacing features. The witch was not only what she had been for centuries in popular imagination—a source of mischief and misfortune. Now, in the eyes of learned judges, she was much more—one of a vast number of devil worshipers who had yielded to Satan in the most repulsive ways and become his sexual servant. This newer definition of the witch as sexual servant and member of a large devil-worshiping cult became even more frightening to those in authority than the witch's power to inflict malefice. The change can be measured in the law. For example, the *Carolina*, the German imperial law code promulgated in the 1530s, punished alleged witches more severely if they could be shown to have brought harm to their neighbors. But the Saxon criminal code of the 1570s, which was widely imitated throughout Germany and Scandinavia, mandated death by fire for *any* dealing with the devil, regardless of whether the accused had brought about harm by magical means.

This reformulation of the law of witchcraft reflected the new view, frequently expressed in witch hunters' manuals published after 1560, that the real root of the witch's crime was her allegiance to Satan. The change can be dated precisely in Scotland, where the statute on witchcraft passed in 1563 defined the crime as malefice. It made no mention of dealings with Satan. But, by the 1590s, the decade of the first large Scottish witch hunts, the meaning of witchcraft had been altered. As on the continent, the offense now lay in the witch's pact with Satan and her promise of servitude. Accusations of malefice usually were not enough to condemn a suspected witch. Because evidence of the demonic pact was essential for conviction, the search for the devil's mark became an inevitable part of Scottish witch trails. . . .

The triumph of this updated image of the witch as the sabbat-attending sexual servant of the devil coincided with a dramatic rise in the rate of witchcraft prosecution. For all of Europe during the last two-thirds of the fifteenth century, about three hundred witch trials have been verified. Between 1560 and 1680 Germany alone experienced thousands of such trials.

The important changes in the meaning of witchcraft and the tremendous increase in trial incidences during the era of religious reform have sometimes been played down by scholars searching for the medieval origins of witch hunting. We should remember, however, that the new stereotype of the witch current among the elites seems to have evoked far more intense fears than had earlier images of witchcraft. This redefinition set the stage for the witch craze.

It was not simply a matter of more witch trials; specifically, more women were accused of trafficking with the devil. Before 1400, when witchcraft meant sorcery, only a bare majority—50 to 60 percent—of accused witches were women. In the fifteenth century, as witchcraft became equated with diabolism, . . . the proportion of female accused rising to between 60 and 70 percent. During the witch craze itself, the preponderance of women increased still further. Over Europe as a whole in this period about 80 percent of witch suspects were women, and in some places women accounted for more than nine out of ten accused witches.

These figures suggest that originally witchcraft was not viewed specifically as a woman's crime. The stereotypical medieval sorcerer said to engage in image magic, spell casting, or the concoction of love potions was frequently perceived as a male figure learned in the arcane and dangerous science of ritual magic. As the crime was redefined in the fifteenth century to stress servitude to the devil, however, witchcraft became a gender-linked offense; women, the witch-hunting manuals repeated, were morally weaker than men and therefore were more likely to succumb to satanic temptation. The linkage thus forged became even stronger when, during the sixteenth and seventeenth centuries, lay and clerical elites came to see the witch as Satan's sexual servant. The one-fifth of witch suspects in Scotland who were men, for example, do not appear to have been accused of any sexual relationship with the devil, unlike their female counterparts. As witchcraft became identified with sexual trespasses in the minds of reforming witch hunters, its gender-linked status was greatly reinforced. . . .

The coming of the witch craze was one manifestation of the impact of spiritual reform in the sixteenth and seventeenth centuries. The twin movements of the Protestant Reformation and the Catholic Counter Reformation (referred to collectively, for convenience, as the Reformation) created a new ideology that profoundly affected all aspects of European life. The reformers—both Catholic and Protestant—saw spiritual matters as the core of human identity. In this they resembled earlier Christian leaders, but they broke decisively with the medieval past in their systematic, persistent attempts to Christianize peasants and other ordinary folk. In the reformers' ideology, Christianity was not just a matter for a few religious specialists, such as monks or priests, as had been the de facto situation in the Middle Ages. Instead, the reformers believed that each member of the community should lead a Christian life. This conviction gave all branches of reform their great stress on missionary work. As evangelists spreading the faith, the godly reformers preached and taught at all levels of European society. Their educational efforts met with considerable success, for members of the lay elites and even lower social groups adopted the values and habits required by the new doctrines of spiritual reform. In this way the ideology of the religious elite came to be a potent political and social force. Embraced by rulers, judges, and other authorities and imposed on popular classes, the ideas of godly reform penetrated deeply into European culture during the era of the witch craze. A "Christianization" of Europe in the sixteenth and seventeenth centuries was probably the major long-term result of the upsurge in spirituality that occurred during the Reformation era.

The reformers, whether Catholic or Protestant, were militants who saw the world as the scene of cosmic conflict between forces of good and evil. They were inclined to detect evidence of deviant practices everywhere. The new stereotype of the witch reflected the religious and lay authorities' concern with religious dissidents in strife-torn Reformation Europe. The witch hunters' image of collective devil worship at the sabbat undoubtedly derived in part from their knowledge of secret religious services that persecuted minorities were resorting to in many areas of Europe. Authorities predisposed to suspicions of clandestine conventicles gathering under their noses were ready to believe that large numbers of devil worshipers were also in their midst. Worth noting in this regard is the symbolism of the witches' sabbat, which reveals the authorities' belief that devil worshipers were reversing Christian ceremonial. Making an obscenity of the holy kiss, turning consecrated bread into devil's food—these, like the diabolical stigmata of the devil's mark, were the blasphemies that the orthodox expected from their heretical enemies, whether they were labeled Catholics, Protestants, or witches.

More generally, the Reformation was the occasion for renewed concern with the power of Satan in the world. Leading Protestant and Catholic reformers, continuing the tradition of late medieval Latin Christianity, laid great stress on satanic imagery. For example, in the catechism of the leading Jesuit reformer Peter Canisius, the name Satan appears sixty-seven times, four more than Jesus' name. Martin Luther believed that the devil was lord of this world; . . . he held that visible reality and all things of the flesh belonged to Satan. . . . And John Calvin,[6] who saw humans so yoked to sin that they could do nothing to save themselves, pictured human will as the captive of Satan's wiles, in most cases abandoned by God to the devil's power. . . .

Mainstream reformers and religious radicals seem to have been equally deeply concerned about Satan. John Rogers, the seventeenth-century Eng-

---

[6]1509–1564, French Protestant theologian, founder of Calvinism and religious leader of Geneva.

lish sectarian, admitted to seeing devils in every tree and bush. For years he slept with his hands clasped in a praying position, so that he would be ready if Satan came for him during the night. As a boy Rogers was haunted by "fear of Hell and the devils, whom I thought I saw every foot in several ugly shapes and forms, according to my fancies, and sometimes with great rolling flaming eyes like saucers, having sparkling firebrands in one of their hands, and with the other reaching at me to tear me away to torments."

It may be hard to take seriously today the idea of a personal devil who brings bad weather, illness, or other misfortune, but the image was vividly real to the religious reformers and those who came under their influence. . . .

Belief in the devil proved a psychological necessity for many people, as the intensely introspective habits and preoccupation with sin encouraged by all branches of reformed Catholic and Protestant Christianity apparently heightened feelings of inadequacy and moral responsibility. Thus, there was created powerful psychological pressure to project the resulting guilt feelings onto an external personage, the devil, if not onto the devil's human servant, a witch. Meanwhile, the Reformation era's profound political and social upheavals seemed clear proof of Satan's increased activity. Rival groups regularly cast their enemies as representatives of the devil, just as they viewed themselves as fighters on the side of God.

After 1560, clerics and other members of the elites who were influenced by reforming ideals came to interpret many folk practices as devilish and heretical. The representatives of reformed religion had little tolerance of the folklorized Christianity that had been the everyday religion of most people in the Middle Ages. Imbued with a new sense of doctrinal purity, they sought to root out all popular practices that did not flow from official teaching. Reformers labored to inculcate Christian doctrine and moral codes of behavior formerly unheard of in the European countryside. These strong missionary efforts brought the reformers into conflict with deeply traditional folk practices. In such combat the godly saw themselves fighting on one of the many fronts in the war against heresy.

Partly because elite culture laid so much stress on satanic imagery, the reformers were predisposed to find heretical dualism in the folkways of the uneducated. What they discovered in the backwoods horrified the missionaries. In Brittany, for example, peasants believed that buckwheat was not made by God but by Satan. When they harvested this grain, the staple of the poor family's diet, they threw handfuls into the ditches around the field as a thanksgiving offering to the devil. Many purifying missionaries were alarmed to discover rural folk who believed that Satan was coequal with God or that good and evil stemmed from separate forces. . . .

. . . Although the Catholic church prescribed sacraments and exorcism for warding off Satan, and Protestants counseled prayer, ordinary people had invented their own remedies. The Breton peasants' buckwheat offering was typical of popular techniques for controlling evil. In general, Satan was not nearly as horrifying in folk imagery as he was in the minds of most theologians. Popular theatricals in medieval towns had featured entertaining demon-figures who danced on the scene amid exploding fire-crackers. Yet these devils were defeated by Christ before the final bows. In the popular plays, even the most degenerate sinner could escape hell through a simple act of devotion to a powerful saint like the Virgin Mary.

Folklore stressed Mary's ability to cheat the devil even of his rightful prey, but to the reforming elites of the sixteenth and seventeenth centuries this was too easy a solution. Even the Catholic Counter Reformation, which, unlike Protestantism, retained the cultic veneration of saints, imagined the devil as a dreadful personage whom God permitted to operate in the world as appropriate punishment for the misdeeds of sinners. Michelangelo's depiction of the Last Judgment in the Sistine Chapel reflects the pessimistic spirit of the reformers in its representation of Christ and demons cooperating in sending the damned to hell, while Mary turns away from the doomed sinners' desperate pleas for intercession with her son. After 1560, the godly reformers labored hard to impress on the populace a much more menacing image of the devil. Popular religious plays were suppressed, and the semicomic folk-demon of the later Middle Ages was replaced by the deadly Satan long familiar in elite culture. . . .

. . . Whether known as wizards, magicians, or cunning men, these were the leading therapeutic operatives of pre-Reformation rural Europe. . . . [T]hey were called on by peasants to heal the sick, recover stolen property, or foretell the future. In general, they functioned as protectors of the community against the invisible world of demonic evil. Magicians used herbal medicines, amulets, incantations, and elaborate rituals as their stock in trade. . . .

The existence of popular magic as a universal feature of medieval and early modern village life is testimony to the failure of institutional Christianity to penetrate into rural Europe before the Reformation era. The functions of protection and reassurance carried out by these popular practitioners paralleled certain of the functions of sacramental Christianity. Many Christian rituals were based on the invocation of God's protection for the participants, as in the priest's blessing of a maritime village's fishing fleet before the boats set out to sea. But, because the pre-Reformation clergy tended to be highly neglectful, the psychologically necessary protective role was often performed by magicians. By turning to these practitioners, the populace was in effect rejecting institutional religion. This, at any rate, was the conclusion drawn by the newly energized reforming clergy in Protestant and Catholic Europe during the sixteenth and seventeenth centuries. In this period individual magicians were regularly denounced and sometimes . . . prosecuted for sorcery. In the duchy of Lorraine, where demonologists were especially adamant about the criminality of magical healing, judges threatened and tortured witch doctors until they admitted satanic origins for their curative skills. This was one side of the war on popular religion waged during the Reformation era, as clerical and lay elites associated folk magic with libertinage, atheism, and heresy in general. Paradoxically, the authorities' campaigns against these practitioners of "white magic" may have strengthened the impulse to hunt out witches. For, if recourse to magical healers was denied, an effective technique of self-help against misfortune disappeared. Only the machinery of official witchcraft trials remained to protect the bewitched and the fearful from malefice. . . .

The foregoing analysis may help explain the rise of a new form of the witchcraft stereotype in the environment of confessional antagonisms and revivified spirituality characteristic of the Reformation era. Yet such a line of argument is really too general to get at the issue of women and witchcraft. The problem remains: why was it generally a female who was identified as the witch? To approach this question from another angle, let us consider some of the main points of Christian tradition on the subjects of woman and sexuality.

Traditions of woman-hatred long antedate the era of the witch craze, of course. Many cultures of the ancient world regarded women as second-class members of humanity or worse, and the male fear of female domination is reflected in myths of diverse cultures. Christian traditions echoed this bias. Despite the strong emphasis placed on the equality of all Christians before God, from earliest times the Catholic church limited the priesthood to men, stressing, as Pope Paul VI reaffirmed in 1977, that the original models of Christian action, Jesus and the apostles, were all males. Although the cult of Mary developed in the Middle Ages, the church insisted that only the status of virginity and the role of motherhood could glorify the female condition. In the serious business of sanctification, even motherhood has disturbed Catholic leaders; there have been very few female saints who were not virgins throughout their lives. . . .

In Christian ideology, antifemale bias is closely linked to fears and suspicions of sexuality. Historically, mainstream Christian teaching has been more or less hostile to the sexual side of humans. Inheriting this characteristic from the Hellenistic world in which it developed, early Christianity was greatly affected by St. Paul's emphasis on a two-sided human nature consisting of a mortal body and an immortal soul. . . . Christianity portrayed the body, and particularly its sexuality, as an obstacle to salvation. In St. Augustine's[7] view, which emerged as the representative Catholic teaching, sexual pleasure could be justified only by a married couple's attempt at procreation, and some medieval and early modern Catholic authorities thought sex sinful even for reproductive purposes. Although during the Reformation Protestant moralists rejected the ideal of celibacy

---

[7]Christian theologian, 354–430, and Bishop of Hippo in North Africa.

and elevated marriage to new heights of respectability, suspicion of sexual pleasure remained a characteristic of all mainstream Christian teaching in the sixteenth and seventeenth centuries.

Jesus' warning, in the Sermon on the Mount, that lusting after a woman in the heart is an adulterous sin became, in the hands of the church fathers,[8] grounds for blaming women for their sexual attractiveness. Origen[9] allegedly castrated himself, an eminently logical solution. But most of the other church fathers, when they found it impossible to banish sexual desire, projected the fault on women, the forbidden objects. Thus, Jerome,[10] who has been called the patron saint of misogyny, discovered that only by studying Hebrew and working on his Bible translation could he sublimate his passion and be rid of the tormenting visions of dancing girls. He characterized woman as "the gate of the devil, the path of wickedness, the sting of the serpent, in a word a perilous object." This view was typical. Tertullian[11] told women, "you are the devil's gateway". . . . These early images established a pattern. In the Middle Ages and the Renaissance, women were consistently portrayed as the more lascivious of the sexes, forever dragging men into the sin of lust and away from the ascetic spirituality of which they might otherwise be capable. The reverse of the Victorian idea of female asexuality, the Christian tradition regarded women as quintessentially sexual beings.

Many such misogynistic ideas were compiled in the *Malleus Maleficarum* for perpetuation in subsequent witch trials. Women, wrote Kramer and Sprenger, are inferior physically, mentally, and morally. Their imperfections cause women extraordinary difficulty in warding off temptation. They have an "insatiable carnal lust," are inclined to deception, resist discipline, and lure men into sin and destruction. Such are the characteristics that make them likely targets for the devil; hence, the preponderance of females among the devil's servants. The authors of the *Malleus* rested their assertions on a jumble of historical half-truths, disfigured etymologies, and mistaken medicine. They derived the word *femina* from *fe* and *minus*, to show that women have little faith. The fall of kingdoms and of virtuous men they blamed on females. Naturally, they attributed to Eve's initiative the fall of the human race in the Garden of Eden. Adducing the accumulated wisdom of the ages, Kramer and Sprenger quoted widely from biblical and Roman sources. Only if all of these authorities were wrong could one deny the inferiority of women. And, once female biological deficiency was accepted, the foundation was set for accusations of witchcraft on the ground that women lacked the moral fortitude to resist temptation.

[8] Authoritative theologians of the early Christian Church who formulated doctrines.
[9] Early church father, 185–254.
[10] Christian theologian and translator of the Bible, c.347–420.
[11] Christian theologian, c.160–231.

The antifemale prejudices of the *Malleus* were echoed repeatedly in the many demonological treatises that appeared during the age of witch trials. Nicolas Rémy, a judge who prosecuted many witches in Lorraine during the 1590s, found it "not unreasonable that this scum of humanity, i.e., witches, should be drawn chiefly from the feminine sex," for women had always been famous as sorcerers and enchanters. And King James[12] explained the disproportion of female witches by reference to Genesis: "The reason is easie, for as that sex is frailer than man is, so it is easier to be entrapped in these grosse snares of the Devile, as was over well proved to be true, by the Serpents deceiving of Eve at the Beginning," which, he thought, had given Satan ready access to women ever since. In the same vein, Henri Boguet, a witch-hunting prosecutor in the Burgundian Franche-Comté, thought it natural that witches should confess to sexual liaison with Satan. "The Devil uses them so," Boguet explained, "because he knows that women love carnal pleasures, and he means to bind them to his allegiance by such agreeable provocations; moreover, there is nothing which makes a woman more subject and loyal to a man than that he should abuse her body."

This highly unflattering image of women was not limited to a small number of enthusiastic witch hunters. The social order of the elites reflected universal and almost entirely unquestioned assumptions about the inferiority and dangerous attributes of females. The best medical opinion, like that of religious thinkers, associated women with sinful sexuality. Dr. François Rabelais gave this idea its classic Renaissance literary formulation in his *Gargantua and Pantagruel*. Expressing the standard medical view, he described the womb (*hysterus* in Greek) in graphic terms as the seat of woman's sexual passion and the dominant part of a literally hysterical female organism:

> For Nature has placed in a secret and interior place in their bodies an animal, an organ that is not present in men; and here there are sometimes engendered certain salty, nitrous, caustic, sharp, biting, stabbing, and bitterly irritating humors, by the pricking and painful itching of which—for this organ is all nerves—and sensitive feelings—their whole body is shaken, all their senses transported, all their passions indulged, and all their thoughts confused. . . .

Although by 1600 advanced medical opinion, spurred by improved understanding of female anatomy, led most leading physicians to discard this Platonic image of the migratory uterus, the female's excessive desire for coitus remained a medical truism. . . . [H]er well-known capacity for multiple orgasms prompted the belief that she habitually exhausted and ran down her mate in satisfying her carnal appetites. As physicians held that only moderate expenditure of semen was compatible with good

[12]King James VI of Scotland from 1567 and, as James I, King of England, 1603–1625.

health, female sexual demands seemed a physical as well as a moral threat to men. But, although women were seen as suffering from overwhelming sexual passion, experts on biology denied them an active role in the reproductive process. Aristotle's[13] theory that semen holds all that is necessary for generation still held sway, and the woman's part was imagined as the entirely passive one of providing a nurturing environment for the developing fetus.

Neither was there much sympathy for woman among other leaders of early modern culture. Theologians, lawyers, and philosophers were nearly unanimous in asserting her inferiority to man, even if a few legal scholars, like some physicians, seem to have been a little embarrassed about expressing antifemale opinions. . . .

A good indicator of the notion of women that was widespread among the intellectual elites during the age of witch trials comes from Jean Bodin, the famous lawyer and political theorist who also penned a ferocious tract denouncing witches. Bodin began his masterpiece, *The Republic*, with a description of the model household. In it the wife was at the bottom. As the ultimate dependent, she came not only after her husband in the domestic order of things, but also behind the children, servants, and apprentices. Bodin's scheme may have been a bit extreme, but almost no one in the sixteenth and seventeenth centuries, not even early feminists, challenged the need for male superiority in the household. Unlike our modern democratic assumptions, the universally accepted conventional wisdom of the time was that hierarchy was necessary for every kind of social arrangement. As God presided over the universe, as humans were lords of creation, and as kings ruled their states, so it was believed that, in the family, men must be the dominant authorities and women their subordinates. . . .

Acceptance of the principle of male superiority and its embodiment in family life, law, and all other social arrangements meant that, throughout European culture, disorder was associated with women on top. The inversion of morality that was a general feature of the witch stereotype is reflected clearly in the lack of dependency on men exhibited in supposed acts of malefice and in night riding to the sabbat. To men, the reversal in sex roles was probably among the most disconcerting elements in the image of the witch. Among theologians, lawyers, and philosophers, discussion of women was almost always linked with marriage. Thinkers seemed unable to imagine a social role for unattached females. This psychological blind spot is one way to explain why a disproportionately high number of accused witches were widows and other unmarried women not under the rule of men. . . .

In general, the religious strife of the Reformation probably had the effect of increasing fear and hatred of women. Females had been singled out as the progenitors of heresy in medieval times, and such accu-

---

[13]Greek philosopher and scientist, 384–322 B.C.

sations resurfaced in the sixteenth century. In fact, earlier dissident sects, including the Cathars,[14] had encouraged women to assume active religious roles, in striking contrast to strict Catholic application of St. Paul's dictum that women must remain silent in church. And enthusiastic sects of the Reformation era regularly featured women among their leading spirits. De Lancre's horror at female participation in religious services betrayed a characteristic tendency of mainstream church and secular authorities of Reformation times to associate women with religious deviance. This association reinforced traditional Christian fears of women and helped to fuel the misogyny that underlay witch hunting.

Of course, de Lancre was not a unique case. If an argument can be made for witch trials as a manifestation of intensified misogyny in the late sixteenth and early seventeenth centuries, the proliferation of witch-hunting godly reformers is among the most impressive kind of evidence. As we have seen, a prominent feature of all branches of reforming Christianity, Catholic and Protestant, was the evangelical impulse. In spreading Christian doctrine to the backwoods, reformers were fighting popular religious practices, including what they saw as witchcraft. The witch hunts spread with the arrival of spiritual militancy. . . .

It is important to realize, however, that this preoccupation with witchcraft and peasant religion was not limited to clerics alone. As the example of de Lancre suggests, such concerns spread to the laity as well. Many of the most active demonological writers and judges were laymen who had become imbued with the values of spiritual reform. For example, the Lorraine witch hunter Nicolas Rémy was a bitter enemy of lax priests and spoke out against the residues of pagan beliefs in Catholic folk religion. Even Jean Bodin characterized witchcraft as "superstitious religion," the same term the godly used to denounce peasant beliefs. And Bodin was far from an orthodox godly reformer in his private religious preferences and his public calls for religious toleration. The imagery of the sabbat, devil worship, and sexual servitude underlay the demonology of many other lay judges. Thus, witch hunting demonstrates the success of reforming efforts to energize the lay elites with the ideology of spiritual purification.

The sexual prejudices expressed in witch hunting are one of the best indicators of this success. The sixteenth century was the first in which it was acceptable for laymen to discuss sexual topics. Secular writers' adoption of traditional Christian ideas about women and sex suggests the considerable degree to which religiously based notions were absorbed into lay culture. Predisposed as they were to identify women with sinful sexuality, lay and clerical authorities came to express misogynistic sentiments on an

---

[14]Medieval sect in southern France and northern Italy that held that a good god had created the world of the spirit and that Satan had created the material world.

unprecedented scale in their campaigns against popular religion. In the process, they gave traditional fears of women a new and sharper focus. Thus, the encounter of high and low cultures in the era of the Reformation became an occasion for transforming the ancient, conventional misogyny of the Western past into a murderous set of prejudices. The witch craze's slaughter of women was the result of the spread of woman-hatred in the spiritually reformed elites and its application in the reformers' campaigns against folk religion. . . .

That prejudice against women was based on sexual fears and guilt feelings can scarcely be doubted. Women were regularly depicted as predators, with sexuality as their weapon. . . . To twentieth-century observers, nothing could be clearer than the erotic emotions that led men, for example, to undress women publicly and minutely examine their genitals. Few people in those days thought in terms of unconscious sexual symbolism, so the possible presence of libidinous impulses in respectable judges was rarely mentioned by contemporary writers. The appeal of sexuality and violence, the mixture of pleasure and pain that we call sadism, was usually not expressed consciously at the time of the witch trials. . . . At least one observer in the era of witch hunting noted the prurient interests that witchcraft investigations could bring out. An astonished eyewitness at Salem recounted how the Puritan divine Cotton Mather publicly exposed and fondled the breasts of a seventeen-year-old girl as she lay writhing in a fit of ostensibly demonic possession. . . .

To understand the predominance of women witches, then, it is not enough to cite the misogynistic sentiments of witch-hunting prosecutors. All too often earlier writers, both clerics and laymen, had given vent to traditional Christian ideas about the inferiority of women. What was new in the Reformation era was the connection of these traditional prejudices to full-fledged ideologically based movements for reform. Catholics and Protestants undertook massive campaigns to alter popular behavior, particularly sexual behavior. The relatively weak social controls characteristic of late medieval Europe were replaced by far more stringent codes and effective enforcement mechanisms.

There are many clues to the meaning of the newly enhanced sexual character of witchcraft in the clash of elite reforming impulses and popular values. As the reform of elite society progressed, many members of the upper classes came to sense a growing distance between themselves and the masses. Traditional attitudes of universal brotherhood gave way to an imagery of social cleavage built on cultural differences. By and large, the European elites grew contemptuous of popular ways and associated them with everything they had learned to despise. The manners of the upper classes, to begin with externals, were becoming notably different from those of ordinary folk. At table they used the newly invented fork instead of their fingers. It was now the mark of a gentleman to carry a

handkerchief on his person at all times. In upper-class domestic architecture bedrooms were turning into private retreats for the first time, with
the corridor introduced as a by-pass.

These elite expressions of individuality were founded on a sense of
privacy and self-discipline that made the physically spontaneous appear
dangerous and low. That which was "natural" did not seem necessarily
desirable, for human nature had an animal-like side that had to be overcome in order for man to lead a moral life. Infants, therefore, were not
allowed to crawl in seventeenth-century upper-class households, because
this habit reminded adults of four-footed beasts. Almost inevitably, then,
popular culture was associated with bestial naturalness and lack of restraint. In particular, the most subjugated groups were consistently linked
with moral licentiousness. Children received hard discipline to drive out
the devil in them. Blacks had a reputation for sexual potency because of
their allegedly low moral status. And women were consistently tied to Satan and sex. It is not hard to see in these stereotypes projections of desires
repressed by European elites ever more thoroughly imbued with the spirit
of religious reform.

Here was one of the key linkages underlying the witch trials. As large
segments of elite society were becoming preoccupied with self-control,
physical restraint, and ascetic demeanor, the sexual aspects of popular
culture caused great concern. Elite convictions that plebeian women were
likely to succumb to any attractive stranger make understandable the injec-
tion of a strong dose of sex into the witchcraft recipe. Women, and particularly women of nonelite social classes, seem to have struck these judges
as fundamentally immoral types who, as slaves to their sexual urges, were
capable of the worst treason against man and God.

... "Whore and witch" was the standard characterization of accused
women from the villages of Luxembourg, and whore meant a woman who
indulged in sex for pleasure, not for money.

The accused witches ... of the fourteenth and fifteenth centuries ...
were frequently males, but the proportion of men continually declined before and during the witch craze, as the crime was reformulated in strongly
sex-linked terms. The one-fifth of witch suspects in Scotland who were
men, for example, do not appear to have been accused of any sexual relationship with the devil, unlike their female counterparts. As witchcraft
became identified with sexual trespasses in the minds of the reforming
witch hunters, its sex-linked status was greatly reinforced.

This association may well be indicative of a psychological process by
which women, as agents of Satan, were held responsible for male sexual
inadequacy and transgressions. Symptoms of what can be termed early
modern machismo include a highly patriarchal family structure, an obsession with codes of sexual honor, and the curious stress on the genital-
emphasizing codpiece in dress and literary expression. All of these may
betray considerable male insecurity. The purifiers' preachments about the

close relationship of sin and sex surely encouraged in their audiences a sense of guilt about sexual feelings. If inability to adhere to newly generalized standards of Christian sexual behavior could be blamed on women as a consequence of satanic intervention, the male sense of guilt would be greatly reduced.

In this may be found one of the principal social and psychological foundations for witch-hunting misogyny in the age of religious reform. ... [I]n the French-speaking territories of the Spanish Netherlands, the villages that experienced witch trials were the ones with parish priests who took religious reform particularly to heart. These clerics' guilt feelings about their repressed physical desires ... made them harp on sexual themes in their sermons and stress the stereotypical image of the witch as the exemplar of dangerous female sexuality. In neighboring communities with priests who behaved more like laymen, the congregants never were taught to associate women and sex with Satan, and trials for witchcraft did not occur.

Guilt feelings stemming from repressed sexuality and unrealized desires for spiritual fulfillment were not limited to men during the Reformation era. Some of the most dramatic episodes of the witch craze originated in convents, where sisters declared themselves possessed by demons and engaged in behavior regarded as lewd and indecent by scandalized observers. The nuns blamed men for their actions, claiming that they had been bewitched. Like other females who held males responsible for their bewitchment, these sisters were in effect reversing the cycle of repression, guilt, and scapegoating that the clerical establishment had burnt into the European consciousness by associating women and sex with Satan.

On the conscious level, the witch hunters and other leaders of godly reform, like the medieval inquisitors before them, saw themselves as inspired primarily by the desire to save souls. They regarded many members of their flocks as mired in sin, but the attractive Christian idea that even the worst sinner is capable of redemption and salvation spurred on the reformers. This motivation is important to remember, because the horrors of witch prosecutions can easily blind us to their judges' ideals. The art of the Catholic Counter Reformation revived the New Testament theme of the harlot redeemed by Christ, and seventeenth-century artists produced many propaganda canvases showing Mary Magdalene and others, sometimes in the dress of contemporary prostitutes. These paintings display sin as fundamentally sexual, and they associate sexuality with women. Yet also present is the theme of repentance and the ever-present possibility of salvation. In the spirit that inspired this art can be glimpsed the Christian charity that moved the godly elites, even in witch trials. The reformers' deep ideological commitment made them welcome confession and repentance. They saw such changes in behavior as a means of opening the gates of heaven to the sinner. Nevertheless, one cannot escape the conclusion that the witch hunters' identification of women with sin, sexuality, and lower-class mores, combined with their ideological zeal, led them to establish a pattern of judicial excess and gross violations of human dignity.

Ironically, the available evidence seems to indicate that, despite the cultural elites' perception of ever-increasing distance between their ethos and that of ordinary folk, plebeian behavior was in fact changing dramatically in response to pressures from above. Beginning in the mid-sixteenth century, the moderate toleration of sexual license that appears to have been the norm in the later Middle Ages was replaced by a far more repressive spirit, not only among the elites but also at lower levels of society. A few examples can illustrate the changes. For the old ways, consider the Pyrenean village of Montaillou in the fourteenth century. There casual premarital sex was accepted, and about 10 percent of the households consisted of unmarried couples living together. Meanwhile, the local priest set the pace in lechery.

Montaillou was an atypical community because of its Catharist tendencies, but a concubine-holding priesthood was standard in pre-Reformation Europe. In Bavaria, for example, only 3 to 4 percent of the parish priests of the mid-sixteenth century had *not* taken concubines. The efforts of the Catholic reformers, however, soon led to the transformation of priestly celibacy from a pious hope to an actual model for imitation. Reform-minded churchmen vigorously combated formerly widespread patterns of concubinage among the clergy and the upper classes. Those who persisted, unless they were very highborn, were subject to denunciation and eventually to excommunication. As a result, the proportion of illegitimate births attributable to concubinage fell dramatically after the sixteenth century.

Such campaigns eventually produced a marked improvement in the moral quality and educational preparation of parish priests. The spread of Protestantism in northern Europe can be understood in part as a symptom of popular revulsion against a priesthood that was badly trained and morally lax. The Protestant pastor received a systematic preparation that stressed knowledge of the Bible and methods for communicating its teaching to his congregants. One of these methods was setting a personal example of moral behavior. All over Catholic Europe, church leaders were similarly concerned with improving the quality of the local clergy. Under Jesuit leadership, the Council of Trent's[15] strictures about the training and behavior of priests gradually took hold. No longer was the local cleric just another member of the community, a good fellow who might join in a Mardi Gras dance. In reformed Europe he became a sacred figure, separated from the profane society that he was constantly trying to remake in his own new image.

[15]Roman Catholic council that met intermittently between 1545 and 1563 to reform the Church, define doctrine, and roll back Protestantism.

Not only clerics found themselves called to higher standards of sexual behavior. As in today's ideologically motivated revolutionary regimes, the magistrates of the time developed an interest in crimes against morality. The Parlement of Rouen, for example, began to hear frequent cases of adultery, bigamy, sodomy, and incest. These kinds of crimes increased from less than 1 percent of the court's business in 1548–49 to 10 percent in 1604–06. The town fathers of the Lutheran imperial free city of Nördlingen also legislated harsher punishments for sexual offenders after the middle decades of the sixteenth century. From 1590, judges in Geneva and the Swiss Catholic canton of Fribourg, moved by exposure to reformed spiritual ideas that classified sexual deviance as heretical, regularly tried offenders accused of sodomy and bestiality. The General Assembly of the Presbyterian Church in Scotland was instrumental in prompting trials of—note the combination—"incest, adulterie, witchcraft, murther and abominable and horrible oaths." The General Assembly protested to the king in 1583 that without punishment for these offenses "daily sinne increaseth, and provoketh the wrath of God against the whole countrie." Between 1574 and 1696 the Scottish Parliament passed ten statutes condemning blasphemy and swearing and fifteen against sabbath-breaking. Adultery and incest were made capital offenses in the 1560s, at the same time that the Parliament legislated against witchcraft. After 1600, English church courts and justices of the peace also conducted many trials of fornicators. These efforts apparently were effective, to judge from English birth records. As late as Elizabeth's[16] reign, the rates of premarital conception and illegitimacy continued high, yet both ratios dropped by a remarkable 50 to 75 percent under Puritan influence during the first half of the seventeenth century.

The active roles taken by lay judges in these areas attest to the breakdown of traditional medieval spheres of clerical and nonclerical activities. It has often been pointed out that the state's intervention in witch trials reflects the secularization of law in early modern Europe. Equally worthy of note is the extent to which witch legislation and prosecution by state authorities responded to religious concerns. By exercising the power of the newly centralized states in cases of witchcraft and other moral offenses, lay elites showed the deep impact on them of spiritual reform.

The godly not only condemned adultery and premarital sex but also objected to strong passion in the marriage bed. "Never on Sunday" or during Lent was the standard clerical admonition, along with detailed instructions about avoiding "sinful" positions and actions while making love. The first natives to be told of the "missionary position" were the villagers of Europe. Reforming French bishops distributed detailed manuals to parish priests to help them implement approved sexual behavior among the congregants. In these handbooks, learned churchmen established an

[16]Queen of England, 1558–1603.

elaborate hierarchy of sexual sins and recommended appropriate penances for violations that ranged in seriousness from "unnatural" sexual positions, including women on top, to incest and sodomy. The content of this sexual advice was not particularly novel, but the vigorous, well-organized enforcement effort of reform-minded authorities was.

In all of these ways, the moral ideology of spiritual reform was given political meaning in the late sixteenth and seventeenth centuries. The emphasis on sexual repression in society made witchcraft a particularly heinous crime, especially when formulated as sexual servitude to the devil. . . .

The reformers' antipathy for popular sexual practices was merely one side of their consistent tendency to identify the folkways of ordinary people with sin and heresy. Popular recreations like dancing, gambling, and playacting were regularly condemned as immoral and in some places were suppressed. The great seasonal festivals, including Carnival, May Day, Michaelmas, and Midsummer's Eve, which were grand occasions in the life of the people, came under heavy attack by reformers, who condemned them as lewd and pagan profanations. For centuries the liberties of Mardi Gras and similar celebrations had served as a useful safety valve in the pressure-filled lives of ordinary people. But to the reformers these festivals seemed circuses of sin. Eating, drinking, sex, and violence were the chief themes of such occasions, and many of the organized activities—parades, contests, and theatricals—celebrated these basic human impulses. The carnality of Carnival implied that it was all right to give free rein to bodily pleasures, at least on some special days of the year. Heavy eating and drinking were part of the ritual, and population records show a clear rise in births nine months after festival seasons. Carnival was playtime, but to godly reformers such play appeared the height of sacrilege.

Repressive authorities were tempted to ban all types of group revelry. In Scotland the church and borough councils repeatedly prohibited large gatherings, such as the "penny bridal" weddings of poor folk who had to ask guests to bring their own refreshment. This kind of deprivation inspired the typical description of witches' sabbats in Scottish and continental trial confessions. The accounts nearly always speak of uproarious disorder—eating, drinking, music, dancing—the activities denied to ordinary people both by their poverty and by the godly elites' suspicion of festive popular gatherings.

In the imagination of the authorities, the witches' sabbat of ordinary folk naturally included unbridled, licentious celebration, because reformers were certain that their social inferiors were greatly susceptible to the enticements of bodily pleasure. . . .

Backing for these efforts at purification came from secular rulers, who saw religious uniformity and cultural conformism as effective props for centralized absolute government. The motivation for the reform of popular culture was thus partly political. Severely traumatized by the revolutionary episodes and civil warfare that were endemic in Reformation Europe, princes were determined to suppress political and social dissidence among the lower classes. For example, secular rulers became conscious of the explosive potential of popular celebrations, for festivals sometimes sparked large-scale rioting and even full-blown rebellions. With the support of state officials, the churches moved to suppress the popular lay associations that often organized these events and substituted the parish as the main unit of urban life. An important instance was the abolition of fraternities of adolescent males, which had long been one of the central sources of community identity in European towns.

As a result, by the end of the age of witch hunting traditional forms of folk culture had either disappeared or been subdued throughout Europe. . . . It may be overstating the case to speak of an extinction of popular culture. Yet the wild atmosphere of Mardi Gras, the licentiousness of May Day, and the liberation from normal restraints that characterized all folk celebrations survived only in domesticated, decorous form under watchful Catholic establishments, while in most Protestant lands they were abolished as ungodly profanations. Among Catholics, formal religious processions replaced unbridled popular spectacles. In Protestant churches, Bible texts covered the walls to hide the sensual images produced by local artists in the Catholic past, and everywhere there was renewed emphasis on sermons (often stressing the horrors of hell) as the medium by which the masses were to be guided. A more rigidly controlled society emerged, organized around absolutist states and hierarchical churches that intruded into every area of community life. The witch craze was one side of this scene of generalized cultural clash.

Once sexual "deviance" was connected with witchcraft and heresy in preachers' sermons as well as in the law, the campaign against licentious behavior must surely have been easier to win. To the extent that the reformers' war against sex was successful, the elites' efforts to introduce diabolism into the stereotype of the witch were seemingly accepted by the populace. In any case, as the trials proliferated, popular culture clearly received demonic imagery as a plausible extension of the witch stereotype. Satanic stereotypes apparently did not take firm root in the folklore of witchcraft and tended to fade from popular tradition after the trials ended. But during the age of the witch hunts, ordinary people were effectively conditioned by the godly elites to accept the reality of devil worship among their neighbors. This is one measure of how thoroughly elite ideas of witchcraft were imposed on lower cultural levels. . . .

Another indicator of the penetration of elite values into lower cultural levels was the widespread acceptance of the sexual stereotype of female witchcraft. The ancient traditions of misogyny, reinforced by a renewed preoccupation among the reformed elites with sexual sinning, were transmitted to the populace through the missionary efforts of godly reformers during the sixteenth and seventeenth centuries. Thus, bias against women, a conventional characteristic of Christian teaching, became uniquely intense during the era of religious reform. In this period alone did the West's traditional misogyny result in the execution of many thousands simply because, as women, they were automatically suspect. Sixteenth- and seventeenth-century reforming impulses found one of their most important applications in the area of sexuality. The quantum leap in witch trials during this era was one outlet for the deep stresses produced at all social levels as the godly reform of sex took hold.

In many regions of Europe, the spread of witch trials accompanied the advent of a reform-minded clergy. These men of God, trained in seminary or university, were apt to see the devil everywhere and to imagine him as the force underlying all heresy. Thus, when encountering peasant beliefs in sorcery-induced illness or crop failure, clerics and lay authorities influenced by the clerical outlook often went beyond the initial charge and began questioning the accused about devil worship and sabbats. The elites placed charges of malefice in a wider explanatory context within which they could understand the dynamics of supernatural evildoing. This kind of bicultural process, overlaying peasant beliefs with learned concepts, began in the relatively infrequent witch trials of the fifteenth century. With the coming of the Reformation and the appearance of a large, well-educated, irrepressibly evangelical clergy in Western and Central Europe, contacts between learned and popular cultures no longer were sporadic and superficial. They became a regular, permanent feature of village life. These frequent contacts made for frequent witch trials.

One way of understanding the witch craze is to see it as a part of the many-sided war on popular culture waged by reforming clerical and lay establishments in the sixteenth and seventeenth centuries. The chronology of witch hunting argues for this thesis, because the onset of large-scale witch trials corresponds almost exactly with the uneven spread of reforming impulses across Christendom. Witch hunts proliferated as the godly began to indoctrinate ordinary people with Christian theological teaching and concepts of moral behavior unknown to country dwellers of earlier generations. In Western Europe, trials for witchcraft became frequent after 1560, but in Poland and the Habsburg lands of Central Europe, where reform commenced later, such trials were rare until after 1600. As for the remote world of Orthodox Russia, Muscovy, untouched by Western spiritual movements, conducted some trials for sorcery but, lacking the concept of the devil-worshiping heretic, never knew a witch craze. Although it is far from a complete explanation of the trials, the evidence for spiritual reform as a precipitant of the witch craze is very powerful.

The Rites of Violence: Religious Riot in Sixteenth-Century France

NATALIE Z. DAVIS

Eight religious wars rocked the kingdom of France from 1562 to 1598. Spurred by the grandiose ambitions of the leading aristocratic families and fueled by the religious fervor so characteristic of the Protestant and Catholic Reformations, these civil wars became international wars as Spain sought to dismember her northern neighbor, and nearly succeeded. The devastation was enormous, as Huguenot (French Protestant) and Catholic armies crisscrossed France. Indeed, by the late 1580s, there were three competing factions: Protestant, ultra-Catholic (receiving support from Spain), and those Frenchmen who placed the state above religion. No wonder, then, that in this ungodly four decades of turmoil, violence and brutality were endemic.

Natalie Davis explores one aspect of violent behavior in late sixteenth-century France: the religious riot. Her article is evidence of the influence of anthropology on history, for she seeks to discover the meaning of the patterns of riot behavior. Davis does not see the riots as class warfare; they drew legitimacy from religious rituals and beliefs. Most notorious of these riots was the St. Bartholomew's Day Massacre of 23–24 August 1572, when Catholics killed perhaps two to three thousand Huguenots in Paris and, later, approximately ten thousand in other parts of France. Davis goes beyond this well-known event to the dynamics of religious riots throughout the kingdom. In attempting to locate common denominators of the many outbreaks of sectarian violence during this very religious period in history, Davis raises important questions. What claims to legality did the rioters have? We are often tempted to dismiss rioters out of hand as lawbreakers, but sixteenth-century participants in crowd violence had quite another perspective. Who participated in the riots? The very poor, hoping to profit from the occasion, or better-placed social groups, committed sincerely to specific goals? What goals did rioters have? Did they simply lash out at random, unreflective as they acted? Were they organized and did they plan their acts of desecration, brutality, and death?

Davis's examination of the idea of pollution places us in the midst of the religious crowd. Sixteenth-century Catholics were certain that Protestants (who in turn believed the same about Catholics) profaned God and the community by their actions and even by their very existence. Was there not, then, an obligation, a duty to society and to God to remove the uncleanliness and profanation? How could a sincere Christian in the sixteenth century permit defilement by others who threatened to overturn society, to rupture what should be, according to both Catholics and Protestants, a society unified by the one faith and only one faith? French people did not believe in the virtue of religious toleration. In fact, religious toleration was thought to be injurious to God and to God's plan. What were the differences between Catholic and Protestant riots? How did the belief systems of each religion determine the types of violence practiced by its adherents? Finally, when did the riots most often occur?

In conclusion, we are left with great insight as to the mentality of these religious people, for we know of their greatest fears and the steps they were prepared to take to alleviate those fears. Were they justified? And was such violence extraordinary or usual in Reformation France?

> These are the statutes and judgements, which ye shall observe to do in the land, which the Lord God of thy fathers giveth thee . . . Ye shall utterly destroy all the places wherein the nations which he shall possess served their gods, upon the high mountains, and upon the hills, and under every green tree:
>
> And ye shall overthrow their altars, and break their pillars and burn their groves with fire; and ye shall hew down the graven images of their gods, and destroy the names of them out of that place [Deuteronomy xii. 1–3].

Thus a Calvinist pastor to his flock in 1562.

> If thy brother, the son of thy mother, or thy son, or thy daughter, or the wife of thy bosom, or thy friend, which is as thine own soul, entice thee secretly, saying Let us go serve other gods, which thou hast not known, thou, nor thy fathers . . . Thou shalt not consent unto him, nor hearken unto him . . . But thou shalt surely kill him; thine hand shall be first upon him to put him to death, and afterwards the hand of all the people. . . .
>
> If thou shalt hear say in one of thy cities, which the Lord thy God hath given thee to dwell there, saying, Certain men, the children of Belial are gone out from among you, and have withdrawn the inhabitants of their city, saying Let us go and serve other gods, which ye have not known . . . Thou shalt surely smite the inhabitants of that city with the edge of the sword, destroying it utterly and all that is therein [Deuteronomy xiii. 6, 8–9, 12–13, 15].

> And [Jehu] lifted up his face to the window and said, Who is on my side? Who? And there looked out to him two or three eunuchs. And he said, Throw her down. So they threw [Jezebel] down: and some of her blood was sprinkled on the wall, and on the horses: and he trode her under foot . . . And they went to bury her: but they found no more of her than the skull and the feet and the palms of her hands . . . And [Jehu] said, This is the word of the Lord, which he spake by his servant Elijah . . . saying, In the portion of Jezreel shall dogs eat the flesh of Jezebel: and the carcase of Jezebel shall be as dung upon the face of the field [II Kings ix. 32–3, 35–7].

Thus in 1568 Parisian preachers held up to their Catholic parishioners the end of a wicked idolater. Whatever the intentions of pastors and priests, such words were among the many spurs to religious riot in sixteenth-century France. By religious riot I mean, as a preliminary definition, any violent action, with words or weapons, undertaken against religious targets by people who are not acting *officially and formally* as agents of political and ecclesiastical authority. As food rioters bring their moral indignation to bear upon the state of the grain market, so religious rioters bring their zeal to bear upon the state of men's relations to the sacred. The violence of the religious riot is distinguished, at least in principle, from the action of political authorities, who can legally silence, humiliate, demolish, punish, torture and execute; and also from the action of soldiers, who at certain times and places can legally kill and destroy. In mid sixteenth-century France, all these sources of violence were busily producing, and it is sometimes hard to tell a militia officer from a murderer and a soldier from a statue-smasher. Nevertheless, there are occasions when we can separate out for examination a violent crowd set on religious goals. . . .

. . . We may see these crowds as prompted by political and moral traditions which legitimize and even prescribe their violence. We may see urban rioters not as miserable, uprooted, unstable masses, but as men and women who often have some stake in their community; who may be craftsmen or better; and who, even when poor and unskilled, may appear respectable to their everyday neighbours. Finally, we may see their violence, however cruel, not as random and limitless, but as aimed at defined targets and selected from a repertory of traditional punishments and forms of destruction. . . .

. . . My first purpose is to describe the shape and structure of the religious riot in French cities and towns, especially in the 1560s and early 1570s. We will look at the goals, legitimation and occasions for riots; at the kinds of action undertaken by the crowds and the targets for their violence; and briefly at the participants in the riots and their organization. We will consider differences between Protestant and Catholic styles of crowd behaviour, but will also indicate the many ways in which they are alike. . . .

What then can we learn of the goals of popular religious violence? What were the crowds intending to do and why did they think they must do it? Their behaviour suggests, first of all, a goal akin to preaching: the defence of true doctrine and the refutation of false doctrine through dramatic challenges and tests. "You blaspheme", shouts a woman to a Catholic preacher in Montpellier in 1558 and, having broken the decorum of the service, leads part of the congregation out of the church. "You lie", shouts a sheathmaker in the midst of the Franciscan's Easter sermon in Lyon, and his words are underscored by the gunshots of Huguenots waiting in the square. "Look", cries a weaver in Tournai, as he seizes the elevated host from the priest, "deceived people, do you believe this is the King, Jesus Christ, the true God and Saviour? Look!" And he crumbles the wafer and escapes. "Look", says a crowd of image-breakers to the people of Albiac in 1561, showing them the relics they have seized from the Carmelite monastery, "look, they are only animal bones". And the slogan of the Reformed crowds as they rush through the streets of Paris, of Toulouse, of La Rochelle, of Angoulême is "The Gospel! The Gospel! Long live the Gospel!"

Catholic crowds answer this kind of claim to truth in Angers by taking the French Bible, well-bound and gilded, seized in the home of a rich merchant, and parading it through the streets on the end of a halberd.

"There's the truth hung. There's the truth of the Huguenots, the truth of all the devils". Then, throwing it into the river, "There's the truth of all the devils drowned". And if the Huguenot doctrine was true, why didn't the Lord come and save them from their killers? So a crowd of Orléans Catholic taunted its victims in 1572: "Where is your God? Where are your prayers and Psalms? Let him save you if he can". Even the dead were made to speak in Normandy and Provence, where leaves of the Protestant Bible were stuffed into the mouths and wounds of corpses. "They preached the truth of their God. Let them call him to their aid".

The same refutation was, of course, open to Protestants. A Protestant crowd corners a baker guarding the holy-wafer box in Saint Médard's Church in Paris in 1561. "Messieurs", he pleads, "do not touch it for the honour of Him who dwells here". "Does your God of paste protect you now from the pains of death?" was the Protestant answer before they killed him. True doctrine can be defended in sermon or speech, backed up by the magistrate's sword against the heretic. Here it is defended by dramatic demonstration, backed up by the violence of the crowd.

A more frequent goal of these riots, however, is that of ridding the community of dreaded pollution. The word "pollution" is often on the lips of the violent, and the concept serves well to sum up the dangers which rioters saw in the dirty and diabolic enemy. A priest brings ornaments and objects for singing the Mass into a Bordeaux jail. The Protestant prisoner smashes them all. "Do you want to blaspheme the Lord's name everywhere? Isn't it enough that the temples are defiled? Must you also profane prisons so nothing is unpolluted?" "The Calvinists have polluted their hands with every kind of sacrilege men can think of", writes a Doctor of Theology in 1562. Not long after at the Sainte Chapelle,[1] a man seizes the elevated host with his "polluted hands" and crushes it under foot. The worshippers beat him up and deliver him to the agents of Parlement.[2] . . .

One does not have to listen very long to sixteenth-century voices to hear the evidence for the uncleanliness and profanation of either side. As for the Protestants, Catholics knew that, in the style of earlier heretics, they snuffed out the candles and had sexual intercourse after the voluptuous Psalmsinging of their nocturnal conventicles. . . . But it was not just the fleshly licence with which they lived which was unclean, but the things they said in their "pestilential" books and the things they did in hatred of the Mass, the sacraments and whole Catholic religion. As the representative of the clergy said at the Estates[3] of Orléans, the heretics intended to leave "no place in the Kingdom which was dedicated, holy and sacred

[1] A Gothic church in Paris, built in the thirteenth century to house relics.

[2] The Parlement of Paris, a sovereign judicial court with jurisdiction over approximately one-half of France.

[3] The Estates in French provinces were assemblies that maintained relations with the central government and dealt with provincial affairs.

to the Lord, but would only profane churches, demolish altars and break images".

The Protestants' sense of Catholic pollution also stemmed to some extent from their sexual uncleanness, here specifically of the clergy. Protestant polemic never tired of pointing to the lewdness of the clergy with their "concubines". It was rumoured that the Church of Lyon had an organization of hundreds of women, sort of temple prostitutes, at the disposition of priests and canons; and an observer pointed out with disgust how, after the First Religious War,[4] the Mass and the brothel re-entered Rouen together. One minister even claimed that the clergy were for the most part Sodomites. But more serious than the sexual abominations of the clergy was the defilement of the sacred by Catholic ritual life, from the diabolic magic of the Mass to the idolatrous worship of images. The Mass is "vile filth"; "no people pollute the House of the Lord in every way more than the clergy". Protestant converts talked of their own past lives as a time of befoulment and dreaded present "contamination" from Catholic churches and rites.

Pollution was a dangerous thing to suffer in a community, from either a Protestant or a Catholic point of view, for it would surely provoke the wrath of God. Terrible wind storms and floods were sometimes taken as signs of His impatience on this count. Catholics, moreover, had also to worry about offending Mary and the saints; and though the anxious, expiatory processions organized in the wake of Protestant sacrilege might temporarily appease them, the heretics were sure to strike again. It is not surprising, then, that so many of the acts of violence performed by Catholic and Protestant crowds have . . . the character either of rites of purification or of a paradoxical desecration, intended to cut down on uncleanness by placing profane things, like chrism, back in the profane world where they belonged. . . .

For Catholic zealots, the extermination of the heretical "vermin" promised the restoration of unity to the body social and the guarantee of its traditional boundaries:

> *And let us all say in unison:*
> *Long live the Catholic religion*
> *Long live the King and good parishioners,*
> *Long live faithful Parisians,*
> *And may it always come to pass*
> *That every person goes to Mass,*
> *One God, one Faith, one King.*

For Protestant zealots, the purging of the priestly "vermin" promised the creation of a new kind of unity within the body social, all the tighter because false gods and monkish sects would no longer divide it. Relations

[4]1562–1563.

within the social order would be purer, too, for lewdness and love of gain would be limited. As was said of Lyon after its "deliverance" in 1562:

. . . .
When this town so vain
Was filled
With idolatry and dealings
Of usury and lewdness,
It had clerics and merchants aplenty.

But once it was purged
And changed
By the Word of God,
That brood of vipers
Could hope no more
To live in so holy a place.

Crowds might defend truth, and crowds might purify, but there was also a third aspect to the religious riot—a political one. . . .

. . . When the magistrate had not used his sword to defend the faith and the true church and to punish the idolators, then the crowd would do it for him. Thus, many religious disturbances begin with the ringing of the tocsin, as in a time of civic assembly or emergency. Some riots end with the marching of the religious "wrongdoers" on the other side to jail. In 1561, for instance, Parisian Calvinists, fearing that the priests and worshippers in Saint Médard's Church were organizing an assault on their services . . . , first rioted in Saint Médard and then seized some fifteen Catholics as "mutinous" and led them off, "bound like galley-slaves", to the Châtelet prison.

If the Catholic killing of Huguenots has in some ways the form of a rite of purification, it also sometimes has the form of imitating the magistrate. The mass executions of Protestants at Merindol and Cabrières in Provence and at Meaux in the 1540s, duly ordered by the Parlements of Aix and of Paris as punishment for heresy and high treason, anticipate crowd massacres of later decades. The Protestants themselves sensed this: the devil, unable to extinguish the light of the Gospel through the sentences of judges, now tried to obscure it through furious war and a murderous populace. Whereas before they were made martyrs by one executioner, now it is at the hands of "infinite numbers of them, and the swords of private persons have become the litigants, witnesses, judges, decrees and executors of the strangest cruelties".

Similarly, *official* acts of torture and *official* acts of desecration of the corpses of certain criminals anticipate some of the acts performed by riotous crowds. The public execution was, of course, a dramatic and well-attended event in the sixteenth century, and the wood-cut and engraving documented the scene far and wide. There the crowd might see the offending tongue of the blasphemer pierced or slit, the offending hands of the desecrator cut off. There the crowd could watch the traitor decapitated and disemboweled, his corpse quartered and the parts borne off for public display in different sections of the town. The body of an especially heinous criminal was dragged through the streets, attached to a horse's tail. The image of exemplary royal punishment lived on for weeks, even years, as the corpses of murderers were exposed on gallows or wheels and the heads of rebels on posts. . . . [C]rowds often took their victims to places of official execution, as in Paris in 1562, when the Protestant printer, Roc Le Frere, was dragged for burning to the Marché aux Pourceaux,[5] and in Toulouse the same year, when a merchant, slain in front of a church, was dragged for burning to the town hall. "The King salutes you", said a Catholic crowd in Orléans to a Protestant trader, then put a cord around his neck as official agents might do, and led him off to be killed.

Riots also occurred in connection with judicial cases, either to hurry the judgement along, or when verdicts in religious cases were considered too severe or too lenient by "the voice of the people". Thus in 1569 in Montpellier, a Catholic crowd forced the judge to condemn an important Huguenot prisoner to death in a hasty "trial", then seized him and hanged him in front of his house. . . . And in 1561 in Marsillargues, when prisoners for heresy were released by royal decree, a Catholic crowd "rearrested" them, and executed and burned them in the streets. . . .

The seizure of religious buildings and the destruction of images by Calvinist crowds were also accomplished with the conviction that they were taking on the rôle of the authorities. When Protestants in Montpellier occupied a church in 1561, they argued that the building belonged to them already, since its clergy had been wholly supported by merchants and burghers in the past and the property belonged to the town. . . .

To be sure, the relation of a French Calvinist crowd to the magisterial model is different from that of a French Catholic crowd. The king had not yet chastised the clergy and "put all ydolatry to ruyne and confusyon", as Protestants had been urging him since the early 1530s. Calvinist crowds were using his sword as the king *ought* to have been using it and as some princes and city councils outside of France had already used it. Within the kingdom before 1560 city councils had only *indicated* the right path, as they set up municipal schools, lay-controlled welfare systems or otherwise limited the sphere of action of the clergy. During the next years, as revolution and conversion created Reformed city councils and governors (such as the Queen of Navarre) within France, Calvinist crowds finally had local magistrates whose actions they could prompt or imitate.

In general, then, the crowds in religious riots in sixteenth-century France can be seen as sometimes acting out clerical rôles—defending true doctrine or ridding the community of defilement in a violent version of

[5]Pig market.

priest or prophet—and as sometimes acting out magisterial rôles. Clearly some riotous behaviour, such as the extensive pillaging done by both Protestants and Catholics, cannot be subsumed under these heads; but just as the prevalence of pillaging in a war does not prevent us from typing it as a holy war, so the prevalence of pillaging in a riot should not prevent us from seeing it as essentially religious. . . .

So long as rioters maintained a given religious commitment, they rarely displayed guilt or shame for their violence. By every sign, the crowds believed their actions legitimate.

One reason for this conviction is that in some, though by no means all, religious riots, clerics and political officers were active members of the crowd, though not precisely in their official capacity. In Lyon in 1562, Pastor Jean Ruffy took part in the sack of the Cathedral of Saint Jean with a sword in his hand. Catholic priests seem to have been in quite a few disturbances, as in Rouen in 1560, when priests and parishioners in a Corpus Christi parade[6] broke into the houses of Protestants who had refused to do the procession honour. . . .

On the other hand, not all religious riots could boast of officers or clergy in the crowd, and other sources of legitimation must be sought. Here we must recognize what mixed cues were given out by priests and pastors in their sermons on heresy or idolatry. . . . However much Calvin[7] and other pastors opposed such disturbances (preferring that all images and altars be removed soberly by the authorities), they nevertheless were always more ready to understand and excuse this violence than, say, that of a peasant revolt or of a journeymen's march. Perhaps, after all, the popular idol-smashing was due to "an extraordinary power (*vertu*) from God." . . .

The rôle of Catholic preachers in legitimating popular violence was even more direct. If we don't know whether to believe the Protestant claim that Catholic preachers at Paris were telling their congregations in 1557 that Protestants ate babies, it is surely significant that . . . Catholic preachers did blame the loss of the battle of Saint Quentin[8] on God's wrath at the presence of heretics in France. . . . And if Protestant pastors could timidly wonder if divine power were not behind the extraordinary force of the iconoclasts, priests had no doubts that certain miraculous occurrences in the wake of Catholic riots were a sign of divine approval, such as a copper cross in Troyes that began to change colour and cure people in 1561, the year of a riot in which Catholics bested Protestants. . . .

[6]A Roman Catholic festival instituted in the thirteenth century to honor the Blessed Sacrament (the body of Jesus).

[7]John Calvin (1509–1564), French Protestant theologian, founder of Calvinism and religious leader of Geneva.

[8]Spanish victory over the French in 1557.

In all likelihood, however, there are sources for the legitimation of popular religious riot that come directly out of the experience of the local groups which often formed the nucleus of a crowd—the men and women who had worshipped together in the dangerous days of the night conventicles, the men in confraternities, in festive groups, in youth gangs and militia units. It should be remembered how often conditions in sixteenth-century cities required groups of "little people" to take the law into their own hands. Royal edicts themselves enjoined any person who saw a murder, theft or other misdeed to ring the tocsin[9] and chase after the criminal. Canon law allowed certain priestly rôles to laymen in times of emergency, such as the midwife's responsibility to baptize a baby in danger of dying, while the rôle of preaching the Gospel was often assumed by Protestant laymen in the decades before the Reformed Church was set up....

... [T]he occasion for most religious violence was during the time of religious worship or ritual and in the space which one or both groups were using for sacred purposes....

Almost every type of public religious event has a disturbance associated with it. The sight of a statue of the Virgin at a crossroad or in a wall-niche provokes a Protestant group to mockery of those who reverence her. A fight ensues. Catholics hide in a house to entrap Huguenots who refuse to doff their hats to a Virgin nearby, and then rush out and beat the heretics up. Baptism: in Nemours, a Protestant family has its baby baptized on All Souls' Day[10] according to the new Reformed rite. With the help of an aunt, a group of Catholics steals it away for rebaptism. A drunkard sees the father and the godfather and other Protestants discussing the event in the streets, claps his sabots and shouts, "Here are the Huguenots who have come to massacre us". A crowd assembles, the tocsin is rung, and a three-hour battle takes place. Funeral: in Toulouse, at Easter-time, a Protestant carpenter tries to bury his Catholic wife by the new Reformed rite. A Catholic crowd seizes the corpse and buries it. The Protestants dig it up and try to rebury her. The bells are rung, and with a great noise a Catholic crowd assembles with stones and sticks. Fighting and sacking ensue.

Religious services: a Catholic Mass is the occasion for an attack on the Host or the interruption of a sermon, which then leads to a riot. Protestant preaching in a home attracts large Catholic crowds at the door, who stone the house or otherwise threaten the worshippers....

But these encounters are as nothing compared to the disturbances that cluster around processional life. Corpus Christi Day, with its crowds, coloured banners and great crosses, was the chance for Protestants *not* to put rugs in front of their doors; for Protestant women to sit ostentatiously in their windows spinning; for heroic individuals, like the painter Denis

[9]Bell used to sound an alarm.

[10]Commemoration of the souls of the departed, celebrated on 2 November.

de Vallois in Lyon, to throw themselves on the "God of paste" so as "to destroy him in every parish in the world". Corpus Christi Day was the chance for a procession to turn into an assault on and slaughter of those who had so offended the Catholic faith, its participants shouting, as in Lyon in 1561, "For the flesh of God, we must kill all the Huguenots". A Protestant procession was a parade of armed men and women in their dark clothes, going off to services at their temple or outside the city gates, singing Psalms and spiritual songs that to Catholic ears sounded like insults against the Church and her sacraments. It was an occasion for children to throw stones, for an exchange of scandalous words—"idolaters", "devils from the Pope's purgatory", "Huguenot heretics, living like dogs"—and then finally for fighting. . . .

The occasions which express most concisely the contrast between the two religious groups, however, are those in which a popular festive Catholicism took over the streets with dancing, masks, banners, costumes and music—"lascivious abominations", according to the Protestants. . . .

As with liturgical rites, there were some differences between the rites of violence of Catholic and Protestant crowds. . . .

. . . [T]he iconoclastic Calvinist crowds . . . come out as the champions in the destruction of religious property ("with more than Turkish cruelty", said a priest). This was not only because the Catholics had more physical accessories to their rite, but also because the Protestants sensed much more danger and defilment in the *wrongful use of material objects*. . . .

In bloodshed the Catholics are the champions (remember we are talking of the actions of Catholic and Protestant crowds, not of their armies). I think this is due not only to their being in the long run the strongest party numerically in most cities, but also to their stronger sense of *the persons of heretics* as sources of danger and defilment. Thus, injury and murder were a preferred mode of purifying the body social.

Furthermore, the preferred targets for physical attack differ in the Protestant and Catholic cases. As befitting a movement intending to overthrow a thousand years of clerical "tyranny' and "pollution", the Protestants' targets were primarily priests, monks and friars. That their ecclesiastical victims were usually unarmed (as Catholic critics hastened to point out) did not make them any less harmful in Protestant eyes, or any more immune from the wrath of God. Lay people were sometimes attacked by Protestant crowds, too, such as the festive dancers who were stoned at Pamiers and Lyon, and the worshippers who were killed at Saint-Médard's Church. But there is nothing that quite resembles the style and extent of the slaughter of the 1572 massacres. The Catholic crowds were, of course, happy to catch a pastor when they could, but the death of any heretic would help in the cause of cleansing France of these perfidious sowers of disorder and disunion. . . .

. . . [T]he overall picture in these urban religious riots is not one of the "people" slaying the rich. Protestant crowds expressed no preference for killing or assaulting powerful prelates over simple priests. As for Catholic crowds, contemporary listings of their victims in the 1572 massacres show that artisans, the "little people", are represented in significant numbers. . . .

. . . Let us look a little further at what I have called their rites of violence. Is there any way we can order the terrible, concrete details of filth, shame and torture that are reported from both Protestant and Catholic riots? I would suggest that they can be reduced to a repertory of actions, derived from the Bible, from the liturgy, from the action of political authority, or from the traditions of popular folk justice, intended to purify the religious community and humiliate the enemy and thus make him less harmful.

The religious significance of destruction by water or fire is clear enough. The rivers which receive so many Protestant corpses are not merely convenient mass graves, they are temporarily a kind of holy water, an essential feature of Catholic rites of exorcism. . . .

Let us take a more difficult case, the troubling case of the desecration of corpses. This is primarily an action of Catholic crowds in the sixteenth century. Protestant crowds could be very cruel indeed in torturing living priests, but paid little attention to them when they were dead. (Perhaps this is related to the Protestant rejection of Purgatory and prayers for the dead: the souls of the dead experience immediately Christ's presence or the torments of the damned, and thus the dead body is no longer so dangerous or important an object to the living.) What interested Protestants was digging up bones that were being treated as sacred objects by Catholics and perhaps burning them, after the fashion of Josiah in I Kings. The Catholics, however, were not content with burning or drowning heretical corpses. That was not cleansing enough. The bodies had to be weakened and humiliated further. To an eerie chorus of "strange whistles and hoots", they were thrown to the dogs like Jezebel, they were dragged through the streets, they had their genitalia and internal organs cut away, which were then hawked through the city in a ghoulish commerce.

Let us also take the embarrassing case of the desecration of religious objects by filthy and disgusting means. It is the Protestants . . . who are concerned about objects, who are trying to show that Catholic objects of worship have no magical power. It is not enough to cleanse by swift and energetic demolition, not enough to purify by a great public burning of the images, as in Albiac, with the children of the town ceremonially reciting the Ten Commandments around the fire. The line between the sacred and the profane was also re-drawn by throwing the sacred host to the dogs, by roasting the crucifix upon a spit, by using holy oil to grease one's boots, and by leaving human excrement on holy-water basins and other religious objects.

And what of the living victims? Catholics and Protestants humiliated them by techniques borrowed from the repertory of folk justice. Catholic crowds lead Protestant women through the streets with muzzles on—a popular punishment for the shrew—or with a crown of thorns. A form of charivari[11] is used, where the noisy throng humiliates its victim by making him ride backward on an ass. . . . In Montauban, a priest was ridden backward on an ass, his chalice in one hand, his host in the other, and his missal at an end of a halberd. At the end of his ride, he must crush his host and burn his own vestments. . . .

These episodes disclose to us the underlying function of the rites of violence. As with the "games" of Christ's tormentors, which hide from them the full knowledge of what they do, so these charades and ceremonies hide from sixteenth-century rioters a full knowledge of what they are doing. Like the legitimation for religious riot . . . , they are part of the "conditions for guilt-free massacre". . . . The crucial fact that the killers must forget is that their victims are human beings. These harmful people in the community—the evil priest or hateful heretic—have already been transformed for the crowd into "vermin" or "devils". The rites of religious violence complete the process of dehumanization. So in Meaux, where Protestants were being slaughtered with butchers' cleavers, a living victim was trundled to his death in a wheelbarrow, while the crowd cried "vinegar, mustard". And the vicar of the parish of Fouquebrune in the Angoumois was attached with the oxen to a plough and died from Protestant blows as he pulled.

What kinds of people made up the crowds that performed the range of acts we have examined in this paper? First, they were not by and large the alienated rootless poor. . . . A large percentage of men in Protestant iconoclastic riots and in the crowds of Catholic killers in 1572 were characterized as artisans. Sometimes the crowds included other men from the lower orders. . . . More often, the social composition of the crowds extended upward to encompass merchants, notaries and lawyers, as well as clerics. . . .

In addition, there was significant participation by two other groups of people who, though not rootless and alienated, had a more marginal relationship to political power than did lawyers, merchants or even male artisans—namely, city women and teenaged boys. . . .

Finally, as this study has already suggested, the crowds of Catholics and Protestants, including those bent on deadly tasks, were not an inchoate mass, but showed many signs of organization. Even with riots that had little or no planning behind them, the event was given some structure by the situation of worship or the procession that was the occasion for many disturbances. In other cases, planning in advance led to lists of targets, and ways of identifying friends or fellow rioters. . . .

That such splendor and order should be put to violent uses is a disturbing fact. Disturbing, too, is the whole subject of religious violence. How does an historian talk about a massacre of the magnitude of St.

[11]Davis defines this elsewhere as "a noisy, masked demonstration to humiliate some wrongdoer in the community."

Bartholomew's Day? One approach is to view extreme religious violence as an extraordinary event, the product of frenzy, of the frustrated and paranoic primitive mind of the people.

A second approach sees such violence as a more usual part of social behaviour, but explains it as a somewhat pathological product of certain kinds of child-rearing, economic deprivation or status loss. This paper has assumed that conflict is perennial in social life, though the forms and strength of the accompanying violence vary; and that religious violence is intense because it connects intimately with the fundamental values and self-definition of a community. The violence is explained not in terms of how crazy, hungry or sexually frustrated the violent people are (though they may sometimes have such characteristics), but in terms of the goals of their actions and in terms of the rôles and patterns of behaviour allowed by their culture. Religious violence is related here less to the pathological than to the normal.

Thus, in sixteenth-century France, we have seen crowds taking on the rôle of priest, pastor or magistrate to defend doctrine or purify the religious community, either to maintain its Catholic boundaries and structure, or to re-form relations within it. We have seen that popular religious violence could receive legitimation from different features of political and religious life, as well as from the group identity of the people in the crowds. The targets and character of crowd violence differed somewhat between Catholics and Protestants, depending on their perception of the source of danger and on their religious sensibility. But in both cases, religious violence had a connection in time, place and form with the life of worship, and the violent actions themselves were drawn from a store of punitive or purificatory traditions current in sixteenth-century France.

In this context, the cruelty of crowd action in the 1572 massacres was not an exceptional occurrence. St. Bartholomew was certainly a bigger affair than, say, the Saint Médard's riot, it had more explicit sanction from political authority, it had elaborate networks of communication at the top level throughout France, and it took a more terrible toll in deaths. Perhaps its most unusual feature was that the Protestants did not fight back. But on the whole, it still fits into a whole pattern of sixteenth-century religious disturbance.

This inquiry also points to a more general conclusion. Even in the extreme case of religious violence, crowds do not act in a mindless way. They will to some degree have a sense that what they are doing is legitimate, the occasions will relate somehow to the defence of their cause, and their violent behaviour will have some structure to it—here dramatic and ritual. But the rites of violence are not the rights of violence in any *absolute* sense. They simply remind us that if we try to increase safety and trust within a community, try to guarantee that the violence it generates will take less destructive and less cruel forms, then we must think less about pacifying "deviants" and more about changing the central values.

Birth and Childhood in Seventeenth-Century France

WENDY GIBSON

Historians have sometimes referred to seventeenth-century France as a zenith of French civilization, the era of absolutism in government, the Baroque in art, and classicism in literature. Yet, the regular and humble processes of birth and childhood were frightful and dangerous times for all in that century, and even more so for females.

Approximately 3 percent of births were stillborn; 25 percent of children died before their first birthday; 25 percent more died by the age of twenty. These figures varied according to social group and geographical location, but it is clear that in all circumstances the life of a child was precarious. How do you account for such a high rate of mortality? How did peasants react to the death of a child?

For girls there was an additional situation: they were as a rule unwanted, unloved, and unappreciated. It is evident from time immemorial that nearly all societies valued boys over girls, but why did seventeenth-century Frenchwomen join with males in disparaging the female sex? Aristocrats in particular bemoaned the birth of a girl. Did the nobility have better reasons than the bourgeoisie or peasants to celebrate the birth of a male infant?

Gibson traces the life of a girl from birth through adolescence. What customs at and soon after birth might have damaged the baby girl? What were the responsibilities of the midwife? Why was speed in baptism so important? Affection toward the child was lacking. Why were mothers so reluctant to nurse their own children? Nursing would have established or tightened bonds between mother and infant. How were children clothed? What games did they play? To what extent did clothes and games distinguish children from the world of adults?

How were children integrated into the life of the community through education and work? Was there children's work? Was there work deemed especially appropriate for girls? Did religion reinforce or condemn the often bestial treatment of the young? What did theologians and writers say about childhood and about girls?

In what ways do you think the French absolutist state reflected these attitudes and practices relating to childhood and to females? After all, child-rearing practices produce a new generation of adults affected by their treatment as children. Was France caught in a cycle of a lack of affection toward the young along with a severe approach toward childhood and especially girls that led inexorably to an authoritarian, patriarchal government and social structure?

'It's a girl!' The midwife's pronouncement was calculated to bring little joy to the exhausted mother or her expectant relatives in seventeenth-century France. Queen Marie de Médicis[1] 'wept loud and long' in 1602 on

---

[1] 1573–1642, wife of King Henry IV.

learning that she had supplied France with a princess, Elisabeth, instead of a second heir to the throne and 'could not reconcile herself to the fact'. In 1662 Louis XIV's[2] first sister-in-law Henriette d'Angleterre (Madame), having impatiently ascertained the female sex of the child that she was in the actual process of bearing, 'said that it would have to be thrown in the river, and showed her extreme disappointment to everyone'. Outside the royal circle the sense of anti-climax was equally keen. Memorialists recording the birth of a girl into an aristocratic family speak of the 'great regret' and 'ordeal' of the father, and of the mother's 'misfortune'. Gazette-writers and other well-wishing versifiers stress that couples will rapidly work to correct their mistake:

'But since it is only a female cherub,
Husband and wife, redoubling their efforts,
Will work all over again
To produce a male cherub afterwards'.

Grandmothers for their part seek to guard against a second 'accident' by stern injunctions to daughters not to let their unborn offspring 'become a girl'.

The general disappointment could take on more palpable forms. When a royal prince was born the occasion was marked by prolonged rejoicings: cannon salvoes, bonfires, pyrotechnic displays, processions and services of thanksgiving, free distributions of wine in the streets, and the release of prisoners. But when, after the birth of his third daughter Henriette in 1609, Henri IV[3] summoned the Paris Parlement[4] to make 'signs of rejoicing in the customary manner' the First President[5] replied 'that it was not the custom to hold any ceremonies for girls, except for the first-born one, and that no such ceremony was registered in the rolls, in the Church of Paris, or in the Town Hall'.

That women should accept and join in the chorus of disparaging remarks which greeted the arrival of a member of their own sex caused some amazement to contemporaries like the Comte de Bussy-Rabutin,[6] who maliciously interpreted it as a tacit admission of male superiority. But there were other, more practical, reasons for the prevailing attitude. In a country such as France, where women were excluded from the right of succession to the throne and from effectively holding public office, and where titles and property were normally passed on from generation to

[2]King of France, 1643–1715.

[3]King of France, 1589–1610.

[4]A sovereign judicial court having jurisdiction over approximately one-half of the kingdom.

[5]The highest-ranking of the presiding judges in the Parlement.

[6]Roger de Rabutin, Count of Bussy (1618–1693), wit and author of a scandalous book.

generation through the eldest male, the absence of an heir could constitute a real disaster. 'The males', as Gui Patin[7] wrote, 'are the props and supports of a big family's lastingness'. Lack of them might necessitate the abandonment of rank and possessions laboriously acquired over the centuries to rival dynasties and households interested in making posterity forget to whom they owed their elevation and lustre. Expressions of chagrin over births of girls are accordingly always most pronounced amongst royalty and the aristocracy, who had most to lose by them. Lower down in the social hierarchy the bourgeoisie note the event with a noncommittal wish for the infant's future virtue:

> God give her the grace to be mindful to fear and love Him, and fill her with His gifts.

> God give her the grace to be pure white in fact as in name, before God and men.

> God give this child the grace to live and die with a holy fear and love of Him.

The reactions of the peasantry, in the absence of direct written records of their sentiments, remain still more inscrutable. But any pleasure experienced at the thought of an extra worker in the family was bound to be tempered by the awareness of an extra mouth to feed, an extra 'establishment' to provide in later life.

For the birth of a daughter meant that sooner or later a dowry would have to be handed over to a husband or to a convent, a consideration which affected every class of society. Whatever the size of the dowry it represented the cession to outsiders of cash and property which, if invested in a son's marriage or career, would either have remained within the bosom of the family or yielded appreciable returns in the form of wages, perquisites and social distinction. The unhappy father had, moreover, the invidious task of safeguarding his daughter's virginity against the stratagems of designing gallants, on pain of sullying the family name and honour.

Born into a society disposed to regard her as more of an encumbrance than a blessing, the little girl began at once a struggle for survival against the host of physical perils and superstitions that beset the seventeenth-century infant. Birth, like the other two major events of human existence, marriage and death, was surrounded by its own age-old set of rituals. Some—the custom of blowing wine into the newborn child's mouth to prevent future inebriation and epilepsy, rubbing the baby's lips with a piece of gold to ensure their redness, inducing fashionable dimples by placing peas under the cheekbones—were comparatively innocuous. Oth-

---

[7] 1602–1672, dean of the faculty of medicine at the University of Paris.

ers risked causing irreparable damage. Infant heads were kneaded to give them a good shape, or tightly bound with narrow bands, producing an elongation by which Parisian children were instantly recognisable. Noses were bound, pulled and pinched to correct real or fancied deformities. A cruel operation was performed on the infant girl's breast in the belief that this would facilitate the suckling of children in later life.

Cleansed without by a mixture of water and wine, and within by means of soap suppositories, the infant had then to submit to the strait-jacket of swathing bands in which it would spend the first eight or nine months of life, sometimes longer in the case of girls. The main purpose of swaddling, apart from that of providing warmth and protection, was to render the body upright and the limbs straight and to accustom the child to stand instead of crawling in an unseemly and unhealthy fashion over floors that were cold, damp and littered with human and animal drop-pings. In practice the reverse effect was often achieved. In their anxiety to develop a plump, well-rounded breast in their nurslings, misguided wet-nurses subjected infant thoraxes to such compression that permanent humpbacks, projecting shoulders and curvatures of the spine resulted. Constriction of the hips, impeding their proper broadening, caused seri-ous problems when the age of child-bearing was reached. Legs emerged from their wrappings bent, twisted and chafed.

To the discomfort of cramped and sore limbs was added that of a diet calculated to extinguish rather than to sustain life. Instances of children in the upper strata of society being suckled by their natural mothers were already sufficiently rare in the sixteenth century to make Marguerite de Valois,[8] future wife of Henri IV, start at the sight of an aristocratic hostess tranquilly calling for her baby to breast-feed before guests at a feast. A powerful coalition of ignorance, vanity and selfishness militated against the performance of what indignant preachers and moralists represented as a fundamental maternal duty. Human milk was popularly supposed to be formed of blood which flowed from the womb to the breasts, where it was mysteriously whitened. Suckling, therefore, could only have a debilitating effect upon the constitution of the mother, draining her of precious life-blood. Worse still, her youthful silhouette was threatened by this messy chore, and just at a time when it was important to have the wherewithal to cajole and mollify a husband impatient for the resumption of normal conjugal services. In consequence, the infant scarcely had time to rejoice in the maternal smiles and caresses over which pedagogues waxed lyrical before being despatched to the arms of a local village wet-nurse whose own frequently scanty milk was quickly supplemented with the notorious *bouillie*.[9] This glutinous concoction of flour and cow's milk worked wonders in silencing cries of hunger, sometimes permanently.

[8] 1553–1615, daughter of King Henry II of France and Catherine de Médicis.
[9] Pap.

Minute prescriptions for the choice of an ideal *nourrice*[10] were listed in every gynaecological treatise of the day. The sum total of opinions was that she should be a brunette of twenty-five to thirty years and of healthy stock, with good teeth, ample but not excessive proportions, a pleasant and virtuous disposition, and clear pronunciation, the last two qualities in order that her nursling would not contract any undesirable habits or modes of speech. Sexual continence during breast-feeding, with a view to maintaining high quality milk, was a further requirement, but one which was likely to be half-heartedly obeyed and to precipitate the introduction of weaning well before the recommended stage of the appearance of teeth.

The paragon of integrity described by the specialists appears in real life to have eluded even the most earnest parental seekers of her services. For private and public journals testify to a negligence of duty on the part of the *nourrice* that caused, at best, disfigurement or crippling, at worst, death. The philosopher John Locke,[11] conversing with a physician at Orléans in 1678, learned that the lameness of the local children was due 'more to the negligence of nurses than anything else, carrying them always wrapped up and on one side, and he thinks this to be the cause, because this lameness lights more on girls that are tenderer, than boys who are stronger and sooner out of their swaddling clothes'. At the opposite end of the century Pierre de l'Estoile[12] made a grim entry in his Journal for 1608 to the effect that 'many little children' had been 'stifled by their wet-nurses', though he failed to specify whether the stifling was done deliberately or came about through the habitual accident of the wet-nurse rolling on the baby in bed. The very person, then, entrusted with the rearing and physical well-being of infants presented yet another threat to their continued existence.

Maladies of different kinds, some arising from congenital malformations and clumsy post-natal care, others contracted in insanitary homes filled to capacity with humans and livestock, and all aggravated by the bleedings and purgings which doctors ordered with gay abandon, accounted for further deaths. All sections of society had a high rate of infant mortality. The Protestant leader Henri, Duc de Rohan, managed to rear to adulthood only one of his nine children, and Henri IV's minister, Sully,[13] only four of his own ten offspring. *Livres de Raison,* diaries kept by the heads of households, depress by their long casualty lists. Simon Le Marchand, a bourgeois of Caen, recorded between 1612 and 1635 the birth of twelve offspring, ten of whom were overtaken by death within a maximum of two years, and mostly within a matter of days or months. Usually the fatal occurrence is just starkly noted, an eloquent testimony to its common-

[10] Wet-nurse.

[11] English philosopher (1632–1704) who traveled to France from 1675 to 1679.

[12] Pierre Taisan de l'Estoile (1546–1611), a lawyer who kept a journal during the reigns of Henry III and Henry IV.

[13] Maximilien de Béthune, duc de Sully (1560–1641), first minister to Henry IV.

place nature. Sometimes a pious ejaculation, touching in its resignation, accompanies the entry:

God grant her peace.

May God through His grace deign to have had mercy upon her, not charging her with the sins of her father and mother, albeit that these sully her profoundly.

God has given, God has taken away, blessed be the name of the Lord. Her soul is in heaven and her body in our tomb, near that of her good mother. May it please the divine majesty that their souls be together in heaven.

Only occasionally does the note of serene acceptance waver a little, betraying a proud parent whose hopes for the future have been cruelly shattered: 'She was well taught and full of promise . . . Had considerable intelligence, knew how to read at five years and had all the good inclinations and sentiments of her late mother'.

The extreme precariousness of infant existence helps to account for the emphasis that was placed on rapid baptism. Such was the concern to avert the tragedy of a Catholic baby's soul being condemned to wander in limbo and the body confided to a specially demarcated portion of the cemetery because death had intervened before the accomplishment of this vital ceremony that provision was made for the administration of a preliminary form of baptism known as the *ondoiement* to any new-born child whose life was considered to be in imminent danger of extinction. Anyone, male or female, lay or ecclesiastic, Catholic or non-Catholic, could perform the *ondoiement,* provided that they used natural water and pronounced in whatever language they knew the formula: 'I baptise you in the name of the Father, and of the Son, and of the Holy Ghost'. It sufficed for only a part of the child to protrude from the mother's body for the emergency baptism to be legitimate, and syringes were invented for use within the womb in cases of obstructed birth.

Formal presentation of the infant at the parochial church font was generally carried out with speed, whether an *ondoiement* had already been performed or not. At eight in the evening on 8 August 1677 Ferdinand Jacque, a Parlement advocate of Dôle, hastened to church the daughter who had arrived just before two o'clock that same day. Boys and girls born into the Froissard-Broissia family, also of Franche-Comté, were rushed to the font within as little as one or two hours after birth, a practice which proved remarkably effective in weeding out the weaker scions. Usually, however, parents managed to curb their zeal sufficiently to give the newly-born twenty-four hours to gather strength before being exposed to the elements.

Fairly frequent exceptions to the rule for speedy baptism were royal and aristocratic children whose official admission to Catholicism was delayed for reasons of state or convenience. Louis XIII[14] and his sister Elisabeth, born respectively in September 1601 and November 1602, were not baptised until 14 September 1606, along with their sister Christine, who had joined the family in February of that year. The Duchesse de Montpensier, Louis's niece, received her baptism in July 1636, at the age of nine. Mlle de Béthune, a grand-daughter of Chancellor Séguier,[15] was obliged to wait fourteen years before being christened.

In the choice of godparents, a considerable amount of latitude was allowed. Children of a very young age are themselves often found acting in this capacity. The grand-daughter of the illustrious Marquise de Rambouillet[16] was allowed to be a godmother at four years because she could answer the necessary questions when interrogated by the local priest. In 1688 Racine's[17] daughter Madeleine had as godparents her elder brother and sister, despite the fact that the latter, aged seven, was unable to sign the baptismal register. Having brothers and sisters serve as godparents, a popular custom, was a useful means of reinforcing with spiritual bonds the ties of blood already existing. Respectable introductions between youngsters of the opposite sex could also be made at the baptism ceremony, forming the basis of future marriages. Just as age was taken very little into account in the selection of godparents, so was social status. The attachment and gratitude of domestics was strengthened by holding their offspring at the font and by permitting them to do likewise with the infants of their employers. The supreme gesture of piety and humility consisted in handing children for baptism to a couple of paupers, and in performing a reciprocal service for the offspring of the poor. Thus Marguerite de Valois acted as impromptu godmother to the son of an Irish beggar-woman delivered one day in her path. Not only individuals but collective bodies also could stand as godfather or godmother. Evidence of this phenomenon is more common in connection with boys, baptised under the aegis of municipal authorities or the Provincial Assemblies (*Etats Provinciaux*). But Tallemant[18] mentions a lady-love of the Duc de Guise who had the town of Marseille as godparent, while the abbess of Sainte Croix at Poitiers, Flandrine de Nassau, Princess of Orange, owed her unusual forename to the fact of being the godchild of the *Etats*[19] of Flanders.

Custom decreed that the infant be given as a first name that of the godmother or godfather, as appropriate. For the Catholic girl the name

[14]King of France, 1610–1643.

[15]Pierre Séguier, duc de Villemor (1588–1672), chancellor to Louis XIII and Louis XIV.

[16]Catherine de Vivonne, Marquise de Rambouillet (1588–1665), hostess of regular gatherings of the cream of Parisian society.

[17]Jean Baptiste Racine (1639–1699), playwright.

[18]Gédéon Tallemant de Réaux (c.1619–1700), author of anecdotal memoirs.

[19]The assemblies of the leading men of Flanders.

would normally be that of a saint whose virtues she might imitate and whose protection she might implore; for the Protestant girl the name of an Old Testament heroine such as Rachel[20] or Sarah[21] would be first choice. The addition of second and third names was regarded by the Church as superfluous. There were, however, few blue-blooded girls without at least a double-barrelled forename, an abuse described towards the end of the century as spreading to the *Tiers Etat,*[22] who considered that the possession of several names conferred on their infants an air of nobility. . . .

It was not at all unusual for several children in a family to bear the same forename. When an elder child died prematurely what seems in retrospect like a pathetic attempt at resuscitation would sometimes be made by passing on the same name to the next brother or sister that came along. But a succession of living children might equally be christened alike, for religious or family reasons. The pious Ducs de Beauvillier and de Noailles bestowed the name of Marie, the former on all of his nine daughters, the latter on seven out of eleven daughters. In the Savelli household to which Mme de Rambouillet belonged the name of Lucine, a saint of the family, was added to that of all daughters on baptism. The usage was not without causing a certain amount of confusion, and was one of the reasons which prompted the authorities to insist on the regular keeping of parish baptismal records.

Baptism being essentially a solemn sacrament, the Church saw little reason for it to be accompanied by merry-making and jollification. The faithful, however, begged to differ, seeing in the occasion a glorious excuse for lavish expenditure, gastronomic indulgence and letting off steam generally. Plenty of noise was obligatory. Music from violins, fifes and tabors (or salvoes from guns in the case of the nobility) would accompany the infant to church. Guests would while away the time that it took the priest to perform the familiar ritual—exorcisms, introduction of salt into the child's mouth (a symbol of wisdom and preservation from vice), aspersion with holy water, anointment with oil, imposition of the christening bonnet . . . , reading from Saint John's Gospel and exhortation to the godparents—by laughing, joking, promenading and exchanging kisses. Peals of bells would signal the termination of the ceremony. At that point the new Christian was apt to be whisked away to the nearest tavern and released only when the parents gave the merry kidnappers the means to wet the baby's head. Parents of substance would seek to render the event more memorable by keeping open house over a number of days and by giving presents to the populace. . . .

Delicate infants, perhaps born before time, or those whose mothers had made special vows in return for a safe delivery, sometimes received,

[20]The second wife of Jacob.

[21]Wife of Abraham and mother of Isaac.

[22]Third Estate, one of the three traditional groupings of French society. The First Estate constituted the clergy, the Second the nobility, and the Third everyone else.

in addition to baptism, an extra form of spiritual protection. This consisted in dedicating them to God, the Virgin Mary, or one of the saints, in honour of whom they would adopt a religious type of raiment for a number of years stipulated by their parents. Madeleine de Sourdis, a future abbess whose precarious health had caused her to be offered at six weeks of age to the Virgin 'in order that it would please her [the Virgin] to be her Protectress, and to agree to let her wear the white habit in her honour, till the age of seven', lived to be an octogenarian. Less fortunate was the prematurely-born daughter of Louis XIV, who died in December 1664, a fortnight after being taken to the Récollettes[23] in the Faubourg Saint Germain and committed to assuming the habit and scapulary of the order for the first three years of her life. White or blue were the usual colours of the garments worn by girls consecrated in this way, and a service in church commemorated the moment when they were formally exchanged for ordinary, worldly clothes.

Children were clothed, as paintings and engravings of the period show, in scarcely modified versions of the heavy dress of their elders. Aristocratic girls bowed beneath the weight of jewels and elaborate coiffures. 'She staggers under gold and jewels', wrote Mme de Maintenon[24] of the tiny young Duchesse du Maine,[25] 'and her coiffure weighs more than her whole person. She will be prevented form growing and being healthy'. To induce them to preserve an upright carriage beneath the load they had stiffening material inserted into the corsage of their dresses and wore a type of bodice similarly strengthened with bone or metal. Hunchbacks like the three daughters of the Maréchale de la Mothe were condemned from childhood onwards to life in an iron corset.

Young and not so young shared games and pastimes too. The meanest little towns boasted of a tennis court in which children outshone mothers and fathers by their precocious dexterity with a racket. Strollers in the gardens of the Tuileries were charmed by the spectacle of groups of girls playing at bowls and skittles, and engaging in jumping competitions terminated by the solemn crowning of the winner with flowers or laurel. Over in the enclosure of the Palais de Justice[26] impoverished girls who assisted the numerous merchants selling their wares there were in the habit of tossing to and fro a ball or shuttlecock while digesting their lunch. Gentlewomen did not disdain shuttlecock, since it was permitted during recreation hours at Mme de Maintenon's aristocratic boarding-school at Saint-Cyr, along with games such as spillikins, chess, draughts and *trou-madame* (played by rolling balls into holes) which the foundress of the

[23] A reformed branch of the Franciscans, a medieval religious order.

[24] Françoise d'Aubigné, Marquise de Maintenon (1635–1719), second wife of Louis XIV.

[25] Louise de Bourbon, duchesse de Maine (1676–1753), wife of Louis XIV's eldest son and hostess of a periodic gathering of literary and political personages.

[26] Palace of Justice, seat of the Parlement and of other law courts in Paris.

establishment regarded as exercising the brain or the memory. Juvenile play-acting, included under the same utilitarian rubric, became as popular at Saint-Cyr as it was in the rest of upper-class society, but it underwent an enforced eclipse after sumptuous performances of Racine's *Esther* before the court in 1689 had stirred dangerous emotions in the bosom of actresses and spectators. Mme de Maintenon continued, however, to let her girls entertain small, select audiences in conditions of strict privacy and sobriety, and did not oppose the theatrical bent of her most important charge, the Duchesse de Bourgogne,[27] whom she schooled after the ten-year-old princess's arrival at court in 1696. She even condescended to the occasional game of blind man's bluff which all the high-ranking ladies of the court had to play in order to amuse the king's effervescent grand-daughter-in-law.

Early participation by children in the social, and especially in the religious, life of the community was encouraged. It was the youngest members of the family who pronounced the benediction at mealtimes and handed round portions of the bean cake traditionally baked on New Year's Eve. Under a watchful maternal eye they distributed alms to the poor and solicited offerings from the congregation in church. Theirs were the hands trusted to select winning tickets in public lotteries. Attired in angelic or other symbolic raiment they marched in pious processions, saluted dignitaries on the occasion of a ceremonial entry into town or installation in office, and paraded at times of national rejoicing. Though contemporary recorders of such events habitually fail to specify the sex and age of the children involved, it is obvious from scattered references that young girls played their part in public ceremonies of welcome, thanksgiving and supplication. They came into their own when it was a question of greeting high-born ladies who had come to take up temporary or permanent residence in the locality.... As members of the so-called 'devout sex', girls were naturally associated with corporate demonstrations of piety. It was they who led a procession to implore the Divinity for rain to fall on their drought-stricken town of Châlons in the summer of 1624. Young daughters of upper-class families of Marseille learned an object lesson in humility when, arrayed in virginal robes, they each escorted a female from the poor-house in a procession of 1688 which ended with some of their mothers waiting upon the impoverished women at table....

It goes without saying that community life was not all play and pageantry. The sober reality of work intervened at an age which struck travellers in France by reason of its earliness: 'the smallest children are trained to work', remarked Elie Brackenhoffer of Strasbourg after a trip to Grenoble. Albert Jouvin of Rochefort made an identical observation at the arsenal of Toulon: 'You see there...even very little children... working'. The poverty of parents who needed every hand available, ev-

---

[27]Marie Adélaïde, duchesse de Bourgogne (1685–1712), wife of Louis XIV's grandson.

ery *sou*[28] earned, in order to maintain the family bread supply was the major factor in turning children out into the fields or the forerunners of the factories as soon as they had sufficient intelligence and strength to be able to mind livestock and perform simple mechanical operations. Seven or eight was the age at which the exercise of reason was thought to commence. But grown-ups were impatient: children in the vicinity of Alençon were employed to manufacture pins at the ripe old age of six. Any qualms over child labour were easily stifled by the reflection that children were not worked to the point of exhaustion. Even in a poor-house like the famous La Charité at Lyons, where indigent and orphaned girls and boys were constrained from the age of seven to rise at five in the morning and busy themselves with silk-making till dark in winter and six in the evening in summer, John Locke felt that 'counting their mass and breakfast in the morning, collation in the evening and time of dinner, their work is not hard'. The idea was firmly ingrained, moreover, that the young needed to be trained and to be preserved from the evils of slothfulness. Parents who suffered no economic duress still believed in delegating household chores to their daughters at the first opportunity and in making sure that every minute of the day was fruitfully filled. 'I observed here one thing as I walked along the streets', wrote Francis Mortoft on a visit to Nantes in 1658, 'that none of the women were idle, but the gentlewomen and little girls, as they sat at their doors or walked about the streets, had their spinning work in their hands.' No devil was going to find mischief for idle young hands to do if mothers like these could help it.

Inevitably children so rapidly established in the adult roles of wage-earners and, if they were well-to-do, of marriage partners, were judged by adult criteria. Judgements were harsh. The great classical writers in general show themselves to be impervious to the charms of childhood, viewing it with some horror as an age of physical and mental weakness, essentially lacking in dignity. 'Childhood is the life of an animal' was the terse verdict of Bossuet[29] when he considered the impotence of the child's will and reason to combat the force of passions. 'Children . . . are already men', that is to say, possessed of all vices, according to La Bruyère.[30] The genial La Fontaine[31] underlines their stupidity, harshness and cruelty. . . .

Manifestations of affection towards these miniature adults appear decidedly inhibited by modern standards. The few brief insights into the sentiments of the peasantry left by seventeenth-century observers attest to a certain detachment between parents and offspring, of the kind which characterises the expressions and stances of the group depicted in the

[28] A coin equivalent to twelve *deniers* (pennies).

[29] Jacques Bénigne Bossuet (1627–1704), Bishop of Meaux, court preacher, tutor to Louis XIV's son, and author of numerous works.

[30] Jean de La Bruyère (1645–1696), author of the *Characters*.

[31] Jean de La Fontaine (1612–1695), French poet.

painting *Famille de Paysans*,[32] attributed to Louis Le Nain,[33] where each figure seems physically withdrawn from the others and immersed in his or her own private world. The ex-soldier turned moralist, Fortin de la Hoguette, cites peasant fathers and children as an example of the purely pragmatic relationship, what he calls 'a very obscure feeling of affection on the part of father towards son, son towards father . . . which subsists only as long as it is necessary for them to work together', that develops when parents tend their progeny like their livestock, nurturing the body at the expense of the soul. At best the generalisation would avowedly apply only to fathers and sons, leaving unsettled the question of whether peasant fathers were equally unfeeling towards daughters, and vice versa. In addition it was penned by an 'outsider' from a higher social bracket who shared with a good many of his equals the propensity for interpreting peasant behaviour in the light of that of animals. The attitude taken by some sections of fashionable society towards demonstrating love for children hardly justified feelings of superiority. Coulanges, Mme de Sévigné's[34] cousin, in a lengthy *Chanson*[35] entitled 'Avis aux Pères de Famille',[36] pleads for fathers to observe public silence about their offspring and to make sure that the latter eat apart from civilised company:

> *Know, furthermore, good people,*
> *That nothing is more intolerable*
> *Than to see your little children*
> *Strung like onions round the big table,*
> *With runny noses and greasy chins,*
> *Poking their fingers in all the dishes.*

The sight of a learned man stooping to play with his own child brought a pitying smile to the lips of Vigneul-Marville:[37]

> Learned men have their ridiculous side as well. Who would not have laughed at seeing Melancthon, the most serious and erudite of the Lutheran theologians, reading from a book held in one hand, and with the other rocking his child to sleep? I saw on one occasion the late Monsieur Esprit in a very similar posture. He was reading Plato, and from time to time he would stop reading, shake his infant's rattle, and play with this kid.

However, as this passage reveals, there *were* fathers willing to brave public

[32]"Peasant Family."

[33]1593–1643, painter of rustic scenes and of common people.

[34]Marie de Rabutin-Chantal, Marquise de Sévigné (1626–1696), famous letter-writer.

[35]Song.

[36]"Advice to Fathers of the Family."

[37]Pseudonym of Noël Bonaventure d'Argonne, author of a late seventeenth-century work on history and literature.

ridicule and the prejudices of what were for the most part childless scholars in order to show affection for, and interest in, their young children.

Letters provide a precious testimony in this respect since, out of the public gaze, in the intimacy of a page designed only for the perusal of a loved one or a friend, a father could abandon himself unashamedly to the promptings of paternal affection. Henri IV confides to his mistress Mme de Verneuil his pleasure in the wit, or naivety, of their four-year-old Gabrielle: 'our daughter conversed with my wife and myself and the whole company for three hours this evening, and nearly made us die laughing'. The Maréchal de La Force preoccupies himself with keeping his daughter's complexion free from sunburn in his absence, and threatens her with the ultimate sanction of no Christmas presents if she persists in talking through her nose and failing to study diligently. In the later part of the century Racine's letters are fully of homely chatter about little Nanette's difficulty in cutting her teeth, the wit and intelligence of young Madelon, and his delight at receiving a bouquet for his *fête*[38] from his youngest daughters while he is busy working. But perhaps the most touching memorial to the bond between a father and his small daughter is that enshrined within the memoirs of Henri de Campion, a nobly-born military man who died in 1663. Louise-Anne entered his life on 2 May 1649, 'so beautiful and so pleasing that from the moment of her birth I loved her with a tenderness that I cannot put into words'. Scarcely had Campion time to savour the joys of paternity before death robbed him of the child on 10 May 1653:

> When I reflected that I was separated for the whole of my life from what was most dear to me, I could find no pleasure in the world, outside of which lay my happiness. I know that many will tax me with weakness and with a lack of fortitude over an accident that they will not consider one of the worst; but to that I would reply that things only affect us according to the feelings that we have for them, and that therefore one should not make blanket judgments as if we all had the same way of thinking. It is necessary to know how highly we rate things before praising the patience we show on losing them. . . . I confess that I would be acting like a woman if I pestered people with my laments; but always to cherish what I loved most of all, to think about her continually and to want to rejoin her, I consider that the sentiment of a man who knows what love is, and who, believing firmly in the immortality of the soul, feels that the departure of his dear daughter is a temporary absence, and not an eternal separation.

Even the fondest of fathers, it seems, was uncomfortably aware of indulging a culpable weakness in loving and grieving for his own child.

It was not, therefore, a very welcoming face that seventeenth-century society presented to the infant girl. From a physical point of view life was fraught with dangers to which her tender constitution often succumbed.

---

[38] Name-day.

From a moral point of view she suffered doubly. As a child she was an object of mistrust to theologians, moralists and certain men of letters who saw in her essentially the product of Original Sin, a wilful animal needing, they urged with some success, to be kept at a distance even from her own parents until the process of reason began to operate. As a female she was a disappointment because she was 'fragile' in all respects and inapt to maintain her family's material status. This initial burden of prejudice was to accompany her continually, and not least throughout the second major phase of existence, her education.

Insanity in Early Modern England

MICHAEL MacDONALD

Insanity, as Michael MacDonald reminds us, is not the same for all times and places, but is culturally defined. Definitions of what constitutes madness reflect the values of a society. Thus, in England, interpretations of madness and the treatment accorded the insane changed between the sixteenth-century Protestant Reformation and the eighteenth-century Industrial Revolution. What were the most significant of these changes? How do developments in English society explain the increased attention given to the mentally ill?

Many early modern Englishmen looked to family life as a cause of mental disorder. Why? Even the government held the institution of the family to be a primary concern in its efforts to deal with the insane. Thus the Court of Wards and Liveries acted rather honestly and "sanely" when it adjudicated the estates of lunatics. How did the government's behavior toward poor lunatics come to be intertwined with the problem of poverty? Just as the state had the poor locked up in workhouses, so by the eighteenth century did governments, as well as private citizens, establish asylums for the insane. Why did society now condone the confinement of these groups of people who formerly had enjoyed a measure of freedom?

There was great competition in England among those who thought they understood mental disorders. Proponents of magic, religion, and science, which interacted and overlapped in the seventeenth century, disagreed on the causes and treatment of insanity. Should we be more surprised that remedies and explanations offered by physicians did not work or that the elite of England gradually came to accept the claims of medical science? At least supernatural explanations for madness, if perhaps misguided, did not normally harm the mentally disturbed. Exorcisms and faith healing, for example, may have had therapeutic value. On the other hand, medical remedies employed techniques that were seen to be, as MacDonald says, "unpleasant, ineffective, and theoretically insupportable." Why did the ruling classes put their faith in those secular priests, the physicians? How did irrationality come to typify the attitude toward the mentally ill, cruelly treated and incarcerated, during the eighteenth-century "Age of Reason"?

Madness is the most solitary of afflictions to the people who experience it; but is the most social of maladies to those who observe its effects. Every mental disorder alienates its victims from the conventions of action, thought, and emotion that bind us together with the other members of our society. But because mental disorders manifest themselves in their victims' relationships with other men and women, they are more profoundly influenced by social and cultural conditions than any other kind of illness. For this reason the types of insanity people recognize and the significance they attach to them reflect the prevailing values of their society; the criteria for identifying mental afflictions vary between cultures and historical periods. The response to the insane, like the reaction to the sufferers of physical diseases, is also determined by the material conditions, social organization, and systems of thought that characterize a particular culture and age. The methods of caring for mentally disturbed people, the concepts that are used to explain the causes of their maladies, and the techniques that are employed to relieve their anguish are all determined more by social forces than by scientific discoveries, even today. Two central problems, therefore, confront historians of insanity. First, they must show how ideas about mental disorder and methods of responding to it were adapted to the social and intellectual environment of particular historical periods. Second, they must identify changes in the perception and management of insanity and explain how they were related to broader transformations in the society.

The history of mental disorder in early modern England is an intellectual Africa. Historians and literary scholars have mapped its most prominent features and identified some of its leading figures, but we still have very little information about the ideas and experiences of ordinary people. Both the unfortunates who actually suffered from mental afflictions and the men and women who tried to help them still inhabit *terra incognita*. Their story, the social history of insanity between the Reformation and the Industrial Revolution, falls into two distinct eras divided by the cataclysm of the English Revolution. During the late sixteenth and early seventeenth centuries, the English people became more concerned about the prevalence of madness, gloom, and self-murder than they had ever been before, and the reading public developed a strong fascination with classical medical psychology. Nevertheless, conventional beliefs about the nature and causes of mental disorders and the methods of psychological healing continued to reflect the traditional fusion of magic, science, and religion that typified the thinking of laymen of every social rank and educational background. The enormous social and psychological significance of the family shaped contemporary interpretations of insane behavior and determined the arrangements that were made to care for rich and poor lunatics alike. . . . During the century and a half following the great upheaval of the English Revolution, the governing classes embraced secular interpretations of the signs of insanity and championed medical methods of curing mental disorders. They shunned magical and religious techniques of psychological healing. Private entrepreneurs founded specialized institutions to manage mad people, and municipal officials established public madhouses. The asylum movement eventually transferred the responsibility for maintaining lunatics out of the family and into the asylum. Madmen were removed from their normal social surroundings and incarcerated with others of their kind; lunatics lost their places as members of a household and acquired new identities as the victims of mental diseases.

Interest in insanity quickened about 1580, and madmen, melancholics, and suicides became familiar literary types. Scientific writers popularized medical lore about melancholy, and clergymen wrote treatises about consoling the troubled in mind. Gentlemen and ladies proclaimed themselves melancholy; physicians worried about ways to cure the mentally ill; preachers and politicians denounced sinners and dissenters as melancholics or madmen. Anxious intellectuals claimed that self-murder was epidemical, and they argued about its medical and religious significance. . . . Heightened concern about the nature and prevalence of mental disorders was fostered by the increasing size and complexity of English society. Population growth and economic change increased the numbers of insane and suicidal people and overburdened the capacity of families and local communities to care for the sick and indigent. Renaissance humanism set new standards of conduct for the nobility, and the turbulent and incomplete triumph of Protestantism fragmented English society into religious groups with sharply differing views about how people ought to behave. The adequacy of traditional codes of conduct was subjected to intense criticism by learned reformers and religious zealots, and both humanist intellectuals and Puritan clergymen were naturally concerned about the causes and significance of abnormal behavior. Although they often looked to the same sources for ideas about insanity, one can say in general that religious conservatives elaborated classical medical psychology, whereas Puritan evangelists revitalized popular religious psychology and set it in a Calvinist theological framework.

In spite of the increased interest in insanity and the growing controversy about its religious implications, the perception and management of mental disorders did not change fundamentally before 1660. Contemporary ideas about the varieties of mental maladies and their characteristic signs were rooted in ancient science and medieval Christianity, and the typology of insanity was similar all over Western Europe. Within the broad framework of medical and religious thought, however, popular stereotypes of mental disorder were adapted to fit English conditions. For example, widely held beliefs about the behavior of mad and troubled people and the immediate causes of their misery reflected the psychological significance of the family in the lives of ordinary villages. Descriptions of the symptoms of violent madness placed great emphasis on irrational threats toward members of one's immediate family. Traditional legal prohibitions against suicide aimed to prevent it by emphasizing the responsibility of potential self-murders for their family's welfare. Common complaints about the causes of overwhelming anxiety and despair included unrequited love, marital strife, and bereavement. This preoccupation with the family was the consequence of its elemental importance in English society. The household was the basic social unit, and at every level of society it performed a myriad of functions. Within the walls of great houses and cottages children were reared and educated, the sick and infirm were nursed and maintained, estates were managed and goods were manufactured. Most households were very small. Except among the wealthy, whose entourages often included dozens of servants, clients and kin, households normally consisted only of a married couple, their young children, and, in many cases, a servant or apprentice. The small size of domestic groups and the high rate of geographical mobility in early seventeenth-century England greatly enhanced the part that the nuclear family played in the emotional lives of people of low and middling status.

The social importance of the family was also recognized in the arrangements for maintaining mad and troubled people. Only a handful of the insane in a nation of five million souls were cast into an asylum before the English Revolution. Bedlamites[1] swarmed through the imaginations of Jacobean playwrights and pamphleteers, but the famous asylum was in truth a tiny hovel housing fewer than thirty patients. Bethlem Hospital was the only institution of its kind, and its inmates languished there for years, living in squalid conditions without adequate medical treatment. Private institutions to house the insane did not begin to proliferate until the last half of the seventeenth century, municipal asylums to rival Bedlam were not founded in major cities for another century, and county lunatic hospitals were not established until after 1808. Tudor and Stuart governments responded to increasing concern about insanity by refurbishing traditional institutions to help families bear the burden of harboring a madman. The welfare of rich lunatics was guarded by the Court of Wards and Liveries, which exercised the crown's feudal right to manage the affairs of minors who inherited land as tenants-in-chief. Children, idiots, and lunatics were siblings in the eyes of the law, because they all lacked the capacity to reason and so could not be economically and legally responsible.

The Court of Wards was notorious for selling its favors to the highest bidder, allowing guardians who purchased wardships to ruin their charges' estates and bully them into profitable marriages. But toward lunatics the court behaved with uncharacteristic delicacy, repudiating rapacity in favor of family and legitimacy. King James[2] instructed the court to ensure that lunatics "be freely committed to their best and nearest friends, that can receive no benefit by their death, and the committees, bound to

---

[1]Bedlam and Gedlamites are names derived from Bethlem Hospital in London.
[2]James I, 1603–1625.

answer for . . . the very just value of their estates upon account, for the benefit of such lunatic (if he recover) or of the next heir." The order was obeyed. The court usually appointed relatives or friends of mad landowners to see that they were cared for and their property preserved. Naturally, there were some sordid struggles for the guardianship of rich lunatics, and sometimes men hurled false accusations of insanity at wealthy eccentrics in hopes of winning a rich wardship. But the court was unusually scrupulous about investigating chicanery when it concerned lunatics, and abuses appear to have been rare. Before a landowner was turned over to a committee of guardians, a jury of local notables was assembled to certify that he had been too mad to manage his estates for a year and more. Such juries relied on common sense and common knowledge to establish that a person was insane, but their chief preoccupation was to discover whether he could perform the necessary economic chores to preserve the family property.

The court and the men who acted as inquisitors and guardians on its behalf behaved more virtuously toward the estates of lunatics than those of minor heirs because there was little profit in the wardship of the insane. Lunacy was regarded as a temporary state and the law decreed that when the madman recovered he should have restored to him all of his property, save the amount the guardians expended for his care. And because lunatics were unreasoning creatures, they could not contract marriages, perhaps the most valuable aspect of the wardship of minors. Legal rules and low incentive to break them effectively protected the rights of insane landowners, and when the Court of Wards was abolished during the Revolution cries were heard that lunatics were now vulnerable to the greed of unscrupulous guardians as never before. . . .

The chief concern of the crown's policy toward insane landowners was to preserve the integrity of their estates so that their lineages would not be obliterated by the economic consequences of their madness. Paupers had no property or social standing to protect, but the Tudor and Stuart state tried also to assist poor lunatics by providing financial relief for their families. After 1601 the government obliged parishes to treat impoverished madmen as "deserving poor," people who, like orphans and cripples, were unable to work through no fault of their own. . . . These allowances were paid out of the funds from local taxation for poor relief, and they were intended to prevent humble families from starvation and fragmentation because the lunatic's labor was lost. A 1658 order by Lancashire justices to provide for Isabell Breatherton illustrates the way the system worked in practice:

> It is ordered by this court that the . . . churchwardens and overseers of the poor within the parish of Wimwick shall . . . take into consideration the distracted condition of Isabell, wife of James Breatherton of Newton and provide for her or allow unto her said husband weekly or monthly allowances as her

necessity requires, so as she may be kept from wandering abroad or doing any hurt or prejudice either to herself or otherwise.

As the population grew and the economy became more specialized in the sixteenth and seventeenth centuries, poverty became a major social problem. Municipal governments experimented with new kinds of institutions, such as hospitals and workhouses, in an attempt to find some solution to the increasingly alarming situation, and the crown began slowly to imitate some features of these experiments. In 1609, for example, counties were ordered to establish houses of correction to confine the able-bodied poor and train them for gainful employment; compliance was slow, but by the 1630s every shire[3] had such an institution. Lunatics were sometimes housed in these local Bridewells,[4] but it appears that incarceration was regarded as an exceptional and undesirable expedient. Lancashire officials were reluctant to confine madmen to the county's house of correction if they could avoid it, preferring to leave them in the care of their families whenever possible. For the poor as for the rich, therefore, the Tudor and early Stuart state left the care and management of the insane largely in the hands of their families and attempted to lessen the social and economic impact of lunacy by helping families either directly through the Court of Wards or indirectly through the parishes.

Early seventeenth-century methods of explaining the natural and supernatural causes of insanity and relieving the suffering of its victims were marked by a traditional mingling of magical, religious, and scientific concepts. Individual cases of mental disorder might be attributed to divine retribution, diabolical possession, witchcraft, astrological influences, humoral imbalances,[5] or to any combination of these forces. Cures were achieved (in theory) by removing the causes of the sufferer's disturbance, and the means to combat every kind of malign effect were dispensed by a bewildering array of healers. Insane men and women were treated by specialists, such as humanistic physicians, who practiced a single method of psychological healing, or they were consoled by eclectics, such as medical astrologers or clerical doctors, who combined remedies from several systems of therapy. The profusion of causal explanations for insanity and of healing methods was not simply the result of the inchoate state of the medical profession. It was also a practical manifestation of the popular confidence that magic, religion, and science could be reconciled. Medieval and Renaissance cosmology provided a systematic model for making such a reconciliation, and on a less sophisticated plane popular religious thought fused religious and magical beliefs.

[3]A district in England coinciding roughly with a modern county.

[4]Jails, named after the London house of correction.

[5]Physicians believed that sickness was caused by an imbalance among the four humors (yellow bile, black bile, phlegm, and blood).

Classical medical psychology became very popular among the educated classes during the sixteenth and seventeenth centuries. It was disseminated by the physicians, who were increasingly articulate and well-organized, and by humanist intellectuals, who were often clerics and medical amateurs.... Although the remedies sanctioned by natural scientific theories were no more effective than religious or magical treatments for mental disorder, the medical approach eventually prevailed over supernatural explanations for the causes of madness. In the early seventeenth century the natural and supernatural approaches coexisted uneasily, championed by rival groups of professionals, to be sure, but not yet incompatible to many minds. Humanistic physicians battled to secure a monopoly over the care of sick and insane people and to make their trade proof against the interloping of clerical doctors, apothecaries, surgeons, astrologers, and village wizards....

... Medical practice was a natural extension of ministers' duty to relieve the afflictions of their flocks, and a great many rural rectors and vicars provided various kinds of medical services for their parishioners. Medicine was an essential aspect of the astrologers' art, and occultists of every degree of rank and learning, from highly educated university graduates to illiterate village wise folk, used astrology as a tool for medical diagnosis and prognostication. The doctors could do little to prevent clergymen from practicing their craft, because the church and the universities had the power to license medical practitioners, and neither was likely to concur that learned clerks who practiced medicine were as culpable as ignorant quacks. Humanistic physicians could not possibly supply all the medical needs of the English people, and so long as clerical doctors, and indeed astrologers and cunning men and women,[6] did not slaughter their patients and garnered reputations for effective treatments, the authorities were inclined to grant them licenses to practice medicine legally. In London and its suburbs, however, the College of Physicians were empowered to fine unlicensed practitioners, and the privilege was used to harass popular astrologers and empirics.... The doctors' efforts to persuade the public that scientific medicine was the only legitimate basis for healing made little headway before the English Revolution: Professional eclecticism and therapeutic pluralism continued to characterize the treatment of physically ill and mentally disturbed people.

During the course of the seventeenth century, religious controversy and the shock of revolution accelerated the triumph of medical explanations for insanity among the governing classes. The Anglican hierarchy repudiated popular demonology for theological reasons, only to discover that Jesuits and Puritans eagerly took up the struggle against the Fiend and his minions. Radical Protestants developed new means for casting

[6]Cunning men and women practiced so-called white witchcraft, which involved predicting the future, healing, preparing love potions, and recovering lost objects.

out devils and uplifting downcast hearts and used them to proselytize as well as to console. They insisted that misery, anxiety, and sadness were the emblems of sin, the normal afflictions of the unregenerate, and they taught that the surest means to overcome them was spiritual self-discipline and godly fellowship. Insanity was the epitome of conduct unguided by a pious and responsible personality. . . . The Puritans produced a literature of anxious gloom in which despair normally preceded conversion, and they naturally bruited about their ability to relieve such suffering. During the Revolution the sects—especially the Quakers—employed their powers of exorcism and spiritual healing to prove by miracles their divine inspiration and refute the charges of the "hireling priests." The orthodox elite seized the healer's gown in which the radicals clothed themselves and turned it inside out, calling religious enthusiasm madness and branding the vexations of tender consciences religious melancholy.

These events coincided with remarkable achievements in physical science and anatomy, and they helped to accomplish the end that physicians had been unable to attain by propaganda and persecution. They prompted the ruling elite to embrace secular explanations for mental disorders and to repudiate magical and religious methods of healing them. The secularization of the elite's beliefs about insanity affected their notions about the nature of mental diseases as well as the causes of such afflictions. . . . The educated classes' gradual rejection of traditional religious ideas about suicide in favor of the medical theory that it was the outcome of mental disease was also fostered by orthodox hatred of religious enthusiasm. Throughout the eighteenth century dissenting sects continued to exorcise people who believed that they were possessed by the Devil. Anglican spokesmen argued that the age of miracles was long past, and the Devil rarely if ever swayed the minds and inhabited the bodies of people in modern times. This argument corroded the traditional stereotype of suicide, which depicted self-murder as a religious crime, committed at the instigation of the Devil, who often appeared personally to urge his victims on to self-destruction.

The rejection of the supernatural beliefs and thaumaturgy of the sectaries fostered scorn for religious and magical therapies. Although the methods of psychological healing practiced by the Dissenters[7] were often effective, the governing classes abandoned them in favor of medical remedies for mental disorders, techniques that were widely recognized to be unpleasant, ineffective, and theoretically insupportable. Magical remedies against supernatural harm, such as astrological amulets, charms, and exorcisms, were discarded by reputable practitioners. By the end of the seventeenth century a loose hierarchy of prestige had been established among the various types of healers who treated insanity, and at its apex were the humanistic physicians, who viewed madness and gloom as natu-

[7]Those who rejected Anglicanism, the state religion.

ral disorders. The dominance of secular interpretations of insanity among the eighteenth-century governing classes was embodied in the asylum movement. Beginning about 1660, scores of entrepreneurs founded private madhouses to care for the insane, and beginning about a century later, some municipal governments established receptacles for pauper lunatics. The therapeutic practices of the new asylums were based mainly on medical theories and remedies. . . .

The governing classes' repudiation of supernatural explanations of the signs and causes of insanity and their rejection of magical and religious therapies were not readily accepted by the mass of the English people. Throughout the eighteenth century ordinary villagers continued to believe that witches and demons could drive men mad and that the Devil could possess the minds and bodies of his victims. They sought the help of a ragtag regiment of increasingly disreputable astrologers and folk magicians to protect them against these evils. The exorcisms and religious cures of the Non-conformist sects,[8] and particularly of the Methodists, appealed to the strong popular attachment to traditional supernaturalism. The deepening abyss between elite attitudes toward insanity and popular beliefs was not simply the consequence of the enlightened scientism of the educated classes. Medical theories about mental disorders were contradictory and controversial; medical therapies were notoriously difficult to justify either theoretically or empirically. They appealed to an elite sick of sectarian enthusiasm because they lacked the subversive political implications that religious psychology and therapy had acquired during the seventeenth century. As the eighteenth century progressed, more and more people were subjected to incarceration in madhouses and to medical brutality. The abolition of family care for lunatics and the abandonment of therapeutic pluralism were the consequences of religious conflict, political strife, and social change. The lunacy reformers of the early nineteenth century drew an exaggerated, but nevertheless genuinely horrified, picture of the terrible suffering that the asylum movement and rise of medical psychology inflicted on the insane. . . .

[8]The Dissenters from Anglicanism (Church of England).

Acknowledgments *(continued)*

"Gladiatorial Combat in Ancient Rome." Jérôme Carcopino. From *Daily Life in Ancient Rome: The People and the City at the Height of the Empire*, pp. 231–247. Copyright © 1940 Yale University Press. Reprinted by permission of the Yale University Press.

"Why Were the Early Christians Persecuted?" G.E.M. de Ste. Croix. World Copyright: The Past and Present Society, 175 Banbury Road, Oxford, England. This article is here reprinted in abridged form with the permission of the Society and the author, from *Past and Present: A Journal of Historical Studies*, no. 26 (November 1963).

Rural Economy and Country Life in the Medieval West by Georges Duby, Cynthia Postan, translator, by the University of South Carolina Press. 1968, pp. 5–11, 15, 21–25, 27. Reprinted by permission of Edward Arnold (Publishers) Ltd.

"The Life of the Nobility." Marc Bloch. From *Feudal Society*, 1961, pp. 293–311. Reprinted by permission of University of Chicago Press.

"Environment and Pollution." Jean Gimpel. From *The Medieval Machine: The Industrial Revolution of the Middle Ages.* Copyright © 1976 by Jean Gimpel. Reprinted by permission of Henry Holt, and Company, Inc.

"Medieval Children." David Herlihy. From *Essays on Medieval Civilization*, Bede Karl Lackner and Kenneth Roy Phillip, eds. Used by permission of the Walter Prescott Webb Memorial Lecture Committee, University of Texas at Arlington.

"Fast, Feast, and the Flesh: The Religous Significance of Food to Medieval Women." Caroline Walker Bynum. Copyright © 1985 by The Regents of the University of California. Reprinted from *Representations*, No. 11 (Summer 1985) pp. 1–25, by permission.

"Vendetta and Civil Disorder in Late Medieval Ghent." David Nicholas. Copyright © 1990 David Nicholas. Reprinted by permission of David Nicholas.

"The Development of the Concept of Civilité." Reprinted from *The History of Manners* by Norbert Elias, trans. by Edmund Jephcott, by permission of Pantheon Books, a division of Random House, Inc. English Translation © 1978 by Urizen Books.

"The Family in Renaissance Italy." David Herlihy. From *Forums in History*. Copyright © 1974 The Forum Press. Reprinted by permission of the publisher, The Forum Press.

"The Early History of Syphilis: A Reappraisal." Alfred Crosby. Reprinted by permission of the American Anthropological Assocaiation for *American Anthropologist* 71:2, April 1969.

"Lost Women in Early Modern Seville." Mary Elizabeth Perry. Reprinted from *Feminist Studies*, Volume 4, Number 1 (1978): 195–211, by permission from the publisher, Feminist Studies, Inc., c/o Women's Studies Program, University of Maryland, College Park, MD 20742.

"Nuns, Wives, and Mothers: Women and the Reformation in Germany." Merry Wiesner. From *Women in Reformation and Counter-Reformation Europe*, ed. by Sharon Marshall, 1989, pp. 8–26. Reprinted by permission of Indiana University Press.

"Sexual Politics and Religous Reform in the Witch Craze." Joseph Klaits. From *Servants of Satan: The Age of the Witch Hunts*, 1985, pp. 48–53, 56–73, 76–85. Indiana University Press. Copyright © Joseph Klaits

"The Rites of Violence: Religous Riot in Sixteenth-Century France." Natalie Z. Davis. The Past and Present Society, 175 Banbury Road, Oxford, England. This article is here reprinted in abridged form, with the permission of the Society and the author, from *Past and Present: a Journal of Historical Studies*, no. 59, (May 1973), pp. 51–91.

"Birth and Childhood in Seventeenth-Century France." Wendy Gibson. From Chapter One: "Birth and Childhood" in *Women in Seventeenth Century France*, 1989. Reprinted by permission of Macmillan London and Basingstoke and St. Martin's Press.

"Insanity in Early Modern England." Michael MacDonald. From *Mystical Bedlam*, 1981, pp. 1–11. Reprinted with the permission of Cambridge University Press.